BASIC
INSTRUMENTATION
Industrial
Measurement

BASIC
INSTRUMENTATION
Industrial
Measurement

PATRICK J. O'HIGGINS

Ryerson Polytechnical Institute

McGraw-Hill Book Company

New York · St. Louis · San Francisco
London · Toronto · Sydney

This book was to have been dedicated to me, but life's path takes unexpected turns, and so, instead, I dedicate it to the very dear memory of my husband. With his children, Linda, Paul, and Rosaleen, and this book, he has left behind a part of himself.

Patricia E. O'Higgins

Preface

All men by nature desire to know.

ARISTOTLE

Technological progress in the field of industrial instrumentation has been extraordinary in the past few decades. No doubt the next decades will see even greater expansion in the technology of instrumentation. For this reason there will be a continued demand for well-trained men to design, produce, service, and operate the variety of industrial instruments which have become so important and vital in our modern industrial society and, in particular, in the process industries.

This text has been written particularly for those studying the fundamentals of the theory and practice of industrial-process instrumentation at the technical-institute and college levels. It is necessary to have a background knowledge of basic physics and the ability to manipulate the usual elementary mathematics. The student should try to investigate the mathematical derivation for himself and to understand the fundamental principle involved with each type of industrial instrument. The next step should be an endeavor to visualize what goes on in the instrument and its operation, purpose, and application in process control.

The entire objective of this approach is to encourage a fundamental understanding of the basic principles of industrial instruments. The technique used is the step-by-step method, starting from the simple ideas and gradually leading to the more complex ones. In this way the student's understanding of the fundamentals grows. With industrial training and experience there will be a completion of knowledge which will lead to a wider vision of things to come in the dynamic technology of instrumentation.

It is advisable that the student should also be receiving laboratory and workshop training. It is essential to study the theory and practice simultaneously, because in this way the student can visualize and then actually investigate the laws and principles governing the operation of the instrument. Workshop training should include, apart from the usual machine workshop techniques and skills, the dismantling, calibration, servicing, assembling, panel hookup, and installation of industrial instruments.

In this book each basic idea and concept is developed and related to practice by numerical examples using step-by-step solutions. Numerous review questions and problems in each chapter have been selected from both theoretical and practical considerations. There are a number of problems and essay assignments which are intended to encourage the student to refer to libraries, technical literature, or current issues of manufacturers' catalogues and publications for fuller details and information.

It should be mentioned at this stage that this book, on such a wide and ever-increasing subject, is just a humble attempt to present some basic ideas and fundamentals of instrumentation. The student is well advised to seek further after grasping the elementary concepts, and thereby "grow the fruits of labor."

Patrick J. O'Higgins

Acknowledgments

The material in this book is an accumulation of the contributions of a great many people and companies. Their cooperation and encouragement has been much appreciated and is gratefully acknowledged. It is a humanly impossible task for one person to assemble and evaluate all the scientific progress in this field over the past years in a single text and to present in detail the numerous trends in design and development work of instrument-research laboratories and manufacturers on this continent.

To the following people I extend my sincere gratitude for their individual assistance in reviewing the material and for providing me with a wealth of constructive and censorious criticism:

J. H. Brace, P.Eng., Vice President, Administration, Honeywell Controls Ltd.

P. H. Byrne (deceased)., M.A.Sc., Ph.D., P.Eng., Department of Physics, Ryerson Polytechnical Institute, Toronto

H. C. Dawson, M.A., Department of Instrument Technology, Ryerson Polytechnical Institute, Toronto

H. D. Forrest, B.Sc., M.A., Department of Physics, Ryerson Polytechnical Institute, Toronto

B. E. Hutchins, B.A.Sc., P.Eng., Department of Mathematics, Ryerson Polytechnical Institute, Toronto

H. W. Jackson, Ontario Department of Education

Manfred Straka, Ph.D., Director, Mathematics and Physics, Northern Ontario Institute of Technology, Kirkland Lake

T. E. Wisz, B.A.Sc., P.Eng., Department of Mathematics, Ryerson Polytechnical Institute, Toronto

The following companies provided technical assistance and diagrams:

Ashcroft Lumber Co. Ltd.
Bailey Meter Company Limited
Baker Instruments Limited
Beckman Instruments Inc.
Bristol Co.
The Bristol Company of Canada Limited
Brooks Instrument Canada Limited

Budenberg Gauge Co., Ltd.
Carrier Air Conditioning (Canada) Ltd.
Crossman Machinery Co. Limited
F. W. Dwyer Mfg. Co.
Edwards High Vacuum (Canada) Ltd.
Evershed & Vignoles Ltd.
Fischer & Porter (Canada) Limited
The Foxboro Company Limited
General Controls Company (Canada) Limited
G. Kent (Canada) Ltd.
Hammel-Dahl & Foster Engineering Divisions, ITT General Controls, Inc.
Henry Troemner Inc.
Hersey-Sparling Meter Co.
Honeywell Inc.
Industrial Instruments Inc.
Instrument Society of America
Instruments Publishing Co.
Mason-Neilan Division of Worthington (Canada) Ltd.
Meriam (Charles) Company
The Meriam Instrument Co.
Ohmart Corp.
Peacock Brothers Limited
The Permutit Company
Ranar Industries Ltd.
Reed Paper Group Ltd.
Rockwell Manufacturing Company of Canada, Ltd.
Rohm & Haas of Canada Limited
Rotameter Manufacturing Co. Ltd.
Schaevitz Engineering
U.S. Gauge, A Div. of Ametek, Inc.

Finally, much credit goes to Patricia, my wife, for typing of the manuscript, consideration of grammatical details, and patience in moments of "trial and tribulation."

Patrick J. O'Higgins

POSTSCRIPT

Someone once said that "A man only begins to grasp the true meaning of life when he plants a tree under whose shade he knows he will never sit." The author knew that he might never see the result of the work he put into the compiling of this book, and unfortunately he never did. Indeed, this book would never have reached its readers were it not for the loyalty and hard work of two of his friends. To John Brace, of Honeywell Controls Ltd., and Peter Dawson, of Ryerson Polytechnical Institute, I owe more than words can express for their sacrifice in time given to complete this book and thus ensure that the work put into it by my husband was not wasted.

Patricia E. O'Higgins

Contents

CHAPTER ONE

The art and science of measurement

When you can measure what you are speaking about, and express it in numbers, you know something about it.

LORD KELVIN

The Need for Measurement

During an address on the subject of measurement, Lord Kelvin, a British scientist, stated a fundamental principle of science: "I often say that when you can measure what you are speaking about and express it in numbers, you know something about it." He clearly stressed that little progress is possible in any field of investigation without the ability to measure. Present-day mass production, processed products, worldwide communications and travel, and scientific and technological progress could not exist without adequate measurement techniques. The progress of measurement is, in fact, the progress of science.

The widespread use of instrumentation in industry started before World War II. It began with the introduction of reliable instruments for the continuous recording of the measurements of such industrial plant variables as temperature, pressure, level, flow, and humidity. The number of variables which require measurement is being continuously extended as new techniques and methods based on newly found physical and chemical phenomena are developed. In addition, existing methods have to be improved to meet the more exacting demands of the process industries, space programs, and research projects.

Standardized calibration. Calibration is the art of testing the validity of measurements by an instrument in normal operation by comparison with measurements made by primary or secondary standards. It is essential for good performance to insist upon a high degree of accuracy and reliability. In regard to the accuracy of an instrument it should be noted

1

that no instrument is accurate in an absolute sense. All measuring devices give only a more or less close approximation to the value of the quantity being measured. It is necessary to use the type of device which will measure to the specified degree of accuracy and to know that it is in condition to do so. The accuracy of meters or instruments used as measuring devices will be considered at length in later paragraphs. Calibration is the act or process of making adjustments or markings on an index scale so that the readings of a measuring device conform to an accepted and certified standard. Errors and corrections are revealed by standardized calibration.

National Bureau of Standards. The National Bureau of Standards in the United States and similar institutes in other countries were established to render essential scientific data and services to government, industry, business, and other institutions. These services are mainly related to standards and methods for accurate measurement of natural phenomena. The Bureau also maintains absolute standards and provides the methods and instruments required to utilize those standards.

Through calibration services, the Bureau ensures the accuracy of a countless number of scientific and industrial instruments by comparison with national and international standards. Continual research is conducted to meet the increasing need for more precise measurement. Full information of the services available can be obtained by writing to the National Bureau of Standards, Washington, D.C.

Measurement Terminology

It is important to become familiar with some of the basic terminology used in measurement work and in instrument practice:

Absolute standards are devices designed and constructed to specifications based on legal international definitions of the various fundamental units of measurement. An example is the standard meter. The term "absolute" is used in the sense of being independent, and not relative, but finite.

Secondary reference standards are designed and constructed from the absolute standards. Sometimes they are referred to as prototypes.

Working standards are calibrated in terms of secondary standards and are generally used directly for on-the-job or field measurements.

Comparison equipment, such as the electric-circuit bridge and the potentiometer, is used in comparing on-the-job or field instruments with working standards.

Environmental conditions must be considered during every standardizing operation. Such variables as temperature, humidity, vibrations, light intensity, supply-line voltage variations, and filtered-air supply must be kept consistent and must conform to specified requirements for recommended practice and acceptable results. Variations in arrangement, procedures, and suggested practices may be employed by different standardization laboratories, but all such laboratories have the common purpose of maintaining standards and instruments of measurement.

Routine calibration means the actual procedure of checking an instrument for accurate and efficient service. The following are some of the main preliminary steps to take:

1. Visual inspection for obvious physical defects
2. Visual inspection for proper installation and application in accordance with manufacturer's specification
3. Zero setting of all indicators
4. Leveling of devices which require this precaution
5. Operational test to detect major defects

Certification of calibration means that equipment has been calibrated, tested, and certified by a recognized standards laboratory as to its degree of accuracy in conforming to a particular standard unit or quantity. A certificate or some marking is usually indicative that the equipment or measuring device has passed a rigid calibration.

Primary-standards laboratories directly relate their measurements to the Bureau of Standards. Only the standards laboratories and Bureau of Standards can certify equipment and standards. The calibration procedures, measuring devices, and reference standards they use have the necessary accuracy for certification. Industrial-standards laboratories relate their measurement to either the primary or secondary standards.

For greater detail or amplified interpretation of the terms used, reference should be made to the glossary at the back of the text and to the publications on nomenclature and definitions of engineering and scientific professional societies or national institutes.

REVIEW QUESTIONS AND PROBLEMS

1-1 Describe the need for and purpose of measurement and the importance of standards.
1-2 Define the following terms: (a) standardized calibration, (b) routine calibration, (c) certificate of calibration.
1-3 In the design, layout, and operation of a calibration laboratory what environmental requirements must be considered?
1-4 Define the following terms: (a) absolute standards, (b) working standards.

The Nature of Measurement; Statements

Generally, a statement can be considered to fall in one of two broad classifications. Statements of the first kind are found in the theorems of geometry, which deal with humanly constructed definitions and formal proofs and are therefore considered incontrovertible. For example, it is stated by Euclid with absolute certainty that the sum of the angles in a triangle is 180°. This is an exact truth because it is just a restatement of Euclid's own definitions. This kind of statement is not a measurement.

On the other hand, measurement, as a statement, is the result of a human operation, and judgment is part of the nature of a measurement. Thus the statement is inexact. The *science of measurement, therefore, is concerned as much with errors and their effects on the end result as with measurement itself.*

When performing precision measurements, it is normal practice to record a series of observations rather than be content with only one value or reading. Errors of different magnitude will enter into the observations. With a sufficient number of readings, simple mathematical techniques can be employed to minimize the effects of error. These techniques consist of finding the average value of a given set of recorded data and determining its probable error.

Common Errors in Measurement

The *error* of a measurement is the numerical difference between the indicated or measured value and the true value. For example, if the barometric pressure is measured as 757 millimeters (mm), whereas a more accurate or standard measurement gave 758 mm, then,

$$\text{Error } E = \text{measured value} - \text{true value}$$
$$= 757 - 758$$
$$= -1 \text{ mm}$$

The *relative error* in any measured value is the ratio of the error to the true value. Therefore, the measured pressure has a relative error of $\frac{1}{758}$. Errors in general measurement work are classified as personal, random, systematic, instrumental, and applicational.

Personal errors are those caused either by carelessness, lack of experience, or bias on the part of the observer. Carelessness is a familiar factor in many human operations. Examples are actually incorrect readings or observations and mistakes in arithmetic. *Bias* is a more subjective type of error that usually results from having some preconceived notion of the magnitude or quality of the variable under measurement. Data are selected to substantiate the results, rather than treated with equal confidence. A common method of overcoming personal errors is to have readings made by more than one observer.

Random errors are indicated when repeated measurements of the same quantity or variable result in differing values. The errors probably exist, but they are considered indeterminate. They occur by pure chance both conditionally and unconditionally.

Systematic and instrumental errors are what can be called built-in errors which result from the characteristics of the materials used in constructing the measuring systems. Such errors can be largely compensated for by algebraic corrections; they are caused by such things as inertia, hysteresis, friction, and backlash in gearing or by the filling capacity of instruments used to measure differential pressure.

Applicational errors are due to incorrect application and faulty installation. An instrument must be applied and used strictly in accordance with design specifications and manufacturer's instructions.

Accuracy and Precision of Measuring Instruments

Accuracy. Attention has been called to the fact that instrument accuracy is purely a relative matter. That is, there is no such thing as absolute accuracy in connection with the measurement of physical quantities. The accuracy of a measurement or reading which is made with a meter or instrument can be defined as the closeness with which the reading approaches the true value or standard. The accuracy of a measurement is the degree of error in the final result. There is an ever-increasing demand for higher-accuracy instruments to meet the requirements of the application.

The accuracy of an instrument can be determined by calibration under operating conditions. One common method of expressing accuracy is to state that the instrument is accurate to within plus or minus a certain specific amount or a certain percent at a certain point on the scale or between specified points on the scale. For example, a thermometer may be described as having an error not in excess of ± 0.5 degrees Fahrenheit (°F) between 100 and 200°F.

Example. A pressure gauge reads 48 pounds per square inch (psi or lb/in.²) when a pressure of 50 psi is applied and 98 psi when 100 psi is applied. Calculate the relative error or inaccuracy at both points.

Solution. The relative error at the lower point is

$$\frac{50 - 48}{50} = \frac{2}{50} = 0.04 \text{ or } 4\%$$

At the higher point

$$\frac{100 - 98}{100} = \frac{2}{100} = 0.02 \text{ or } 2\%$$

Precision. Precision refers to the degree of agreement of a set or group of measurements among themselves. It should be understood that in instrument practice accuracy and precision have two distinct meanings. For example, if two voltmeters of the same make, date, and model are compared, it may be found that each has carefully ruled circular scales, knife-edge pointers, and probably mirror-backed scales to avoid parallax errors. The two meters may be read to the same precision. However, if the resistor in one meter becomes slightly defective, perhaps because of contamination, the meter readings will be subject to an error.

As explained previously, accuracy is determined by calibration against a standard, so that in the case of the two voltmeters it is possible for the two instruments to have different accuracies. The precision of reading may be the same, but the precision is no guarantee of accuracy, which can be determined only by comparative test measurement. On the other hand, the detection of possible inaccuracies presupposes a high degree of precision. It is up to the observer or experimenter to take the necessary precautions to ensure that the instruments used are functioning properly and that no controllable outside phenomenon is influencing the accuracy of measurements taken.

Sources of Inaccuracy

Parallax. The effect of parallax is a very common personal source of error. Parallax occurs when an observer measures a given position by means of scale and indicator (pointer). The measured value will change with the relative position of the observing eye. This point is best illustrated by means of the diagram in Fig. 1-1, which shows the ideal position B where the pointer and image in a mirror-backed meter coincide.

Controllable and uncontrollable effects. Some of the controllable errors which must be considered are errors present in measuring instruments because of their physical structure. Inaccuracy may be due to a great number of different causes acting singly or jointly:

1. Imperfect material, such as variation in bore of tubing and variation in the molecular structure of the materials used for coil springs or linkages
2. Unavoidable physical phenomena, such as capillary and surface-tension effects, imperfect refraction of light, and frictional effects
3. Imperfect construction which can be improved, such as excessive friction or inertia, lost motion, and poorly cut gears and cams

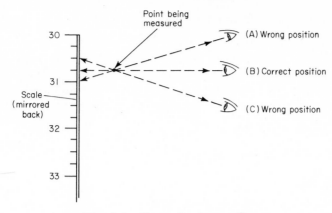

Fig. 1-1 Error due to parallax.

4. Unavoidable or partly unavoidable properties of materials, such as aging of metals, the gradual yielding of materials to physical stress, the aging of permanent magnets, and the effects of corrosion and erosion

Inaccuracies arising from such causes as friction of rest and motion, clearances in bearings and gears, and aging of materials are more or less regular in character and are responsible for what is referred to as the *hysteresis loop* of an instrument. This is the loop which is obtained by plotting instrument readings against true or known standard values. The instrument is used first in ascending steps and then in descending steps. A typical hysteresis loop is shown in Fig. 1-2.

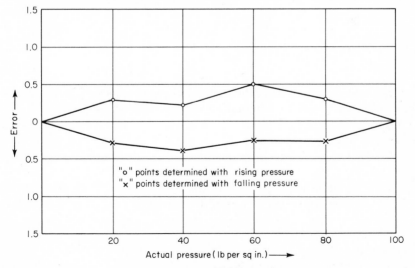

Fig. 1-2 A hysteresis loop and statement of accuracy.

Static Errors, Drift, and Reproducibility

The *static error* of measurement is the deviation of the instrument reading from the true value at any point on the scale where a steady reading has been obtained, i.e., under equilibrium conditions. Large static errors are undesirable. The graph in Fig. 1-3 shows the calibrated scale and

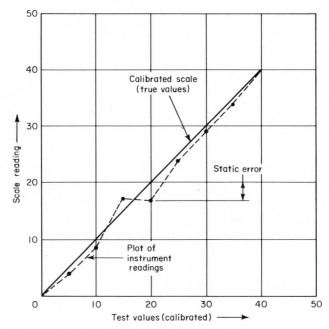

Fig. 1-3   Correction chart for static error.

actual instrument readings. The curves plotted are based on hypothetical data and are intended to illustrate the meaning of static error.

Reproducibility is the degree of closeness with which the same value of a variable can be measured at different times. Perfect reproducibility signifies that the instrument has no *drift*. "Drift" in this sense means a gradual separation of the measured value from the calibrated value, usually after a long interval of time during which the value of the variable does not change. Drift can be caused by permanent set, stress, or fatigue in metal components. Alternatively, it can be due to wear, erosion, or general deterioration as a function of time.

Example 1. The measuring scale shown in Fig. 1-4 shows the error in measurement. Calculate the percent error of full scale and of actual point.

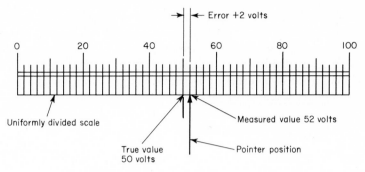

Fig. 1-4   Error in instrument measurement.

Solution. A positive error denotes that the measured value is algebraically greater than the true value. Full scale is 100 volts; error is +2 volts:

$$\tfrac{2}{100} \times 100\% = +2\% \text{ of full-scale value}$$
or
$$\tfrac{2}{50} \times 100\% = +4\% \text{ of actual point value}$$

Example 2. If a pyrometer, an instrument for measuring high temperatures, is used to measure a furnace temperature at 1650 degrees Celsius (°C) and it is accurate to ±5°C, calculate the percent error. If the same error of ±5°C occurs in the measurement of the temperature of boiling water at 100°C, show how serious the error becomes.

Solution. An accuracy of ±5°C gives a percent error of

$$\pm \tfrac{5}{1650} \times 100\% = \pm 0.3\%$$

In the case of measuring the temperature of boiling water at 100°C the percent error is

$$\pm \tfrac{5}{100} \times 100\% = \pm 5\%$$

which is a much more serious error.

Example 3. An instrument with a range of 200 to 1200°C is said to have an accuracy within ±0.25%. What does this mean?

Solution. An accuracy within ±0.25% means that the static error at any point of the scale never exceeds 3.0°C, that is, 0.25% of full scale (1200°C). If the accuracy is referred to span (1200° − 200° = 1000°C), the figure becomes 2.5°C.

Sensitivity

Sensitivity may be defined as the magnitude of displacement of the indicating element of an instrument per unit change in the measured quantity.

$$\text{Sensitivity} = \frac{\Delta\theta \text{ (small displacement change of indicator)}}{\Delta R \text{ (small change of the measured quantity)}}$$

Sensitivity is an important property of instruments which is determined by design. The numerical value of the sensitivity is influenced by the requirements of instrument application. The choice will be decided by the smallest subdivision required by the conditions of the test measurement.

Sensitivity and responsiveness are frequently confused, as in speaking of a thermometer which is "sensitive to 0.1°C." In accordance with the definitions of the two terms, it is correct to say that the thermometer will "respond to a change of ±0.1°C."

Responsiveness

The term *responsiveness* denotes the amount of displacing or actuating effect required to cause motion of the indicating part of the meter. It is determined by noting the smallest alteration in the quantity being measured that will produce a perceptible change in the indication of the meter.

Example. A pressure gauge at 200 psi requires a change of ±2 psi to cause a change in indication. Evaluate the percent responsiveness of the gauge.

Solution

$$\text{Responsiveness} = \tfrac{2}{200} \times 100\% = 1.0\%$$

It is quite possible that the value of the factor may and probably will be different for all points within the range of the instrument.

The responsiveness may be partly controllable and partly uncontrollable. Controllable responsiveness refers to time lag. For example, a pressure gauge measuring a pulsating pressure may have its responsiveness increased by connecting it to the pressure source through a long capillary tube to absorb pulsations and thus give a steady reading. Uncontrollable responsiveness may be due to inertia and friction, which can be minimized by proper lubrication and adjustment of the indicating mechanism.

Span, Range, and Significant Figures

Span and range. If the highest point of calibration is X units and the lowest point is Y units and if the calibration is continuous between these two points, then the *range* is said to be from Y to X units. The instrument *span* is given by $X - Y$ units.

Example 1. A high-temperature instrument is calibrated to measure from 0 to 2000°F. What are the range and span?

Solution. The range is 0 to 2000°F; the span is

$$2000°F - 0°F = 2000°F$$

Example 2. An instrument similar to the one of Example 1 is calibrated from 100 to 500°F. What are the range and span?

Solution. The range is 100 to 500°F; the span is

$$500°F - 100°F = 400°F$$

Significant figures. The number used in recording the reading of an instrument is partly determined by the sensitivity of the instrument. In writing a measured value as a series of digits, certain of these digits will have an element of doubt associated with them. The total number of significant figures is the number of figures that should be retained as valid and is dependent on the probable error associated with the observation or reading. For example, if the reading is interpreted by an observer as being 3.6834 and the probable error of this particular reading is given as ±0.05, then the reading should be taken as 3.68 ± 0.05.

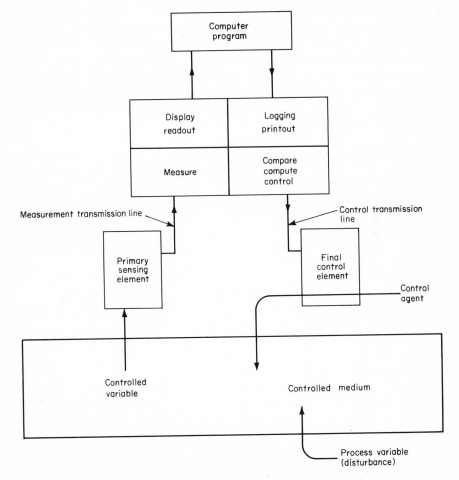

Fig. 1-5 Basic elements of a centralized instrumentation system.

Basic Functions of an Instrumentation System

Instrumentation may be defined as the art and science of applying measuring instruments and controlling devices to a system or process for the purpose of determining the identity or magnitude of certain varying physical quantities or chemical phenomena. The purpose of instrumentation is the control of physical quantities or variables within specified quality limitations at the maximum possible efficiency and at the minimum cost.

A typical arrangement of the basic elements and functions of a centralized instrumentation system is shown, as a block diagram, in Fig. 1-5. The fundamental elements and functions of instruments and control systems are described in Chap. 7, which deals with the art and science of instrumentation. The reason for this deferment is to allow time for the reader to become acquainted with some of the actual measurement fundamentals such as density, pressure, vacuum, and level. By gaining experience in the instrumentation laboratory and workshop, the reader will become aware of some of the implications of instrumentation. For maximum benefit to the reader, theory and practice must, if possible, be closely allied.

REVIEW QUESTIONS AND PROBLEMS

1-5   If the barometric pressure is measured as 759 millimeters of mercury (mm Hg) by using the laboratory barometer, whereas a more accurate standard measurement gave 758 mm Hg, calculate the relative error.

1-6   Define the following and give examples of each: (a) personal error, (b) instrumental error, (c) applicational error.

1-7   Distinguish between accuracy and precision.

1-8   List four possible sources of error in instrument measurements.

1-9   Define static error and reproducibility and give examples of each.

1-10   An instrument for measuring high temperatures is used to measure temperature at 1650°F, and it is accurate to ±5°F. Calculate the percent error if the same error of ±5°F occurs at 100°F. Show how serious the error becomes.

1-11   (a) Define the terms "sensitivity" and "responsiveness," and discuss their application in instrument measurement work.
(b) A pressure gauge at 100 psi requires a change of ±1 psi to cause a change in indication. Compute the percent responsiveness of the gauge.

1-12   An instrument is calibrated from 100 to 500°C. What are the (a) range and (b) span?

CHAPTER TWO

Dimensional analysis and engineering units

The way to get at the nature of any subject matter you're looking at is by analysis . . . by logic until you get to the atom of the matter.
BERTRAND RUSSELL

Applied science is based to a large extent upon a combination of physical analysis and experimental observations. The invariable objective is to provide dependable practical results and a thorough understanding of fundamental variables. In this chapter are described dimensional analysis and engineering units, two very useful and practical tools in organizing, interpreting, correlating, and checking experimental data and proving the interrelationship of physical quantities. The techniques described will be found useful in performing ordinary calculations and evaluating laboratory or test results involving various physical quantities, each having a variable nature, such as flow rate, viscosity, fluid pressure, and humidity.

Fundamental Dimensions

The fundamental dimensions of any mechanical or physical quantity are conventionally expressed in terms of a set of three primary quantities: mass, length, and time. *Mass* is denoted by $[M]$, *length* is denoted by $[L]$, and *time* is denoted by $[T]$. The square brackets in each case imply the *dimension*. For example, since area possesses both length and breadth, the dimensions are $[L^2]$, and typical units are square inches and square feet. Similarly, the dimensions of a volume are $[L^3]$, and typical units are cubic inches and cubic feet.

Since velocity is a displacement per unit time, e.g., feet per second, the dimensions are $\left[\dfrac{L}{T}\right]$ or $[LT^{-1}]$. Similarly, acceleration is defined as the

13

rate of change of velocity, e.g., feet per second per second, and the dimensions are $\left[\dfrac{L}{T^2}\right]$ or $[LT^{-2}]$.

Flow rate is usually given as a certain volume flowing through a pipeline in a unit of time. The dimensions for flow rate are then $\left[\dfrac{L^3}{T}\right]$, and typical units are cubic feet per second.

Engineering Units for the Fundamental Dimensions

All measurements are actually relative in the sense that they are comparisons with some standard. While "dimension" is a descriptive word, a *unit* is a definite standard or measure of dimension. A unit is defined as a particular amount of the quantity to be measured. For example, the inch, foot, and meter are different units indicating different but definite lengths, while the dimension common to all these units is length. The following are some basic units used in the applied sciences and in instrument technology:

Measurement of time. The second (sec) is the fundamental unit of time. Both the English and metric systems of measurement employ this unit.

Measurement of length. The primary standard of length in the United States is the United States prototype meter 27, a platinum-iridium (90 percent platinum, 10 percent iridium) line standard having an X-shaped section. This bar is kept at the National Bureau of Standards in Washington, D.C. The international prototype meter is kept at the International Bureau of Weights and Measures at Sèvres, near Paris, France.

The yard is defined as 1 yard = 0.9144 meter (m). The inch is therefore exactly equal to 25.4 mm. The foot (ft) is the fundamental unit of length and is defined as $\frac{1}{3}$ yard.

The inch is subdivided into smaller units in two ways. Where precision is not required, the subdivisions are fractional, that is, $\frac{1}{2}$, $\frac{1}{4}$, $\frac{1}{8}$, $\frac{1}{16}$, $\frac{1}{32}$, $\frac{1}{64}$. However, precision measuring instruments used in instrument practice are calibrated to read in thousandths of an inch and ten thousandths of an inch. In some workshops and test laboratories instruments can measure accurately to one millionth (0.000001, or 1.0×10^{-6}) of an inch, referred to as a *microinch*.

Measurement of length (metric system). Most of the countries in the world, except the United States, Canada, and the British Commonwealth of Nations, use a system of length measurement based on the meter. By international agreement, the wavelength of the orange-red light of krypton 86 is the world's length standard. The standard meter is defined as 1,650,763.73 wavelengths of the orange-red line of krypton 86.

The metric system is decimal; the meter, for example, has as subdivisions the centimeter (0.01, or 1.0×10^{-2}, m), the millimeter (0.001, or 1.0×10^{-3}, m), and the micron (0.000001, or 1.0×10^{-6}, m). Because of the ease with which decimal calculations can be made, the metric system is becoming recognized as the measuring system of science.

Measurement of mass and weight. *Mass* is the property of matter which causes the matter to resist acceleration. Mass is independent of the earth's gravity; *weight*, on the other hand, depends on both gravity and mass. The mass contained in one pound, or the pound mass (lb_m), is the fundamental unit of mass. This unit is defined as 0.45359237 kilogram (kg). The kilogram (1,000 grams) is, by international agreement, the prototype mass of platinum-iridium located in Sèvres, France.

Weight is the force exerted on a given mass by the gravitational attraction of the earth. When a body is weighed on a beam scale, it is directly balanced by a known and calibrated mass. This weighing operation is a measure of the mass in the body, because the attraction of gravity on both the known and the unknown masses is the same. However, when a pound mass is weighed on a spring scale, the deflection of the pointer on the dial scale will be influenced by the local value of the earth's gravitational attraction. Figure 2-1 shows the arrangement of a simple scale, which is a means of measuring weight. The weight of a body can be described as the force the body exerts on its supports owing to its mass and gravity.

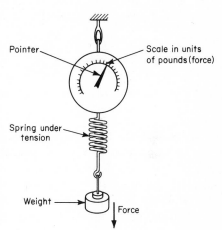

Fig. 2-1   A simple scale to measure weight.

Measurement of force. A force is a push exerted on a body, and it has magnitude and direction. If an unbalanced force acts on a body, the body accelerates in the direction of the force. Conversely, if a body is accelerating, there must be an unbalanced force acting upon it in the direction of the acceleration. This unbalanced force acting on the body is proportional to the product of the mass of the body and the acceleration.

Newton's law of motion. An unbalanced force F acting on a body produces in the body an acceleration a, which is in the direction of the force and is directly proportional to the force and inversely proportional to the mass m of the body. In mathematical form

$$ka = \frac{F}{m} \qquad \text{or} \qquad F = kam$$

where k is a proportionality constant. If suitable units are selected so that $k = 1$, then $F = ma$. Figure 2-2 shows how an unbalanced force can be found from the vector addition of forces.

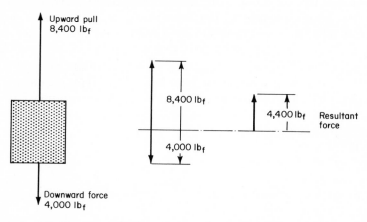

Fig. 2-2   Finding an unbalanced force by using vector addition of forces.

Units of force. In the equation $F = ma$ it is desirable to make $k = 1$, that is, to have units of mass, acceleration, and force such that $F = ma$. To do this, two fundamental units from which a third unit may be derived are specified. In the centimeter-gram-second (cgs) system, the fundamental unit of mass is the gram and the unit of acceleration is the centimeter per second per second. The corresponding derived unit of force, called the dyne, is the unbalanced force which will accelerate a mass of one gram at the rate of one centimeter per second per second.

In the meter-kilogram-second (mks) system, the fundamental unit of mass is the kilogram (kg) and the unit of acceleration is the meter per second per second. The corresponding derived unit of force, called the newton, is the unbalanced force which will produce an acceleration of one meter per second per second in a mass of one kilogram.

In the English gravitational system the fundamental unit of force is the pound force (lb$_f$) and the unit of acceleration is the foot per second per second. The corresponding derived unit of mass, called the slug, is that mass which, when acted on by one pound force, acquires an acceleration of one foot per second per second.

The three systems of consistent units may be used with the Newtonian equation $F = kma$, where $k = 1$:

cgs system F (dynes) $= m$ (grams) $\times\ a$ (cm/sec²)
mks system F (newtons) $= m$ (kilograms) $\times\ a$ (m/sec²)
English system F (pounds) $= m$ (slugs) $\times\ a$ (ft/sec²)

Example 1. Compute the force required to give a block weighing 24 lb$_f$ an acceleration of 10 ft/sec².

Solution. Force, mass, and acceleration are related by

$$F = ma = \frac{W}{g}\,a$$
$$= \frac{24\ \text{lb}_f}{32.2\ \text{ft/sec}^2} \times 10\ \text{ft/sec}^2$$
$$= 7.5\ \text{lb}_f$$

It should be noted that $m = W/g$ is the mass of the block, in slugs.

Example 2. When a force of 1,000 lb$_f$ acts on it, a body is found to acquire an acceleration of 20 ft/sec². Compute the mass and weight of the body.

Solution

$$F = ma$$
$$1{,}000\ \text{lb}_f = m\ \text{slugs} \times 20\ \text{ft/sec}^2$$
$$m = 50\ \text{lb}_f\,\frac{\text{sec}^2}{\text{ft}} = 50\ \text{slugs}$$

By rearrangement, the units for 1 slug are $\dfrac{1\ \text{lb}_f\ \text{sec}^2}{\text{ft}}$.

From the equation $m = \dfrac{W}{g}$ the weight (W) is

$$W = mg$$
$$= 50\,\frac{\text{lb}_f\ \text{sec}^2}{\text{ft}} \times 32.2\,\frac{\text{ft}^2}{\text{sec}}$$
$$= 1{,}610\ \text{lb}_f$$

Example 3. If a body weighs 64.4 lb$_f$ at a place where $g = 32.2$ ft/sec², then its mass is

$$m = \frac{W}{g} = \frac{64.4\ \text{lb}_f}{32.2\ \text{ft/sec}^2}$$
$$= 2.0\ \text{slugs}$$

If a body weighs 49 newtons at a place where $g = 9.8$ m/sec², its mass is

$$m = \frac{W}{g} = \frac{49\ \text{newtons}}{9.8\ \text{m/sec}^2} = 5\ \text{kilograms}$$

Engineering System of Units

A satisfactory set of three fundamental dimensions are, as mentioned previously, mass, length, and time. The selection of these primary dimensions is governed, to some extent, by convenience. It is possible and preferable in the engineering dimensional system to employ the dimension "force."

The corresponding three fundamental units are the pound of force [F] (or pound weight), the foot of length [L], and the second of time [T]. The unit for mass in the engineering system is the slug, and it is derived from the units of force and acceleration. In the case of a freely falling body in vacuum the acceleration is that of gravity ($g = 32.2$ ft/sec² at sea level) and the only force acting is the weight of the body.

Using Newton's second law of motion, which states that force is proportional to the product of mass and acceleration,

Force F, in pounds (lb$_f$) = mass, in slugs, $\times$ acceleration, in ft/sec²

Then,

weight W, in pounds force (lb$_f$) = mass, in slugs $\times g$

where $g = 32.2$ ft/sec² or

$$\text{Mass } m, \text{ in slugs} = \frac{\text{weight } W, \text{ in pounds}}{g \ (32.2) \ \text{ft/sec}^2}$$

The following is an example to distinguish between units of mass and force. The *mass density* of a body is defined as the mass per unit volume ρ (rho), or $D = \dfrac{m}{V}$. In the metric system the mass density of water is one gram per cubic centimeter at 4°C. The weight density of water is used more frequently in problems and analysis work dealing with instrumentation. The weight density of water is 62.4 lb$_f$ per cubic foot in the English engineering system of units. The mass density of water is therefore

$$\frac{62.4 \ \text{lb}_f/\text{ft}^3}{32.2 \ \text{ft/sec}^2} = 1.94 \ \text{slugs/ft}^3$$

The mechanical quantities are

Force = mass $\times$ acceleration
Impulse = mass $\times$ velocity (change of momentum)
Work done = force $\times$ distance (change of kinetic energy)

By using the three fundamental dimensions [M], [L], and [T] or, in the engineering dimensional system, [F], [L], and [T], these mechanical quantities can be represented as shown in Table 2-1.

Table 2-1 Fundamental dimensions for mechanical quantities

Quantity	Dimensions	
	M-L-T	*F-L-T*
Mass	$[M]$	$\left[\dfrac{F}{L/T^2}\right]$ or $\left[\dfrac{FT^2}{L}\right]$
Force	$\left[\dfrac{ML}{T^2}\right]$	$[F]$
Impulse or momentum	$\left[\dfrac{ML}{T}\right]$	$[FT]$
Work or energy	$\left[\dfrac{ML}{T^2}\right]$ $[L] = \left[\dfrac{ML^2}{T^2}\right]$	$[FL]$

The kilopond. The kilopond (K_p) is frequently used, and it competes with the newton for popularity in the metric system. A kilopond is the force exerted by a kilogram mass (physical sense) upon its support in a gravitational field of $g = 9.80665$ m/sec². The following is a typical engineering application.

Example 4. A mass of 100 kg is suspended from a rope having a cross-sectional area of 10 cm². Compute the stress in the rope.

Solution. Since a mass of 1 kg exerts a force of 1 K_p, the stress σ (sigma) in the rope will be

$$\sigma = \frac{100 \ K_p \ (\text{force})}{10 \ \text{cm}^2 \ (\text{area})} = 10 \ K_p/\text{cm}^2$$

Figure 2-3 shows the comparison of the mass-force equivalent, in grams, of the newton, the pound force, and kilopond.

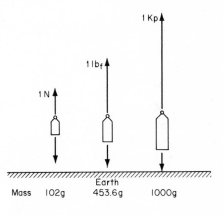

Fig. 2-3 The newton, pound, and kilopond are related to one another approximately as 1:5:10.

Dimensional Analysis

Scientific methods are based upon a combination of physical analysis and experimental observation. The objective is to provide dependable results and an understanding of how they were derived. This section is introduced to show the importance and advantage of dimensional analysis and units in the organization, correlation, and interpretation of experimental data.

Dimensional analysis is very useful in determining dimensionless ratios. For example, the common trigonometric functions, such as the sine and tangent, may be regarded as dimensionless ratios of lengths. The measure of inclination of an angle, as shown in Fig. 2-4, is a function of the ratio of any vertical side to the corresponding base. Trigonometric functions, expressed as dimensionless ratios, afford a convenient method of setting up tables which can be used for a wide range of problems. Specific gravity is also an example of a dimensionless ratio useful for comparison purposes. The frequently used term "efficiency" is another example of a dimensionless ratio. In instrumentation and scientific engineering work it is becoming usual to express experimental results in terms of dimensionless ratios or just as numbers.

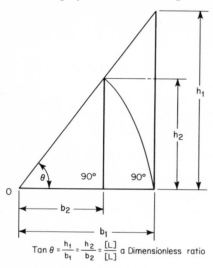

$$\text{Tan } \theta = \frac{h_1}{b_1} = \frac{h_2}{b_2} = \frac{[L]}{[L]} \text{ a Dimensionless ratio}$$

Fig. 2-4   The tangent as a measure of inclination.

Dimensional analysis is a mathematical method found very useful in checking equations, investigating the validity of formulas, checking units, and determining a convenient arrangement of variables having a physical relation. In any equation used in the applied sciences which expresses a physical relation between variables of a set, complete numerical and dimensional equality must exist if the equation is to be valid. If the dimensions and units do not balance, then the equation is rendered invalid and is rejected.

A study of dimensions and dimensional analysis often aids in making a description of physical phenomena easier and more convenient. Dimensional analysis results in a sound, orderly arrangement for solving problems dealing with the result of a set of variables in practical formulation or in experimentation work.

Applications of dimensions and dimensional analysis are made in the fundamental approach to problems in dynamics, rigid-body mechanics, thermodynamics, hydraulics, fluid mechanics, and other fields of pure and

Table 2-2   Dimensional analysis of various quantities and variables

Quantity	Symbol	M-L-T	F-L-T	Typical units
Area	A	L^2	L^2	ft^2
Volume	v	L^3	L^3	ft^3
Velocity	V	LT^{-1}	LT^{-1}	ft/sec
Acceleration	a or g	LT^{-2}	LT^{-2}	ft/sec^2
Angular velocity, in radians	ω (omega)	T^{-1}	T^{-1}	sec^{-1}
Mass	m	M	FT^2L^{-1}	lb$_f$ sec^2/ft
Mass density	D or ρ (rho)	ML^{-3}	FT^2L^{-4}	lb$_f$ sec^2/ft^4
Weight	W	MLT^{-2}	F	lb$_f$
Force	F	MLT^{-2}	F	lb$_f$
Weight density or specific weight	w	$ML^{-2}T^{-2}$	FL^{-3}	lb$_f$/ft^3
Discharge	Q	L^3T^{-1}	L^3T^{-1}	ft^3/sec
Weight rate of flow	G	MLT^{-3}	FT^{-1}	lb$_f$/sec
Intensity of pressure or stress	p or σ (sigma)	$ML^{-1}T^{-2}$	FL^{-2}	lb$_f$/ft^2
Modulus of elasticity	E	$ML^{-1}T^{-2}$	FL^{-2}	lb$_f$/ft^2
Absolute or dynamic viscosity	μ (mu)	$ML^{-1}T^{-1}$	FTL^{-2}	lb$_f$ sec/ft^2
Kinematic viscosity	ν (nu)	L^2T^{-1}	L^2T^{-1}	ft^2/sec
Power	P	ML^2T^{-3}	FLT^{-1}	ft-lb$_f$/sec
Torque	T	ML^2T^{-2}	FL	ft-lb
Shear stress	τ (tau)	$ML^{-1}T^{-2}$	FL^{-2}	lb$_f$/ft^2
Surface tension	σ (sigma)	MT^{-2}	FL^{-1}	lb$_f$/ft

applied science. The word "dimension" is frequently used to denote both the numerical magnitude of a measurement and its dimensional class. For the benefit of the reader, Table 2-2 lists numerous physical quantities in terms of $[M]$, $[L]$, and $[T]$ and also in terms of $[F]$, $[L]$, and $[T]$. The symbols and a set of typical engineering units are also listed.

Explicit substitution of units in all engineering equations should quickly give familiarity with basic ideas of dimensional analysis. For each physical quantity a number and unit must be substituted in an equation for each term. In this way the equation must balance dimensionally to be valid and for the units to be correct.

The following examples provide illustrations of dimensional analysis with equations and concepts of functions.

Example 1. Check that the following displacement equation balances dimensionally

$$S = V_0 t + \tfrac{1}{2}at^2$$

where S = distance traveled
V_0 = velocity
a = acceleration
t = time

Solution. The dimensional equation becomes

$$[L] = [LT^{-1}][T] + [LT^{-2}][T^2]$$

By grouping indices of like terms,

$$[L] = [LT^{-1+1}] + [LT^{-2+2}]$$

Since any term having the index of zero is 1, that is, $T^0 = 1$,

$$[L] = [L] + [L]$$

Hence the dimension of length exists on both sides of the equation. Appropriate units could be feet or meters.

Example 2. The following equation is used to determine the viscosity μ of a liquid having a certain volume flow rate Q through a capillary of internal diameter D.

$$\mu = \frac{1}{128} \frac{\Delta p}{L} \frac{D^4}{Q}$$

The pressure drop across a length of the capillary is given by $\Delta p/L$. Check that the equation balances dimensionally and prescribe appropriate units.

Solution. Using the set of $[M]$, $[L]$, and $[T]$, and by adding indices of like terms, the dimensional equation for the variables becomes

$$[ML^{-1}T^{-1}] = \left[\frac{ML^{-1}T^{-2}}{L}\right][L^4]\frac{1}{[L^3T^{-1}]}$$
$$[ML^{-1}T^{-1}] = [ML^{-2}T^{-2}][L^4][L^{-3}T^1]$$
$$[ML^{-1}T^{-1}] = [ML^{-2+4-3}][T^{-2+1}]$$
$$= [ML^{-1}T^{-1}]$$

Hence the equation balances dimensionally. Typical units for viscosity are grams per centimeter per second, or grams per centimeter second (g/cm sec).

Alternative method. Using the $[F]$, $[L]$, and $[T]$ dimensions, the dimensional equation for the variables becomes, with indices of like terms added,

$$[FTL^{-2}] = \frac{[F/L^2]}{[L]}[L^4]\frac{1}{[L^3T^{-1}]}$$
$$= [FL^{-3}][L^4][L^{-3}T^{+1}]$$
$$= [FTL^{-3+4-3}]$$
$$= [FTL^{-2}]$$

Hence the equation balances dimensionally. Typical units for viscosity are lb$_f$ sec/ft². Other units are discussed in the section dealing with the measurement of viscosity.

Example 3. Consider the time of one swing or oscillation of a simple pendulum. The quantities or variables describing the swing are listed in Table 2-3.

Table 2-3

Variables (dimensions)	Symbol	Dimensional formula
Time of swing	t	T
Length of pendulum	L	L
Mass of pendulum	m	M
Acceleration of gravity	g	LT^{-2}
Amplitude of swing (radians)	θ	None

$$t = f(Lmg\theta)$$

where f is any function of these four variables.

For dimensional homogeneity (uniformity) the dimensions of T must be equal to those in $f(Lmg\theta)$. The dimensional equation for the function becomes

$$[T] = [L]^a[M]^b[LT^{-2}]^c$$

where a, b, and c represent the numerical powers to which L, m, and g may have to be raised to establish the final expression.

Simultaneous equations can be used to solve for a, b, and c by equating the indices of like dimensions in the dimensional equation for the function.

Time $[T]$ $1 = -2c$ $c = -\frac{1}{2}$
Length $[L]$ $0 = a + c$ $a = \frac{1}{2}$
Mass $[M]$ $0 = b$ $b = 0$

Since $b = 0$, the mass is not a factor to be considered, because

$$M^0 = 1$$

Hence $t = k \left(\dfrac{L}{g}\right)^{\frac{1}{2}}$ or $t = k \sqrt{\dfrac{L}{g}}$

Experimentally, k is found to be equal to the constant 2π:

$$t = 2\pi \sqrt{\frac{L}{g}}$$

It should be observed carefully that the method of dimensional analysis only systematically arranges the variables that presumably influence the event under investigation. If one or more of these quantities or variables is omitted, the result should be significant only to the degree that the missing variables are significant.

Example 4. The discharge Q of a liquid, in volume per unit time, through a horizontal capillary tube is thought to depend upon the pressure drop per unit length $\Delta p/L$, the diameter D, and the dynamic viscosity μ. Establish, by applying dimensional analysis, the form of the equation for discharge in terms of the other variables.

Solution. The functional equation is

$$Q = f\left(\frac{\Delta p}{L}\, D\mu\right)$$

The dimensional equation is

$$\left[\frac{L^3}{T}\right] = \left[\frac{M/LT^2}{L}\right]^a [L]^b \left[\frac{M}{LT}\right]^c$$

$$[L^3 T^{-1}] = [ML^{-2}T^{-2}]^a [L]^b [ML^{-1}T^{-1}]^c$$

Equating the respective powers for time, mass, and length,

Time $[T]$	$-1 = -2a - c$	$a = 1$
Mass $[M]$	$0 = a + c$	$b = 4$
Length $[L]$	$3 = -2a + b - c$	$c = -1$

Therefore, the final relationship becomes

$$Q = k\,\frac{\Delta p}{L}\,\frac{D^4}{\mu}$$

where k is a nondimensional constant found by experiment to be $1/128$. Hence

$$Q = \frac{1}{128}\,\frac{\Delta p}{L}\,\frac{D^4}{\mu}$$

Example 5. The velocity of sound V in a gas depends upon the mass density ρ, pressure p, and dynamic viscosity μ. Establish, by dimensional analysis, the form of the equation for the velocity in terms of the other variables.

Solution. The functional equation is

$$V = f[\rho p \mu]$$

The dimensional equation is then

$$\left[\frac{L}{T}\right] = \left[\frac{M}{L^3}\right]^a \left[\frac{M}{LT^2}\right]^b \left[\frac{M}{LT}\right]^c$$

$$[LT^{-1}] = [ML^{-3}]^a [ML^{-1}T^{-2}]^b [ML^{-1}T^{-1}]^c$$

$$= [M^a L^{-3a}][M^b L^{-b} T^{-2b}][M^c L^{-c} T^{-c}]$$

Equating the respective powers for time, mass, and length,

Time $[T]$	$-1 = -2b - c$	$a = -\frac{1}{2}$
Mass $[M]$	$0 = a + b + c$	$b = \frac{1}{2}$
Length $[L]$	$1 = -3a - b - c$	$c = 0$

which makes the final expression

$$V = k \sqrt{\frac{p}{\rho}}$$

where k is some arbitrary constant determined by actual experimental results

Table 2-4   Common units and approximate conversion factors values

Length

1 kilometer (km)   = 1,000 meters
1 meter (m)   = 100 centimeters
1 centimeter (cm)   = 10^{-2} m
1 millimeter (mm)   = 10^{-3} m
1 micron   = 10^{-6} m
1 angstrom (A)   = 10^{-10} m
1 inch (in.)   = 2.54 cm
1 foot (ft)   = 30.48 cm
1 meter (m)   = 39.37 in. (approx)
1 mile (mi) statute = 1.609 km
1 mil   = 10^{-3} in.

Volume

1 liter (l) = 1,000.027 cm^3 = 1.057 qt = 0.03432 ft^3
1 cubic meter (m^3) = 1,000 (l) = 35.32 ft^3
1 cubic foot (ft^3) = 7.481 U.S. gal
1 U.S. gal = 0.833 imp gal = 231 $in.^3$ = 3.785 liters

Mass

1 kilogram$_m$ (kg) = 1,000 g$_m$ = 0.06852 slug
1 lb$_m$ = 453.5924277 g$_m$

Mass Density

1 g/cm^3 = 1.940 slug/ft^3

Weight Density

1 lb$_f$/ft^3 = 16.02 kg$_f$/m^3

Force

1 newton (N) = 10^5 dynes = 0.2248 lb$_f$ = 0.102 kg$_f$
1 pound force (lb$_f$) = 0.4536 kg$_f$
1 U.S. short ton = 2,000 lb$_f$
1 long ton = 2,240 lb$_f$
1 kilopond (K$_p$) = 1 kilogram force (kg$_f$)

REVIEW QUESTIONS AND PROBLEMS

2-1   Explain what is meant by the expressions (a) fundamental dimensions, (b) fundamental units, (c) engineering units, (d) mks units.

2-2   Define the following terms and give the dimensions in each case: (a) slug, (b) force, (c) pound force, (d) pound mass.

2-3   Compute the force necessary to accelerate a mass of 10 slugs at the rate of 10 ft/sec².

2-4   Evaluate the mass m of a body whose weight W is (a) 19.6 newtons, (b) 96 lb, (c) 1,960 dynes. Assume $g = 32$ ft/sec² $= 980$ cm/sec².

2-5   Compute the force required to give an object weighing 12 lb$_f$ an acceleration of 8 ft/sec².

2-6   Determine the force of 1 lb$_f$ in terms of newtons.

2-7   Evaluate the magnitude of the gravitational force acting on a 9-kg body at a place where the gravitational acceleration is 9.79 m/sec².

2-8   (a) Explain the practical applications of dimensional analysis.
(b) Give the dimensions of mass, force, pressure, and torque.
(c) If the equation for the time of swing of a simple pendulum is

$$t = 2\pi \sqrt{\frac{L}{g}}$$

where L = length of pendulum
g = gravitational acceleration
show that the dimensions balance on both sides of the equation.

2-9   Reynolds number is used as a criterion of flow and is given by

$$\mathrm{Re} = \rho \frac{DV}{\mu}$$

where ρ = mass density
D = diameter
V = velocity
μ = dynamic viscosity
Show that this group of variables is nondimensional.

2-10   The velocity V of an airstream is alleged to be related to the pressure difference Δp across a Pitot static tube by the equation

$$V = \sqrt{\frac{2g\,\Delta p}{w}}$$

where w is the weight density of the air and g is the gravitational acceleration. Carry out a dimensional-analysis check on the validity of this expression.

2-11   Develop an expression for the frequency of a simple pendulum, assuming it is a function of the mass of the pendulum, the length of the pendulum, and the gravitational acceleration.

2-12   It is assumed that flow Q over a rectangular weir as shown in Fig. 2-5 varies directly with the length $[L]$ and is a function of the

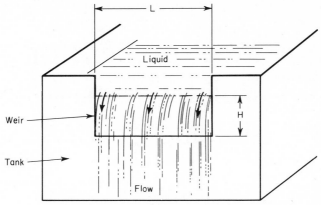

Fig. 2-5   Flow through a rectangular weir.

head H and gravitational acceleration. Show that by dimensional analysis the flow equation is

$$Q = kLH^{3/2}g^{1/2}$$

where k is a constant.

2-13   The diagram in Fig. 2-6 shows a rotating shaft in a bearing of a control mechanism. If the torque is a function of the diameter D, the axial length L, the rotating speed N, the dynamic viscosity of the oil μ, and the load per unit of projected area in the bearing p,

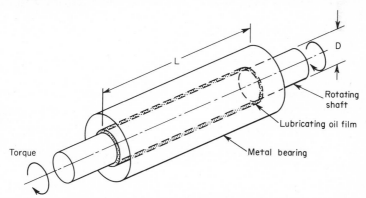

Fig. 2-6   Rotating shaft in bearing.

establish, by dimensional analysis, the equation

$$T = CD^3N\mu$$

where C is an arbitrary constant.

CHAPTER THREE

Measurement of weight, density, and specific gravity

Weights and measures are necessary to every occupation of human industry.

JOHN QUINCY ADAMS

In industrial processes and scientific work it is frequently desirable and often necessary to know the mass density, weight density, or specific gravity of materials. Materials are commonly classified as solids, liquids, and gases. The term *fluid* is applicable to both liquids and gases.

If small cubes of different metals having the same volume are obtained, it will be found that they all have different weights. Referring to Fig. 3-1,

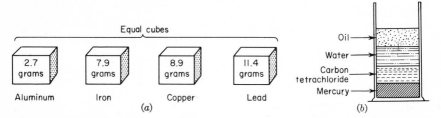

Fig. 3-1 (a) *Comparison of heaviness of metals.* (b) *Comparison of heaviness of liquids.*

aluminum is one of the lightest metals and lead is one of the heaviest. In order to compare the relative heaviness of different substances, the term *density* is used. Because of its common occurrence, water is generally used as the basis for comparison. The temperature must also be specified because of volumetric changes. Water has its greatest density at 39°F, and some comparison scales refer to that temperature.

Mass Density

In scientific work "mass density" means the mass per unit volume. In the metric system mass density is expressed in grams per cubic centimeter; in the British system, as slugs per cubic foot.

$$\text{Mass density } D, \text{ or } \rho = \frac{\text{mass } m}{\text{volume } V}$$

Dimensionally, the units of mass density are $\left[\dfrac{M}{L^3}\right]$, that is, slugs per cubic foot or grams per cubic centimeter.

Weight Density

In the applied sciences the *weight density* is used. It is defined as the weight force per unit volume.

$$\text{Weight density } w = \frac{\text{weight force } W_f}{\text{volume } V}$$

Dimensionally, the units of weight density are $\left[\dfrac{F}{L^3}\right]$, that is, pounds force per cubic foot.

Newton's law, which states that force is proportional to the product of mass and acceleration, gives a simple relation between mass and weight. Symbolically

$$W_f = mg \qquad \text{or} \qquad m = \frac{W_f}{g}$$

where m is the mass, W_f is the weight force, and g is the earth's gravitational acceleration at a particular location. Weight is the force exerted on a given mass by the gravitational effect of the earth. Hence,

$$\text{Weight density } w = \frac{mg}{V} = \rho g$$

The dimensions of ρg are the same as for the weight density, because the product mg is considered to be a force F.

When a body is weighed on a beam balance or scale, it is directly balanced by a known and calibrated mass. This weighing operation is, in fact, a measure of the mass of the body, because the attraction of gravity on both the unknown and known masses is the same. On the other hand, when a pound mass is weighed on a spring scale, the deflection of the scale will be influenced by the local value of the earth's gravitational attraction. The weight of a body is dependent upon this attraction of gravity, whereas the mass of the body is not dependent upon it.

Specific Gravity

Specific gravity (sp gr) is defined as the ratio of the mass or weight density of a substance to the mass or weight density of a selected reference material such as water under prescribed conditions of constant volume and temperature.

$$\text{Sp gr} = \frac{\rho}{\rho_w} = \frac{w}{w_w}$$

Example. The weight of a cubic foot of mercury is 847.0 lb, while that of water is 62.3 lb at the same temperature.

$$\text{Specific gravity of mercury} = \frac{847.0 \text{ lb}}{62.3 \text{ lb}} = 13.6$$

Specific gravity is a dimensionless term because it is the result of a ratio operation and the dimensions cancel out. Mercury, as the example shows, is 13.6 times heavier than water.

Laboratory Measurement of Density and Specific Gravity

In order to find the density of wood or metal which is in the form of a rectangular block, it is necessary to find the weight and volume of the block. The weight may be found by means of an ordinary balance, and the volume may be found by measuring the length, width, and depth and multiplying the three together. For accurate results, vernier calipers must be used in determining the dimension of the block.

One of the easiest methods for determining specific gravity is to weigh a given volume of the material and then to find the weight of an equal volume of water. The ratio of the weight of the material to that of water gives the specific gravity.

Hydrometer. An instrument which is used for finding the density or specific gravity of a liquid directly is called a *hydrometer*. The common hydrometer consists of a glass float which is weighted at the bottom, generally with mercury or lead shot. The float has a hollow stem inside which is a graduated scale. The arrangement is shown in Fig. 3-2. To find the density of a liquid, the hydrometer is floated in the liquid and the position of the surface of the liquid on the hydrometer scale indicates the liquid density.

The hydrometer is based on the application of Archimedes' principle of floatation, which states that the weight of a floating object is equal to the weight of the fluid which it displaces. The float increases the buoyancy of the hydrometer because of the liquid displaced. Hydrometers used for liquids which are lighter than water have a large float, and scale graduations start with a specific gravity of 1.00 at the bottom. A variety of hydrometers based on the principles discussed are available on the market.

Hydrometers are used in the laboratory and in industry for testing

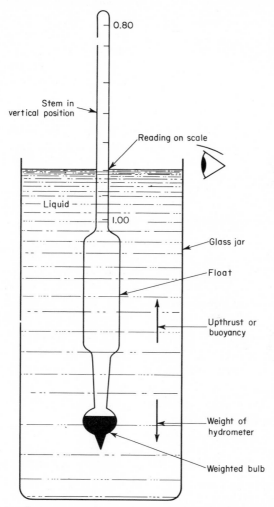

Fig. 3-2   Structure and operation of a simple hydrometer.

liquids such as salt solutions, petroleum products, and acids. The storage-battery hydrometer is used to test the specific gravity of the acid solution and thereby estimate the degree to which the battery should be charged. Hydrometers are also used in the testing of antifreeze mixtures, of milk for possible dilution, and for estimating the strength of wines and beers.

Density or specific-gravity bottle. The specific-gravity bottle is another method used for measuring liquid densities. In Fig. 3-3 is shown a small

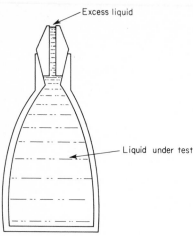

bottle fitted with a ground-glass stopper having a central hole. The liquid under test is poured into the bottle. As the stopper is inserted, the excess liquid is forced out through the hole. Care should be taken to exclude air bubbles and to wipe liquid from the outside of the bottle. The bottle is then weighed on an analytical balance, and its weight is recorded. The weight of the bottle when empty must also be determined. In this way the net weight of the liquid can be found.

The internal volume of the bottle is found by taking standard tests with distilled water, using a graduated jar. From these data, both the

Fig. 3-3   Specific-gravity bottle.

density and specific gravity of the liquid at standard temperatures can be found.

$$\text{Specific gravity} = \frac{\text{net weight of liquid in the bottle}}{\text{net weight of water in the bottle}}$$

Westphal balance. The Westphal balance is based on the definition of specific gravity and on Archimedes' principle. If a body of constant volume is immersed in different liquids, the corresponding losses of weight of the body are proportional to the weights of equal volumes of the liquids. If one of these liquids is water, then the specific gravity of the unknown liquid may be found.

The Westphal balance is shown in Fig. 3-4. The instrument can be standardized in distilled water. The specific gravity of an unknown liquid can then be read directly by adding up the beam-rider weights when the beam is truly balanced at the index end. The plummet must be fully immersed in the liquid under test. Accurate results can be obtained with this balance if great care is taken with the apparatus.

The plummet of the Troemner model displaces 5 grams (g) of distilled water at 20°C. The weights supplied are 5 g and 500, 50, and 5 milligrams (mg). The 5-g rider is suspended from the same loop as the plummet, and the plummet is immersed in distilled water at 20°C. The balance should be in equilibrium, this indicating a specific gravity of 1.000. The 5-g rider is left in the same position for liquids which are denser than water, and it is removed and used on the beam for liquids which are less dense than water.

The riders are used one at a time in order of decreasing weight. If the 5-g rider is in notch 7 of a beam balance, the 0.5-g rider is in notch 6, the

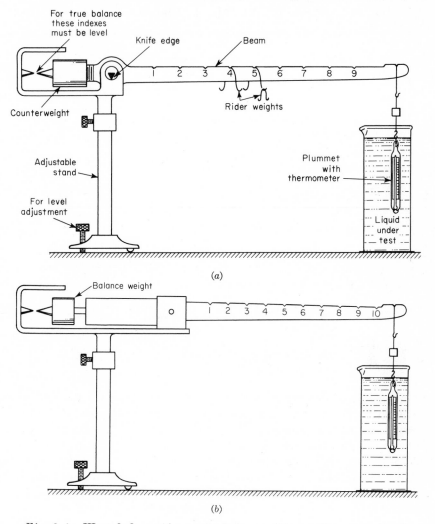

Fig. 3-4   Westphal specific-gravity balance. (Henry Troemner Inc.)

0.05-g rider is in notch 4, and the 0.005-g rider is in notch 3, the specific gravity is read as 0.7643. The specific gravity of liquids less than 1 can be measured by suspending a plummet from an analytical balance and using weights on the opposite side to obtain balance.

Industrial Measurement of Density and Specific Gravity

Air bubbler method. This arrangement, which is shown in Fig. 3-5, gives a continuous indication or record of specific gravity. The method necessitates drawing a sample of the liquid from the process system. The container provides a fixed depth of liquid into which is inserted a stand-

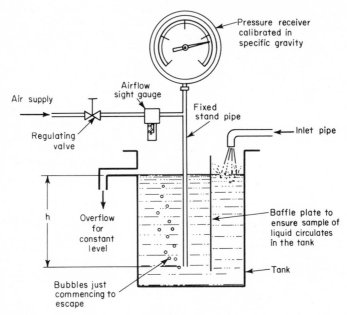

Fig. 3-5   Arrangement of bubbler system to measure specific gravity.

pipe at constant immersion. Air is fed past a regulating valve and a sight gauge into the standpipe. Bubbles are just permitted to escape from the bottom end of the standpipe; then the pressure in the system and the standpipe equals the pressure due to the head of liquid above the lower end of the standpipe. This pressure will vary with the specific gravity of the liquid, and the receiving instrument is calibrated in terms of specific gravity. The air pressure, in pounds per square foot, equals the pressure head of liquid in the same units. Symbolically

$$p = h \times 62.4 \times \text{sp gr}$$

where p = pressure of the air in the system and standpipe, lb/ft^2
      h = height of liquid above the opening at the bottom of the stand-
          pipe, ft
  sp gr = specific gravity of the liquid

The weight density of water, in pounds per cubic foot, is 62.4. Using dimensional analysis on both sides of the equation,

$$\left[\frac{F}{L^2}\right] = [L]\left[\frac{F}{L^3}\right] = \left[\frac{F}{L^2}\right]$$

Example. During a test run to determine the specific gravity of a liquid by using a bubbler system, the air-line pressure was 0.6 lb/in.², or 86.4 lb/ft², for bubbles to escape at the open end of a pipe immersed in the liquid at fixed depth of 2.0 ft. Compute the value of (a) the specific gravity and (b) the weight density of the liquid.

Solution. (a) $p = h \times 62.4 \times$ sp gr

$$\text{sp gr} = \frac{p}{h \times 62.4}$$
$$= \frac{86.4 \text{ lb/ft}^2}{2 \text{ ft} \times 62.4 \text{ lb/ft}^3}$$
$$= 0.7 \qquad \text{no dimensions or units}$$

(b) To compute the weight density w of the liquid

$$w = 62.3 \text{ lb/ft}^3 \times 0.7$$
$$= 43.4 \text{ lb/ft}^3$$

Differential-pressure method. Figure 3-6 shows the operating principle of a density-measuring system. The chamber contains the liquid whose weight density (w_l) is under measurement. Two bubble tubes are im-

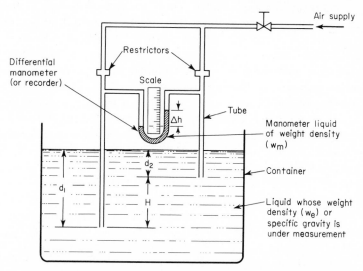

Fig. 3-6 Principle of the differential-pressure type of density meter. (The Foxboro Company Limited)

mersed at distances d_1 and d_2, respectively, as indicated. Air is bled through a restrictor to each tube, and it builds up pressure until it equals the heads wd_1 and wd_2. The escape of air, which bubbles out through the holes at the bottoms of the tubes, holds the pressure constant at this value.

If, as shown in the diagram, a manometer is attached in order to measure the differential pressure in the bubble tubes, then the differential pressure

$$\Delta p = w_m \, \Delta h$$

where w_m is the weight density of the manometer liquid and Δh is the differential head.

$$w_m \, \Delta h = w_l(d_1 - d_2) = w_l H$$

Hence
$$w_l = \frac{w_m}{H} \Delta h$$

and $w = k \, \Delta h$, where k is a constant, since H is a fixed spacing and w_m is also constant. The reading is a measure of the density, and a suitable instrument or device can be calibrated in density units.

Naturally, there are further requirements to be added to the basic scheme in order to accommodate the range of densities from 0.9 to 1.0. An added pressure head is introduced in the low-pressure side of the differential manometer by means of a reference chamber. This provides full-scale travel of the measuring device for the density range under measurement.

Electrical recording hydrometer. There are various designs of electrical recording specific-gravity meters. The electrical recording hydrometer is only one of them, and it has been selected for discussion because of its simplicity. The schematic arrangement is shown in Fig. 3-7a. The hydrometer is contained in a glass cylinder in which the overflow sill and outlet maintain a constant liquid level.

At the top of the hydrometer is attached a length of iron wire which acts as a core for the differential transformer containing two equal secondary windings (Chap. 12). As the specific gravity or density of the liquid which is under measurement varies, the hydrometer will rise or fall, and this movement will adjust the position of the iron-wire core of the transformer. This, in turn, will change the ratio of the voltages developed in the two secondaries. A circuit can be set up to indicate or record on an electrical instrument. A typical installation of a transmitting type of specific-gravity test with a constant-head chamber is shown in Fig. 3-7b.

Electrical and pneumatic transmitting density meters. In Fig. 3-8a is shown the arrangement of one particular design of a measuring and controlling density meter used with clear liquids and industrial slurries. The working operation is, briefly, as follows: The liquid under measure

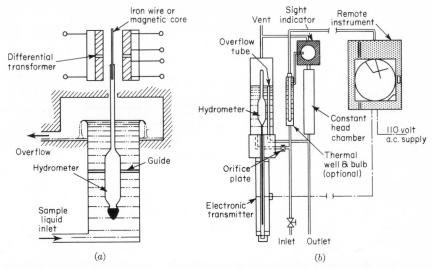

Fig. 3-7 (a) *A differential transformer, having its magnetic core positioned by a hydrometer, provides a way of converting specific-gravity values into electrical equivalents.* (b) *Transmitting-type specific-gravity tester with constant-head chamber.* [Fischer & Porter (Canada) Limited]

ment flows through a hairpin loop of tube *A*. Tube *A* is pivoted on the axis *B–B*, which intersects the flexible connections *C*. The weight of the tube and its contents is transmitted to a weighbeam *D* and is balanced by the counterweight *E*, which is adjustable along the beam. A change in the density of the fluid disturbs a state of equilibrium, and it is detected by the force balance *F*, the output of which is proportional to the change in density. Sensitivity is adjusted by movement of the rider *G*, which transmits the weight changes to the force balance. A calibrating weight *H*, hung on the weighbeam, permits the sensitivity to be verified. A damping device (not shown) is incorporated to prevent oscillation of the moving parts. The density indications are independent of the rate of flow through the instrument. In the case of a slurry the rate of flow must be such as to prevent deposit of the solid material.

The force balance is pneumatically operated and gives an output signal of the standard pressure range which can be indicated or recorded on a conventional pneumatic receiver. A supply of clean compressed air is required. Variations from the standard arrangement are possible in respect of the materials which are in contact with the fluid. The tube loop can be hard rubber or glass; the flexible connectors can be in the form of bellows.

An electrical force balance is also available as an alternative to the pneumatic system. It gives an output signal, in milliamperes, that is

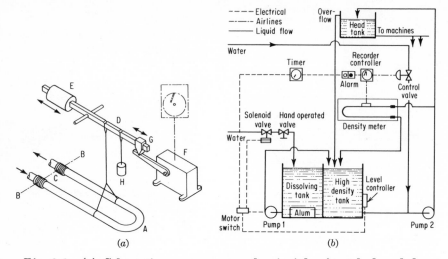

Fig. 3-8   (a) *Schematic arrangement and principle of a tube-loop balance density meter.* (Rotameter Manufacturing Co. Ltd.) (b) *Continuous alum density control.* (Albert E. Reed & Co. Ltd.)

proportional to density variations. Although the meter assembly is very sturdy in design and construction, it is sensitive enough to detect density changes as small as 0.00025 g/cm³. A typical automatic density-control scheme used in the paper industry is shown in Fig. 3-8b.

A wide variety of electrical, electronic, and pneumatic transmitting density and specific-gravity meters are available. Each has unique features in design and operation, but all are based on the same fundamental concepts of measurement.

Weight-volume method. A simple method of measuring density of liquid is to weigh continuously a fixed volume of the liquid under test. The weighing is done by using either a mechanical balance or an electrical load cell, as shown in Fig. 3-9a and b. A load cell is an electromechanical

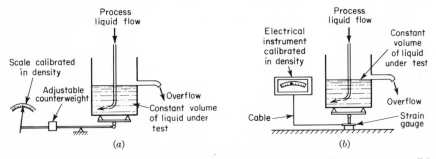

Fig. 3-9   (a) *Mechanical balance method of determining liquid density.* (b) *Electric strain gauge method of determining liquid density.*

device called a strain-gauge transducer (Chap. 14). When the mechanical portion is deflected by a weight, the strain gauge is distorted, causing a change in an electrical resistance. The strain gauge is employed as the variable resistance in an electric bridge network. In this way it is possible to have remote indicating or recording of the density. The scheme can be used for continuous measurement, in which case the fixed volume can be enclosed in a small container through which the process liquid flows at a fixed rate. Details of metallic and semiconductor strain gauges and electrical and electronic transducers are given in Chap. 9.

Radioisotope method. The density of a liquid can also be measured by using a radioactive technique. A source of radioactive energy, e.g., cobalt 60 or radium, is placed at one side of a tank with its rays directed across the tank. A radioactive sensing cell or unit, such as a Geiger tube, is placed on the opposite side of the tank to act as a receiver. The amount of radioactive energy remaining after passing through the tank walls and the liquid is a function of the density of the liquid.

The Ohmart Corporation is one of several companies manufacturing a range of radioactive density meters. Arrangements shown in Fig. 3-10*a* and *b* are typical. Gamma radiation energy from the radioactive source

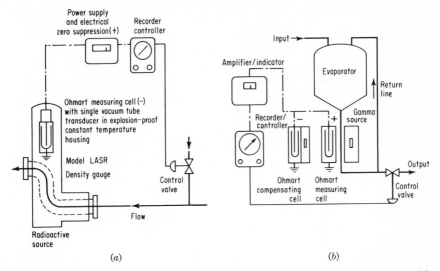

Fig. 3-10 (a) *Typical density control system. Density gauges provide measurement and control of optimum material density in any processing operation requiring small pipes. Diagram shows control of liquid density by actuation of a control valve.* (Ohmart Corp.) (b) *A typical evaporator control system. Evaporator output is measured for density by an Ohmart SG gauge. As variations from optimum are detected, the signals open or close the control valve to control hold-up time to maintain optimum density.* (Ohmart Corp.)

passes through the material which is going through a pipeline. The amount of energy attenuated by the material is proportional to the density of the material. The radiation which is not attenuated is detected by a unique cell which changes radioactive energy directly into electric energy.

Electrical zero suppression is obtained from a regulated power supply, which produces a current opposite in polarity to the current of the measuring cell. Current values are balanced so that at the predetermined minimum density the signal from the measuring cell is nullified. A calibration potentiometer on the power supply adjusts the full-scale setting. If the material becomes more or less dense than optimum, the output from the transducer, a function of density change, can be applied through standard recorders, or recorder-controllers, and can control valves, agitators, or pumps. The density of solids or liquids or the percent solids of slurries can be measured with a precision and repeatability of ± 2 percent of full scale.

Specific-gravity meters for gases usually operate on the same basis as meters used for liquids. In one design, gas of known volume and weight is enclosed within a float. The float is placed on a balance beam to detect variations in density of the sample gas by the actual deflection of the balance beam. It is necessary, with this method, to have automatic compensation for ambient (surrounding) temperature and atmospheric pressure changes. In view of the small forces involved, a very delicate balance is required.

Another method which is frequently used to determine specific gravity

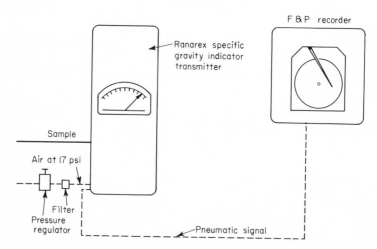

Fig. 3-11 Schematic diagram of specific-gravity indicating-recording system. [The Permutit Company and Fischer & Porter (Canada) Limited]

of a gas is to compare the weight of a column of the sample gas with the weight of a column of air of the same height and at the same temperature. The Ranarex instruments for gas-specific-gravity measurement operate as follows: A fan draws in a sample of gas to be tested, sets it in rotation, and creates a torque in its companion impulse wheel located in the same chamber. This torque, which is proportional to the gas density, is compared with the torque produced by atmospheric air in an identical upper chamber, the impeller of which rotates in the opposite direction. The difference between these opposing torques is a measure of the specific gravity and causes the pointer to move over the scale. The general arrangement is shown in Fig. 3-11.

Temperature and Pressure Effects on Density

Temperature effects. When a substance is heated, its volume increases but its weight remains unchanged:

$$\text{Density} = \frac{\text{weight}}{\text{volume}}$$

Therefore, on heating, the density of a substance decreases. Now let

V_0 = volume of the substance at 0°C
V_t = volume of the substance at any temperature t°C
W = weight of substance
γ (gamma) = coefficient of volumetric expansion

At t°C, $V_t = V_0$; hence,

$$\frac{W}{V_0} = \text{weight density at 0°C} = w_0$$

$$\frac{W}{V_t} = \text{weight density at } t°C = w_t$$

By substituting these terms in the volume-expansion equation

$$V_t = V_0(1 + \gamma t)$$

the result is

$$w_t = \frac{w_0}{1 + \gamma t}$$

From this result, the weight density of the substance decreases when temperature increases.

If the mass density is considered, then the corresponding equation becomes

$$\rho_t = \frac{\rho_0}{1 + \gamma t}$$

Pressure effects. In the equations for mass density, $\rho = m/V$, and for weight density, $w = W_t/V$, it should be noted that volumetric variations will certainly cause density change. If the pressure is either increased or decreased, particularly in the case of gases, there will be a corresponding change in the volume in accordance with the gas law $PV = $ constant.

Specific-gravity and Density Values

The specific-gravity values of certain solids and liquids are listed in Table 3-1. Density values of the more common gases are given in Table 3-2.

Table 3-1   Specific gravities

(Referred to water at 39°F = 4°C, max density, and at standard atmospheric pressure)

Lead	11.34
Mercury	13.546
Tool steel	7.70–7.73
Oils	0.88–0.94
Water at 39°F = 4°C (max density)	1.00
Petroleum, gasoline	0.70–0.75

Table 3-2   Weight-density values, in lb/ft³, of some gases at 32°F and 1 atm pressure

Air	0.0807
Carbon dioxide	0.1234
Nitrogen	0.0780
Oxygen	0.0892

Specific-gravity scales. Generally, the specific gravity of a liquid is expressed as the ratio of the weights of equal volumes of the liquid and water at a constant temperature. There are some scales which depart from this basis. Examples are the American Petroleum Institute (API) and the Baumé scales, both of which are expressed in degrees.

$$\text{Degrees API} = \frac{141.5}{\dfrac{\text{Sp gr of liquid at 60°F}}{\text{Sp gr of water at 60°F}}} - 131.5 \qquad (1)$$

For liquids less dense than water

$$\text{Degrees Baumé} = \frac{140}{\dfrac{\text{Sp gr of liquid at 60°F}}{\text{Sp gr of water at 60°F}}} - 130 \qquad (2)$$

For liquids denser than water

$$\text{Degrees Baumé} = 145 - \frac{145}{\dfrac{\text{Sp gr of liquid at 60°F}}{\text{Sp gr of water at 60°F}}} \tag{3}$$

REVIEW QUESTIONS AND PROBLEMS

3-1 Define the following terms and state the dimensions and units in each case: (a) mass density, (b) weight, (c) weight density, (d) specific gravity.

3-2 The specific gravity of mercury is 13.6. Compute the density of mercury (a) in grams per cubic centimeter and (b) in pounds per cubic foot.

3-3 The mass of a cork is 10 g and its volume is 40 cm³. What is its mass density?

3-4 The weight of a substance is 966.0 lbf and its volume is 10.0 ft³. What are its (a) weight density and (b) mass density? Assume the earth's gravitation acceleration to be 32.2 ft/sec².

3-5 If the weight of a cubic foot of aluminum is 167 lbf at room temperature, while that of water is 62.3 lbf, compute the specific gravity of aluminum.

3-6 Describe the application of Archimedes' principle of floatation in the design and operation of a hydrometer.

3-7 A hydrometer sinks in water to a depth of 15.0 cm. Calculate how far it would sink in liquid with a specific gravity of 0.80.

3-8 Describe, with the aid of a neat diagram, the operation of determining specific gravity of a liquid by using either the specific-gravity bottle or the Westphal balance method. Point out some of the precautions that must be observed for accurate results.

3-9 During a test run to determine the specific gravity of a liquid by using a bubbler pressure gauge system, the air-line pressure was 144.0 lb/ft² (1.0 lb/in.²) and the open end of the pipe was 4.0 ft below the level of the liquid. Compute the specific gravity of the liquid.

3-10 (a) State why temperature must be kept constant when determining specific gravity and density values of any substance.
(b) The density of mercury at 0°C is 13.60 g/cm³, and its coefficient of volumetric expansion is 1.8×10^{-4} per °C. Compute the density of mercury at 100°C.

3-11 Describe, with the aid of a neat diagram, any density or specific-gravity measurement and control scheme you know.

CHAPTER FOUR

Basic concepts
of pressure
measurement

Fluid pressure acts in all directions.

PASCAL

The basic concepts and physical behavior of pressure are reviewed briefly in this chapter. The purpose is to emphasize the principles used in the measurement of pressure, which is one of the most common variables in any industrial process plant. Measuring instruments have to be designed to measure pressures lower than 10^{-4} mm of mercury (Hg) and pressures so great that very tough constructional materials are permanently distorted by them.

Water flows out of a faucet or tap because of pressure in the pipe. The pipeline pressure is supplied by a pump, reservoir, or water tower. The force which causes the water to come out of the tap will depend upon the pressure in the pipe. That water finds its own level is well known. Suppose that two glass containers of different cross-sectional area, as shown in Fig. 4-1, are connected together by a tube at the base. If water

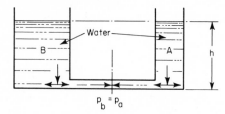

Fig. 4-1   Pressure equilibrium.

is poured into one container, it will flow into the other through the connecting tube. When pouring is stopped, both water columns will be at the same height.

Consider why it is that the comparatively greater weight of water in *B* does not drive the smaller weight of water in *A* straight out of the tube. Although the weight of water in *B* is greater than the weight of water in *A*, it has a larger area to push down upon. The weight or force resting on a unit area at the bottom of *B* is equal to the weight resting on a unit area at the bottom of *A*. This weight or force per unit area is called the *intensity of pressure*. The pressure at the bottom of *B* is equal in intensity to the pressure at the bottom of *A*. This pressure is transmitted in all directions in accordance with Pascal's law, as will be explained shortly. Therefore, along the center line of the tube which connects the two containers, the pressures coming from opposite directions are the same, and hence the two columns of liquid balance.

Intensity of Pressure

Intensity of pressure is defined as the force per unit area. Force in this sense has the same meaning as that given by the physicists under Newton's second law, i.e., in terms of mass and motion ($F = Ma$).

$$\text{Intensity of pressure } p = \frac{\text{force } F}{\text{area } A}$$

that is, pounds per square inch, pounds per square foot, or grams per square centimeter. The intensity of pressure of a fluid (liquid or gas) is analogous to stress in a tie rod.

Example. A man weighs 180 lb$_f$ and stands on skis each having an effective area 90 in. long by 4 in. wide. What pressure will he exert on the snow when standing on one foot?

Solution

$$p = \frac{F}{A} = \frac{180 \text{ lb}}{(90 \times 4) \text{ in.}^2} = \tfrac{1}{2} \text{ lb/in.}^2, \text{ or psi}$$

If now the man is wearing ice skates, each blade having an effective area 12 in. long and $\tfrac{1}{8}$ in. wide, when standing on one foot his pressure on the ice becomes

$$p = \frac{180 \text{ lb}}{(12 \times \tfrac{1}{8}) \text{ in.}^2} = 120 \text{ lb/in.}^2, \text{ or psi}$$

Pressure in a liquid increases with the depth and is extended in all directions. If a long glass cylinder with two holes at the side, as shown in Fig. 4-2, is filled with water, it will be observed that water will issue with greater force from the lower hole than from the upper one. This demonstrates that the pressure in a liquid column increases directly with depth. There is a greater weight of water forcing the water out of the lower hole

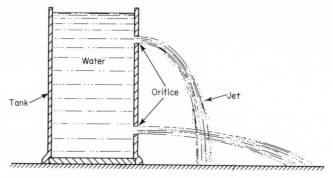

Fig. 4-2   Pressure increase with depth.

than out of the upper one, and therefore a greater pressure occurs at the level of the lower hole. From this simple experiment another fact may be observed: the water is being forced out sideways. The pressure due to the weight of the water is transmitted through the water not only downward but sideways as well.

Pascal's Law

Pascal's law states that pressure in a liquid is transmitted equally in all directions. This can be readily confirmed by means of a rubber ball punctured with a number of holes. Soak the ball in water and then lay it on a table and press down upon it. Water will squirt in all directions, although the ball is being pressed in one direction only.

It was shown previously that intensity of pressure is proportional to the depth. Hence $p = w_l h$, where w_l is the weight density of the liquid, or $p = w_w$ sp gr h, where w_w is weight density of water and sp gr is the specific gravity of the liquid. By dimensional analysis,

$$\left[\frac{F}{L^2}\right] = \left[\frac{F}{L^3}\right][L] = \left[\frac{F}{L^2}\right]$$

Figure 4-3 shows a tank of cubic shape having 1-ft sides that is completely full of water. The weight density of the water is 62.4 lb/ft³. The pressure acting on the bottom of the tank is 1 ft head of water, and the intensity of pressure is

$$p = \frac{F}{A} = \frac{62.4 \text{ lb}}{144 \text{ in.}^2}$$
$$= 0.433 \text{ lb/in.}^2, \text{ or psi}$$

Therefore, this is the same as saying that 1 ft head of water is equivalent to a pressure of 0.433 psi.

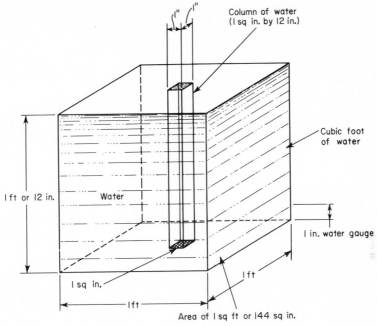

Fig. 4-3 Reference diagram.

Pressure Head

Pressure head h represents the height of a column of a homogeneous fluid that will produce a given intensity of pressure, from the equation $p = wh$

$$h \text{ (ft)} = \frac{p \; (\text{lb}_f/\text{ft}^2)}{w \; (\text{lb}_f/\text{ft}^3)}$$

By dimensional analysis,

$$[L] = \frac{[F/L^2]}{[F/L^3]} = [L]$$

Important Conversions

1 in. water gauge (w.g.), or a head of water 1 in. high

$$= \frac{62.4 \; \text{lb}_f/\text{ft}^3}{1,728 \; \text{in.}^3/\text{ft}^3} \times 1 \text{ in.} = 0.0361 \; \text{lb}_f/\text{in.}^2, \text{ or psi}$$

1 ft w.g. $= 0.0361 \; \text{lb}_f/\text{in.}^3 \times 12 \text{ in.} = 0.433 \; \text{lb}_f/\text{in.}^2$, or psi

1 in. Hg $= 0.0361 \; \text{lb}/\text{in.}^2 \times 13.60 = 0.491 \; \text{lb}_f/\text{in.}^2$

$$1 \; \text{lb}_f/\text{in.}^2 = \frac{1}{0.03614 \; \text{lb}_f/\text{in.}^3} = 27.7 \text{ in. water (w.g.)}$$

or 1 lb/in.² will support a column of water 27.7 in. high.

$$1 \text{ lb}_f/\text{in.}^2 = \frac{1}{0.491 \text{ lb}_f/\text{in.}^3} = 2.036 \text{ in. Hg}$$

or 1 lb$_f$/in.² will support a column of mercury 2.036 in. high.

> 1 standard atmosphere = 760 mm (29.92 in.) Hg at 0° (32°F) having a
> (air pressure at   density of 13.6 g/cm³
> sea level)
> = 14.7 lb/in.²
> = 1.033 kg/cm²

The reader should verify that a pressure of 14.7 lb/in.² will support a column of mercury 760 mm high.

Example. Calculate the pressure on a diver at a depth of 100 ft in seawater (weight density 64 lb/ft³).

Solution. Suppose the diver's helmet is exactly 100 ft below the water surface; then each horizontal square foot of helmet will support a column of water 100 ft high and 1 ft² in cross section.

Weight of water pressing down on one square foot of the helmet

$$= 100 \text{ ft} \times 1 \text{ ft}^2 \times 64 \frac{\text{lb}_f}{\text{ft}^3}$$

$$= 6{,}400 \text{ lb}_f$$

Intensity of pressure = 6,400 lb/ft²
= 44.4 lb/in.² (where 1 ft² = 144 in.²)

Then there will be an additional pressure acting on the diver's helmet owing to the atmosphere of, for example, 14.7 lb/in.²

Total pressure = pressure due to head of water + atmospheric pressure
= 44.4 + 14.7
= 59.1 psia

where psia is pounds per square inch absolute, or the absolute pressure intensity.

REVIEW QUESTIONS AND PROBLEMS

4-1   Define the following terms and give an example of the units in each case: (a) intensity of pressure, (b) stress, (c) pressure head, (d) weight density.

4-2 Calculate the pressure, in pounds per square inch, of a fire hydrant that must send a jet of water to the top of a building 340 ft high.

4-3 Convert a pressure of 15.0 ft of water to feet of oil having a specific gravity of 0.75.

4-4 Calculate the pressure, in pounds per square inch, at a depth of 20.0 ft below the free surface of a body of water having a weight density of 62.4 lb/ft³.

4-5 (a) State Pascal's law.

(b) A column of water 6 ft high is enclosed in a square tube 2 in. on each side. Calculate the pressure, in pounds per square inch at the bottom of the column.

(c) If the column of water of part (b) remains at 6 ft but the square tube is increased to 12 in. on each side, calculate the pressure at the bottom of the column, in pounds per square inch.

4-6 (a) Express 100 ft w.g. in pounds per square inch.

(b) Find the pressure, in pounds per square inch, at the bottom of a vertical tube containing a column of mercury 20.0 in. high.

4-7 (a) Describe, with the aid of a diagram, an experiment to demonstrate how pressure at a point in a liquid increases with the depth below the surface.

(b) Explain the statement: "Pressure of a liquid varies with specific gravity."

4-8 The diagram of Fig. 4-4 shows a simple type of water-gauge tester. If the combined weight of piston and load is 240 lb and the area of the piston is 30 in.², what should the gauge read in (a) pounds per square inch and (b) inches of mercury?

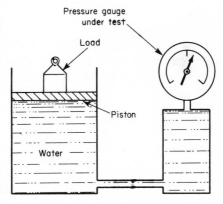

Fig. 4-4 Transmission of pressure in a closed system: simple gauge tester.

Air Pressure

Although the density of air is very low, it does have weight. Its mass density is about 0.0012 g/cm³, and its weight density is 0.0752 lb/ft³ at 68°F and a pressure of one atmosphere. Air is attracted by the earth, as is every other substance. Since air has weight, it exerts force on any object immersed in it, and the force per unit area is the air pressure. This pressure, under normal conditions, is about 14.7 lb/in.² On an ordinary shop window which measures 10 by 10 ft the total force is

$$\frac{10 \text{ ft} \times 10 \text{ ft} \times 144 \text{ in.}^2/\text{ft}^2 \times 14.7 \text{ lb/in.}^2}{2,000 \text{ lb}_f/\text{ton}} = 106 \text{ tons (approx)}$$

Fortunately, this large force is balanced by another force, equal in magnitude but opposite in direction, on the other side of the shop window. During a tornado, the exterior pressure suddenly falls drastically, and the greater interior pressure could actually cause the shop or house to explode; therefore, windows should be kept open during a bad storm.

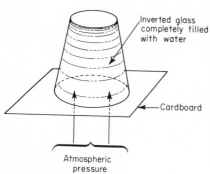

Inverted glass completely filled with water

Cardboard

Atmospheric pressure

Fig. 4-5 Atmospheric pressure experiment.

Figure 4-5 illustrates a simple experiment. A glass is filled to the brim with water and a piece of cardboard is so placed on the top that there are no air bubbles beneath it. If the glass is now turned upside down, the water will not run out, because the pressure of the atmosphere under the cardboard is greater than that of the water above it.

Vacuum

A vacuum is considered, under perfect conditions, as a space in which there are very few atoms or molecules. A perfect vacuum, i.e., one in which no atoms are present, is unobtainable since every material which surrounds a space has a definite vapor pressure. Therefore, the term "vacuum" is generally taken to mean a space containing air or other gas at well below atmospheric pressure.

Atmospheric Pressure

Evangelista Torricelli, an Italian scientist, obtained a vacuum by filling a long glass tube, sealed at one end, with mercury and inverting it over mercury in a trough. The mercury did not remain in the tube, but ran down a certain distance. Since there was nothing above it, Torricelli had created a vacuum. He found that, whatever length of tube he used, the mercury would stand only at a vertical height of about 76 cm, or 30 in. If the tube was tilted from the vertical position, the mercury would run up until its vertical height was again 76 cm. This is shown in Fig. 4-6. Torricelli put forward the theory that the mercury falls in the tube until

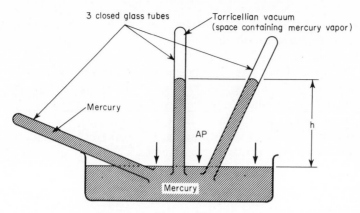

Fig. 4-6 Torricellian vacuum.

the weight of the column is exactly balanced by the pressure of the surrounding atmosphere:

$$AP = hw \quad \text{or} \quad AP = h\rho g$$

where AP = atmospheric pressure
w = weight density of the liquid
ρ = mass density of the liquid

Example. Express one standard atmosphere (29.92 in. Hg or 76.00 cm Hg) in (a) pounds per square inch and (b) dynes per square centimeter.

Solution

(a) $AP = hw = 29.92 \text{ in.} \times 13.6 \times \dfrac{62.4}{12^3} \text{ lb/in.}^3$

$AP = 14.7 \text{ lb/in.}^2$, or psi

(b) $AP = h\rho g = 76.00 \text{ cm} \times 13.6 \text{ g/cm}^3 \times 980 \text{ cm/sec}^2$
$= 1.013 \times 10^6 \text{ dynes/cm}^2$

Since the dyne per square centimeter is a very small unit, a larger unit of pressure, the bar, is used. A bar is 1.0×10^6 dynes/cm². A common unit, the millibar, is used in weather records. The millibar is a thousandth of a bar or 1.0×10^3 dynes/cm².

Atmospheric-pressure Measurement

The simple mercury barometer is an instrument for measuring the pressure of the atmosphere. The simplest type is the Torricelli tube. It is filled carefully, so that there are no air bubbles in the mercury, and then inverted in a trough or small basin of mercury. The height of the mercury column, termed the barometric height, is a measure of the atmospheric pressure. The average barometric height is 76 cm of mercury or about 30 in.

The *Fortin barometer* has a scale graduated in both centimeters and inches, and there is a moving vernier that permits accurate reading to two decimal places. Most laboratories possess an instrument of this type, and the reader should make a point of inspecting one.

The *aneroid barometer*, as shown in Fig. 4-7, works on a principle entirely different from that of the mercury barometer. The word "aneroid" means

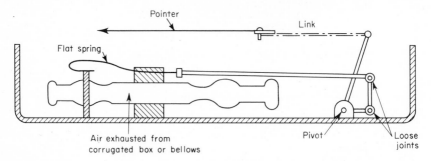

Fig. 4-7   Sectional view of a simple aneroid barometer.

without liquid. The instrument consists of a partially evacuated box or bellows, made of thin spring metal, which is corrugated in concentric circles to permit it to cave in at the center. (See also Chap. 5.) A spring prevents the bellows from collapsing completely. In operation, when the atmospheric pressure increases, the box or bellows is pushed in slightly more than usual at the center. This movement is magnified by a system of levers and linkages which cause a pointer to move over a circular scale. When the atmospheric pressure decreases, the spring pulls the center of the box or bellows out a little, and the movement is transmitted to the pointer, which goes in the opposite direction. The aneroid barometer is not very accurate and should be tested frequently and checked against a Fortin barometer.

The barograph is a form of aneroid barometer which automatically records the atmospheric pressure on a rotating drum driven by a clock mechanism. The recording paper around the drum is replaced once a week, during which time the drum makes one revolution.

Physical Properties of Gases

Many substances are found in the gaseous state. Air is the most common one. It is a mixture of several gases in which oxygen and nitrogen predominate. Air pressure is used in a number of applications such as pneumatic machines, air brakes, and pneumatic control mechanisms in instrumentation control schemes. For this reason it is important to consider some of the basic characteristics of air as a gas.

Gases are assumed to be elastic, and they can be readily compressed. The combination of these two properties is called *resiliency;* i.e., a gas has the ability to yield to a force and to return immediately to its original conditions upon release of the force.

Variation of volume with pressure. Whenever a sample of gas is confined in a closed container, it exerts a pressure in all directions. Suppose a cylinder contains an enclosed quantity of gas, as shown in Fig. 4-8,

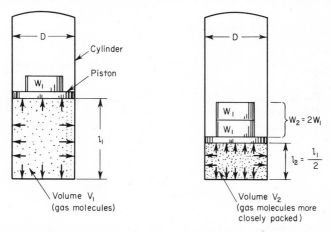

Fig. 4-8 Illustrating pressure-volume relationship by means of a piston and cylinder.

the volume of which is subjected to variation by means of a movable weighted piston. The intensity of bombardment of molecules in the cylinder is due to the pressure variation. The molecules of the gas are continually bombarding each other, the sides of the cylinder, and the bottom of the piston supporting the weight W_1. The impact of these gas molecules on the piston develops a total force equal to the area of the piston times the pressure. Suppose the volume of the gas under this condition to be V_1. When the weight W_1 is replaced by a weight W_2 equal to twice W_1, the pressure P_2 necessary to support W_2 is twice the original pressure. The piston is forced down until the volume V_2 of the confined gas is halved.

The relationship between pressure and volume was first stated as a scientific law in 1662 by the Irish scientist Robert Boyle, and it became known as Boyle's law. The law states that, if the temperature of a contained gas is not permitted to change, the product of the pressure and volume is constant. Symbolically, $PV =$ constant, and the graph of the pressure P against volume V follows that of a hyperbolic curve. Boyle's law holds true for a wide range of pressures, but extreme pressures cause a deviation from it. The relationship is expressed as

$$\frac{\text{Original volume } V_1}{\text{New volume } V_2} = \frac{\text{new absolute pressure } P_2}{\text{original absolute pressure } P_1}$$

$$P_1V_1 = P_2V_2 \qquad \text{at constant temperature}$$

Example. A volume of air is stored in a cylinder 4 ft long and 2 ft in internal diameter. The air is at an absolute pressure of 300 lb/in.^{2}. Calculate the volume, in cubic feet, that the air would expand to if released to atmospheric pressure. Assume atmospheric pressure = 14.7 lb/in.^{2} absolute (lb/in.^{2} abs, or psia).

Solution. Solving for the original volume of the gas,

$$V_1 = \pi r^2 h$$
$$= 3.1416 \times (1 \text{ ft})^2 \times 4 \text{ ft}$$
$$= 12.6 \text{ ft}^3$$

Now, $P_1 = 300$ lb/in.^{2} abs and $P_2 = 14.7$ lb/in.^{2} abs. Using the equation $P_1V_1 = P_2V_2$ and solving for V_2,

$$V_2 = V_1 \frac{P_1}{P_2}$$

$$= 12.6 \text{ ft}^3 \times \frac{300 \text{ lb/in.}^2}{14.7 \text{ lb/in.}^2}$$

$$= 257 \text{ ft}^3$$

Gas storage under pressure. When a quantity of oxygen, nitrogen, or hydrogen is ordered from a supplier, the gas is delivered in steel cylinders at a pressure of about 130 atm. Since the pressure is 130 times the atmospheric pressure, the gas will escape and expand to 130 times the internal volume of the cylinder when the valve of the cylinder is opened.

Variation of volume with temperature. By experiment it has been found that, since an increase in its temperature will cause a gas to expand if the pressure is kept constant, it is reasonable to expect that, if a certain mass of gas were heated in a closed container so that its volume had to remain constant, there would be a consequent increase in the gas pressure. This relationship between volume and temperature is stated as a scientific law, known as Charles' law, which states that the volume of a given mass of an ideal gas kept at constant pressure expands by $\frac{1}{273}$ of its volume at 0°C for each 1°C rise in temperature. Similarly, it contracts by $\frac{1}{273}$ of its volume at 0°C for each 1°C drop in temperature at constant pressure. Symbolically,

$$V_t = V_0(1 + \tfrac{1}{273}t) \qquad \text{at constant pressure}$$

$$V_t = \frac{V_0}{273}(273 + t) = KT$$

where V_0 = volume at 0°C

V_t = volume of same mass of gas at t°C

$K = \dfrac{V_0}{273}$ a constant

T = absolute temperature, degrees Kelvin

    = 273 + t°C

Although this generalization breaks down at conditions of extremely low and extremely high temperatures, it holds true for conditions normally encountered in industrial instrumentation.

General Gas Law

The two gas laws can be combined to yield, for a given mass of gas,

$$\frac{PV}{T} = \text{constant}$$

This expression indicates that the product PV, which is an energy term, increases directly with absolute temperature T. For a given mass of gas

$$\frac{P_1 V_1}{T_1} = \frac{P_2 V_2}{T_2}$$

Since both the volume and density of any gas are affected by changes of temperature and pressure, it is customary to reduce all gas volumes to *standard conditions* for purposes of comparison. Standard conditions are a temperature of 0°C (273° abs, or 273° Kelvin) and a pressure of one atmosphere.

A *vapor* is the gaseous form of any substance. The term is usually used to describe only those gases that exist as liquids or solids at ordinary temperatures or pressures. Examples are gasoline vapor, alcohol vapor, mercury vapor, and water vapor.

A *mole* is, by convention, the molecular weight of a substance expressed in grams. Thus 1 mole of oxygen is 32 g of oxygen because 32 is the molecular weight of oxygen. One mole of any (ideal) gas occupies approximately 22.4 liters at standard pressure and temperature (STP) conditions. For example, 32 g (1 mole) of oxygen occupies 22.4 liters at 273° abs and 1 atm.

The universal gas constant. The general gas law may also be written for one mole of gas

$$pV = RT$$

where R, called the universal gas constant, is the same for all gases provided a mole is used. If n moles of gas are considered, the equation becomes

$$pV = nRT$$

To evaluate R, consider the following

1. One mole of a gas occupies 22.4 liters at 1 atmosphere (atm) and 273° abs or degrees Kelvin (°K).

$$R = \frac{PV}{nT} = \frac{1 \text{ atm} \times 22.4 \text{ liters}}{1 \text{ mole} \times 273°\text{K}} = 0.0821 \text{ liter atm/mole °K}$$

2. Since 1 atm = 1.013×10^5 newtons/m², 22.4 liters = 0.0224 m³, and 1 m-newton = 1 joule (heat unit)

$$R = \frac{pV}{nT} \frac{1.013 \times 10^5 \text{ newtons/m}^2 \times 0.0224 \text{ m}^3}{1 \text{ mole} \times 273°\text{K}}$$
$$= 8.3 \text{ joules/mole °K}$$

Example 1. A quantity of nitrogen occupies 20 ft³ at 5°C and 760 mm Hg. Compute its volume at 30°C and 800 mm pressure.

Solution. Since the mass of gas is constant,

New volume = old volume × pressure correction ratio

$$\times \text{ temperature correction ratio}$$

$$V = 20 \text{ ft}^3 \times \frac{760 \text{ mm}}{800 \text{ mm}} \times \frac{303°\text{K}}{278°\text{K}} = 21 \text{ ft}^3$$

Example 2. By using the ideal-gas equation

$$pV = nRT$$
$$R = 0.082 \frac{\text{liter-atm}}{\text{mole °K}}$$

compute the volume of oxygen occupied by 8.00 g of oxygen at 20°C and 750 mm Hg. The molecular weight of oxygen is 32.0.

Solution

$$\text{number of moles} = \frac{\text{mass of gas, in grams}}{\text{molecular weight of gas}} = \frac{m}{M}$$

$$V = \frac{mRT}{MP}$$

$$= \frac{8 \text{ g} \times 0.082 \text{ liter atm/mole °K} \times 293°\text{K}}{32 \text{ g/mole} \times {}^{750}\!/_{760} \text{ atm}}$$

$$= 6.1 \text{ liters}$$

Dalton's Law of Partial Pressures

Dalton's law of partial pressures states that the total pressure of a gaseous mixture is equal to the sum of the partial pressures of the components. The partial pressure of a component of a gas mixture is the pressure which the component would exert if it alone occupied the entire volume. Dalton's law is very accurate for ideal gases, which obey the gas laws exactly. Applications of Dalton's law are found in the vapor-filled thermal systems described in Chap. 14, which deals with temperature measurement.

Example. In a gaseous mixture at 20°C the partial pressures of the constituents are as follows: hydrogen 200 mm Hg, methane 320 mm Hg, carbon dioxide 150 mm Hg, ethylene 105 mm Hg. Calculate the total pressure of the mixture and the volume percent of hydrogen.

Solution

$$\text{Total pressure} = \text{sum of partial pressures}$$
$$= (200 + 320 + 150 + 105) \text{ mm Hg}$$
$$= 775 \text{ mm Hg}$$
$$\text{Volume of hydrogen} = \frac{\text{partial pressure of hydrogen}}{\text{total pressure of mixture}}$$
$$= \frac{200 \text{ mm Hg}}{775 \text{ mm Hg}} \times 100\%$$
$$= 25.8\%$$

Scales for Pressure Measurement

Pressure intensities can be expressed with reference to any arbitrary data, and the usual ones are absolute zero and local atmospheric pressure. The common scales are (1) gauge pressure, psig, (2) absolute pressure, psia, (3) vacuum scale, usually stated in inches of water or inches of mercury below atmospheric pressure.

Gauge and absolute pressures. The difference between the gauge-pressure scale and the absolute-pressure scale is the location of the zero point. On the gauge-pressure scale, the zero point is at the atmospheric-pressure line. Figure 4-9 shows the three scales and their relationship to

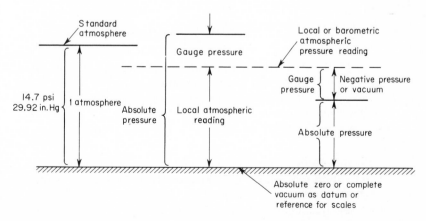

Fig. 4-9   Scales for pressure measurement.

each other. On the absolute-pressure scale, the zero point is at the absolute-zero pressure mark.

Absolute pressure = gauge pressure + atmospheric pressure

Vacuum. Vacuum measurement is the measurement of pressure below atmospheric, and the scale is usually graduated in inches of mercury or inches of water.

Table 4-1   Conversion of units

1 atmosphere (atm) = 14.7 lb/in.^{2}, or psi
= 29.92 in. Hg
= 76 cm Hg
= 34 ft of water (H_2O)
= 1.013 × 10^5 newtons/m^2

Table 4-2   Relation between gauge pressure, absolute pressure and atmospheres

Gauge pressure, psig	Absolute pressure, psia	Atmospheres, atm
−14.70	0	0
0	14.70	1
10.00	24.70	1.67
14.70	29.40	2

REVIEW QUESTIONS AND PROBLEMS

4-9   Define the following terms and give examples when they are appropriate: (a) Torricellian vacuum, (b) atmospheric pressure, (c) absolute pressure, (d) gauge pressure.

4-10   (a) Describe, with the aid of a neat diagram, any type of barometer that you are familiar with.

(b) Describe how you would set up and use a simple mercury barometer.

(c) Why is water an unsuitable liquid for use in a barometer?

(d) Why does the diameter of the barometer tube make no difference in the readings?

(e) Is the reading affected if the barometer is inclined to the vertical?

4-11 The height of a mercury barometer is 76 cm. Calculate the height, in meters, if oil of density 0.90 g/cm³ is used instead of mercury, which has a density of 13.6 g/cm³.

4-12 (a) State Boyle's law for gases and describe briefly how you would verify it experimentally.
(b) A short cylinder closed at one end was sunk, open end downward, to the bottom of a lake. After drawing it up again, it was noticed that the inside had been wetted for two-thirds of its depth. Calculate the depth, in meters, of the lake if the barometric reading was 75 cm and the specific gravity of mercury was 13.5.

4-13 A volume of air is stored in a steel cylinder 8 ft long and 2 ft in internal diameter. The air is at an absolute pressure of 300 psi. Calculate the volume, in cubic feet, to which the air would expand if released to atmospheric pressure.

4-14 The volume of air in a car tire is 1,200 in.³ at 32 lb/in.². Calculate the volume this air would occupy at a standard pressure of 14.7 lb/in.².

4-15 Air is trapped in a uniform U tube sealed at one end by mercury, as shown in Fig. 4-10. When the mercury levels in the two limbs

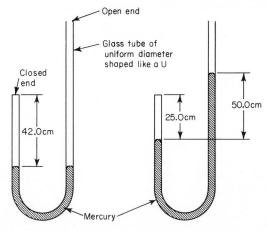

Fig. 4-10 A simple method of finding atmospheric pressure.

are the same, the length of the air column is 42.0 cm. When more mercury is poured in so that the difference in levels is 50.0 cm, the length of the air column is 25.0 cm. Compute the pressure of the atmosphere.

4-16 A liter of gas measured at 1 atm and −20°C must be compressed to ½ liter when the temperature is 40°C. Calculate the new pressure, in atmospheres.

It should be recalled that Pascal's law concerning pressures on liquids in closed systems states that the pressure exerted at any point upon a confined liquid is transmitted in all directions. This principle is applied in the operation of the dead-weight tester and liquid-column tester, which give a direct measurement of pressure or vacuum. The great need for high-precision pressure gauges for use in pneumatic telemetering and control systems has created a large demand for an equally high precision instrument for checking these gauges. Both the liquid-column tester and the dead-weight tester are used for checking pressure gauges; the dead-weight tester is the more reliable.

The Dead-weight Gauge Tester

The fundamental standard of pressure measurement for pressures higher than those for which a heavy liquid column can be conveniently used is the dead-weight free-piston gauge tester. The basic principle of this instrument is to produce the pressure by means of a screw-operated piston and to balance it with a piston of known area loaded with standard weights and working in a closely fitting vertical cylinder. The pressure is equal to the total weight divided by the piston area.

$$p = \frac{\text{total weight } F}{\text{area of piston } A}$$

that is,

$$= \frac{\text{force (lb)}}{\text{area (in.}^2)} \quad \text{or lb/in.}^2$$

Operation of a dead-weight tester. Figure 4-11 shows the component parts of a typical dead-weight gauge tester. It is a sturdy instrument, and with diligent care it should have lifelong accuracy. The reservoir holds enough mineral oil to fill the passageways of the tester. There is a needle valve at the bottom of the reservoir so that the oil can be trapped and held in the passages. On the left in the diagram it can be seen that there is a means of connecting the pressure gauge to the tester. A second screw valve is used to lock pressure in the gauge during a test reading.

In the center there is a free piston which consists of a rod of hardened and polished metal ground and lapped to size. Attached to the piston is a round platform for supporting additional weights. A hand-operated piston is provided; it has hydraulic cup washers and can move the oil in either direction. It is important that the fittings and connections to the pressure gauge under test be tightened to withstand the maximum pressure to be applied and to prevent oil leakage.

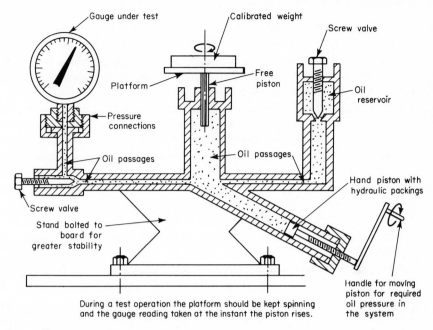

Gauge under test

Calibrated weight

Screw valve

Platform

Free piston

Oil reservoir

Pressure connections

Oil passages

Oil passages

Hand piston with hydraulic packings

Screw valve

Stand bolted to board for greater stability

Handle for moving piston for required oil pressure in the system

During a test operation the platform should be kept spinning and the gauge reading taken at the instant the piston rises.

Fig. 4-11   Sectional view of an Ashcroft dead-weight tester.

In operation, oil is moved from the reservoir into the tester by opening the valve and moving the hand piston outward. The reservoir valve is then shut off, thus trapping the oil in the tester. The crank is then turned so as to move the hand piston inward. Pressure will be generated in the oil and transmitted to all parts of the tester.

Oil is practically incompressible; and if the tester is filled with oil, only a few turns of the screw are needed to produce a large pressure. However, if a great deal of air is trapped in the gauge, it will be compressed and the hand piston may have to move some distance in order to produce the high pressure required. It is advisable to run the oil up to the top of the pipe before connecting the gauge to the tester. When the pressure generated by the oil reaches a certain magnitude, it will lift the measuring piston. The weight of the piston, including the platform and effective area of the piston, will determine the lowest pressure which can be measured. The usual minimum pressure is 5 psi for the low-range testers.

The pistons range from $\frac{1}{8}$ to $\frac{1}{80}$ in.^{2} in area, and a very close fit between the piston and its cylinder is essential, because no packing is used. It is important that, during a test reading, the piston be kept revolving by hand to minimize frictional forces. Sliding friction is less than static friction, and, for this reason, if the platform is given a slight twist, the effect of the sliding of the piston in its cylinder will reduce friction to an insignificant amount. If the platform is not given a spin, pressure will build up underneath until such point that the platform is forced up. This will result in errors. It is advisable to keep the platform revolving when test readings are being taken and to record the pressure value the instant that the platform has a tendency to rise.

The usual practice is to supply weights calibrated in pounds per square inch. However, weights calibrated in other units such as in kilograms per square centimeter, atmospheres, or feet of water are also supplied. It is important that these weights be treated carefully; otherwise, they may lose their weight and effective calibration values. The dead-weight tester is portable and consumes only the energy supplied by the human arm. Its accuracy, specified by the manufacturers, is maintained only if it is handled with care. The tester is used in instrument practice to calibrate master gauges. There is a variety of designs on the market with ranges up to 100,000 psi.

Air-operated dead-weight pressure gauge tester. The air-operated dead-weight tester is similar in principle to the tester already described, except that air from a compressed-air line is required. The air supply pressure must be above the highest pressure to be tested, and, if an air cylinder is used, a reducing valve is required. Nitrogen may be used instead of air.

In testing oxygen gauges no oil must enter the gauges because of the high risk of explosion. In fact, no oxygen instrument or equipment should be lubricated with oil.

In testing gauges for certain atomic-energy requirements, where helium is the gas whose pressure is to be measured a helium pressure test is required because many metals are porous to helium.

Liquid-column Testers

Mercury-column testers for low pressure and vacuum gauges are available. Each tester is a self-contained unit which includes a small hand pump. No external supply of electricity, compressed air, or vacuum is required. The three main components are the liquid column (usually mercury), the gauge stand, and the small hand pump.

Vacuum tester. A vacuum of 27 in. Hg is easily obtained with two or three movements of the pump. The vacuum can be lowered or released by opening a needle valve on the side of the gauge stand.

Low-pressure tester. A vertical hand pump is generally used to fill an air reservoir in the base of the tester. From this source air is admitted to the tester by a single needle valve, while another needle valve permits the pressure to be reduced or released. A low-pressure gauge tester normally incorporates a mercury column graduated up to 20 psi.

REVIEW QUESTIONS AND PROBLEMS

4-17 Why is the dead-weight tester used as a laboratory standard for pressure gauge calibrations?

4-18 (a) Describe, with the aid of a neat diagram, the construction and operation of a dead-weight tester.

(b) Why is it that the smaller the piston diameter in a gauge tester the higher the pressure created in the system?

4-19 (a) Why is static equilibrium necessary for Pascal's law to hold true?

(b) Why should fluids differ from solids when it comes to transmitting forces?

4-20 Find the pressure at the bottom of a tube containing a column of mercury 20 in. high.

4-21 The basic design of a piston gauge is given in Fig. 4-12. The diameter of the oil-filled passages is $\frac{1}{4}$ in. During a test reading, the total weight was 15.0 lb. Calculate the gauge reading of the instrument, in pounds per square inch.

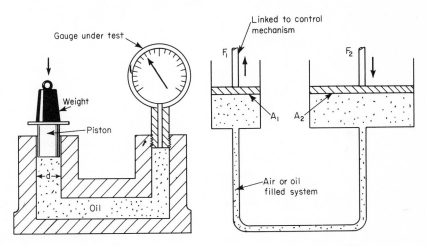

Fig. 4-12   Basic design of a gauge tester.

Fig. 4-13   Simple hydraulic or pneumatic pressure-transmission system.

4-22 In a simple hydraulic press, as illustrated in Fig. 4-13, $A_1 = 10$ in.² and $A_2 = 100$ in.². If $F_1 = 100$ lb, determine the value of F_2 and the ratio of movement of piston 1 to piston 2.

4-23 The effective area of the piston in an air power cylinder used for control purposes is 15.0 in.². Calculate the force required to give an air pressure of 10 lb/in.².

Manometers

Open U-tube manometers. The simplest manometer consists of a tube made of glass or other transparent material bent into the shape of a U and with both ends left open. A few spoonfuls of water poured into the tube is all that is required to make a manometer. The liquid-filled manometer is one of the most useful and inherently accurate instruments for measuring any variable that is a function of pressure. This includes pressure differential, vacuum, draft, level, and flow, to mention a few. Because of its simplicity and accuracy the manometer is widely used, and for that reason it should be thoroughly understood.

The U tube is generally filled about halfway with distilled water, oil, mercury, or any other liquid which flows easily. Figure 4-14a and b shows

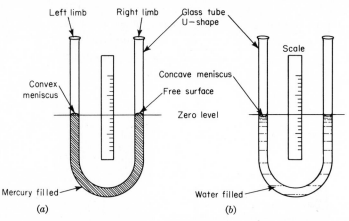

Fig. 4-14   The U-tube manometer. When no pressure is applied to either limb, the manometer liquid remains at zero reading on the scale. The level of the meniscus in the left limb is the same as that in the right limb.

two liquid-filled manometers. For low pressure or vacuum ranges water or oil is used as the liquid. The densities of such liquids are very low as compared with mercury, and thus the liquids are more sensitive to slight changes in pressure. For higher pressure ranges mercury is used.

Liquids used in manometers. Highly refined mineral seal oils of various densities are used in manometry for small pressure differences. Water is not generally used because it evaporates and, unless it is distilled and demineralized, leaves a lime deposit on the tube wall which makes subsequent readings difficult. If the liquid will wet the wall of the glass tube, as water will, the free surface, or *meniscus*, will be concave: the liquid at the center of the tube will be lower than at the side. Clean, highly refined mercury will not wet the tube wall, owing to its high surface tension, and the meniscus of mercury is convex. Figure 4-14a and b shows the meniscus in each case. When the meniscus is concave, the liquid column should be measured to the *bottom* of the meniscus. When the meniscus is convex, as when mercury is used, the column should be measured to the *top* of the meniscus.

Applications of U-tube manometers. When no pressure is applied to either limb of the manometer, the liquid remains at the zero reading on the scale; the level in the left limb is exactly the same as that in the right limb. Figure 4-14*a* and *b* illustrates these conditions. When a pressure intensity *p* is applied to the left limb, the manometer liquid is pushed down in the left limb and up in the right limb until equilibrium or static conditions are achieved. This occurs when

$$p = hw_m$$

where *h* is the height of the liquid column in the right limb above the height of that in the left limb. The weight density of the manometer

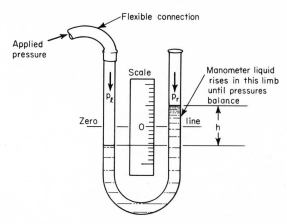

Fig. 4-15   The U-tube manometer. The pressure is applied in the left limb and pushes the manometer liquid into the right limb.

liquid is represented by w_m. Figure 4-15 shows the general arrangement when only one pressure is applied to the manometer.

Example 1. A pressure was applied to one limb of a mercury-filled manometer and the level difference was found to be 10.0 in. Compute the value of the pressure, in pounds per square inch.

Solution. Using the pressure equation for equilibrium

$$p = hw_m$$

$$p = 10.0 \text{ in.} \times \frac{62.4 \times 13.6 \text{ lb}_f}{12^3 \text{ in.}^3}$$

$$= 4.9 \text{ lb/in.}^2, \text{ or psi}$$

By dimensional analysis,

$$\left[\frac{F}{L^2}\right] = [L]\left[\frac{F}{L^3}\right] = \left[\frac{F}{L^2}\right]$$

When two different pressures are applied and p_l is greater than p_r, the level will be higher in the right-hand limb. The difference between these two pressures, that is, $p_l - p_r$, is referred to as the *differential pressure*, symbolized by Δp (delta p).

$$p_l - p_r = \Delta p = hw_m$$

Example 2. If $p_l = 8.0$ lb/in.^{2} and $p_r = 6.0$ lb/in.^{2} and the manometer sealing liquid is mercury having a weight density of 0.488 lb$_f$/in.^{3}, calculate the difference in levels of the two columns.

Solution. Using the pressure equation for equilibrium

$$p_l - p_r = \Delta p = hw_m$$

$$h = \frac{p_l - p_r}{w_m} = \frac{(8.0 - 6.0) \text{ lb/in.}^2}{0.488 \text{ lb/in.}^3}$$

$$= 4.1 \text{ in. Hg}$$

Now, if water is substituted for mercury, the new height becomes

$$h = \frac{(8.0 - 6.0) \text{ lb/in.}^2}{0.036 \text{ lb/in.}^3}$$

$$= 55.8 \text{ in. H}_2\text{O}$$

From a comparison of the results in Example 2 it will be noticed that, for the same differential pressure, a height of only 4.1 in. is obtained if mercury is used and a height of 55.8 in., or about 13.6 times that with mercury, is obtained if water is used. From this it can be concluded that, as previously mentioned, mercury should be used for a high differential pressure. However, if low differential pressures are applied across the manometer, distilled water or mineral seal oil should be used.

Accuracy of the Manometer

Accuracy is not affected by the shape or size of the tube. The U-tube manometer is one of the simplest and most accurate of instruments for measuring pressure. Variations in the size or shape of the U tube have no effect on the accuracy, because the difference between the levels of the two columns will be the same. It would appear that both columns should vary exactly the same amount in height; one column going up, the other down. This is true only when the glass tube has a perfectly uniform cross section.

Figure 4-16*a* and *b* shows three U-tube manometers of different sizes. The left-hand manometer has uniform, precision-bore tubing, the center one has an enlarged limb or leg, and the right-hand one has an exagger-

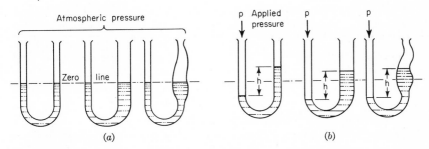

Fig. 4-16   When the applied pressure is the same, the distance moved by the liquid levels in the manometer is identical in each case regardless of tubing irregularities. (The Meriam Instrument Co.)

ated irregular leg. When no pressure is applied, or both ends are open to atmosphere, the manometer liquid level is the same in both limbs.

If an identical pressure is applied to the left limb of each manometer, the distances moved by the liquid columns are different because of tube irregularities. However, the hydrostatic balance provides that, regardless of any difference in the size or shape of the two limbs of the tube, the difference between the column heights remains equal to represent a true measurement of the unknown pressure. This is due to the fact that the constant applied pressure in the left leg displaces sufficient liquid to create a difference in height $h = \dfrac{\rho}{\omega}$. Nevertheless the volume of manometer liquid which moves down in the left leg must be the same as that which moves up in the right leg regardless of its shape or size. It is important to read the level several times for accurate work and to take the statistical average of the observed readings.

Factors in Manometer Accuracy

Insufficient knowledge of the manometer liquid used could affect the accuracy of the measurement. The importance of further considerations depends upon the accuracy requirement and the units specified. When liquids having low specific gravities are used to measure large units, the errors involved are negligible. However, when high-specific-gravity liquids are used to measure extremely small pressures, the following important variables affect the accuracy:

Density. A manometer, no matter how carefully constructed, can be no more accurate than the known accuracy of the density or specific gravity of the manometer liquid.

Vapor pressure. The increased application of manometers to measure vacuum requires consideration of the vapor pressure of the manometer liquid.

Temperature. All liquids change in density with changes in temperature. Since the most important factor in the manometer instrument is density, it is obvious that temperature must be a serious consideration. During calibration and laboratory tests, temperature must be controlled. The average temperature of the manometer liquid can be found, and proper corrections can then be applied to the scale readings.

Other factors which should be considered are the viscosity and surface tension effects of the manometer liquid. The viscosity of a liquid governs the flow characteristic of the liquid. Viscosity is relatively unimportant in a vertical instrument, but more important in an inclined gauge. Surface tension effects are not generally serious and are controlled in the actual design of the instrument by the use of special large-bore tubing and specified liquids. Full details, standards, and recommended practices are published by the Instrument Society of America (ISA).

Manometer-filling Liquids

When it is necessary to measure pressures of liquids which must not come into contact with the manometer liquid because of possible chemical reaction, a sealing liquid is poured into each limb on top of the manometer liquid. The sealing liquid must not mix chemically with either the manometer liquid or the liquid whose pressure is being measured. The sealing liquid must also be lighter than the manometer liquid but heavier than the measured fluid. The same amount of sealing liquid must be added to each limb of the manometer so that the two amounts balance and their pressure heads cancel out.

A good example of this is found in instrument practice in the use of seal pots or chambers as shown in Fig. 4-17. These seal pots are reservoirs which have much larger diameters than the tube diameter of the manometer. In this way the level of sealing liquid will not change significantly when a differential pressure is applied. The bypass valve is used to equalize the levels without disturbing the manometer liquid. For the conditions shown in the diagram

Sum of pressures acting in left-hand limb
    above reference level X–X = sum of pressures acting in
            right-hand limb above reference level X–X

This is true because, according to Pascal's law for equilibrium, the pressures at the lowest point of the U tube are equal and opposite in direction. Hence, at the reference or datum line X–X taken along the

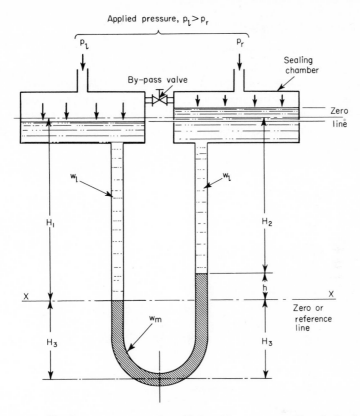

Fig. 4-17   U-tube manometer installed with separate identical chambers containing sealing liquid.

surface of the depressed manometer liquid, the pressures in the left-hand limb balance those in the right-hand limb:

Pressures in left-hand side above line X–X

= pressures in right-hand side above X–X

$$H_1 w_l + p_l = h w_m + H_2 w_l + p_r$$
$$p_l - p_r = h w_m - w_l(H_1 - H_2) = h w_m - w_l h$$
$$p_l - p_r = h(w_m - w_l)$$

This expression is true if the seal-pot diameters are large and the depression in the top-left seal pot or chamber is slight and insignificant, which is the usual technique in instrument practice.

The formula indicates that the effective weight density of the manometer liquid has to be reduced by the weight density of the sealing liquid. If mercury is used as the manometer liquid, and a light oil for the sealing liquid, then there will be only a slight change in the density factor.

Closed U-tube Manometer

In order to measure pressures of several atmospheres, one limb of the manometer would have to be very long to accommodate the range. This would be very clumsy and impracticable. The difficulty can be overcome by closing one limb of the manometer. Dry air is normally trapped in the closed side of a uniform manometer by the liquid, and at the open end of the other limb the applied pressure is connected. Figure 4-18 shows two

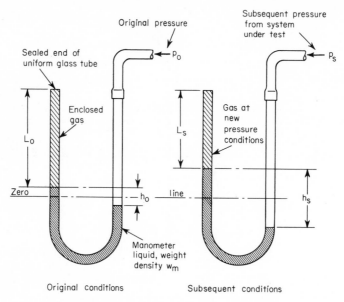

Fig. 4-18 The closed U-tube manometer.

stages of using the closed U-tube manometer. The formulas involved are derived in the following way.

For original conditions the pressure of the air or gas trapped in the closed limb is given by

$$p_l = p_o \pm hw_m$$

The volume of this entrapped air or gas is

$$V_o = L_o a$$

where L_o = length of gas enclosed in the limb

a = uniform cross-sectional area of the limb

The subscripts l and r indicate left and right sides of the manometer, and the subscript o and s indicate values at original and subsequent conditions.

For subsequent conditions the pressure p_o increases to p_s owing to a pressure change in the system under investigation. The new volume becomes

$$V_s = L_s a$$

Applying Boyle's law, pressure $\times$ volume = constant,

$$p_l L_o a = p_s L_s a$$
$$p_s = p_l \frac{L_o}{L_s}$$

Usually p_l is at atmospheric pressure; and by measuring the two lengths L_o and L_s, the new pressure p_s can be readily computed. This type of instrument becomes insensitive at very high pressures because of the compressibility of the trapped air or gas, which causes little change in volume. As mentioned previously, at high pressures Boyle's law does not hold true, and results are very noticeably in error.

Example. A closed U-shaped manometer of constant cross-sectional area is shown in Fig. 4-19. A length of air column AB is initially sealed off at atmospheric

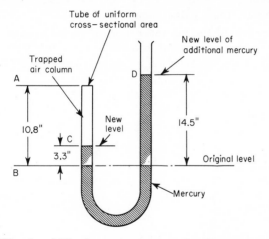

Fig. 4-19   The closed U-tube manometer used to find atmospheric pressure.

pressure with mercury. More mercury is then poured into the open limb until the new levels are at C and D. Calculate, to the nearest 0.1 in., the original atmospheric pressure p_a.

Solution. Let a represent the constant cross-sectional area of the tube. Hence

$$\text{Original volume } V_1 = 10.8a \text{ in.}^3$$
$$\text{Original pressure } p_1 = h \text{ in. Hg}$$
$$\text{Subsequent volume } V_2 \text{ of enclosed air column} = (10.8 - 3.3)a \text{ in.}^3$$
$$\text{Subsequent pressure } p_2 = h + (14.5 - 3.3)$$

By Boyle's law,
$$p_1 V_1 = p_2 V_2$$
$$h \times 10.8 \times a = (h + 11.2) \times 7.5 \times a$$
$$\text{Original atmospheric pressure } h = 25.5 \text{ in. Hg}$$

REVIEW QUESTIONS AND PROBLEMS

4-24 (a) Name several applications of the glass U-tube manometer for pressure measurement in laboratory and industrial work.

(b) How could the simple type of U-tube manometer be adapted for high-pressure ranges?

(c) When is a dimineralized-water-filled manometer used?

(d) Why is it that the shape or size of a manometer does not affect the readings?

4-25 Define the following terms: (a) differential pressure, (b) concave and convex meniscus, (c) negative pressure.

4-26 State clearly what is meant by the pressure-balance equation in solving pressure problems with U-tube manometers.

4-27 If a mercury manometer is used to measure a differential pressure of 2.0 psi, calculate the height between the two levels of the mercury columns.

4-28 In Question 4-27 what would be the difference if water instead of mercury were used in the manometer?

4-29 (a) State some of the limitations of the closed type of manometer used for high-pressure measurement.

(b) A closed manometer tube, as shown in Fig. 4-20, has a uniform cross-sectional area. A column of air is trapped in the closed side at

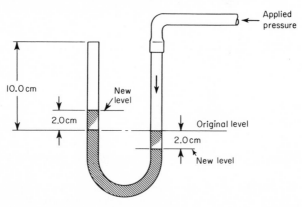

Fig. 4-20   The closed U-tube manometer used to find applied pressures.

atmospheric pressure of 14.7 psi with mercury. The original levels are indicated. Now an additional pressure is applied, such as to cause the mercury to climb 2 cm in the closed limb. Calculate the value of this applied pressure, in pounds per square inch, absolute and gauge.

CHAPTER FIVE

Fluid pressure and vacuum measurement

What I have done is the fruit of simple experience, which is the true teacher.

LEONARDO DA VINCI

MANOMETERS

Well or Reservoir Manometers

U-tube manometers are usually not convenient for pressure measurement, because two readings must be taken and added algebraically to obtain the final pressure. The simple U-tube manometer presents difficulties when it is necessary to use a float or other device for continuous indicating or recording purposes. In order to overcome these difficulties, a well or reservoir is substituted for one of the columns of the U tube. The general arrangement is shown in Figs. 5-1 and 5-2. The left-hand limb is replaced

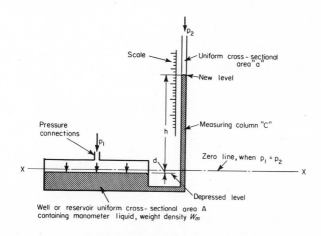

Fig. 5-1   Simple well manometer.

73

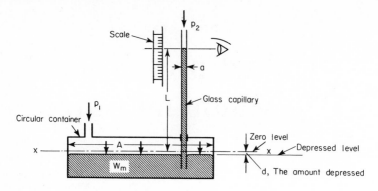

Fig. 5-2   Basic principle of the well manometer.

by a reservoir or well which has an area much larger than the area of the tube.

The pressure is applied to the liquid in the reservoir, which forces the level down a small amount. The displaced liquid enters the measuring column, which causes the level to rise. If p_1 is greater than p_2, then the liquid level is forced down in the reservoir and rises in column C until the pressure is balanced. The pressure-balance equation for the forces acting on each side of the system and taken from the same datum line X–X is

$$p_1 = p_2 + (d + h)w_m$$

Volume of liquid displaced in reservoir

$$= \text{volume of liquid gained in measuring column}$$

$$A_1 d = ah$$

hence

$$h = \frac{A_1 d}{a}$$

By substitution in the pressure-balance equation,

$$\text{Differential pressure } p_1 - p_2 = w_m \left(d + \frac{A_1 d}{a} \right)$$

or

$$p_1 - p_2 = w_m d \left(1 + \frac{A_1}{a} \right)$$

If d is now substituted by h, that is, $d = \dfrac{a}{A_1} h$,

$$p_1 - p_2 = w_m h \left(\frac{a}{A_1} + 1 \right)$$

If now the area A_1 of the reservoir or well is 10 times the area of the measuring column a, then for every inch the mercury rises in the measuring column the level in the reservoir will go down $\frac{1}{10}$ in. In the equation for the displaced volume

$$\frac{h}{d} = \frac{A_1}{a} = \frac{10}{1}$$

hence
$$h = 10d$$

This means that a 1-in. reading on the scale is an indication that an actual pressure of $1\frac{1}{10}$ in. has been applied. The graduations would be too far apart to read correctly. Therefore, the inch divisions on the scale are made $\frac{9}{10}$ in. apart. In this way they will read an actual applied pressure of 1 in. The larger the ratio of the area of the reservoir to that of the tube, the lower will be the correction factor needed to be applied to the scale.

Example. In a reservoir or well-type manometer the sealing liquid is mercury having a weight density of 0.488 lb/in.^{3}. If the area of the well is 30 in.^{2} and that of the tube is $\frac{1}{16}$ in.^{2}, calculate the height of the measuring column if the applied differential pressure is 10.0 lb/in.^{2}. The arrangement is similar to that shown in Fig. 5-2.

Solution

Mercury displaced in large reservoir = mercury gained in manometer tube

The pressure-balance equation is

$$p_1 = (L + d)w_m + p_2$$

$$p_1 - p_2 = (L + d)w_m = L\left(1 + \frac{a}{A_1}\right)w_m$$

Hence
$$10 \text{ lb/in.}^2 = L \times 0.488\left(1 + \frac{\frac{1}{16}}{30}\right) = 0.488L$$

since the fraction $\frac{\frac{1}{16}}{30}$ is negligible. Then

$$L = \frac{10}{0.488}$$
$$= 20.4 \text{ in. Hg}$$

Practical considerations. In actual instrument practice two errors are encountered if small-bore glass tubing is used in the measuring column. These are capillary and surface tension effects of very narrow tubing. When clean mercury is used, the diameter of the tubing should be not less than 1 cm. For water and other liquids which wet the sides of the tube, the diameter can be slightly less than 1 cm. Examples of actual sizes of a typical industrial well-type manometer are:

Glass tubing diameter or bore $\frac{1}{4}$ in.

$$\text{Area } a = 0.05 \text{ in.}^2, \text{ approx}$$

Reservoir internal diameter 4 in.

$$\text{Area } A_1 = 12.5 \text{ in.}^2, \text{ approx}$$

Hence
$$\frac{a}{A_1} = \frac{0.05}{12.5} = \frac{1}{250}$$

which indicates that the scale correction factor is insignificant.

Figure 5-3 shows a typical well-type manometer used for laboratory and industrial purposes. There are many varieties of the well-type ma-

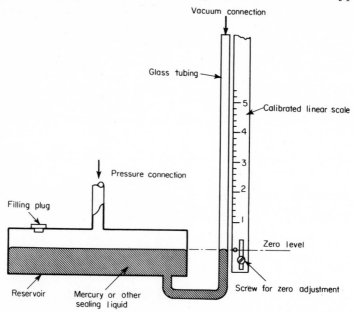

Fig. 5-3 Sectional view of typical commercial well manometer.

nometer on the market; all are based on the principles discussed. Each manometer is, however, individually calibrated and uses different zero-adjustment techniques. The main precaution to take before using a manometer for measuring a pressure or vacuum is to make certain that zero adjustment is made before taking test readings. It is also important to make sure that the instrument is leveled by means of an attached level gauge. Another variety of reservoir or well type of manometer is the inclined manometer, which is used when a higher sensitivity and readable accuracy are required.

The Inclined-tube Pressure Gauge

The inclined-tube gauge is a special development of the ordinary U-tube manometer. It has one limb that is inclined at an angle to the horizontal plane and a vertical limb that consists of a relatively large well. The sloping tube carries a scale adjacent to it. The main purpose of the inclined tube is to achieve a longer scale than the ordinary U-tube manometer for the same pressure differentials. Figure 5-4 shows the main features

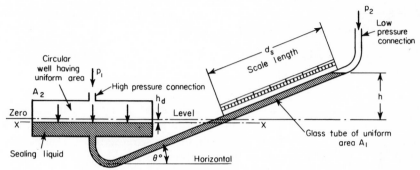

Fig. 5-4   Basic principle of inclined-tube gauge.

of the inclined-tube gauge. If p_1 is greater than p_2, the liquid in the large bulb is depressed and forced up the inclined tube.

$$\text{Volume displaced} = A_2 h_d = A_1 d_s$$

hence
$$h_d = d_s \frac{A_1}{A_2}$$

Using the line X-X as the reference,

Total pressure on left-hand limb = total pressure on right-hand limb
$$p_1 = p_2 + (h + h_d)w$$

where w is the weight density of the manometer liquid. Hence

$$p_1 - p_2 = wd_s\left(\sin\theta + \frac{A_1}{A_2}\right)$$

since
$$h = d_s \sin\theta$$

Suppose the tube is inclined to the horizontal at an angle such that 5 units are measured along the tube for 1 unit vertically, as shown in Fig. 5-5. Then a rise of h in. in the level of the liquid in the tube will produce a movement of the liquid along the tube 5 times as great. Therefore, the movement for a small change in level is more readily detected than in a vertical type of manometer. The increased sensitivity and readable accuracy of the inclined-tube manometer can be appreciated when one considers that a 6-in. range (range is always expressed in terms of a vertical column height) can be expanded by an inclined-tube manom-

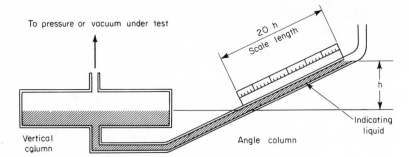

Fig. 5-5   An inclined manometer having an expanded scale of 20:1.

eter to cover a 48-in.-long scale. The reading accuracy in such a case is very high, because there are 8 in. of scale for a 1-in. range. An instrument of this type lends itself to a scale directly graduated in hundredths of an inch. Use of water as an indicating liquid would make the graduations a full tenth of a linear inch apart, equal to 0.0005 psig.

Practical considerations. Great care and attention must be taken to keep the manometer tube clean if readings are to be accurate; otherwise, errors occur because of the force of adhesion between the liquid and the tube. For precision work, allowance must be made for the change in level in the large tube. If the diameter of the bulb is large in comparison to the diameter of the tube, the change of level in the bulb will be very small and can be considered negligible. The tube can be made of glass or plastic material. The liquid used is normally a light oil so selected that the line of the meniscus and the lines of the scale form a straight line as shown in Fig. 5-6.

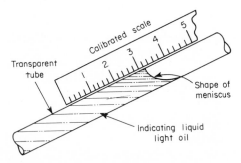

Fig. 5-6   Scale and shape of meniscus.

The inclined-tube manometer is used mostly for low-pressure differential measurements of boiler draft, furnace pressure, and static pressures in air-conditioning systems and also for determining the differential pressures across air filters and fans. It is a portable instrument and therefore useful for checking and troubleshooting purposes in large industrial plants.

Selection of an instrument range. Instrument range is selected on the following bases:

1. The overall vacuum, pressure, or pressure differential range to be measured
2. Readable accuracy specified
3. Convenience in handling the instrument

The pressure range can be readily converted to inches of various standard fluids. The Meriam Instrument Company supplies a variety of manometer fluids of different color, specific gravity, and vapor pressure, together with special conversion tables for the manometer fluids used.

Readable accuracy increases as the scale is expanded by using indicating fluids having lower specific gravities. A highly refined mineral seal oil, red in color, having an approximate vapor pressure at 25°C of 1 mm Hg, and useful over a range of 40 to 120°F has a specific gravity of 0.827 at 60°F compared with water at 4°C.

Convenience in handling requires a compromise between desired readability available in a longer instrument range and the physical ability to handle the longer range. An expanded scale means that more graduations for an inch of vertical height are obtained. It is also possible to read the scale much more accurately and easily.

The Ring Balance

The ring-balance instrument has a larger application to gas-flow metering than to purely differential-pressure measurement. It consists of a hollow or annular circular ring internally divided into two sections by a partition (Figs. 5-7 and 5-8). On each side of the partition are flexible connections leading to the two applied pressures. The ring is pivoted at the center on a knife-edge groove. When a pressure differential is applied to the partition, it sets up a rotating moment. The ring starts to rotate on its pivot in a direction away from the higher pressure. This rotating action continues until the opposing moment, created by the counterweight W at the foot of the ring, balances the rotating moment. The liquid in the ring acts as a seal and may be mercury, water, or an oil. Whichever liquid is used acts as a seal.

$$\text{Rotating moment} = (p_a - p_b)AR_1$$

where A is the area of the partition separating the two pressures.

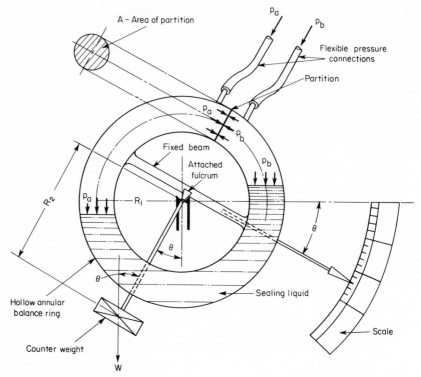

Fig. 5-7   Principle of the ring-balance manometer.

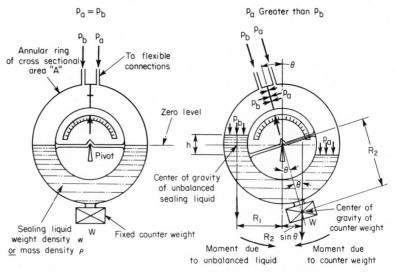

Fig. 5-8   Principle of the ring-balance manometer.

$$\text{Restoring moment} = WR_2 \sin \theta$$

where θ is the angle of tilt.

$$p_a - p_b = \frac{WR_2}{AR_1} \sin \theta$$

By dimensional analysis,

$$\left[\frac{F}{L^2} \right] = \frac{[F]}{[L^2]} \frac{[L]}{[L]} = \left[\frac{F}{L^2} \right]$$

There is another method of formulating an equation for the differential pressure by using the ring-balance principle. Taking moments on both sides of the fulcrum, as shown in Fig. 5-8,

$$\text{Counterclockwise moment} = \text{clockwise moment}$$
$$hAwR_1 = WR_2 \sin \theta$$
but
$$p_a - p_b = wh$$
$$h = \frac{p_a - p_b}{w} = \frac{WR_2}{AR_1} \frac{\sin \theta}{w}$$

By dimensional analysis

$$[L] = \frac{[F/L^2]}{[F/L^3]} = \frac{[F]}{[L^2]} \frac{[L]}{[L]} \frac{1}{[F/L^3]} = [L]$$

The angle of tilt or rotation is thus a measure of the differential pressure, and a pointer attached to the ring may be used with a circular scale for measurement purposes.

In the equation established, it should be noted that there is no density factor involved, so that the instrument is free of any variation in density due to temperature changes. No overload device is necessary for this type of manometer, because the excessive pressure will equalize by depressing the sealing liquid on one side down to the bottom of the ring, so that the gas on the high-pressure side will escape or bubble through to the low-pressure side.

Ring-balance differential gauge application. Usually the ring-balance differential gauge is used for low-pressure ranges such as those frequently encountered in the gas industries. The ring may be of glass, metal, or plastic depending upon the nature and pressure of the gas.

The tilting manometer gauge. Another instrument using the same principle as the ring-balance manometer is the tilting U-tube manometer shown in Fig. 5-9. The pressure is admitted to the ends of the tube containing the sealing liquid. The crosspiece of the U-shaped tube is balanced on a pivot. In this case a spring attached to the tube acts as the restoring moment. The angle of tilt of the tube may be indicated on a scale graduated in units of differential pressure.

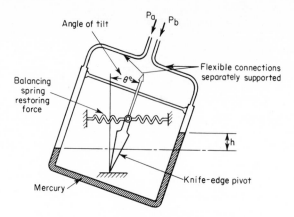

Fig. 5-9   The tilting manometer gauge.

Performance characteristics. Some of the performance characteristics of ring-balance meters are:

1. Low-pressure ranges are from 0.5 to 25 in. of water.
2. Basic differential ranges may be obtained by varying the cross-sectional area of the ring. Intermediate ranges can be obtained by altering the value of the restoring weight. However, the weight density of the sealing liquid decides the pressure at which the sealing liquid will allow short-circuiting from the high-pressure to the low-pressure connections. $P = hw$.
3. Normally, calibration adjustments are effected by changing the position of the weight or its value.
4. The sensitivity of the instrument is of the order of 1 part in 1,000.

Applications. The major applications for the ring-balance manometer are in connection with flowmeters used for gas- and air-flow measurements.

REVIEW QUESTIONS AND PROBLEMS

The well manometer

5-1   (a) Describe briefly, and with the aid of a neat sketch, the principle of operating a simple well-type manometer.

(b) How do the vertical scale divisions relate to the area of the well and bore of tubing used?

(c) What is meant by the zero adjustment of a manometer?

5-2   The application of the principle of the well-type manometer is shown in Fig. 5-10. The vertical travel of the float causes the pointer or pen to indicate or record the variation in movement. If $p_1 = 210$ lb/in.^{2} and $p_2 = 225$ lb/in.^{2} and if the area of the narrower tube is 15 in.^{2} and that of the large meter body is 60 in.^{2}, calculate the travel d of the float, in inches.

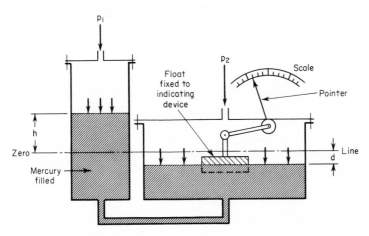

Fig. 5-10   The well manometer used to measure differential pressure.

5-3   In a well-type manometer the sealing liquid is mercury. If the area of the well is 30.0 in.^{2} and that of the measuring tube is $\frac{1}{16}$ in.^{2}, calculate the height of the mercury reading if a differential pressure of 5.0 lb/in.^{2} is applied.

5-4   A manometer has a vertical measuring column glass tube $\frac{3}{16}$ in. bore. The tube is attached at the bottom to a rectangular-shaped well 6 in.^{2} in area. Calculate the height of glass tubing required if the maximum pressure to be measured is 10 lb/in.^{2}.

The inclined gauge

5-5   (a) What liquid column would accurately measure very low pressure differentials over an extended scale?
(b) Give three applications for the use of the inclined-tube manometer.

5-6   Calculate the differential head in inches demineralized water used in an inclined-tube manometer. The angle of inclination is 30° to the horizontal, and the diameter of the large bulb is 4 in. and that of the tube $\frac{1}{4}$ in. The extended scale adjacent to the inclined tube is 4 in. The following equation is given:

$$p_2 - p_1 = wd\left(\sin\theta + \frac{A_1}{A_2}\right)$$

where w is the weight density of water.

5-7   If the ratio $\frac{A_1}{A_2} = \frac{1}{256}$, calculate the scale length if the maximum differential pressure is 1.0 in. w.g., $\theta = 30°$, and the weight density of water used in the manometer is $w = 0.036$ lb/in.³.

5-8   (a) List some of the precautions that must be taken with the inclined-tube pressure gauge.
(b) If light oil is used in the gauge, sketch the shape of the meniscus and indicate where the reading should be taken from the scale.

5-9   Suppose the manometer in Question 5-6 had an inclined length to vertical length ratio of 20:1. How would this affect the result previously obtained with the gauge?

5-10   For the inclined-tube draft gauge shown in Fig. 5-11, compute the gauge pressure, in pounds per square inch, at B if the right-hand

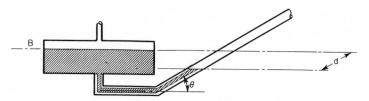

Fig. 5-11   Inclined manometer gauge.

limb is open to atmosphere. The oil used has a specific gravity of 0.870, $d = 5.00$ in., and $\theta = 20°$.

Ring balance and tilting gauge

5-11   Describe, with the aid of a neat diagram, the operation of either the ring-balance or tilting U-tube manometer as a differential pressure gauge.

5-12   In the design of a ring-balance manometer, θ varies from 0 to 30°, $R_2 = 12$ in., $R_1 = 7$ in., and the radius of the partition in the hollow ring is 1 in. A counterweight of 454 g is used. Calculate the maximum differential pressure value, in inches water gauge, which the instrument will indicate.

5-13   Why is no overload device necessary for the ring-balance or tilting U-tube manometer?

5-14   If the maximum differential pressure for a ring-balance manometer is to be 10 in. w.g., calculate the value of the counterweight to be used in Question 5-12 if the only other modification is that θ for maximum rotation is now 90°.

5-15 A ring-type manometer has a mean diameter of 20.0 cm, and the cross-sectional area of the tube is 3 cm². The liquid used in it is mercury. The center of gravity of a mass of 200 g used as a counterweight is 15.0 cm from the pivot point. Calculate the value of the differential pressure, in dynes/cm², which will cause the ring to tilt 30°. *Note:* Be careful of units.

5-16 In the design of a ring-balance manometer, calculate the angle of deflection if the mean radius of the hollow annular ring is 15 cm and the cross-sectional area of the ring is 1.0 cm². The counterweight is 400 g and its center of gravity is 17 cm from the pivot. The differential pressure is 2.23×10^5 dynes/cm².

BELL–TYPE MANOMETERS

The principle used in the bell-type manometer involves the force produced by the difference of pressures on the inside and outside of an inverted bell, which has a thin metal or plastic wall. The bell is partly immersed in a sealing liquid. The higher-pressure connection is led to the inside of the inverted bell. The lower-pressure connection is led in at the top of the container. The upward or downward movement of the bell can be determined and calibrated in terms of the differential pressure. The general arrangement is shown in Fig. 5-12, which is a cross-sectional view of a

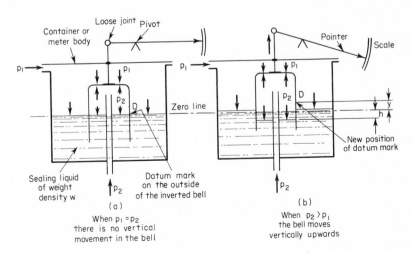

Fig. 5-12 The basic principle of the bell-type manometer.

typical industrial type of inverted bell manometer. The nomenclature is as follows:

$A_{\bullet}$ = outer area of inverted bell (radius R_o)
A_1 = inner area of inverted bell (radius R_1)
y = vertical travel of inverted bell
w = weight density of the sealing liquid
$p_2 - p_1 = \Delta p$, the differential pressure
R = radius of the container of the manometer

To ensure that the difference in levels of the liquid inside and outside the inverted bell does not have a significant effect in the calculation of the differential pressure, the radius R of the container is very much larger than either the inside or the outside radius of the bell. In instrument practice, the radius of the container or meter body is about 2.5 times as large as the radius of the inverted bell. For example, $R_o = 1.7$ in., $R_1 = 1.6$ in., and R is approximately 4.0 in. Under these conditions, when the pressures are applied, the level of the zero or datum mark on the inverted bell rises a distance y and the level of the surface of the liquid inside the bell will be depressed a distance h. The gain of liquid outside the bell, although equal to the loss of liquid from inside the bell, causes a negligible increase in the outside level because of the much larger value of the radius R of the container in comparison to the radius of the bell.

Differential pressure on top area of the inverted bell
= loss of upthrust on the bell

The loss of upthrust is in accordance with Archimedes' principle, which states that the upthrust or buoyancy acting on an object immersed in a fluid is equal to the weight of the liquid displaced by the object. As the bell rises, less of its length is immersed in the liquid, thus the upthrust on it due to buoyancy is reduced. In the case of the inverted bell manometer with a thick wall the equation is

$$(p_2 - p_1)\pi R_1{}^2 = \pi(R_o{}^2 - R_1{}^2)wy$$

$$y = \frac{p_2 - p_1}{w(R_o{}^2 - R_1{}^2)} R_1{}^2$$

By dimensional analysis,

$$\left[\frac{F}{L^2}\right][L^2] = [L^2]\left[\frac{F}{L^3}\right][L]$$
$$[F] = [F]$$

This equation yields approximate results as long as $R_o{}^2 - R_1{}^2$ is much smaller than R^2. The pressure at which the sealing liquid will limit range can be found from

$$p_2 - p_1 = \Delta p = hw$$

Inverted-bell-type differential-pressure meters are normally used when the actual differences of pressure are small. There are a variety of different designs; Fig. 5-13 shows one of them. The sealing liquid separates the two

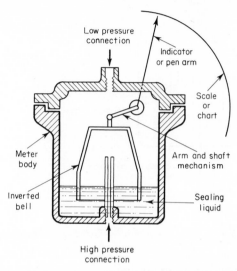

Fig. 5-13 Sectional view of a typical industrial inverted-bell manometer.

pressures in the meter body. The higher pressure on the underside causes the inverted bell to rise. A higher pressure on the outside of the bell, which acts down upon it, would cause the bell to travel downward. The vertical motion of the inverted bell is transmitted by means of an arm and shaft into a rotary movement. The shaft extends through a pressure-tight bearing into the meter case, where it is then used to drive an indicating pointer or pen arm of a recording instrument across a properly graduated scale or chart.

Thin-wall inverted bell. Instead of a thick-wall bell a thin-wall bell suspended from a spring, as shown in Fig. 5-14, can be used. Usually, the effects due to displacement of the sealing liquid are small, because the radius of the meter body is much larger than that of the inverted bell. In addition, the effect of buoyancy can be neglected.

With this type of instrument, it is usual practice to apply the high pressure to the outside of the bell, while the low pressure is led to the inside of the bell. The difference between the force due to the pressure on the outside acting downward on the top of the bell and the force due to the pressure acting upward inside the bell is equal to $A_o(p_2 - p_1)$ lb, where A_o is the effective outside area of the thin-wall manometer. This is balanced by the force exerted by the spring. (Refer to p. 90.)

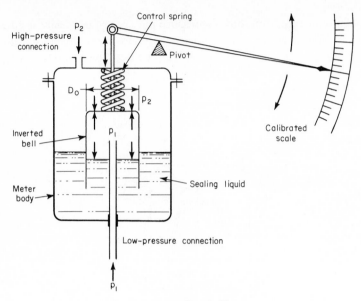

Fig. 5-14   Spring-controlled bell-type manometer.

Net applied force acting on top of bell

= change in length of spring × spring rate

Symbolically,

$$A_o(p_2 - p_1) = (L_1 - L_o)S$$

By dimensional analysis,

$$[L^2]\left[\frac{F}{L^2}\right] = [L]\left[\frac{F}{L}\right] = [F]$$

But $L_1 - L_o$ is, in fact, the vertical travel y of the bell, and

$$y = \frac{A_o}{S}(p_2 - p_1)$$
$$= K(p_2 - p_1)$$

where K is the constant A_o/S. From this expression, it may be stated that travel of the bell is proportional to the differential pressure to be measured. Thus this principle can be used to design an industrial type of manometer.

No overload device is necessary because, in the case of gas measurement, when the differential pressure becomes great enough to force the sealing liquid down to the level of the edge of the bell, the gas will bubble through the liquid. This has the effect of equalizing the pressure until such time as the differential returns to a measurable quantity. The range of the instrument will depend on the value of the spring rate. For high ranges mercury is used as the sealing liquid, and, in the case of low pressure down to a few inches of water gauge, an organic liquid may be used as a seal.

The methods used to transmit the motion of the bell to the outside of the meter body can be the same as those used to indicate the position of the float in instruments described earlier. For example, a pressure-tight bearing, segmental lever, or rotary arm movement can be used to measure differential pressures.

Inverted-bells Balance Manometer

Figure 5-15 is a cross-sectional view of a pressure-measuring device which consists of two identical bells inverted in a bath of oil. These inverted

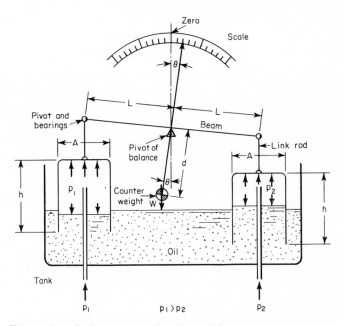

Fig. 5-15   Balance type of differential-pressure manometer.

bells are suspended from the balance beam by means of rods. The rods are carried on pivot-socket-type bearings having small contact surfaces in order to minimize frictional effects. The two pressures which are to be compared are led through the bottom of the oil bath into the inside of the inverted bells. The pressure differential is indicated by the pointer, which moves with the rotation of the beam balance. The scale usually has a range of 0.00 to 0.20 in. w.g., although a larger range is possible, according to the application requirements. The nomenclature is as follows:

$p_1 - p_2 =$ differential pressure
$W =$ counterweight with pointer attached to the beam
$L =$ distance from beam pivot to the bell support
$d =$ distance from the center of gravity of the counterweight to the pivot of the beam
$\theta =$ angle of tilt, or deflection from the vertical
$A =$ internal area of the top of each inverted bell

Taking moments about the pivot of the beam

$$\text{Rotating moment} = \text{restoring moment}$$
$$(p_1 - p_2)AL \cos\theta = Wd \sin\theta$$
$$p_1 - p_2 = \frac{Wd}{AL} \tan\theta$$

By dimensional analysis,

$$\left[\frac{F}{L^2}\right] = \frac{[F]}{[L^2]}\frac{[L]}{[L]} = \left[\frac{F}{L^2}\right]$$

Hence the differential pressure is a function of the angle of deflection.

The restoring force is small and is produced by the change in the position of the center of gravity of the counterweight, which is attached to the beam. As the beam rotates, the position of the counterweight is altered. The instrument is sensitive to small changes of pressure. Variations as small as 0.001 in. w.g. can be detected on a quality instrument of this type. The two bells may be either metal or plastic, and in operation they are subject to the same changes of temperature. The area of the oil surface in the bath is relatively larger than the circular area of the bells in order to minimize the effect of the oil level inside each of the bells. The oil surface should be parallel to the plane of the bell mouths to avoid buoyancy effects.

Applications. This type of manometer is used in the steel industry for measuring and controlling open-hearth-furnace pressures. The movement of the beam for a differential-pressure change actuates a pneumatic unit which can be used to control the pressure conditions inside the furnace.

Spring Characteristics

In the field of instrument practice springs play a very important role. They are used in various shapes and sizes, from small coil springs to the large springs which are used for damping purposes in industrial instruments or automatic control equipment. It will be necessary to discuss some of the characteristics of springs so that the application and importance of springs in instrument practice may be better understood.

Hooke's law. Any elastic material that undergoes distortion, elongation or change of position does so in a manner directly proportional to the applied force. The Bourdon tube, which is the very heart of so many pressure- and temperature-measuring instruments, is a typical example. The fundamental law of springs states that, so long as the material operates over the linear portion of its range, the elongation or angular movement is directly proportional to the applied force.

An important characteristic of a spring is stiffness factor or spring rate, which is defined as the force divided by the distortion. For example, if a coiled spring requires a force of 20 lb to stretch it 4 in., then the spring stiffness factor or spring rate becomes

$$\text{Spring rate } S = \frac{\text{force (lb)}}{\text{elongation (in.)}} = \frac{20 \text{ lb}}{4 \text{ in.}} = 5 \text{ lb/in.}$$

The spring rate, then, is given as the force required to extend the spring one inch.

Stress-strain relationship. Instruments which depend for their calibration upon the stress produced in an elastic component or member when it is strained must be checked at regular intervals against a standard in order to guarantee accuracy. If an elastic measuring element such as a helical or Bourdon tube, metallic bellows, diaphragm, or spring is stressed repeatedly, it will be observed that the zero shift is greatest at first and then decreases gradually after each stressing. Such elements are stressed through their maximum range several times before they are calibrated. Stress is the force per unit area of the member:

$$\text{Stress} = \frac{\text{force } F \text{ (lb)}}{\text{area } A \text{ (in.}^2)} = \frac{F}{A} \qquad \text{lb/in.}^2, \text{ or psi}$$

Strain is an indication of the distortion or elongation due to the stress and is expressed in inches per inch length of the member.

$$\text{Strain} = \frac{\text{change in length (in.)}}{\text{original length (in.)}} = \frac{\Delta L}{L_o} \qquad \text{in./in.}$$

The relation between stress and strain is shown in Fig. 5-16a and b. During a series of tests on a steel wire, a record is kept of the applied forces

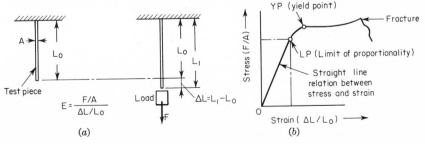

Fig. 5-16 (a) *Experiment to find Young's modulus of elasticity.* (b) *Typical plot of stress vs. strain for an elastic metallic material.*

or loads, together with the corresponding elongations. The important conclusions from such tests are:

1. The initial relationship of stress and strain is essentially a straight line; i.e., the slope is practically constant. For example, T_1, T_2, and T_3 are three of several sets of test results taken on the steel wire the values for which are as tabulated:

Test	Stress, lb/in.^{2}	Strain, in./in.
T_1	5,000	0.0016
T_2	10,000	0.0033
T_3	15,000	0.0048

The slope is given by the ratios:

$$\frac{\text{Stress}}{\text{Strain}} = \frac{5{,}000 \text{ lb/in.}^2}{0.0016 \text{ in./in.}} = \frac{10{,}000 \text{ lb/in.}^2}{0.0033 \text{ in./in.}} = \frac{15{,}000 \text{ lb/in.}^2}{0.0048 \text{ in./in.}}$$
$$= 30{,}000{,}000 \text{ lb/in.}^2, \text{ or psi (approx)}$$

This ratio, or slope of the line, is called *Young's modulus of elasticity*, usually designated by E. In the above case, for steel, $E = 30{,}000{,}000$ psi, and this is an important characteristic of the quality of the steel. This slope of the plotted line is fairly constant from 0 to LP, as shown in Fig. 5-16b.

2. The point at which the strain is no longer linearly proportional to the stress is called the *limit of proportionality* (LP).
3. From point LP to point YP the material is within the elastic range, but the strain or elongation is not readily calculated.
4. When the *yield point* (YP) is reached, the sample test piece will continue to strain without any increase in load. Fracture will then occur.

Elastic properties of some materials commonly used in instrument work are given in Table 5-1.

Practical considerations. It is very important to observe that an instrument should on no account be subjected to a pressure or stress greater than the designed values; otherwise, its original accuracy will be jeopardized.

Hysteresis. No material will return exactly to its original form when a deforming stress or pressure on it is removed. That is because there is no absolutely elastic material. All materials have an internal friction which must be overcome before elongation commences, and this internal frictional force varies according to the properties and characteristics of the material. Steel, copper, and brass, for example, develop small internal

Table 5-1   Elastic properties of some materials

Material	Young's modulus of elasticity E, lb/in.^{2} elongation per inch of original length	Stress at elastic limit, lb/in.^{2}
Annealed brass	14,000,000	16,000
Bronze	14,500,000	40,000
Copper	18,000,000	10,000
Aluminum	10,000,000	25,000
Steel	30,000,000	20,000*

* Average value; depends on the quality of steel.

frictional forces for small displacements, and for that reason they are used in instrument practice. Also, these metals nearly repeat their performance with either increasing or decreasing forces. That is to say, each has a small hysteresis loss. Rubber, on the other hand, has a high hysteresis loss.

The hysteresis loop shown in Fig. 5-17 represents the amount of energy required for the material to go through a complete cycle of pressure or

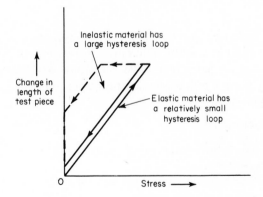

Fig. 5-17   Hysteresis loops of elastic and inelastic materials.

stress changes. An ideal elastic material has no hysteresis loop. An inelastic material has a relatively large hysteresis loop and, therefore, a high hysteresis loss. Because of inaccuracies in readings caused by hysteresis, it is recommended in instrument practice to use materials with as little hysteresis loss as possible. Also, a material with a high hysteresis loss is likely to fail under repeated operation. A piece of tin sheet can be broken by continual bending; the work put into it is to overcome internal friction, with the result that the metal becomes quite warm.

Springs can operate repeatedly under high stresses and still yield little heat because of the small amount of internal friction. For this reason, as already mentioned, steel, bronze, and copper are among the metals used in the manufacture of springs.

REVIEW QUESTIONS AND PROBLEMS

Bell-type manometer

5-17   (a) State Archimedes' principle of floatation.
(b) If the depth of immersion of the inverted bell, outside diameter (OD) = $1\frac{3}{4}$ in., inside diameter (ID) = $1\frac{1}{2}$ in., is 3 in. in mercury, calculate the weight of the bell when the differential pressure is zero.

5-18   If the area of the manometer container is considered large compared with the area of the inverted bell, calculate the travel of the bell (OD = $1\frac{3}{4}$ in., ID = $1\frac{1}{2}$ in.) if water is used as the sealing liquid and the differential pressure is 0.01 psi. Use the expression

$$y = \frac{p_2 - p_1}{w(R_o{}^2 - R_1{}^2)} R_1{}^2$$

5-19   The water in Question 5-18 is now replaced by mercury as the sealing liquid and the differential pressure is 1.0 psi. Calculate the travel of the same bell under these new conditions.

5-20   Why is no overload device necessary for the inverted-bell-type manometer?

Spring characteristics

5-21   (a) Define the terms spring rate, Young's modulus of elasticity, and hysteresis.
(b) Discuss some of the applications you know of high-quality springs used in instruments.

5-22   If a spring is required to stretch $\frac{3}{4}$ in. and the spring rate is 6 lb/in., calculate the necessary applied force.

5-23   During a test on a brass link rod 10 in. long with a cross-sectional area of $\frac{1}{4}$ in.², an elongation of 0.030 in. was detected and recorded. Calculate the force applied to the test piece.

5-24   A force of 200 lb compresses a spring 4 in. Calculate the spring rate, in pounds per inch.

5-25   A bellows pressure unit has a spring rate of 50 lb/in. What effective diameter should the bellows have if 10 lb/in.² produces a movement of $\frac{1}{2}$ in.?

5-26 In industrial instrument practice, hysteresis is often measured along with lost motion and friction. Comment on this statement and give practical cases of its application.

Spring-controlled bell-type manometer

5-27 Calculate the travel of an inverted-bell type manometer if the outer diameter of the bell is $1\frac{3}{4}$ in. and the applied differential pressure is 10.2 lb/in.^{2}. The control spring incorporated in the instrument is made of steel and has a spring rate of 15 lb/in. Use the expression $A_o(p_2 - p_1) = (L_1 - L_o)S$.

5-28 Calculate the value of the spring rate required in a thin-wall inverted-bell-type manometer if the following data are specified:

> Maximum differential pressure $= 80$ psi
> Outside diameter of the thin-walled bell $= 2$ in.
> Maximum bell travel permitted $= 4$ in.

5-29 Why does the range of an instrument such as the one described in Question 5-28 depend upon the spring and the specific weight of the sealing liquid?

5-30 Describe, with the aid of diagrams, three methods of transmitting the travel of the bell floats to read changes in differential pressure outside the meter body.

Inverted-bells balance-type manometer

5-31 The counterweight weighs 20 oz and its center of gravity is 3 in. from the fulcrum of a balance beam supporting identical inverted bells. The bells are 1 in. in radius, and each is positioned 5 in. from the fulcrum. If the angle of tilt is 10°, calculate the differential pressure in (a) pounds per square inch, (b) inches water gauge.

5-32 (a) Describe, with the aid of a diagram, the construction and operation of the inverted-bells balance-type manometer.
(b) Give reasons why the instrument of part (a) is sensitive to very small differential-pressure changes of the order of 0.001 in w.g.

MECHANICAL PRESSURE-MEASURING ELEMENTS

Bourdon-tube Pressure Gauges

A variety of pressure-measuring elements are used in process and other industrial plants. All pressure elements are designed to operate under a pressure change by bending, deforming, or deflecting or by moving some device an amount which depends upon the pressure variation. Such elements are termed *transducers*, because they can take one form of energy from the measuring source and supply energy of a different kind to an indicating, recording, or controlling system. For example, a pressure gauge may take energy from the air compressed in a cylinder and supply enough mechanical power to move a pointer across a scale to indicate or record the pressure in the cylinder.

Bourdon tubes. The bourdon-tube type of gauge for measuring pressure or vacuum is one of the oldest instruments used in industry. It dates to the early days of steam power development. Its effectiveness and reliability are so good that it is still used in steam plants and chemical process and other industries. The component parts and mechanism of a typical Bourdon-tube gauge are shown in Fig. 5-18.

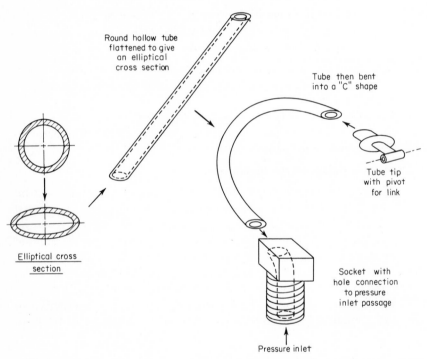

Fig. 5-18   Construction and component parts of a Bourdon-tube gauge.

Eugene Bourdon invented this type of gauge in 1851. He stated that a round tubing which has been flattened and bent into a circular arc will tend to return to its original shape when a pressure is applied inside it. The operation is similar to that of the paper coiled-tube blowers used at parties. In its simplest form it consists of a length of thin-walled metal tubing which has been flattened to approximately an elliptical cross section and then rolled into a C shape, having an arc span of about 270°.

This tube is then supported in a socket which contains the pressure-inlet passageway to the inside of the Bourdon tube. The free end of the tube is sealed; it is called the *tip*. The tube, socket, and tip are welded, brazed, or soldered together according to the applied-pressure range.

From experience it has been found that the deflection of the tip of the tube depends upon the radius of the bend, the total tube length, the wall thickness of the tube, the major and minor axes of the cross section, and Young's modulus of elasticity of the tube material. Under pressure the elliptical or flattened section tends to change its shape to a circular form. Stresses are set up and the tube begins to straighten out.

Motion studies. In a pressure gauge the problem is to change a nearly straight line motion of about ¼ in., for maximum pressure reading, into a full-scale deflection of 270° of the pointer shaft. Figure 5-19 shows how this

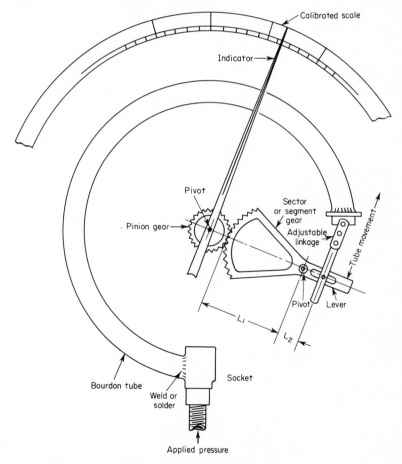

Fig. 5-19 Bourdon-tube gauge.

is accomplished. A small pinion gear which is attached to the pointer meshes with a much larger segment or sector gear which pivots about a fixed point in the instrument case. The segment gear has an extension, called the lever, beyond the pivot. At the end of the lever there is an adjustable link connection to the tip of the Bourdon tube. Any motion of the tip will be transmitted by means of the link to the lever, the segment gear, and in turn to the pinion gear, which rotates the spindle containing a lightweight pointer. The pointer rotates clockwise when the Bourdon unwinds and indicates, on a suitably calibrated scale, the magnitude of the applied pressure under measurement.

Suppose the gear ratio is 13.5:1; then the segment will have to rotate through $270° \div 13.5 = 20°$ about the pivot. If L_1 is 1.40 in., L_2 is 0.70 in., and the Bourdon yields a deflection length of $\frac{1}{4}$ in., then the angle of

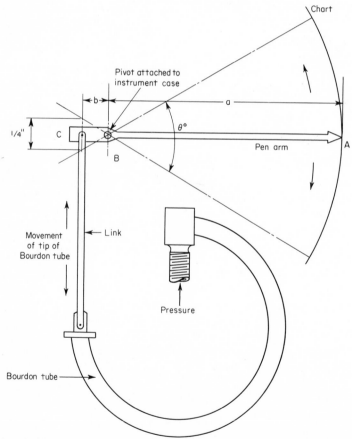

Fig. 5-20   Use of lever principle and linkage to magnify reading.

rotation of the segment will be nearly 20°. Adjustment devices are provided so that the correct angle of rotation may be obtained. In the case of pressure-recording instruments, as shown in Fig. 5-20, a pen arm moves over a circular chart. The pen arm is pivoted at B, the pen well being at A recording on a circular chart. At the other end, C, the pen arm is linked to the tip of the Bourdon tube. Any deflection of the Bourdon is magnified at A by the ratio a/b.

Now consider some actual values. If the Bourdon movement for full-scale deflection, i.e., for the full pressure range, is $\frac{1}{4}$ in. at the tip, $a = 6$ in., and $b = \frac{3}{8}$ in., then the arc movement of the pen well or indicator will be $(\frac{1}{4} \times 6/\frac{3}{8}) = 4$ in. The angle which the pen traces out in moving from one extreme of the chart to the other is normally about 40°. Figure 5-21 shows the relative position and sweep of a pen arm on a

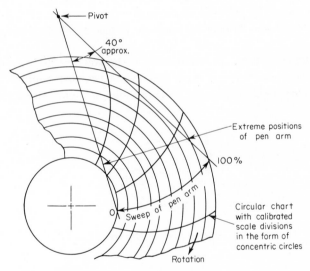

Fig. 5-21   Position of pen arm.

circular recording chart. Very frequently a gauge may be in perfect calibration at both ends of the scale and still show high errors near the center of the scale. This is *error of angularity*, which is the distortion resulting from converting an approximate straight-line motion into an angular motion with a single set of levers. Angularity errors must be kept to a minimum by improving the linkage and leverage in the system.

The component parts of industrial pressure gauges are precision-made, particularly the gears, which are machined to close tolerances. The higher-quality instruments incorporate hardened bushings for the pivot and spindle. Any errors due to wear or loose-fitting bearings are referred to as "lost motion," and errors caused by play in the meshing gear teeth are referred to as "backlash."

Pressure range. Bourdon tubes will measure up to and above 80,000 psi; they are produced by various manufacturers. The lower-range limit varies with the manufacturer, but it may be as low as 0 to 15 psi. 0 to 50 psi is a quite common range.

Materials used. The most common materials used for the Bourdon tube are trumpet brass, phosphor bronze, beryllium copper, alloy steel, and stainless steel. The selection of a material will depend, apart from the maximum pressure and modulus of elasticity, upon cost and the possibility of corrosion. The higher pressures demand materials with a high elastic limit. A tough steel, such as chrome molybdenum, will take a pressure of about 3,000 psi. Beryllium copper, which has an elastic limit of about 1.15×10^5 psi, will also withstand a pressure of 3,000 psi and has lower hysteresis. Beryllium copper is also used for lower pressure ranges.

Spiral Bourdon tube. In some designs the free end of the Bourdon is wound round several times with the socket-pressure connection at the center. Figure 5-22 shows the general idea of such an element. The

Fig. 5-22   *Spiral Bourdon tube.*

amount of movement varies directly with the angle subtended by the total arc. By increasing the number of turns in the spiral or helix, a greater movement of the tip is obtained.

Helical Bourdon tube. The advantage of the helical type of Bourdon is that the mean diameter of the turns can be kept fairly constant over a wide range of pressure. This means that a large instrument case is not necessary. Helical elements are therefore frequently used where multiple recordings are required on the same chart. A typical arrangement is shown in Fig. 5-23. Most of the Bourdon tubes may be used in liquid-, vapor-, or gas-filled thermal systems for measuring temperature. This will be discussed later in connection with temperature measurement.

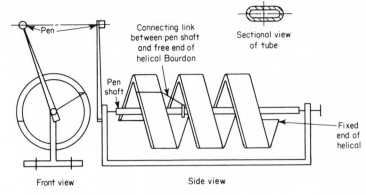

Fig. 5-23   A helical Bourdon tube.

Pressure Bellows

The pressure-measuring element takes the form shown in Fig. 5-24. It is like a cup with a number of corrugations along its sides. In order to dis-

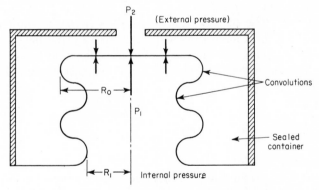

Fig. 5-24   Differential-pressure bellows.

tinguish this curved surface from that of the capsule element, the word "convolution" is sometimes used instead of "corrugation." The bellows is usually formed by special hydraulic presses. Bellows elements are used in larger indicating gauges, recorders, pneumatic controllers, and control valves, where space is not a limiting factor. The main characteristics of metallic bellows are discussed in the following paragraphs.

Flexibility. This is similar in character to that of a helical coiled compression spring. The increases in load and deflection changes are linear up to the elastic limit. This is true only when the bellows is under compression, and for this reason it is necessary to arrange the travel of the bellows to be made on the compression side. In instrument practice the bellows must be opposed by a spring. The resultant deflection or travel of the bellows will depend upon the characteristics of the spring and bellows. The flexibility of the bellows is found in practice to depend upon these physical characteristics:

1. Directly with the number of convolutions
2. Directly as the square of the outside diameter of the bellows
3. Inversely as the modulus of elasticity of the material used
4. Inversely as the cube of the wall thickness

If thicker walls are required to withstand higher pressures, the flexibility will be greatly reduced. Where this is a serious factor, the flexibility may be increased by using a double-walled bellows.

Deflection. The deflection of the bellows is defined as the amount of compressive movement that can be applied before a "permanent set" results; i.e., when the stress is increased beyond the elastic limit and then removed, a permanent set or strain occurs. The bellows then does not return to its original length or shape. Deflection depends upon the number of convolutions in the bellows, and amounts to about 10 percent of bellows length to avoid distortion.

Effective area. The effective area of a bellows must be known in order to calculate the total force that will be exerted by the bellows under a known pressure intensity. The effective area may be found from the following formula, which will give only approximate results (Fig. 5-24).

$$A = \pi \left(\frac{R_o + R_1}{2} \right)^2$$

where A = effective area of bellows
  $R_\bullet$ = outside radius of bellows
  R_1 = inside radius of bellows

More accurate expressions for the effective area may be found in advanced texts, ISA or similar bulletins, and in manufacturers' publications.

Pressure Diaphragms

From the preceding information on Bourdon tubes it is evident that, below a range of 0 to 15 psi, an alternative and more sensitive means of pressure measurement must be considered. It has been found in instrument practice that single metallic diaphragms are suitable for measuring low pressure and vacuums. In its simplest form a diaphragm consists of a thin flexible material, e.g., beryllium copper, leather, or rubberized fabric as shown in Fig. 5-25. Usually there is a thin metallic disk or other rigid material at the center. The diaphragm need not be circular, and some manufacturers used an elongated shape in their instruments.

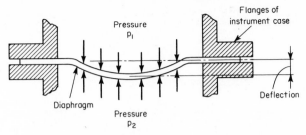

Fig. 5-25 A diaphragm measuring element.

Low pressure or vacuum gauge. The common low-pressure, low-vacuum range is about ± 2.0 in. w.g., as used for the measurement of furnace draft. Figure 5-26 shows schematically the arrangement of a

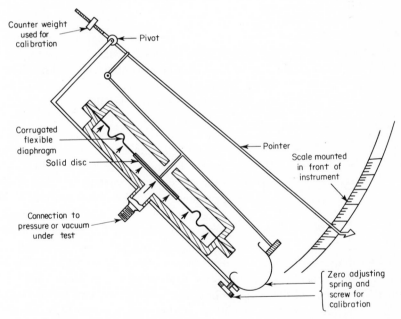

Fig. 5-26 Details of a low-pressure or vacuum gauge.

typical low-pressure or vacuum diaphragm gauge which is frequently used in industry.

Stiff metallic diaphragm. This consists of a hardened and tempered diaphragm of about 3 in. diameter held by flanges, as shown in Fig. 5-27. Pressure is applied to the underside, and the vertical movement is trans-

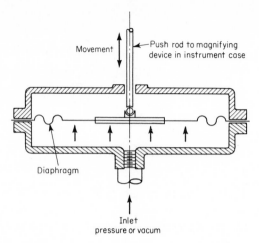

Fig. 5-27   A simple diaphragm gauge.

mitted to the ball-socket joint. With suitable linkage, high magnification may be given to the pointer by a linkage and lever system similar to that shown in Fig. 5-26. The range of the instrument is about 0 to 20 psi. The diaphragm is found to be difficult to protect from overloading.

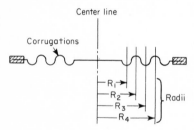

Fig. 5-28   A simple diaphragm.

If, as shown in Fig. 5-28, corrugations are pressed into the thin metallic diaphragm, the effect will be greater flexibility and sensitivity to slight pressure or vacuum variations. However, provided that the movement is not excessive, the deflection may be considered to be in a linear relationship with the applied pressure.

Stacked diaphragm unit. The usefulness of corrugated diaphragms is especially found when the diaphragms are assembled in stack form. A number of corrugated diaphragms having a central hole are pressed and punched out. They are then welded or soldered together so as to be airtight. The assembled unit, shown in Fig. 5-29, looks like a metallic concertina. Pressures are applied at the two connections as indicated, and the differential pressure is transmitted to a pointer pen or control mechanism. Normally the unit is called a "capsule" or low-pressure bellows. It is also used a great deal in pneumatic control systems.

Bourdon-tube pressure transducer. It is a relatively simple matter to produce, from a Bourdon pressure gauge, an electrical output which is proportional to the pressure being measured. The expansion and contrac-

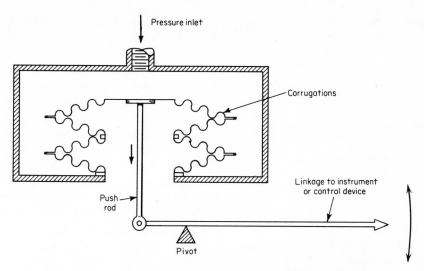

Fig. 5-29   *A stack diaphragm or corrugated bellows element.*

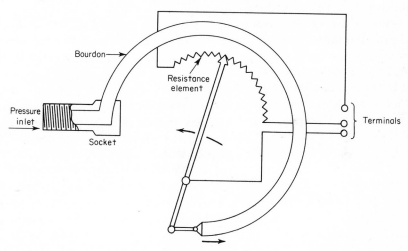

Fig. 5-30   *A transducer with Bourdon pressure tube.*

tion of the Bourdon tube actuates the voltage divider in a potentiometer circuit as indicated in Fig. 5-30. The resulting electrical signal can then be transmitted to a remote-indicating device.

Gauge Accessories and Notes on Installation

Important accessories. In closing this section a few comments will be made about gauge accessories and installation. Gauges, when used on steam drums, steam pipelines, or on any steam equipment must be so installed that live steam does not enter the Bourdon-tube measuring element. The reason is that the high heat content of steam will weaken the

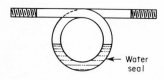

Fig. 5-31   A pigtail siphon.

tube and, because of expansion effects in the component parts, cause the gauge to read low. In order to prevent steam from entering the Bourdon tube, an accessory known as a pigtail, or more precisely a siphon, is installed at the entrance to the pressure connection of the gauge. The pigtail siphon is nothing more than a coiled pipe, as shown in Fig. 5-31. Steam condenses in the loop and provides an effective water seal. The air trapped in the pressure line and Bourdon tube acts as a cushion for transmitting the pressure.

Rapid pulsations in the pressure system, as from a high-speed compressor, cause wear on the gear type of gauge. To prevent this cruelty to the gauge, a restriction or baffle should be installed in the pressure connection line. The throttling effect will tend to make the gauge read the average value of the pressure instead of the peaks and valleys of the alternating pulses. One common type of damping device is a fine screen or wire mesh. The simple needle-valve dampener is also a good device for smoothing out pulsations.

Notes on installation. As always, common sense is an important asset. Pipe wrenches have a crushing effect when used to tighten pressure-gauge connections. Wrenches are to be used on gauges only when the manufacturer has supplied flat surfaces on the socket for the purpose. The pressure tubing should be long enough that it can be coiled a turn or two to prevent vibration from having an effect in loosening the connections and causing strain in the pipework. Periodic inspection and testing will help to maintain accurate instrument readings. Records should be kept to make sure that all instruments in the plant have been checked regularly.

REVIEW QUESTIONS AND PROBLEMS

5-33   (a) Describe, with the aid of a diagram, the principle of operation and construction of any C-type Bourdon-tube gauge that you know.

(b) Sketch a typical pinion-gear movement used in the C-type Bourdon-tube gauge.

(c) If the gear ratio is 14.2:1, calculate the angle through which the segment would have to rotate about the pivot in order that the pointer shaft will revolve through 270°.

5-34   In a pressure-recording instrument the linkage is set up in a way similar to that shown in Fig. 5-20. If the maximum movement for full pressure range of the C-type Bourdon tube is ⅜ in. and the lengths from the pivot are $a = 7$ in. and $b = \frac{1}{4}$ in., calculate (a) the approximate linear length of the pen arc and (b) the approximate angle of sweep.

5-35   Compare the advantages and disadvantages of the spiral and helical Bourdon-tube pressure-measuring elements.

5-36   (a) Describe, briefly, the operation of a diaphragm pressure-vacuum gauge.

(b) If a pressure of 6.0-in. water gauge is acting on an effective area of 30.0 in.² of the diaphragm, calculate the force, in pounds, acting on the push rod.

5-37   (a) Point out the main physical differences and applications of the capsule and bellows elements.

(b) Define the term "flexibility of a bellows."

(c) If the approximate effective area of a bellows is given by $A = \pi[(R_o + R_1)/2]^2$, calculate the effective force acting on a central push rod if a differential pressure of 3.0 psi is applied to the unit. $R_o = 1\frac{1}{2}$ in. and $R_1 = 1\frac{1}{4}$ in.

5-38   (a) What are some of the factors which determine the deflection range of corrugated diaphragms and convoluted bellows?

(b) Evaluate the important physical characteristics of beryllium copper in instrument practice.

Measurement of Gauge Pressure, Absolute Pressure, and Vacuum

Bellows and stacks are used for the measurement of gauge pressure, absolute pressure, and vacuum. It is suggested that the reader review the data on these pressure-measuring elements in order to get a clearer understanding of the following.

Absolute pressure. As already mentioned, in the basic concepts of pressure measurement the zero of the absolute-pressure scale corresponds to a complete absence of pressure. Consider the cylinder shown in Fig. 5-32a to be completely exhausted of all air or gases. The pressure inside it would then be 0 psi absolute, or 0 psia. Let air be admitted into the cylinder, as shown in Fig. 5-32b, at the same pressure as the atmospheric pressure outside the cylinder. If the atmospheric pressure is, at the time, 14.7 psi, a normal value, then the internal pressure inside the cylinder will be 14.7 psia or 14.7 psi above zero on the scale.

Gauge pressure. If now a pressure gauge is connected to the inside of the cylinder as shown in Fig. 5-32b, no reading will be indicated because pressure gauges normally measure pressure above atmosphere. Hence,

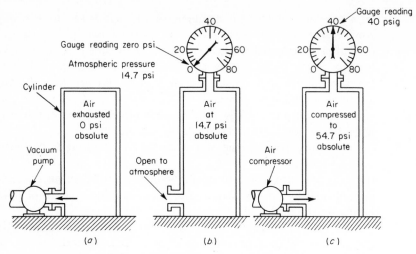

Fig. 5-32   Diagrams illustrating absolute and gauge pressure.

there is no deflection or movement in the Bourdon tube. However, if compressed air, at 40 psi, for example, is admitted into the tank, the gauge will read 40 psig, since this pressure is 40 psi above that of the atmosphere. The gauge pressure is, therefore, the pressure in excess of that of the atmosphere. This may be expressed by the following equation, which is valid only at the time and location of measurement, because atmospheric pressure is a variable.

Absolute pressure = gauge pressure + local atmospheric pressure

Examples

$$\begin{aligned}
\text{Gauge pressure} &= 40.0 \text{ psi}\\
\text{Local atmospheric pressure} &= \underline{14.7} \text{ psi}\\
\text{Absolute pressure} &= 54.7 \text{ psia (Fig. 5-32}c)
\end{aligned}$$

$$\begin{aligned}
\text{Gauge pressure} &= 40.0 \text{ psi}\\
\text{Local atmospheric pressure} &= \underline{14.3} \text{ psi}\\
\text{Absolute pressure} &= 54.3 \text{ psia}
\end{aligned}$$

The greatest proportion of industrial pressure indicators or recorders are designed for gauge-pressure operation, and it is common practice to omit the word "gauge." However, if absolute pressure is required, make certain that the word "absolute" or the abbreviation abs or a is included.

It is very important to note that, with the exception of the closed manometer and the Bourdon tube, all the pressure-measuring devices described are connected on one side to atmosphere and therefore measure the difference between atmospheric pressure and the pressure to be measured. The resultant reading, therefore, is a true gauge pressure. The Bourdon tube, however, will respond to changes in atmospheric pressure if its one connection is left open to atmosphere.

Vacuum. A Bourdon gauge can, in fact, be used as a rather insensitive altimeter. To recapitulate on some of the earlier basic concepts, a state of vacuum exists in a cylinder or in a given system when the absolute pressure within the cylinder or system is below the load atmospheric pressure. A few examples will be considered to illustrate two methods used for determining vacuum or negative pressure. In vacuum work it is convenient to use the metric scale, e.g., millimeters of mercury instead of pounds per square inch. The latter unit is fairly large, and it is usual in vacuum technology to use smaller units of variations and magnitude.

Example. If the atmospheric pressure is 760 mm Hg and the absolute pressure in the system is 100 mm Hg, calculate the vacuum.

Solution. If the difference in pressure between the atmospheric pressure and the actual absolute pressure is taken in the system, then, using the atmospheric pressure as a reference, datum, or zero line, the result is a measure of the degree of vacuum:

760 mm Hg $\doteq$ 100 mm Hg = 660 mm Hg or 660 mm Hg of vacuum

An alternative solution is to consider the absolute pressure itself as an indication of the value of the vacuum existing in the system. In this case the absolute pressure of 100 mm Hg is taken as a measure of the degree of vacuum.

Check   760 mm Hg − 660 mm Hg = 100 mm Hg

Units of Low-vacuum Measurement

Inches water gauge. The scale or unit of vacuum measurement adopted depends on the research, laboratory, or industrial process under investigation. In the steel and metal industries, where furnace conditions are very important, a draft gauge of the type described in a preceding section is frequently used to indicate suction, draft, or vacuum. This is only relative to the local atmospheric pressure. The degree of vacuum generally found in furnace work is up to 1.0 in. w.g.

In many chemical processes there is a great demand for the measurement of vacuum which is not affected by any variables, and for this reason the absolute-pressure scale is used.

Micron. A convenient unit used in high-vacuum techniques and measurements is the micron, which is 1×10^{-6} m Hg, 1.0×10^{-4} cm Hg, or 1.0×10^{-3} mm Hg.

Torr. The torr, 1 mm Hg, is frequently used in measuring vacuum. The unit is named after Torricelli, the Italian physicist.

Absolute-pressure Instruments

To measure absolute pressure, the double-bellows unit used to measure gauge pressure must now be modified, as shown in Fig. 5-33. A common design is based on two opposing identical bellows, one of which is exhausted to a very low pressure by a vacuum pump and the other of which is connected to the absolute-pressure system which is to be measured.

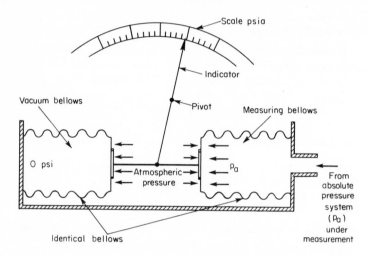

Fig. 5-33   Double-bellows unit to measure absolute pressure.

In the absolute-pressure unit shown in Fig. 5-33 it should be noticed that the local atmospheric pressure effect is canceled out because it acts on each of the top circular surfaces of the identical bellows, which operate in opposition to each other. Also, any change in ambient temperature has no effect on the reading, because any movement resulting from thermal expansion is the same in each bellows. Springs are incorporated to prevent excessive expansion of the bellows caused by overloading or faulty application. Also, as mentioned earlier, the bellows deflection is proportional to the combined result of the calibrating spring and bellows flexibility.

The vacuum-side bellows of the double-bellows unit may be reduced to about $\frac{2}{10000}$ in. Hg abs pressure, which is approximately equivalent to $\frac{5}{1000}$ mm Hg or 5 microns. This value is so low as to be insignificant, and the vacuum bellows can be said to approach zero absolute pressure. With the external atmospheric effects balanced out and nearly zero absolute pressure in one bellows, the deflection of the pointer or pen arm must be proportional to the total pressure in the other bellows. An alternative arrangement is shown in Fig. 5-34. It is basically the same but contains the bellows system in one housing.

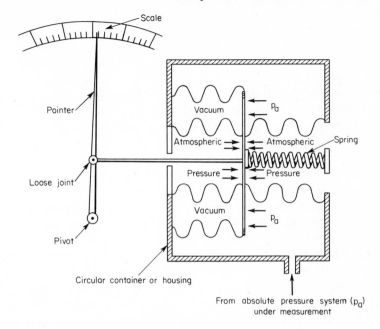

Fig. 5-34 Double-bellows unit in one housing.

The instruments described may also be designed for measuring absolute pressures up to approximately 40 psi. The minimum working range for some industrial applications would be about 0 to 5 in. Hg. For very low absolute-pressure or vacuum measurement, i.e., in microns of mercury, other methods must be used. The basic principle of some of them will be described briefly in the next section. Mechanical, electrical, and electronic gauges and transducers for pressure and high vacuum are described in Chap. 14.

REVIEW QUESTIONS AND PROBLEMS

5-39 Define the following terms: (a) gauge pressure, (b) absolute pressure, (c) suction, (d) vacuum, (e) micron, (f) torr.

5-40 (a) Why does the diaphragm gauge measure only gauge pressure and not absolute pressure?

(b) If the atmospheric pressure is 14.6 psi and the gauge pressure reads 30.0 psig, what is the absolute pressure?

5-41 A bellows gauge used on a cylinder of air reads 4.30 psig when the barometer indicates 30.60 in. Hg. Assuming that the temperature remains constant, what will the gauge read, in psig, if the barometer falls to 28.8 in. Hg?

5-42   (a) If the atmospheric pressure is 770 mm Hg and the absolute pressure is 100 mm Hg, what is the vacuum, in mm Hg?

(b) In what alternative way could the vacuum be expressed?

5-43   Convert a pressure of 10 cm of water to a (a) psi, (b) g/cm², (c) microns Hg. *Note:* 1 cm w.g. = 0.073 cm Hg.

5-44   Describe, with the aid of neat diagram, some instrument with which you are familiar which is used to measure absolute pressure.

Vacuum Measurement

Vacuum. The dictionary defines a vacuum as a "space entirely devoid of matter; a space from which air has almost been exhausted by an air pump." Excellent as these definitions may be in popular usage, in the applied sciences it is important to be more specific. Space from which all matter has been removed cannot be achieved; even the interstellar space of the outer universe is not entirely devoid of matter.

If air is exhausted from a tank or vessel, it is important to specify the degree of vacuum, and for this reason units of measurement are used, as previously mentioned. Air has mass, and the weight of the air leads to the atmospheric pressure on the earth's surface. As already discussed, the atmospheric pressure is conveniently specified in terms of the height of the barometer, which, at sea level, is normally 760 mm Hg.

If air is removed from a cylinder by a pump, the pressure inside is reduced to below that of the atmosphere, i.e., it is less than 760 mm Hg. As the air pressure is reduced in a vessel a vacuum is created and the number of molecules per cubic centimeter in the vessel decreases. At a given temperature this number is directly proportional to the air pressure. For example, at 760 mm Hg there are 2.7×10^{19} molecules/cm³, and at 1 mm Hg there are $(2.7 \times 10^{19}) \div 760 = 3.6 \times 10^{16}$ molecules/cm³. At 10^{-7} mm Hg the number is reduced to 3.5×10^9. The probability of collisions between the molecules is reduced as the pressure decreases, and consequently an electron in such a high vacuum or in very low pressures will travel considerable distances with little chance of hitting a molecule of the residual gas. The following are approximate ranges used in vacuum technology:

Medium high vacuum	1 to 10^{-3} Torrs (mm Hg)
High vacuum	10^{-3} to 10^{-7} Torrs (mm Hg)
Very high vacuum	Less than 10^{-7} Torrs (mm Hg)

High vacuum has always been of fundamental importance in the electronics industry in the fabrication and processing of radio and television tubes, X-ray tubes, and magnetrons. With highly efficient vacuum rotary and vapor diffusion pumps the air may be evacuated to about a hundred-millionth of an atmosphere, allowing the stream of electrons to pass practically unimpeded from cathode to anode. High-vacuum techniques are also used in metallurgy and in the manufacture and preservation of pharmaceutical products such as penicillin and other antibiotics and blood plasma and serums.

Production of Vacuum

Medium vacuum. The production of a medium to high vacuum is normally undertaken by means of a mechanical rotary pump. In brief, as the rotor turns and the edge of the vane passes the intake port, a space is created behind it, and air from the vessel enters this space. The air in front of the vane is compressed during the rotation and is dispelled through the outlet valve. The air displacement depends on the dimensions of the pump, particularly the volume capacity between the rotor and the stator, and on the speed of the rotor.

High vacuum. To obtain lower pressure than that possible with a rotary pump alone, a vapor diffusion pump is added. This takes over when the rotary pump, acting in series as a forepump, has already decreased the pressure to approximately $\frac{1}{10}$ mm Hg. The diffusion pump contains a reservoir of liquid, normally mercury. A heating element vaporizes the mercury, which boils at a low temperature because of the already reduced pressure. The vapor, upon rising, is deflected by an inverted cone so that the stream of mercury molecules passes downward in the chamber of space containing the molecules of the gas being exhausted. There the mercury vapor is condensed by a water jacket surrounding the pump and is circulated back for revaporization. The gas molecules are hit by the downward action of mercury and impelled toward the outlet. These gas molecules are then replaced by other molecules from the vessel until nearly all have been dispelled.

A commercial diffusion pump is made of metal or glass, and the mercury may be seen returning to the reservoir. Mercury has a vapor pressure of about $\frac{1}{1000}$ mm at room temperature. In order to prevent this vapor from spoiling the vacuum, a cold trap is filled with liquid air to reduce the temperature to about $-175°C$. The vapor pressure is then insignificant. Since the cold trap may be inconvenient, special oils (such as the apiezon and silicone oils) having a vapor pressure of 10^{-6} mm Hg at room temperature are used in oil diffusion pumps instead of mercury diffusion pumps.

Gauges and Methods for Measuring Medium and High Vacuum

U-tube closed manometer. The mercury U-tube manometer is a simple vacuum gauge. The closed limb is filled with mercury, and the other limb is connected to a vacuum pump. As the pressure falls the level of mercury sinks in the closed limb and rises in the other until, at low pressures, the levels are practically the same. The difference in the two levels would be about 1 mm Hg, and this indicates the pressure of the pump. As mentioned earlier, the torr, 1 mm Hg, is frequently used in vacuum technology.

The McLeod gauge. To measure pressures of below 1 mm Hg to about 0.00001 mm Hg or to measure absolute pressures as small as 0.001 mm Hg, a special development of the closed manometer has been devised. It is known as the McLeod gauge. The basic elements and general arrangement of the gauge are shown in Fig. 5-35. The McLeod gauge is a practical

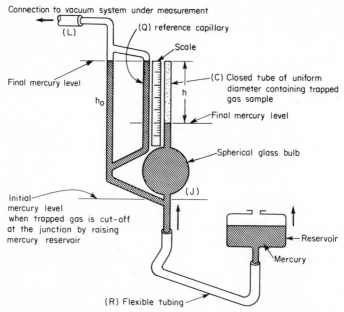

Fig. 5-35   The barometric type of McLeod gauge.

method for measuring vacuum; the calibration is independent of the nature of the gas and can be directly related to physical dimensions of the gauge. There are many varieties of the McLeod gauge, and a few of them will be described. The advantages of this gauge have made it the most acceptable standard for calibrating other gauges.

Principle of the McLeod gauge. The principle of the McLeod gauge is quite simple. It involves trapping a known volume of gas at the pressure which is to be measured and compressing this volume to a new pressure. The calibration is performed by applying Boyle's law, which states that if the temperature is kept constant, then

Initial volume × initial pressure = final volume × final pressure

By knowing the original volume, the final volume, and the final pressure it is possible to evaluate the original pressure in the vacuum system under measurement. Generally, mercury is used for trapping and compressing a known sample volume of gas. Gauges using a low-vapor-pressure oil instead of mercury are also available. Because the levels of mercury must be observed, the construction is of tough glass to withstand sudden high-pressure changes.

Operation of a McLeod gauge. The tube L is connected to the vacuum system under investigation, and the tube R leads to the mercury reservoir, which may be lowered or raised. Initially, the mercury level in the tube is set just below the junction at J. When some equilibrium pressure has been reached in the system and a sample gas volume has been allowed to enter the gauge, the mercury in the reservoir is forced up the tube R. As the mercury passes the junction J it isolates the gas sample in the closed limb, which was at the same pressure (p_x) as the vacuum system under test. The volume V_o of the trapped gas at this junction is known and equal to the volume of the bulb (V_b) plus that of the closed capillary tube (V_c).

As the mercury is raised it fills the spherical bulb and begins to enter the left-hand tube, the capillary Q (open), and the capillary C (closed). The gas in capillary C is then compressed as the reservoir is raised, the amount of compression being given by the ratio of the volume of the bulb and capillary C to the volume in the capillary C after compression. Since the mercury in capillary Q is still exposed to the original pressure in the system, it will rise above the mercury level in capillary C.

There are two fundamental methods used for making measurements with a McLeod gauge. Each involves raising the mercury to a fixed reference point and then measuring the difference in the two mercury levels in the capillaries Q and C. These methods are based on the nonuniform (square-law) scale and uniform (linear) scale.

Nonuniform-scale method. The scale used in this method is shown in Fig. 5-36. When a pressure measurement is being made, the mercury is raised in capillary Q to a level even with the top of capillary C. The difference in mercury levels (h) in capillaries Q and C is noted and recorded. If the cross-sectional area of the capillary C is uniform and represented by a, then the volume of the compressed gas is ah. The pressure of this compressed gas, neglecting the insignificantly low pressure on the mercury in the limb Q, is the difference in mercury levels h. Generally, this difference is measured in millimeters and the vacuum is expressed as absolute pressure in millimeters of mercury.

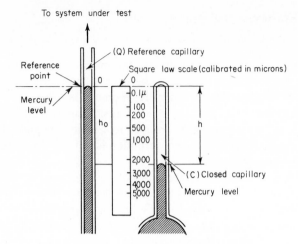

Fig. 5-36   Nonuniform-scale method.

If V_o represents the original volume of gas, i.e., the volume in the closed leg above the cutoff junction J, then the pressure (vacuum) p_x being measured can be obtained by the use of Boyle's law:

$$V_o \times p_x = \text{new volume} \times \text{new pressure (after compression)}$$
$$= ah \times (p_x + h_o)$$
$$= p_x ah + (h_o \times ah)$$
$$p_x(V_o - ah) = h_o \times ah$$
$$p_x = \frac{h_o \times ah}{V_o - ah}$$

but $h_o = h$

therefore $p_x = \dfrac{ah^2}{V_o - ah}$

In many cases ah, the volume of the capillary above the mercury in the closed leg, is negligible compared to V_o, in which case the equation can be written

$$p_x = \frac{ah^2}{V_o} = kh^2$$

where $k = \dfrac{a}{V_o}$

referred to as the compression ratio or gauge constant.

It should be noted that the pressure increases as the square of the difference h in mercury levels, and the scale then becomes nonuniform or parabolic in shape. Such a scale indicates a spread-out at low pressures, as shown in Fig. 5-36.

Example. The closed limb of a McLeod gauge has a diameter of 1 mm and a volume V_o above the cutoff junction of 200 cc. If, at the time that a vacuum reading is being observed, the difference h in mercury levels is noted to be 4 mm, calculate the pressure of the system under test. Also calculate the gauge constant in this case.

Solution. The cross-sectional area a of the closed capillary is $(\pi/4)d^2 = 0.79$ mm^2, and the difference h in mercury levels is 4 mm. The original volume V_o of the gas sample is 2.0×10^5 mm^3. Hence, using the expression for the unknown vacuum,

$$p_x = \frac{ah^2}{V_o}$$
$$= \frac{0.79 \text{ mm}^2 \times (4 \text{ mm})^2}{2.0 \times 10^5 \text{ mm}^3}$$
$$= 6.3 \times 10^{-5} \text{ mm Hg}$$

The gauge constant k in this case is approximately equal to

$$\frac{0.79 \text{ mm}^2}{2.0 \times 10^5 \text{ mm}^3} = 4.0 \times 10^{-6} \text{ mm}^{-1}$$

For accurate work the top of the capillary C is made as flat as possible to satisfy the term h^2; otherwise, the effective values of both heights must be taken. The capillary must also be of high quality and uniform in cross section.

Uniform-scale method. In this case the measuring pressure is indicated on a linear scale as shown in Fig. 5-37. The method involves raising the mercury to a fixed reference point on capillary C and then measuring the difference in the mercury levels in capillaries Q and C. Generally, the reference point is taken close to the junction or cutoff point. (Note, however, that a series of index marks against which a multiplying factor is shown can be provided.) Consider h to represent the height from the reference point to the end of the closed tube and h_o the difference in mercury levels. Also, as previously, let a be the uniform cross-sectional area of the closed capillary C and V_o the original volume of the gas sample being compressed at the pressure p_x.

Using Boyle's law, the relationship, as before, becomes

$$V_o p_x = ah \times (p_x + h_o)$$
$$p_x = \frac{h_o \times ah}{V_o - ah}$$

where ah is the volume of the compressed-gas sample.

It is evident in this case, since a, h, and V_o are constants, that the gauge reading is a linear function, or is directly proportional to h_o. The scale shown in Fig. 5-37 illustrates the uniform divisions used with this method.

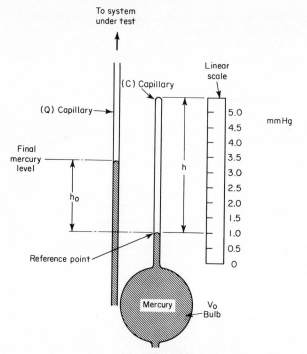

Fig. 5-37   Uniform-scale method.

Example. The closed limb of a McLeod gauge has a diameter of 2 mm and a cutoff volume of 200 cm³. If the height in the closed capillary from the reference index to the end of the tube is 20 cm and the mercury-level difference is 7 cm, calculate the pressure of the system under test. Also calculate the compression ratio or gauge constant.

Solution. The cross-sectional area a of the closed capillary is $(\pi/4)d^2 = 3.14$ mm², and the difference in mercury levels h_o is 70 mm. The height h of the closed capillary above the reference point is 200 mm. Using the expression for the unknown pressure,

$$p_x = \frac{ah \times h_o}{V_o}$$

$$= \frac{3.14 \text{ mm}^2 \times 200 \text{ mm} \times 70 \text{ mm}}{200,000 \text{ mm}^3}$$

$$= 0.22 \text{ mm Hg}$$

The gauge constant or compression ratio $= \dfrac{ah}{V_o}$

$$= \frac{3.14 \text{ mm}^2 \times 200 \text{ mm}}{200,000 \text{ mm}^3}$$

$$= 3.14 \times 10^{-3}$$

The maximum pressure that can be measured by using this gauge is approximately $3.14 \times 10^{-3} \times 200$ mm = 0.63 mm Hg.

In order to increase the maximum pressure value to be measured, either h or a may be increased within practical limitations. By careful selection of capillary diameter and fixed reference points, it is possible to include a total pressure range of about 20 to 1.0^{-5} mm Hg by using both the nonuniform and uniform scales.

One of the other problems in the design of McLeod gauges is the method of moving the mercury up into the capillaries. By using the arrangement shown in Fig. 5-35, the mercury level is controlled by raising and lowering the reservoir, which is filled with mercury. The gauge is at atmospheric pressure; hence, the levels of mercury in the gauge and reservoir are the same. At low pressures the reservoir will have to be lowered at least 760 mm below the cutoff junction (at sea level) so that mercury does not enter the spherical bulb. For this reason this type of gauge is referred to as a "barometric gauge."

The difficulties connected with the gauge are that it is awkward to operate the mercury reservoir for steady readings, the overall size of the gauge is bulky, the mercury becomes easily contaminated, and rubber connections, if used, may be porous and let air into the gauge. To overcome these difficulties, the most common arrangement is to use a vacuum pump in combination with atmospheric pressure to manipulate the mercury levels in the gauge. Many commercial designs make use of two-way stop valves, and some manufacturers supply suitable metal-to-glass seals so that metal tubing can be used. The auxiliary vacuum pump used to operate the gauge does not have to produce low pressures—a few millimeters of mercury is adequate—and its pumping speed can be quite low, because the gauge volume is normally small.

The gauge has some disadvantages for general use. If the gas whose pressure is being measured contains any condensable vapors, Boyle's law does not hold and errors occur. Precautions must be constantly taken to prevent the mercury from reaching the vacuum pump or system under test.

Tilting model. There is a third type of McLeod gauge which is more portable; it is called the tilting gauge. Figure 5-38 shows its operating position. In position 1 the mercury has run into the reservoir, exposing the junction of the measuring tube M. The measuring tube will now have the same pressure as the system under investigation connected at C. The gauge is then tilted 90° to the position 2 as shown. The mercury now traps a sample of the gas in the measuring tube M and compresses it to the certain mercury level. The reference column R, which is a capillary of the same diameter as the measuring tube to nullify meniscus effects, has risen to the top scale index. That is, the meniscus is at the same level as

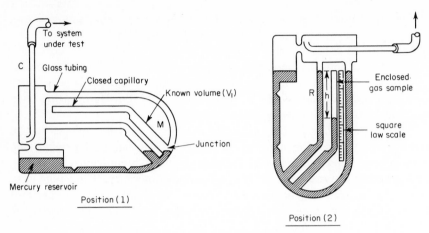

Fig. 5-38   The tilting McLeod gauge.

the top of the closed capillary. The difference in height h of the column is a measure of pressure according to the formula

$$p_x = \frac{ah^2}{V_o - ah}$$

and, since ah is very small and considered insignificant,

$$p_x = \frac{ah^2}{V_o}$$

Concluding Remarks

The McLeod gauge measures gases at absolute pressure down to about 10^{-5} microns Hg. The gauge does not measure pressure directly, but instead takes in a sample of the system gas and compresses it to obtain a reading. An instrument of this type, when accurately made and calibrated, is used to read as low as 0.01 micron Hg and is also used as a master gauge for the purpose of checking other vacuum-pressure-measuring instruments.

It should be restated that accurate operation assumes that no condensable gas, primarily water vapor, is present. If water vapor is present, it will condense when the gas sample is compressed, resulting in a lower than actual pressure reading. Also, the compression of the gas must not be so great that the volume is changed by the molecular packing effect. Boyle's law will then not hold true, and a fairly large error will occur at very low vacuum.

Electrical and electronic methods incorporating transducers for measuring pressure and vacuum are described in Chap. 14.

REVIEW QUESTIONS AND PROBLEMS

5-45   (a) State the scientific concept of vacuum.

(b) Define micron and torr.

(c) There are, at 760 mm Hg, 2.7×10^{19} molecules/cm³, and at a given temperature this number is directly proportional to the pressure. Compute the number of molecules present if the pressure is now 1 mm Hg.

5-46   The pressure in a vacuum system is found to be 2×10^{-4} mm Hg. What is the pressure in microns?

5-47   The closed limb of a U-tube manometer was initially filled with mercury and its open end was connected to a vacuum system under test. If the level in the closed limb falls to 20 mm and is 2 mm above the mercury level in the limb connected to the vacuum system, what is the pressure in the system under test?

5-48   In a McLeod gauge the area of the measuring capillary tube is 1×10^{-2} cm². The volume of the bulb is 300 cm³. By using the equation $p_x = ah^2/V$, calculate the test pressure when h is found to be 7.75 cm.

5-49   (a) Describe the principle and operation of a simple McLeod gauge based on the uniform and nonuniform scales.

(b) During a laboratory test on a vacuum pump based on a uniform-scale McLeod gauge, the following results were recorded:

Length of enclosed gas sample = 12.00 cm
Cross-sectional area   = 0.40 cm²

The volume of spherical bulb and closed capillary was specified as 160 cm³. Calculate the pressure p_x of the system.

5-50   The closed limb of a McLeod gauge has a total volume of 100 cm³ made up of a spherical glass container and a uniform vertical glass capillary similar to that shown in Fig. 5-35. The capillary is 20.0 cm long and has a volume of 10.0 cm³. Compute the pressure of the system under test when the mercury level is (a) at the bottom of the closed capillary, (b) halfway up the capillary.

5-51   Discuss briefly the advantages and limitations of the McLeod gauge, particularly at low vacuum measurement.

5-52   A gas has a volume of 5 ft³ at a temperature of 20°C. Calculate the volume of the gas at 100°C if the pressure is kept constant.

5-53   A gas occupies a volume of 200 liters at a pressure of 10^{-4} mm Hg and a temperature of 20°C. Compute the volume of the gas if the pressure is increased to 10^{-3} mm Hg and the temperature is raised to 50°C.

Electrical and Electronic Methods of Measuring Absolute Pressure and Vacuum

As discussed earlier, absolute pressure and gauge pressure differ by a constant only when the barometric pressure reading is constant. The error in measuring absolute pressure with a pressure gauge depends on the change in the barometric pressure from the normal reading. The error involved is approximately 0.5 psi for each inch of mercury of barometric pressure change.

There are, as already described, many different means of measuring absolute pressure; to these the following must be added in order to cover the complete range as shown in Fig. 5-39. The McLeod gauge (small- and

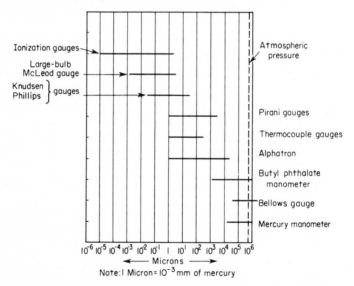

Fig. 5-39   Bar chart showing approximate spans of various types of gauges for measuring low absolute pressure or vacuum.

large-bulb type), the mercury manometer, and bellows and diaphragm gauges have already been discussed in some detail. However, the Pirani, thermocouple, and thermionic gauges are also used to measure high vacuum where continuous measurement is required. These will be briefly described. For details of other special high-accuracy gauges reference should be made to texts on advanced physics or applied electronics or manufacturers' publications.

The Pirani gauge. As early as 1906, M. V. Pirani designed a vacuum gauge consisting of hot-wire elements connected in a Wheatstone bridge in which the out-of-balance current indicated the amount of vacuum achieved. Another type is based on the use of a thermocouple fixed to a hot wire, as found in the thermal-emf type of current meters.

The Pirani and thermocouple vacuum gauges depend on the cooling effect of gas surrounding a heated element. Heat flows from the element by conduction and convection in the gas, so that, if the power dissipation is constant, the temperature of the element will be lower than that of a similar element sealed in a reference vacuum. The resistance of the Pirani element and the thermal-emf output from the thermocouple element are functions of the temperature of the element, and so they are functions of the pressure of the gas surrounding the element.

The Pirani vacuum gauge is shown schematically in Fig. 5-40. The measuring element (in the vacuum to be measured) and the temperature-

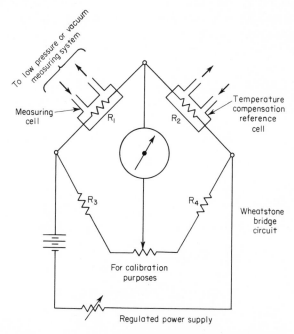

Fig. 5-40   Simple circuit for a Pirani gauge.

compensating reference element (sealed in a reference environment) are incorporated into a Wheatstone bridge circuit so that changes in resistance of the measuring element cause changes in the unbalance current of the bridge. These are indicated by a galvanometer. In the temperature-compensation reference cell, the pressure is normally reduced to approximately one micron of mercury.

Any energy lost by the heated element will be transmitted by radiation or by conduction along the input lead. The measuring cell receives the same power, but it can also lose heat by convection and conduction to any gas which is enclosed. Since the same energy or power is supplied to each arm of the bridge, the measuring cell, having a greater cooling capacity, will have the lower temperature, owing to a decrease in resistance, as compared to the reference cell. Under such circumstances there is a condition of voltage unbalance which can then be measured in any one of a number of ways, of which the Wheatstone bridge is the simplest. The unbalance voltage of the bridge is measured by an instrument similar in design to the automatic-balance potentiometer.

The main advantages of the Pirani gauge are simplicity in design and ease of operation. The disadvantage is that its calibration depends upon the gas of which the vacuum is measured; argon, air, carbon dioxide, hydrogen, helium, or acetylene may be used. In addition, the scale is non-linear. Pirani gauges have an approximate range of 2 to 200 microns Hg.

The thermocouple vacuum gauge. This gauge resembles the Pirani gauge, apart from the constructional aspect and measuring range, in that it depends upon the heat loss by conduction and convection through the gas surrounding the heated element or filament. Figure 5-41 shows the schematic arrangement of a simple thermocouple vacuum gauge. In the

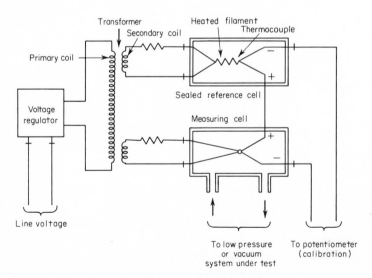

Fig. 5-41   A thermocouple vacuum gauge.

gauge the temperatures of the filaments, or elements, are measured by fine-wire thermocouples in direct contact with the filaments. Figure 5-41 shows the reference or compensating cell and measuring cell connected in "series opposition" so that the output is the difference between their emfs. It is about 20 mv for a vacuum of 450 microns Hg. The thermocouple vacuum gauge has the same features and handicaps as the Pirani gauge.

The Ionization Gauge

Thermionic type. The range of the thermionic type of ionization vacuum gauge is approximately 10^{-7} to 10^{-9} mm Hg. The gauge is shown schematically in Fig. 5-42. In its simplest form the gauge consists of a

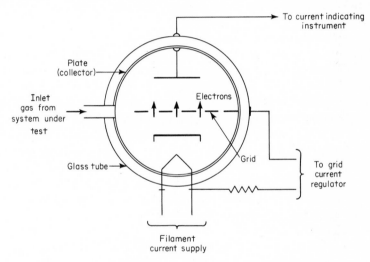

Fig. 5-42 Ionization gauge for vacuum measurement.

closed tube or bulb connected to the vacuum system under measurement. Inside the bulb is a thermionic triode assembly consisting of the filament, a source of electrons, an electron collector (plate) maintained at a positive potential with respect to the filament, and an ion collector to which is applied a negative potential with respect to the filament.

Electrons emitted from the hot filament collide with the gas molecules present and will ionize them. The charged ions will be collected by the electrode at negative potential. The rate of collection is measured as a current in the collector circuit by a current-indicating meter, i.e., a microammeter. This ionization current reading is a measure of the amount of gas inside the tube and is proportional to the number of molecules in the gas, which in turn is a measure of the absolute pressure, provided the electron current is constant. The relationship between pressure and currents can be expressed approximately as

$$p = KP\frac{I_1}{I_2}$$

where p = absolute pressure

K = a constant depending on the potentials used and design of electrodes

I_1 = ionization current

I_2 = electron current

When the potentials and electron current remain constant, the absolute pressure is proportional to the ionization current.

The ionization current is measured by a suitable electrical meter. This type of gauge permits low pressures to be measured continuously. The range of measurement is from nearly zero absolute to one micron. A thermionic ionization gauge may be calibrated by using various inert gases, but it is not reliable with hydrogen, oxygen, and other gases which decompose at the hot filament. Electrons emitted at the hot cathode owing to thermionic emission are attracted toward the grid. These electrons pass through the grid (kept at about 150 volts) and start toward the plate. Ions are formed by collision of the electrons with the molecules of the surrounding gas in the tube. The positive ions are collected on the plate, and thus a positive ion current exists. This ionization current is proportional to the amount of gas inside the tube—and, in turn, to the pressure—provided the electron current is constant. The electrons return to the grid and are collected.

An alternative method of using the thermionic ionization gauge is to make the grid negative and the anode positive. The original method is said to be of higher sensitivity, owing to the fact that the electrons which oscillate around the positive grid generally have an increased path.

It is important, in order to maintain a stable electron current during a test measurement, to introduce stabilizing circuits. Figure 5-43 shows a circuit for the hot-cathode ionization gauge. The emission current passes through the range resistors to achieve the negative bias voltage for the collector, which can, in turn, be operated at ground potential. The developed voltage is compared with a reference voltage, and the difference in values helps to regulate the power supply to the filament.

One difficulty associated with the hot-ionization gauge is the tendency to produce X rays when the ionizing electrons strike the grid. This causes a secondary emission at the collector, resulting in a current which flows in the same direction as the ions. Because of this the design of a single gauge to have linear sensitivity between 1 and 10^{-10} mm Hg is not feasible.

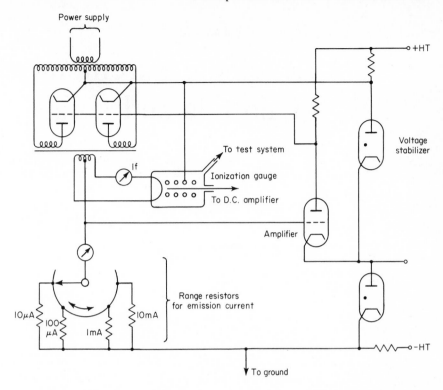

Fig. 5-43 A circuit diagram using a thermionic (hot) cathode ionization gauge. [Edwards High Vacuum (Canada) Ltd.]

Radioactive type. The radioactive-source type of ionization gauge is like the thermionic type with the exception that the ionization is created by the collision of gas molecules and the alpha-particle radiation from a very small radium or other, similar source instead of by electron collision. In this case the positive ions produced by collision of the alpha particles with the gas in the tube are collected. The resulting positive ion current is then measured, and the gauge is then calibrated in terms of low-pressure units.

REVIEW QUESTIONS AND PROBLEMS

5-54 On what principle do the Pirani and thermocouple vacuum gauge operate and in what respect do these two types of gauges differ?

5-55 Why does the analysis of the gas whose vacuum is to be measured affect the calibration of the Pirani or thermocouple vacuum gauge?

5-56 Describe the basic principles on which the ionization vacuum gauge works.

CHAPTER SIX

Level measurement of liquids and solids

Those who fall in love with practice without science are like a sailor who steers a ship without a helm or compass, and who never can be certain whither he is going.

LEONARDO DA VINCI

The vast quantity of water which is used by industry alone, as well as that of the solvents, chemicals, and other liquids which are required for processing materials and products, makes liquid-level measurement and control essential to modern manufacturing plants. Instruments for the measurement of liquid level in storage tanks can be classified as follows:

Mechanical; direct and indirect methods
Pneumatic techniques
Electrical methods
Nucleonic gauges
Ultrasonic systems

The type of instrument or gauge which is to be used in any particular installation depends upon the liquid-level range, the nature of the liquid, operating pressures, and also the cost involved.

Direct Mechanical Measurement of Liquid Level

Dipstick method. By the direct methods the actual varying level of the liquid itself is measured. The most common of these methods is called sticking or dipping. A dipstick is used to measure the oil level in the car engine or the height of fuel oil in a uniformly shaped storage tank. In the bob-and-tape method the bob weight is lowered to the bottom of the tank containing the liquid, and the level is found by noting the point on the tape reached by the liquid surface. It is important in this case to keep the

128

tape vertical and taut when the reading is taken. Obviously, this method is unsuitable for continuous measurement.

For a storage tank which is uniformly shaped the relationship between level and volume on a percent basis is linear. This is shown in Fig. 6-1. In the case of a horizontal cylindrical tank with flat ends, the graph of volume against liquid level or depth is as plotted in Fig. 6-2. Notice that, toward the halfway line, the curve flattens out: the volume increases more rapidly than the level because of the larger surface. A cross-sectional view of the cylindrical tank is also shown to indicate the volume at corresponding levels.

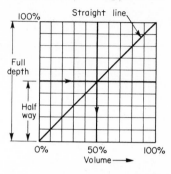

Fig. 6-1   Level-volume rela-tion in uniform tank.

Sight-glass method. A very common example of this means of measurement is the coffee urn seen in cafeterias. The sight tube usually consists of a graduated glass tube mounted on the outside of the tank. As the liquid level alters inside the tank, so does the level in the glass tube. The arrangement is shown in Fig. 6-3. The measurement is simple and direct. When the glass tube is fixed to tanks containing liquids at very high temperatures, corrections must be made because of density variations. The tem-

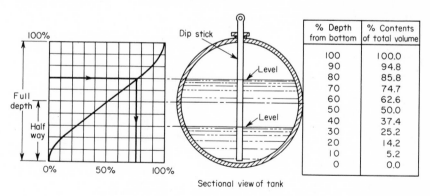

Fig. 6-2   Level-volume relation in horizontal cylindrical tank with flat ends.

perature surrounding the glass tube will be much lower than that in the tank, thus causing a difference in density and influencing the actual level reading. A correction factor will have to be applied, as in the case of sight tubes installed in boiler drums.

Hook gauge. Sometimes it is necessary to measure with high accuracy a very small change in level. In a large tank a small change in level will mean a considerable volumetric change. The hook gauge is suitable for use in such cases. The schematic arrangement is shown in Fig. 6-4. The gauge consists of a vertical tubular rod carrying a scale and terminating in a hook. The tubular rod can move in a guide bracket which locates the gauge. The vertical rod can be raised or lowered by rotating a milled head. The hook gauge is also used in back-water-level measurement and in the measurement of flow of rivers and the levels of reservoirs.

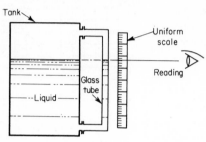

Fig. 6-3   Sight-glass level gauge.

In practice, the instrument must be fixed at a datum or reference level for the changes to be measured. The hook is raised or lowered until the tip of the hook just breaks the liquid surface, when a small standing wave will be formed. A reading is then observed on the scale and vernier, and the accuracy expected is to $\frac{1}{100}$ in.

Float gauges. Archimedes observed that a floating body is buoyed by a force equal to the weight of the liquid it displaces. There are many kinds

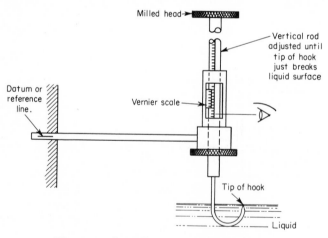

Fig. 6-4   Installation of the hook gauge.

of float-operated devices for continuous, direct level measurement. The primary element is a float which, because of its buoyancy, will follow the varying liquid level. A transducer or converting device can relay the float travel to a pointer or pen arm of a recorder.

The instrument shown in Fig. 6-5 consists of a float, a counterweight, and a flexible connection which can be a chain or thin metallic tape. The counterweight keeps the chain under tension and takes up the slack when

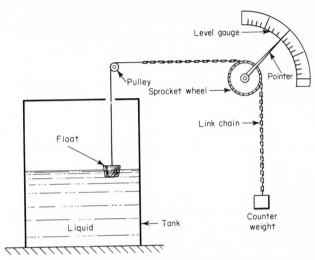

Fig. 6-5   Float level gauge.

the float rises. The chain link may be used to run over the teeth of a gear or sprocket wheel to which a pointer is attached. Any movement of the gear will indicate on a suitably calibrated scale the level of the liquid in the tank. Another type of float-operated instrument has the float attached to a shaft, as shown schematically in Fig. 6-6. The motion of the float travel on the surface of the liquid is transferred to the shaft, and the level is indicated on the dial.

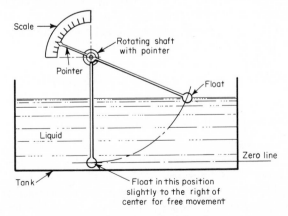

Fig. 6-6   Rotating shaft level gauge.

The floats described are normally partly submerged in the liquid. The weight of the float is adjusted by an internal or external counterweight to maintain a half-submerged position in order to obtain maximum operating force. This is frequently referred to as the constant-displacement type of float. In a liquid of a given specific gravity, the weight displacement remains constant regardless of the level position. The float rises and falls the same distance as the actual liquid level, and the position of the float is a direct indication of level.

With the variable-displacement type of float the action is similar to that described above, except that vertical movement of the float is more restricted. The weight of the displacer is always greater than that of the liquid displaced at full immersion. As the liquid level varies, more or less of the displacer is covered by the liquid. Reference to Fig. 6-7a and b will help to clarify the principle involved.

In accordance with Archimedes' principle (that the apparent loss in weight of a body totally or partially immersed in a liquid is equal to the weight of the liquid displaced), the more the displacer is submerged, the greater is the force created by the displacer, owing to buoyancy. Although the displacer rises and falls with level changes, the movement is very much less than the actual level variation. The difference in movement between displacer and liquid depends upon the cross-sectional area of the displacer, the stiffness or spring rate of the supporting spring or torque tube, and the specific gravity of the liquid.

When a pneumatic signal is required for remote reading or for movements control system, the force created by the displacer owing to buoyancy is generally transferred through a twisting or torque tube. The pneumatic system is so designed that, for each angular position of the tube, there is a corresponding air-pressure signal to the indicator or controller. The main application for the variable-displacement type is when measurement is required for small level changes. The instrument is more sensitive to small level changes, and it is also subject to less mechanical friction.

Float-operated schemes with electrical transmission. The float-operated methods of measuring level can be equipped for electrical transmission. A variety of methods and designs are available.

Indirect Mechanical Methods of Liquid-level Measurement

The simplest arrangement of an indirect method of level measurement is the pressure gauge connected at the bottom or side of a uniform tank containing liquid. The diagram in Fig. 6-8 shows the details of such an installation. The rise or fall of the level causes an increase or decrease of pressure, which is transmitted to the gauge. The dial or scale of the instrument is calibrated in units of level measurement (feet or inches).

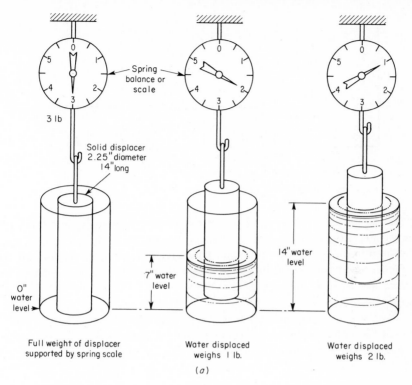

Spring balance or scale

3 lb

Solid displacer
2.25" diameter
14" long

0" water level

7" water level

14" water level

Full weight of displacer
supported by spring scale

Water displaced
weighs 1 lb.

Water displaced
weighs 2 lb.

(*a*)

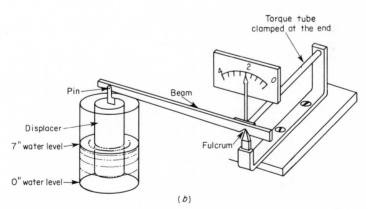

Torque tube
clamped at the end

Pin

Beam

Displacer

7" water level

0" water level

Fulcrum

(*b*)

Fig. 6-7 (a) *Principle of the variable-displacement gauge.* (b) *Basic operation of the variable-displacement gauge.* [Mason-Neilan Division of Worthington (Canada) Ltd.]

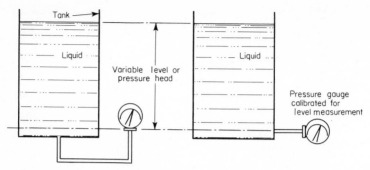

Fig. 6-8   Simple arrangements for level-pressure measurement.

If the nature of the liquid under measurement is such that the liquid must not enter the actual gauge, then a transmitting fluid (e.g., oil) must be used between the liquid and the gauge mechanism. Air is also frequently used and sealed in as the transmitting medium. The air-pressure variation due to change in the liquid level is thus transmitted to a pressure receiver.

Pressure-sensing elements. A diaphragm or bellows (as described in the section on pressure measurement) may be used as the primary sensing element. The schematic arrangement in Fig. 6-9 shows a typical industrial

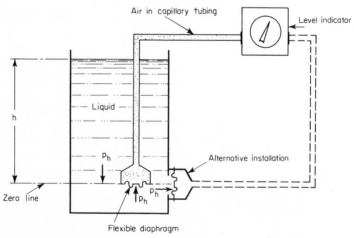

Fig. 6-9   Diaphragm unit and level indicator.

application. The diaphragm is slack; it is made of a flexible material such as rubber or neoprene secured in the flanges of a container. The diaphragm acts as the partition. The pressure due to the height of the liquid is exerted against the lower surface of the diaphragm. The air in the upper section of the diaphragm, and in turn in the capillary tubing leading to a pressure instrument (Bourdon, stack, or bellows type), is compressed as the level increases. The weight of liquid above the diaphragm exerts a pressure on the diaphragm proportional to the height (or head):

Pressure = height of liquid × weight density of liquid

$$p_h = hw$$

By dimensional analysis,

$$\left[\frac{F}{L^2}\right] = [L] \times \left[\frac{F}{L^3}\right] = \left[\frac{F}{L^2}\right]$$

It is seen that the equation balances dimensionally, and appropriate units may now be inserted.

The pressure p_h causes the deflection of the diaphragm and therefore controls the pressure within the enclosed container from the top side of the diaphragm to the pressure instrument. The internal air pressure is then observed on the pressure instrument, which is calibrated in units of liquid level above the diaphragm. Alternatively, the dial may be calibrated in terms of capacity, gallons, or cubic feet of liquid in the storage tank.

Example. A storage tank containing oil of specific gravity 0.9 has its free surface level 10 ft above the bottom of the tank. Calculate the pressure, in pounds per square inch, at the bottom of the tank.

Solution

$$p_h = hw \text{ sp gr}$$
$$= 10 \text{ ft} \times 62.4 \text{ lb/ft}^3 \times 0.9$$
$$= 561.6 \text{ lb/ft}^2 = \frac{561.6 \text{ lb/ft}^2}{144 \text{ in.}^2/\text{ft}^2} = 3.9 \text{ lb/in.}^2$$

or 4 psi to the nearest whole number.

Pneumatic Methods

The bubbler technique. In this method the air pressure in a pipeline is so regulated that the air pressure in the bubbler tube, as shown in Fig. 6-10, is minutely in excess of the liquid pressure in the tank. The bubbler tube is installed vertically in the tank with its open end at the zero level. The other end of the tube or pipe is connected to a regulated air supply and to a pressure gauge. To make a level measurement, the air-supply regulator or valve is so adjusted that the pressure is slightly greater than the pressure (due to the height) exerted by the liquid in the tank. This is achieved by adjusting the air-pressure regulator until bubbles can be seen slowly leaving the open end of the tube. There is, of course, a minimum airflow required to achieve these conditions, and often a small airflow meter is fitted in the line so that a check is more readily available.

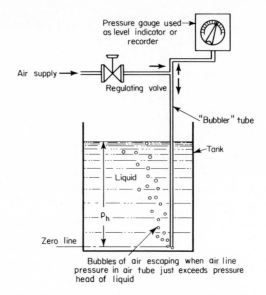

Pressure gauge used → as level indicator or recorder

Air supply →

Regulating valve

"Bubbler" tube

Tank

Liquid

P_h

Zero line

Bubbles of air escaping when air line pressure in air tube just exceeds pressure head of liquid

Fig. 6-10   Principle of bubbler level gauge.

The pressure gauge then measures the air pressure required to overcome the pressure of the liquid head above the open end of the pipe. Normally, the gauge is calibrated in feet or inches. If the tank is uniformly shaped, the calibration may be in units of volume.

Example. In the arrangement shown in the diagram of Fig. 6-11 the air supply is so regulated that bubbles just begin to form in the tube immersed 10.0 in.

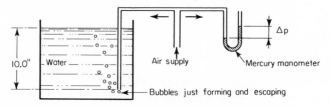

10.0"

Water

Air supply

Mercury manometer

Δp

Bubbles just forming and escaping

Fig. 6-11   Illustration of bubbler level gauge.

in the vessel filled with water. The manometer shows a deflection in the mercury levels. Calculate this head in inches of mercury and in pounds per square inch.

Solution. Since mercury is 13.6 times heavier than water, the head, in inches of mercury,

$$\Delta p = \frac{10.0 \text{ in.}}{13.6}$$

$$= 0.74 \text{ in. Hg}$$

Since 29.92 in. Hg is equivalent to 14.70 psi, the pressure head, in pounds per square inch,

$$\Delta p = \frac{0.74}{29.92} \times 14.7 \text{ lb/in.}^2$$
$$= 0.37 \text{ lb/in.}^2$$

or 0.4 psi to the nearest whole number. Conversely, if Δp were observed to read 0.74 in. Hg, the height of the water column above the bubbler tube would be 10 in.

Differential-pressure level meter. When the liquid is in a pressure vessel, the liquid-column pressure does not give the true measurement, owing to the pressure above the free surface. In order to measure such systems, differential-pressure meters are used. A typical installation is shown schematically in Fig. 6-12. The manometer type of indicator

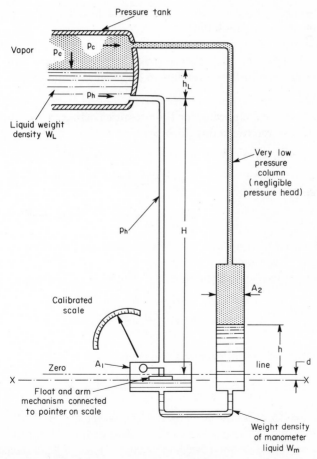

Fig. 6-12 Typical arrangement of differential-pressure level gauge.

shown works on the principle of the reservoir type of manometer discussed in Chap. 5. Referring to the diagram of Fig. 6-12, consider the various pressures acting on the surface of the manometer liquid. In the wide limb they are:

1. The pressure p_c of the fluid (vapor, gas, or liquid) in the space above the free surface of the liquid in the vessel
2. The pressure p_h due to the height of the liquid (level) above the outlet connection O
3. The pressure p_H due to the tank liquid below the outlet O filling the connecting pipe and space above the meter liquid

In the other limb, which is narrower and referred to as the range side, the various pressures acting are:

1. The pressure p_c of the fluid (vapor, gas, or liquid) in the space above the free surface of the liquid in the vessel
2. A possible pressure due to the column of fluid filling the connecting pipe to the narrow limb and the space above the meter liquid
3. The pressue due to the difference in levels of the manometer liquid in the meter

The mathematical equation for the pressures acting in each limb of the meter above the reference line X–X is

$$p_c + h_L w_L + (H + d)w_L = p_c + (h + d)w_m$$

Hence
$$h_L = \frac{(h + d)w_m - (H + d)w_L}{w_L}$$

$$h_L = \frac{(h + d)w_m}{w_L} - (H + d)$$

If A_1 is the area of the wide limb of the meter and A_2 is the area of the narrow limb of the meter, then the volume of mercury displaced in the wide limb is equivalent to the increase of mercury in the right limb.

$$A_1 d = A_2 h$$

hence
$$h = \frac{A_1}{A_2} d$$

If h is substituted in the previous equation,

$$h_L = d \left[\frac{w_m}{w_L} \left(1 + \frac{A_1}{A_2} \right) - 1 \right] - H$$

The difference in pressure detected by the meter is due to the changing level of the liquid in the pressure vessel. Most of the differential-pressure-measuring devices described in Chap. 5 can be used for level measurement.

Normally the connecting pipe to the narrow limb is filled with the liquid and a head vessel or condenser is installed at the top of the limb to provide a constant head. The head on the wide limb then becomes the variable and the differential head-reading gives a measurement of fullness rather than emptiness, i.e., zero reading corresponds to a full vessel and maximum reading to an empty vessel.

Electrical Method (Capacitance Level Gauge)

A simple capacitor consists of two electrode plates separated by an insulator called the dielectric. Therefore, the capacitor type of level instrument is suitable for liquids which can act as the dielectric.

When an electrical potential is applied across the capacitor plates, there will be a removal of electrons from one plate and an addition of the same number of electrons to the other plate. The passage of electrons depends upon the space between the plates, the area of the plates, and the nature of the dielectric between the plates. The capacitance of a two-parallel-plate capacitor is expressed mathematically as

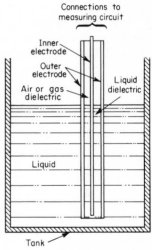

$$C = \frac{2.3 \times 10^{-1} \times KA}{S}$$

where C = capacitance, $\mu\mu$f (10^{-12} farad)
A = area of the plate, in.^{2}
S = space between the plates, in.
K = dielectric constant

As the spacing between the plates becomes smaller, the potential, in volts per inch, increases. The available amount of electrons between the electrode plates is inversely proportional to the space between the plates.

Capacitance, which varies directly with liquid level in tubes, can be applied for measurement and used for control purposes. The schematic arrangement in the diagram of Fig. 6-13 shows the variation of capacitance of a probe or tube immersed in a liquid under level measurement. The capacitance will be at a minimum when the tubes contain only

Fig. 6-13 Capacitance of the probe varies with liquid level.

air and at a maximum when the liquid fills the entire space between the electrodes. By using a suitable measuring unit such as the Wheatstone bridge circuit (which is described in the section dealing with measuring circuits), the liquid level can be measured by adjusting one arm of the bridge to obtain a balance. However, the output of the bridge can be fed to an amplifier and servomotor which will rebalance the bridge automatically and thus indicate the level reading.

In a simpler type of installation a rodlike metal electrode is placed inside the tank and insulated from it. The tank contains a lead to ground.

The capacitance, as in the previous case, becomes a function of the liquid level, which may be registered by an electric bridge circuit and readout instrument. The range of the capacitance level-measuring gauge is from a few inches to several hundred feet. The material of the electrode varies according to the application. For corrosive liquids, stainless steel may be found suitable, and for noncorrosive liquids most common metals are satisfactory.

When the level of solids is to be measured, the general scheme is the same: the storage tank or container becomes one electrode plate and the actual material becomes the dielectric. The other electrode plate is an insulated wire positioned vertically in the center of the tank or container.

A basic electrical level-control scheme. An interesting control scheme is based on the original Evershed Noflote principle. This utilizes the fact that many industrial liquids are electrical conductors. The arrangement consists of two or more electrodes and a special relay operated from an alternating-current (a-c) supply designed to give low voltages across the electrodes.

The general layout of the installation is shown in Fig. 6-14. Two electrodes suspended from insulated fixtures project into the liquid under level control. The electrodes are of different lengths, the lengths being adjusted

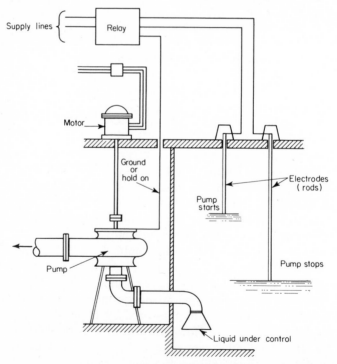

Fig. 6-14   A simple drainage-control scheme. (Evershed & Vignoles Ltd.)

to correspond with the two levels between which the pump is required to operate. The relay is connected by wires to the electrodes, and the sequence of operations is briefly as follows: The liquid, on rising, completes an electrical circuit through the start electrode, thereby actuating the relay. The relay, in turn, operates the pilot coil of the automatic starter, and this starts the motor to the pump. The motor continues to run, owing to the hold-on circuit through ground, until the level falls below the stop electrode, when the pump will stop.

In the installation shown for drainage control, when the liquid level reaches the higher electrode, the pump will start and continue pumping until the level falls below the bottom of the lower electrode. The pump will then stop, and restarting commences only when the level again reaches the upper electrode. The hold-on circuit is obtained from a ground connection which often consists of a third electrode. This same principle is used with certain boiler drum level gauges.

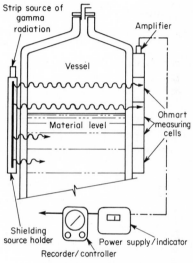

A typical Ohmart level gaging system

Radiation from a strip source of gamma rays is measured by a stack of ohmart measuring cells. The output current from the cells, which varies with the level of the material being measured, is inversely proportional to level change.

Fig. 6-15 Nuclear gauging systems for measuring level or interface position of liquids, solids, or slurries. (Ohmart Corp.)

Nucleonic Gauges

Nucleonic-type level-measuring units consist of a radioactive source, a radiation detector, and electronic measuring circuits incorporating an amplifier and receiving readout instrument or recorder-controller. Nuclear gauges cover a wide range of applications. Installations range from indicating high- and low-level alarms on storage tanks as large as 50 ft in diameter, using gamma switches, through continuous measurement of heights of 20 ft and over to ±1 percent repeatability.

The radioactive source is placed externally on one side of the tank and the detector on the opposite side. The liquid, upon rising and falling inside the tank, absorbs radiation, and the change in intensity received by the detector is a function of the liquid level. A typical level-gauge installation is shown in Fig. 6-15.

The radioactive sources normally used are strontium 90 for beta radiation and cobalt 60 and cesium 137 for gamma radiation. A small radioactive source consists of a rod approximately 1 in. long and ⅛ in. in diameter. For a high-level variation a strip source of short rods placed end to end to make up the required length is used. The strip source is housed in shielded containers, generally with a rotary shutter for transmission purposes.

For level measurement and/or control applications, the detector used is normally a measuring cell that converts radioactive energy directly into electric energy. The output is then fed either to a single vacuum-tube direct-current (d-c) amplifier or to a vibrating-capacitor a-c amplifier that is remotely mounted. In the Ohmart nuclear gauging systems, models LG and MDLV use a model VC vibrating capacitor, feedback-stabilized a-c amplifier-indicator featuring solid-state plug-in circuit modules, and a single vacuum tube. The variable time constant is 1 to 30 sec, and current output is from 0 to 1 ma at 1 volt.

The advantages of the nucleonic gauging systems are:

1. No part of the gauge is in contact with the material under measurement. For this reason the gauge is not affected by conditions of high and low temperature, pressure, viscosity, corrosion, and abrasion.
2. The repeatability in some models varies from ±1 percent range to ±4 or ±2 percent of scale, depending upon the radiation-field intensity. The zero shift is frequently less than 1 percent of scale in 7 days.
3. The level gauges provide sensitive measurement and control without the use of complex components.
4. The gauges are ruggedly constructed to withstand severe industrial conditions.
5. Adequate shielding limits radiation-field intensity well below Atomic Energy Commission (AEC) tolerance.

Ultrasonic Method

A typical ultrasonic system for measuring level changes is shown in Fig. 6-16. Sound waves are sent out to the free surface of the liquid under

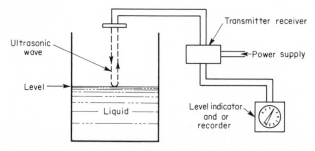

Fig. 6-16   Ultrasonic system for level measurement.

measurement and are reflected back to the receiving unit. Level variations are very accurately measured by detecting the time interval taken for the waves to travel to the surface and back to the receiver. The longer the time interval the farther away is the liquid surface, which, in turn, is an indication of the level measurement.

It should be stated that these systems have been described and illustrated very simply and briefly. Some are highly complicated in design, application, and operation, and also quite expensive.

Measurement of the Level of Solid Substances

Capacitor-probe, nucleonic, and ultrasonic methods. There is a great need in industry for the continuous indication of the levels of granular substances in storage bins or tanks between full and empty conditions. One very common example is the measurement of the level of flour in a silo. The majority of methods described for liquid-level measurement cannot be used satisfactorily for solid-level measurement. Generally, the three exceptions are the capacitor probe, the nucleonic, and ultrasonic methods.

Determination of level by weighing; mechanical and electrical methods. The weight of a material in a tank or storage bin is an indirect method of determining level, since variations in level produce corresponding variations in weight. The storage tank can be weighed on mechanical scales, or it can be weighed electrically by using load cells as shown in Fig. 6-17. The load cells are specially designed and constructed units containing strain gauges. The strain gauges provide a measurable electrical output proportional to the stress applied by the weight acting upon the load cells. As the pressure on the load cells due to variations in the weight of the material inside the tank changes, the electrical resistances of the strain gauges also change. The strain gauge is connected to a measuring bridge circuit containing an electrical meter calibrated in units of level measurement. Full details of the strain gauge are given in the section dealing with electrical transducers.

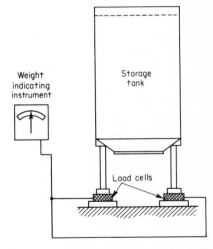

Fig. 6-17 Storage tank weighed electrically by using strain gauges.

It should be clearly noted that the weight level method is accurate only if the density and the granular or particle size of the material being weighed are uniform. Also, the moisture content should be fairly constant for true level measurement. In the case of coal or coke these conditions are seldom realized.

REVIEW QUESTIONS AND PROBLEMS

6-1   (a) Distinguish between direct and indirect methods of level measurement.

(b) Give examples of each of these methods.

6-2   Describe the application of Archimedes' principle in the constant- and variable-displacement types of float.

6-3   What type of primary sensing element would you use to measure the level of a corrosive liquid?

6-4   (a) What is the importance of weight-density or specific-gravity values in computing liquid-level pressures?

(b) Compute the pressure, in pounds per square inch, of a column of liquid 20 ft high if the weight density is 100 lb/ft³.

(c) If the pressure gauge connected at the bottom of a liquid storage tank indicates 10 psi and the specific gravity of the liquid is 0.9, compute the level of the liquid, in feet.

6-5   (a) Describe, with the aid of a neat schematic diagram, the principle of the bubbler type of level gauge. Mention examples of its application.

(b) In a bubbler type of level-measuring system the span is to register 10 to 50 ft of water. Compute the equivalent pressures, in pounds per square inch. What would be the desirable minimum value of the supply pressure?

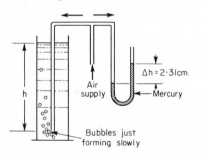

Fig. 6-18   Bubbler principle.

6-6   In the diagram of Fig. 6-18 illustrating the "bubbler" level gauge, what is the level h of the water above the tube, in centimeters, if the differential pressure on the mercury manometer reads 2.31 cm Hg?

6-7   Gasoline in a uniform tank is filled to a depth of 25 ft. What is the pressure, in pounds per square inch, halfway down and at the bottom of the tank? Assume the specific gravity to be 0.70.

6-8   (a) Sketch a graph showing the relationship between pressure and depth in a uniformly shaped storage tank containing liquid.

(b) If you had a sensitive pressure gauge, how would it provide a means for determining the level of the gasoline in the tank?

(c) Sketch a graph showing the relationship between pressure and depth in a horizontal cylindrical tank with flat ends.

(d) With the same gauge, what would now be the nature of the scale divisions for determining the gasoline level?

6-9   For the system indicated in Fig. 6-19 show that

$$H = d\left[\frac{w_m}{w}\left(1 + \frac{A_1}{A_2}\right) - 1\right] - H_1$$

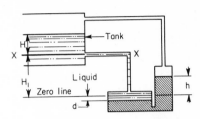

where H = head of liquid above X–X
w_l = density of the tank liquid
w_m = density of the instrument liquid
A_1 = area of the wide tube
A_2 = area of the narrow tube
H_1 = head of tank liquid below X–X to the zero level of the instrument liquid

Fig. 6-19   Differential-pressure method.

6-10   Describe an industrial installation for the measurement of the level of a corrosive fluid in a closed tank by using a differential-pressure mercury-filled meter.

6-11   Several electrical methods are available for level measurement. Describe the operation of one and include a diagram of the arrangement.

6-12   Describe a suitable method which you would use to measure the bin level of iron ore, which is magnetic and very abrasive.

6-13   The tank shown in Fig. 6-20 will discharge liquid at a constant rate so long as the liquid surface within the tank lies above the bottom of the air inlet. Determine the liquid level in the glass piezometer tubes A and B under the conditions indicated. What is the pressure intensity of the

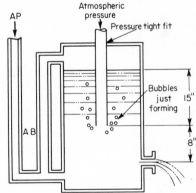

Fig. 6-20   Tank of Question 6-13.

air in the tank if the specific weight of the liquid is 85.0 lb/ft³? Give your answer in pounds per square inch and mark in the levels of A and B in the sketch.

CHAPTER SEVEN

Viscosity measurement

Experimentation is the gateway to scientific progress.

ANONYMOUS

The Nature of Viscosity

The internal friction, or resistance to flow, set up within a fluid (liquid or gas) is called *viscosity*. The water on the surface of a river moves more rapidly than the water near the sides or bottom. Water flow in a pipeline, or airflow in a shaft (or ducting) has greater velocity at the center than it has next to the metal surfaces. This difference in velocity is partly due to the friction between the fluid and the boundary surface, which causes the adjacent layers of fluid to move slowly. These slowly moving layers of fluid, because of internal friction, in turn tend to retard the motion of adjacent layers. Viscosity is responsible for most of the dissipation of energy in transporting liquids and gases in pipelines. For this reason viscosity, or internal friction, is a very important factor in fluid flow.

The property of viscosity is particularly significant in the study of oil. In industry, oils which have the higher viscosity are the "heavier" oils. This term does not bear any relation to their densities. The effectiveness of lubricating oils depends, among other factors, upon the viscosity of the oils. Generally, lubricating oils should be sufficiently viscous that they will not be squeezed out of bearings and yet not so viscous as to increase the resistance to the motion of the moving parts which are being lubricated.

For these reasons the study of viscosity and its measurement is very important. Viscosity is a comparative measure of the ease with which particles in a fluid can change their relative positions and yield to an external force. For example, a thick liquid like honey offers more resistance to flow than does water. More specifically, the viscosity of a liquid or gas is that physical property which determines the magnitude of the resistance of the fluid to a shearing force.

146

Viscometers. The viscosity of a fluid is determined by several methods, one of which is to measure the time required for a known quantity of the fluid to escape through a long tube of small diameter. For determining the viscosity of paints, varnishes, nail polish, and similar liquids a common test is to time the flow of the liquid through a standard opening. Instruments used to determine viscosity values are called *viscometers* or *viscosimeters*.

Each technique for measuring viscosity has its characteristic assumptions and equipment. The operating principles and applications of laboratory and plant viscometers will be described in later paragraphs. The basic concepts, with simple illustrations of the meaning of viscosity, will be described in this section.

Newtonian Assumptions

Consider a fluid to be in laminar or viscous motion, i.e., moving in such a way that adjacent planes or layers (thin-sheet type) of the fluid move slowly in one direction, as shown in Fig. 7-1. If the adjacent layers are

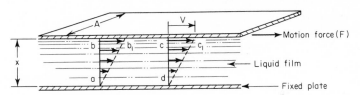

Fig. 7-1   Enlarged view of the deformation of a substance under constant shear.

moving with different velocities, the constant interchange of molecules and momentum creates resistance to the relative motion of the layers. Slippage occurs as the faster-moving layer moves over an adjacent layer.

A fluid is considered to be a substance which deforms continuously when subjected to a shear stress, regardless of how small that shear stress may be. A shear force is the force component tangent to the surface where slippage or cleavage occurs. This force, divided by the area of the surface, is the average shear stress over the area.

In Fig. 7-1 a liquid is shown bounded by two plates. One of the plates is stationary, and the other is moving parallel to the surface of the first one with constant velocity V. The plates are assumed to be large so that the flow is considered as two-dimensional. Newton's first assumption was that whenever a fluid is in contact with a solid boundary, there is no slip or motion of the actual fluid particles immediately adjacent to that boundary. In the case of Fig. 7-1 the velocity of the fluid in contact with the stationary plate is zero and the velocity of the fluid at the upper plate surface is equal to V. This means that the fluid particles at the uppermost layer are carried with the moving plate. This moving layer, in turn, imparts a forward motion to the layer immediately below it, and so on, with diminishing magnitude that reaches zero at the lower plate.

Newton's second assumption was that the shearing stress between adjacent layers of fluid of infinitesimal thickness is proportional to the rate of shear in the direction perpendicular to the motion. In fluids, according to this second assumption, the shearing stress is proportional to the shear velocity.

$$\frac{F}{A} = \mu \frac{V}{x}$$

by rearrangement,

$$F = \frac{\mu A V}{x}$$

where F = pulling force on the upper plate
$\quad\quad A$ = area of the upper plate
$\quad\quad x$ = distance between the two plates
μ(mu) = proportionality constant
The shear stress is given by

$$\tau \text{ (tau)} = \frac{\text{force } F}{\text{area } A}$$

$$\tau = \mu \frac{V}{x}$$

In the differential form $\tau = \mu \, dV/dx$, which is Newton's equation for viscosity and applies to any constant force.

The proportionality factor μ is called the coefficient of absolute or dynamic viscosity of the liquid. The velocity gradient at any point is dV/dx, where dV is the small difference in velocity between two points at right angles to the flow and separated by a small distance dx. An ideal plastic substance is one such that an initial shear stress must be overcome before a continuous distortion sets in, i.e., the relation of τ to dv/dx is linear. If sand were to be placed between the two plates (Fig. 7-1), dry friction would necessitate a finite force to cause a continuous motion. For this reason sand does not fulfill the definition of a fluid.

Newtonian and Non-Newtonian Fluids

Fluids are classified as Newtonian if there is a linear relation between the magnitude of the applied shear stress and the resulting rate of deformation, that is, $\tau \propto dv/dx$. Many lubricating oils are in this category. In non-Newtonian fluids, there is a nonlinear relationship between the magnitude of the applied shear stress and the rate of deformation. This type of fluid is also called *pseudoplastic*. Rubber suspensions and some synthetic oils are in this category. Thermosetting plastics are also a good example of non-Newtonian fluids. An ideal plastic is one with a definite shear stress and a constant linear relation of τ to dv/dx.

Gases and thin liquids tend to be Newtonian fluids, whereas thick liquids and gases near their critical points tend to be non-Newtonian. In gases whose particles have relatively large separations, the cohesive forces are small. Each layer exerts a drag on the other, and the magnitude of this drag depends on the momentum of the particle. For this reason an increase in temperature means an increase in speed and momentum, which results in an increase in the viscosity of the gas.

Rheology is the study and investigation of the deformation and flow of substances under varying conditions of applied forces. Typical rheological graphs of Newtonian and non-Newtonian fluids, as well as the ideal plastic and thixotropic substances, are plotted in Fig. 7-2 to distinguish the

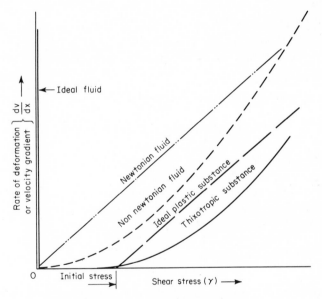

Fig. 7-2   Rheological graphs.

difference in characteristics. A thixotropic substance is one such that its viscosity changes with time. Certain liquids, e.g., some paints and printers' ink, possess the property of increasing in viscosity with the passage of time if left undisturbed. It is believed that all plastics are thixotropic to some extent.

Fluidity is a term sometimes used to describe the property of liquids. It is simply defined as the reciprocal of the absolute viscosity, that is, $1/\mu$.

Units of Absolute and Kinematic Viscosity

Consider a fluid in motion such that adjacent planes or layers are moving with different velocities. A shearing action is set up between the layers. The arrangement is shown in magnified view in Fig. 7-3. The figures *abcd*

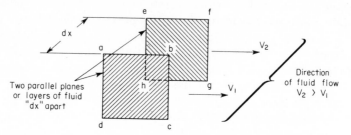

Fig. 7-3   Parallel layers of a fluid in viscous flow.

and *efgh* are two parallel planes of a fluid in motion of equal area A separated by a small distance dx. The velocity of *abcd* is V_1, and that of *efgh* is V_2. By using Newton's equation, an expression for the viscosity is obtained:

$$F = \mu A \; \frac{V_2 - V_1}{dx} = \mu A \; \frac{dv}{dx}$$

$$\text{Absolute viscosity } \mu = \frac{F/A}{V/dx} = \frac{\tau}{dv/dx}$$

where τ = sheer stress
dv/dx = velocity gradient

Units in the fps system. In the foot-pound-second system the units for absolute viscosity are derived by using dimensional analysis and engineering units described in Chap. 2.

$$\frac{\text{lb}_f/\text{ft}^2 \times \text{ft}}{\text{ft/sec}} = \frac{\text{lb}_f \text{ sec}}{\text{ft}^2}$$

which is read pound force second per square foot. The dimensional analysis expression is $[FTL^{-2}]$. The unit of viscosity (which has no special name in the fps system) is 1 $\text{lb}_f \text{ sec/ft}^2$ or 1 slug/ft sec.

Units in the cgs system. In the cgs system the unit of viscosity is the poise (in recognition of the early research work done by Poiseuille, a French physician and scientist), which is 1 dyne sec/cm^2. The coefficient of absolute viscosity of one poise is defined as the tangential force of one dyne for each square centimeter of surface to maintain a relative velocity of one centimeter per second. Small viscosities are expressed in centipoises (1 centipoise = 10^{-2} poise); a centipoise is one-hundredth of a poise. The micropoise is one-millionth of a poise (1 micropoise $= 10^{-6}$ poise). Water at 68°F has an absolute viscosity of 1.008 centipoises.

A second coefficient is kinematic viscosity, which is equal to the absolute viscosity divided by the mass density. Most laboratory viscometers measure kinematic viscosity. Symbolically,

$$\text{Kinematic viscosity } \nu = \frac{\text{absolute viscosity } \mu}{\text{mass density } \rho}$$

$$\nu = \frac{\mu}{\rho} = \frac{\mu}{w/g} = \frac{\mu g}{w}$$

where ν (nu) $=$ kinematic viscosity
μ $=$ absolute viscosity
ρ $=$ mass density
w $=$ weight density
g $=$ acceleration of gravity

The units of kinematic viscosity are

$$\frac{\text{lb}_\text{f} \text{ sec}}{\text{ft}^2} \frac{\text{ft}}{\text{sec}^2} \frac{\text{ft}^3}{\text{lb}_\text{f}} = \frac{\text{ft}^2}{\text{sec}}$$

The dimensional-analysis expression is $[L^2 T^{-1}]$.

Units. In the fps system the unit of kinematic viscosity is 1 ft²/sec and has no special name. In the cgs system the unit is 1 cm²/sec and is called the stoke. Viscosities are listed in handbooks as poises and stokes (cgs system of units). Viscosities of lubricating oils are frequently expressed on an arbitrary scale established by the Society of Automotive Engineers (SAE). An oil which has an SAE rating or number of 10 has a viscosity at 130°F of about 160 to 220 centipoises. SAE 20 oil has a viscosity of between 230 and 300 centipoises.

Conversions. The following are examples of conversion problems.

Example 1. Convert fps units to poises (measured in dyne sec/cm²).

Solution.   1 lb$_\text{f}$ $= 444{,}800$ dynes   (454 g $\times$ 981 cm/sec²)
    1 ft $= 30.48$ cm   (2.54 cm/in. $\times$ 12 in./ft)

Hence $\dfrac{1 \text{ lb}_\text{f} \text{ sec}}{\text{ft}^2} = \dfrac{444{,}800}{(30.48)^2}$ dyne sec/cm²

$= 478.7$ poises

If the viscosity of water at 20°C is 0.01008 poise and the specific gravity of water is 0.998 at this temperature, then

$$\mu \text{ (lb}_\text{f} \text{ sec/ft}^2) = \frac{0.01008}{478.7} = 2.1 \times 10^{-5}$$

$$\nu \text{ (ft}^2/\text{sec)} = \frac{\mu g}{w}$$

$$= \frac{2.1 \times 10^{-5} \text{ lb}_\text{f} \text{ sec/ft}^2 \times 32.2 \text{ ft/sec}^2}{62.4 \text{ lb}_\text{f}/\text{ft}^3 \times 0.998} = 1.09 \times 10^{-5}$$

Example 2. Convert 10.2 poises of a liquid to kinematic viscosity in ft²/sec units, given that the specific gravity of the liquid is as 0.80.

Solution.
$$1 \text{ poise} = \frac{1}{478.7} \frac{\text{lb}_f \text{ sec}}{\text{ft}^2}$$

$$\text{Kinematic viscosity } \nu = \frac{10.2}{478.7} \times \frac{32.2}{62.4} \times \frac{1}{0.80} = 13.7 \times 10^{-2}$$

Temperature Effects on Viscosity

Liquids. Of all the physical conditions, temperature has the greatest effect on viscosity. An increase in temperature causes a greater separation among the liquid molecules, a reduction in the shear stress, and therefore a decrease in viscosity. Many lubricating oils may fail to form a protective film at low temperatures. The large decrease in absolute viscosity with increasing temperature will be observed in Figs. 7-4 and 7-5. For example,

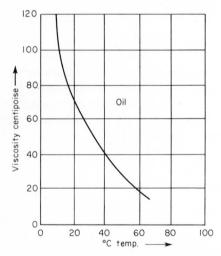

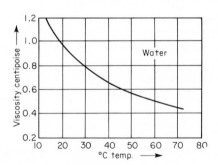

Fig. 7-4   Viscosity variation of an oil with temperature.

Fig. 7-5   Viscosity variation of water with temperature.

tar at 15°C has a viscosity of 1.65×10^6 poises, whereas at 45°C its viscosity is 1.3×10^3 poises. For a temperature span of 30°C the viscosity changes by a factor of a thousand.

There are a number of formulas for the variation of viscosity of a liquid with respect to temperature. Poiseuille's expression is given by

$$\mu_t = \frac{\mu_0}{1 + C_1 t + C_2 t^2}$$

where μ_t = absolute viscosity at $t°C$

μ_0 = absolute viscosity at $0°C$

and C_1 and C_2 are constants.

Gases. As already mentioned, temperature exerts a major influence on the viscosity of gases owing to its effect on the speed of the gas particles. Figure 7-6 shows the variation of viscosity with air temperature. It is seen that the viscosity increases with temperature owing to the increase in momentum of the particles.

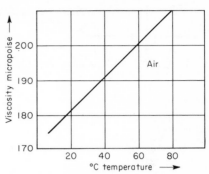

Fig. 7-6 *Viscosity variation of air with temperature.*

Laboratory Methods of Viscosity Measurement

Laminar flow in tubes.[1] A simple and basic method for measuring viscosity is the flow of a liquid through a capillary or small-diameter tube such as used for thermometers. Provided that flow is truly laminar or viscous, all the necessary conditions for viscosity measurement are easily achieved. Figure 7-7 shows two laboratory methods of determining viscosity. In each case certain provisos must be adhered to. There must be no radial flow, and the pressure must be kept constant over the length of the horizontal tube. Also, the liquid in contact with the walls of the tube must be at rest. In this way the viscous resistance is kept proportional to the velocity gradient.

If all conditions are as stipulated, the rate of flow through a tube complies with the Hagen-Poiseuille equation for laminar flow:

$$Q = \frac{\pi R^4 \, \Delta P}{8\mu L}$$

where Q = volume of liquid passing through the tube per second

L = length of capillary tube

R = radius of capillary tube

μ = coefficient of absolute viscosity

ΔP = pressure drop between the ends of the tube

Since the radius is raised to the fourth power in the equation, it is essential to measure it as accurately as possible, and the traveling microscope affords an excellent laboratory method. The discharge rate Q can be found by using a graduated jar to measure the volume of liquid and a stopwatch

[1] See also p. 171.

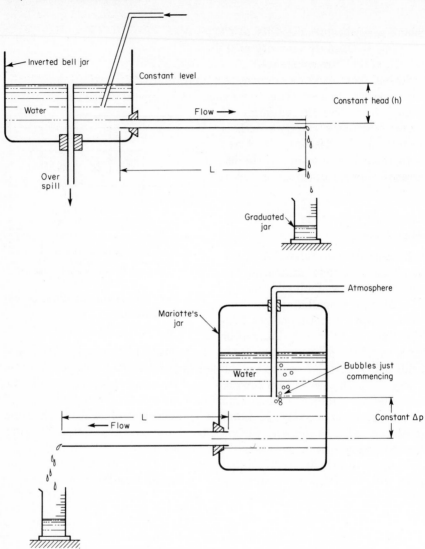

Fig. 7-7   Some laboratory methods of determining viscosity.

to determine the time. The coefficient of absolute viscosity can then be computed.

$$Q = \frac{\text{volume collected}}{\text{time taken}} \quad \text{and} \quad \mu = \frac{\pi R^4 \, \Delta P}{8QL}$$

But
$$\Delta P = h\rho g$$

where ρ is the mass density of the liquid at the temperature prevailing at the time of the experiment.

To verify the units in the Hagen-Poiseuille equation, dimensional analysis should be used:

$$\mu = \frac{\pi R^4 \, \Delta P}{8QL} = \frac{\pi R^4 h \rho g}{8QL}$$

The dimensional equation becomes

$$\left[\frac{FT}{L^2} \right] = \frac{[L^4][(L)(M/L^3)(L/T^2)]}{[L^3/T][L]}$$

$$\left[\left(\frac{ML}{T^2} \right) \left(\frac{T}{L^2} \right) \right] = \left[\frac{M}{LT} \right]$$

$$\left[\frac{M}{LT} \right] = \left[\frac{M}{LT} \right]$$

Hence the equation balances dimensionally and the appropriate engineering units may now be applied.

In utilizing the capillary flow method for determining viscosity it is well to check that the velocity is not near the critical value, above which the flow is turbulent. The expression for the critical velocity having a Reynolds number of 2,000 is

$$V_c = \frac{2,000\mu}{\rho d} *$$

where d is the diameter of the tube. For laminar or viscous flow the velocity must be less than the critical velocity.

The loss of head due to friction is given by the Hagen-Poiseuille law for viscous flow in tubes:

$$h_f = \frac{\Delta P}{w} = \frac{32\mu L v}{wd^2}$$

where v is the mean velocity of the liquid flow. The remarkable feature of the Hagen-Poiseuille equation is that it involves no empirical coefficients or factors, except for the physical properties of the liquid such as viscosity and weight density. The absolute viscosities of some common fluids are listed in Table 7-1, and the kinematic viscosities and specific gravities in Table 7-2.

Hagen, a German engineer, and Poiseuille, a French physician and scientist, experimented on the flow of liquids through capillary tubes and published their results in 1840. Poiseuille was interested in the blood flow through the veins of the human body, and he extended his investigation into pipe-flow problems.

* See also p. 171.

Table 7-1   Absolute viscosity of certain fluids, in cgs units

Substance	Temp, °C	Absolute viscosity, cgs or poise units	Substance	Temp, °C	Absolute viscosity, cgs or poise units
Water	0	0.0179	Mercury	20	0.016
	10	0.0131	Alcohol	20	0.012
	15	0.0114	Glycerine	20	8.5
	20	0.0100	Paraffin	19	0.02
	50	0.0056	Syrup	12	1.4×10^3
	100	0.0029	Asphalt	15	1.31×10^{10}

Table 7-2   Kinematic viscosity and specific gravity of certain fluids, in fps units

Substance	Temp, °F	Sp gr	Kinematic viscosity, ft²/sec
Water	70	0.998	1.060×10^{-5}
Carbon tetrachloride	70	1.582	0.650×10^{-5}
Lubricating oil	70	0.890	125.0×10^{-5}
Heavy fuel oil	70	0.908	157.0×10^{-5}
Gasoline	70	0.724	0.690×10^{-5}
Air	68		16.0×10^{-5}

Consistency Measurement

It should be noted that in the pulp and paper industry one of the most important measurements required is that of consistency of the stock, i.e., weight of dry fiber per gallon of liquid. Direct measurement presents obvious difficulties, and for fixed conditions and over a limited range viscosity is therefore used as an equivalent. Many of the methods outlined above have been adapted for the purpose, and an additional method, using a strain gauge to measure the shearing force, has been put on the market.

REVIEW QUESTIONS AND PROBLEMS

7-1   Define the following terms: (a) viscous flow, (b) coefficient of dynamic viscosity, (c) non-Newtonian fluids, (d) kinematic viscosity.

7-2   Absolute viscosity has the dimensions of (a) $FL^{-2}T$, (b) $FL^{-1}T^{-2}$, (c) FL^2T, (d) or none of these. Kinematic viscosity has the dimensions of (a) L^2T^1, (b) L^2T^{-1}, (c) $FL^{-2}T$, (d) or none of these.

7-3   (a) Give the meaning and units of (a) a poise, (b) a centipoise, (c) a stoke.

(b) If air at atmospheric pressure and at 60°F has a mass density of 0.00237 slugs/ft^3 and an absolute or dynamic viscosity of 3.75×10^{-7} lb$_f$ sec/ft^2, evaluate the kinematic viscosity in ft^2/sec units.

(c) Convert 3.75×10^{-7} lb$_f$ sec/ft^2 into poises.

7-4   A medium lubricating oil at 60°F has a specific gravity of 0.89 and a kinematic viscosity of 188.0×10^{-5} ft^2/sec. Evaluate the absolute viscosity, in lb$_f$ sec/ft^2.

7-5   (a) Describe, briefly, the way in which the viscosity of liquids and gases changes with respect to temperature and pressure changes.

(b) Describe, with the aid of a neat diagram, the laboratory apparatus for one method of determining absolute viscosity of water or other liquid.

7-6   A liquid has a viscosity of 0.05 poise and a specific gravity of 0.85. Evaluate (a) the viscosity, in fps units, (b) the kinematic viscosity, in stokes, and (c) the kinematic viscosity, in fps units.

7-7   Given the Hagen-Poiseuille formula for viscous flow

$$\mu = \frac{\pi D^4 \, \Delta P}{128QL}$$

calculate the viscosity μ of water if, during an experiment, the following data are collected: volume of water collected, 15.6 cm^3; time taken, 10 sec; pressure head, 13 cm H$_2$O; diameter of the tube, 0.200 cm; length of the tube, 30 cm; gravitational acceleration $g = 981$ cm/sec^2.

7-8   The Reynolds number for 10.0 ft^3/sec of water at 68°F through a 12-in. circular pipe is (a) 2,460, (b) 980,000, (c) 1,177,000, (d) 14,100,000, or (e) none of these answers.

7-9   An oil with a kinematic viscosity of 0.005 ft^2/sec flows through a 3.0-in.-ID pipe with a velocity of 10 ft/sec. Determine whether the flow is viscous or turbulent. If the oil weighs 58 lb/ft^3, calculate the friction drop, in pounds per square inch, over 3,000 ft of pipe length.

METHODS OF MEASURING VISCOSITY

Rotating Concentric-cylinders Viscometers

Inner cylinder fixed. The rotating concentric-cylinders viscometer consists basically of two vertical concentric cylinders separated by a small annular space. One cylinder can be rotated with respect to the other. The

liquid under test fills the annular space. In operation the liquid in this
space will rotate in layers, the layer in contact with the rotating cylinder
moving at the same speed as the cylinder and the liquid in contact with
the other cylinder remaining stationary. When the viscometer is in operation, a viscous force which tends to retard the motion of the rotating
cylinder is set up. If the speed is constant, i.e., there is no acceleration,
then the torque causing rotation is equal to that arising from the viscous
retarding force.

The arrangement in Fig. 7-8 shows the concentric-cylinders viscometer.
When the speed of rotation of the outer surface is N revolutions per min-

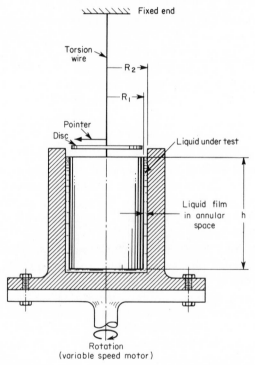

*Fig. 7-8   Sectional view of a concentric-cylinders viscometer with inner
cylinder fixed.*

ute (rpm) and the radius is R_2 ft, then the tangential velocity of the
liquid at the surface of the outer cylinder is $2\pi R_2 N/60$ ft/sec. The tangential velocity is equal to the product of the radius and the angular
speed. The clearance or liquid film thickness between the cylinders is equal
to the difference in the radii, that is, $R_2 - R_1$.

The velocity gradient, using the established notation, is

$$\frac{dv}{dx} = \frac{2\pi R_2 N}{60(R_2 - R_1)}$$

where $dx = R_2 - R_1$.

The torque T on the inner cylinder, which is caused by the viscous force set up, is measured by a torsion wire from which the cylinder is suspended. If a disk is attached to the wire, its rotation may be found by means of an attached pointer or indicator. If the torque due to the fluid below the bottom of the inner cylinder is considered negligible, the shear stress

$$\tau = \frac{T \ (\text{force})}{2\pi R_1^2 h \ (\text{area})}$$

where h is the length of the inner cylinder. If now, these two expressions for dv/dx and τ are substituted in Newton's equation:

$$\mu = \tau \frac{dx}{dv}$$

$$= \frac{15T(R_2 - R_1)}{\pi R_1^2 R_2 h N}$$

Using dimensional analysis to check for correct dimensions,

$$\left[\frac{FT}{L^2}\right] = \frac{[LF][L]}{[L^2][L][L][1/T]} = \left[\frac{FT}{L^2}\right]$$

Outer cylinder fixed. In this case the inner cylinder is rotated at a constant speed while the outer cylinder is stationary. The rotation of the inner cylinder is produced by a couple. A wire or thread is wound around a drum fixed to the spindle of the two pulleys placed as shown in Fig. 7-9. Weights at each end of the wire are suspended and the couple is thereby produced. If

d = diameter of the drum
W = weight, lb force
C = couple produced (dW)

then the viscosity is found from the relation

$$\mu = \frac{Ct(R_2^2 - R_1^2)}{8h\pi^2 R_1^2 R_2^2} \quad \text{in} \left[\frac{FT}{L^2}\right] \text{dimensions}$$

where t is the time of one revolution observed from an indicator attached to the shaft of the inner cylinder.

From these basic ideas various technical developments have been made. One of them is the Stormer Viscometer used for liquids and particularly for plastic material. Either a cylinder or paddle is used as the inner rotating device. The number of revolutions is recorded on a mechanical counter;

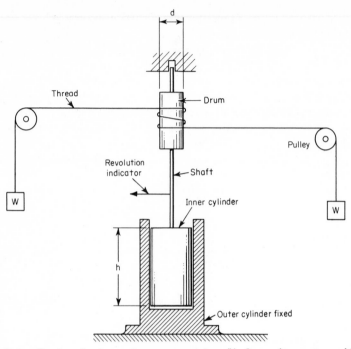

Fig. 7-9 Sectional view of a concentric-cylinders viscometer with outer cylinder fixed.

and by taking the time for 50 or 100 revolutions, t_1 may be computed. If a comparison of the viscosities of different liquids or plastic materials is required, the couple is kept the same in each test and the time for a fixed number of revolutions is measured. The time will be proportional to the viscosity and is therefore the basis of comparison. Commercial viscometers based on the forces created by two magnets to drive the spindle of a standard cylinder which is immersed in the process liquid under test are available.

   Rotating spindle. In the rotating-spindle method for measuring viscosity a spindle is rotated in a container of the sample liquid under test. The basic principle involved is that the viscosity is directly proportional to the torque required to drive the spindle. Continuous viscosity-measuring meters have a provision for the flow of the test liquid into and out of the container.

Stokes' Method

When a viscous liquid flows past a sphere with a Reynolds number of less than 1, or when a sphere moves slowly through a viscous liquid which is at rest, a resisting force is exerted on the sphere. Sir George Stokes, in 1845, performed a series of experiments to determine viscosity by means of the measurement of the time taken for a steel ball to fall through a viscous liquid. He observed that the falling sphere would at first accelerate but that the resistance to its motion increased with its velocity until the resistance just balanced the pull of gravity on the sphere. After this condition was reached, the sphere fell with a constant velocity only (Fig. 7-10).

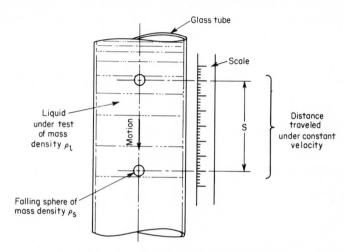

Fig. 7-10   Falling-sphere viscometer.

Stokes proved by mathematical analysis that the resistance to a sphere moving through a noncompressible fluid is given by

$$R = 6\pi r v \mu$$

where r = radius of the sphere

v = velocity of the sphere in the fluid

By equating this resistance to the pull of gravity on the sphere, after the condition of uniform velocity has been attained, the value of μ can be computed.

Pull of gravity = fluid resistance on the sphere at the uniform velocity

$$\tfrac{4}{3}\pi r^3(\rho_s - \rho_e)g = 6\pi r v \mu$$

hence

$$\mu = \frac{2r^2 g(\rho_s - \rho_e)}{9v}$$

By dimensional analysis, using the $[M]$, $[L]$, and $[T]$ dimensions,

$$\left[\frac{M}{LT}\right] = [L^2]\left[\frac{L}{T^2}\right]\left[\frac{M}{L^3}\right]\left[\frac{T}{L}\right] = \left[\frac{M}{LT}\right]$$

where ρ_s = mass density of the sphere

ρ_e = mass density of the liquid whose viscosity is under investigation

The velocity v is obtained by measuring the time taken by the sphere to fall through a known distance in the liquid after the condition of uniform velocity has been achieved. This method of calculating the viscosity gives accurate results only if the uniform velocity v is low. Precautions must be taken to make certain that no eddies are caused by the falling sphere and that the cylinder containing the liquid has a diameter great enough that the cylinder surface will not affect the motion of the sphere.

Example. Calculate the viscosity of glycerine if, during a laboratory test, the uniform velocity of a steel ball falling through a tank of glycerine is found to be 7.0 cm/sec. The radius of the ball is 2 mm. The mass densities of the steel and glycerine are 8 and 1.3 g/cm³, respectively.

Solution. Using Stokes' equation, the viscosity

$$\mu = \frac{2r^2 g(\rho_s - \rho_e)}{9v}$$

$$= \frac{2}{9} 0.2^2 \frac{981}{7}(8 - 1.3)$$

$$= 8.3 \text{ poises}$$

Saybolt Viscometer

In view of the fact that it is difficult to measure accurately the pressure in the tube, the diameter of the tube, and the uniformity along the tube length, an adaptation of the capillary tube is used for industrial measurement of viscosity. It is called the Saybolt viscometer (Fig. 7-11). A short capillary of specified length and diameter is used. A volume of 60 cm³ of the fluid is allowed to flow through the tube under a falling head, and the time of flow is recorded. The time, in seconds, is the Saybolt reading. This instrument measures kinematic viscosity, which is apparent from the equation,

$$Q = \frac{\Delta P \, \pi D^4}{128 L \mu}$$

where   rate of flow $Q = \dfrac{\text{volume collected } V}{\text{time taken } t}$

$$\Delta p = \rho g h$$

Separating the variable terms that are the same regardless of the fluid under test,

$$\frac{\mu}{\rho t} = \frac{gh \pi D^4}{128 V L} = K_1$$

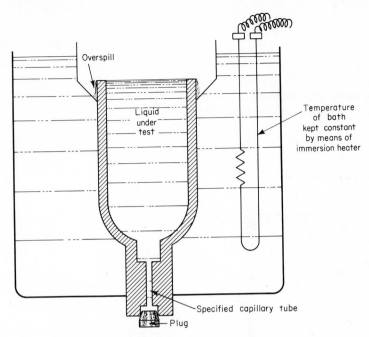

Fig. 7-11 Schematic view of Saybolt viscometer.

Although the head h varies during the test as the fluid level falls, it varies over the same range for all liquids. For this reason the terms on the right side of the equation may be considered as a constant K_1 of the particular instrument. Hence $\nu = K_1 t$, which indicates that the kinematic viscosity varies directly as the time t, in seconds. The capillary tube in the viscometer is short, so that the velocity distribution is not attained. The flow tends to enter uniformly and then, owing to viscous drag at the walls, slow down at the edges and increase in the center. In view of this, a correction must be made to the earlier equation for the instrument:

$$\text{kinematic viscosity } \nu = K_1 t + \frac{K_2}{t}$$

The approximate relationship between viscosity and Saybolt seconds for limited ranges is given by

$$\text{In stokes} = 0.0022t - \frac{1.80}{t} \text{ (SSU)} \text{ or } 0.0224 - \frac{1.9}{t} \text{ (SSF)}$$

$$\text{In poises} = \left(0.0022t - \frac{1.80}{t}\right) \text{sp gr (SSU)} \text{ or } \left(0.0224 - \frac{1.9}{t}\right) \text{sp gr (SSF)}$$

To convert stokes (cm²/sec) to ft²/sec units, divide by 30.48², or 929.

Falling-piston Viscometer

In the falling-piston viscometer, the time required for a piston to fall a certain distance in a cylinder containing the liquid under test is a function of the viscosity. The principle and assembly are shown in Fig. 7-12. The subsequent time required varies with changes in viscosity; the higher the viscosity rating the longer the time.

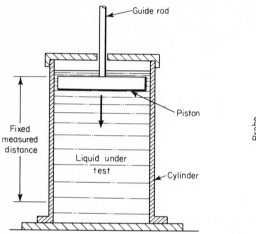 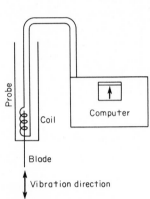

Fig. 7-12   Falling-piston method of determining relative viscosities.

Fig. 7-13   A continuous viscosity measurement and control unit.

Ultrasonic Method

The Bendix Corporation has designed a continuous viscosity measurement and control unit, given the trade name Ultra-Viscoson, which continuously measures the viscosity of a liquid as a function of the damping effect or viscous drag of the liquid on a small vibrating reed constructed of magnetostrictive iron and enclosed in a probe (Fig. 7-13). This metal is used because it changes its physical dimension depending upon the magnetic field to which it is subjected. The ultrasonic probe exposed to the process is stainless steel.

The concentric probe coil is inside the probe assembly, together with the reed. A short current pulse at 28,000 cycles/sec is sent through the probe coil, which rapidly changes the magnetic field around the reed element. This causes the probe reed to be activated into vibration, thus shearing the liquid in which it is immersed. The viscosity of the fluid damps the amplitude of vibration. When the amplitude falls to a given point, the element is automatically pulsed again. Since the damping influence is the absolute viscosity times the density, the rate of pulsation is an indication of the viscosity. The frequency of vibration is fed through a compact electronic analogue computer. The signal at the input to the computer is first the spike type, and then the damped waveform results, owing to the damping effect of the viscous liquid on the vibrating reed.

The computer acts much like a frequency-controlled pulse generator which sends out a driving pulse to the probe coil each time the energy output from the probe diminishes to a low value. The higher the viscosity value, the more rapid the damping and the more frequent the driving pulse. The average current which results from these driving pulses is a measure of the viscosity. Connection terminals provide d-c millivoltage output for operation of standard potentiometric recorders, indicators, and controllers. This equipment is suitable for laboratory, batch-instantaneous, batch-continuous, and continuous-flow viscosity measurement, and it may be used in either Newtonian or non-Newtonian fluids.

Measurement of the Viscosity of Gases

Of several methods available for determining the viscosity of gases the Rankine one is perhaps the earliest. The apparatus consists of two tubes, one on each side and one slightly larger in diameter than the other. The tubes are joined together in a loop as shown in Fig. 7-14. The gas under test is permitted to circulate through the loop when the outlet valve is closed. A globule of mercury is now inserted into the larger tube, and the inlet valve is closed. The time it takes for the mercury globule to fall between two graduated marks A and B is recorded. In its fall the globule displaces the gas (whose viscosity is being measured) through the narrow capillary, since the two tubes form a closed system. Here again, as with the Stokes apparatus, certain provisos are necessary. The pressure difference due to the pellet is insignificant compared with the total pressure of the gas inside the tube. From experimental results, the following equation is derived:

$$\mu = \frac{\pi d^4 t \, \Delta P}{128 L V}$$

where d = diameter of the capillary

L = length of capillary

ΔP = pressure difference across the globule

t = time taken for the globule to fall between the two graduated marks A and B

V = volume displaced by the globule in its downward motion

ΔP is equal to the weight of the pellet divided by the cross-sectional area of the tube if no surface tension effects are present; otherwise, corrections have to be made.

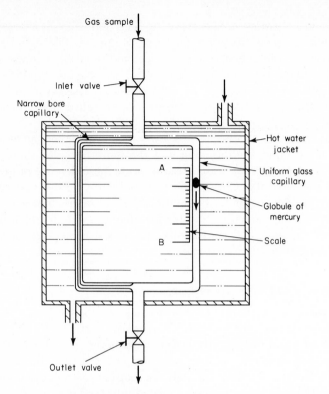

Fig. 7-14   The early Rankine apparatus for determining gas viscosity.

Provision is made for a jacket in order that the apparatus can be adapted for studying the effects of temperature and pressure variations. Other methods are used for measuring the viscosity of gases; examples are the coaxial cylinder and oscillating disk methods. In addition, the variable-area method, which is primarily a flowmeter, is used as a viscometer.

Variable-area viscometer. For continuous viscosity measurement a design based upon the principle of the variable-area flowmeter is used (refer to the section on measurement of flow). A sampling or meter pump draws some of the liquid from the main process stream and pumps it through the variable-area meter, which has a flow-rate-setting float and viscosity-measuring float. The differential pressure across the meter is kept constant, and therefore any movement of the viscosity-measuring float is due to a change in viscosity. This viscosity-measuring float is specially designed with a sensitivity to viscosity variations, whereas the flow-rate-setting float is sensitive to flow variations. For a constant flow rate the rate-setting float will occupy one position in the tapered glass tube.

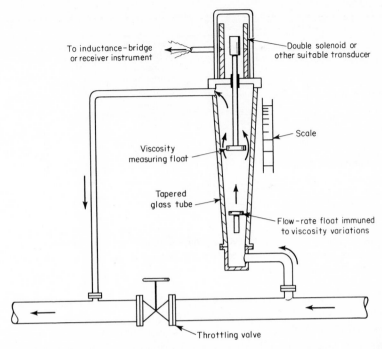

To inductance-bridge
or receiver instrument

Double solenoid or
other suitable transducer

Scale

Viscosity
measuring float

Tapered
glass tube

Flow-rate float immuned
to viscosity variations

Throttling valve

Fig. 7-15   If the flow rate is kept constant, only the viscosity float will be subject to movement to indicate viscosity variations. [Fischer & Porter (Canada) Limited]

The general schematic arrangement is shown in Fig. 7-15. This type of viscometer is useful where telemetering (transmitting metered values) is required. One design incorporates a double solenoid at the top of the float shaft. The variation in inductance is then a function of the viscosity, which is detected on a receiving instrument. Another design employs a unit containing transmission coils which are part of an electronic transmission system.

The float shaft can also be designed to operate a controlling mechanism. A viscosity recorder-controller directly positions the control valve. Figure 7-16 shows a blending control system in which the flow of cutter stock is directly controlled by a viscosity recorder-controller.

Miscellaneous Viscosity Data and Terminology

The *specific viscosity* of a liquid is the ratio of the absolute viscosity of the liquid to that of a standard liquid such as water, both at the same temperature. The *relative viscosity* of a liquid is the ratio of the absolute viscosity of the liquid to that of water at 68°F (20°C), because the absolute viscosity of water at that temperature is very nearly one centipoise.

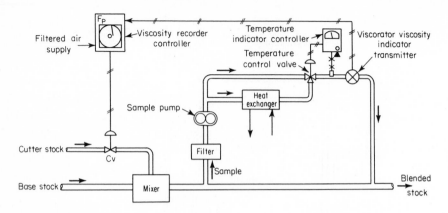

Fig. 7-16   Scheme for continuous fuel oil blending to a constant viscosity. The viscosity recorder controller directly positions the control valve. [Fischer & Porter (Canada) Limited]

Seconds Saybolt Universal (SSU) are values obtained with the Saybolt Universal viscometer, which is used for light oils.

Seconds Saybolt Furol (SSF) are values obtained for viscous liquids such as tar or a heavy fuel oil. The orifice in the Saybolt Furol viscometer is changed, and the resultant measurement is expressed as seconds Saybolt Furol.

Conversion factors

$$1 \text{ lb}_f \text{ sec/ft}^2 = 478.8 \text{ poise}$$
$$= 47,880 \text{ centipoise}$$
$$= 0.00209 \text{ lb}_f \text{ sec/ft}^2$$

Kinedynamic Units (KDU) are units used with fluids which vary in both viscosity and density. These two characteristics can be read accurately on a scale employing the kinedynamic units.

$$\text{KDU} = \text{centistokes} \times \sqrt{\frac{7.02\rho}{8.02 - \rho}}$$

$$\text{KDU} = \text{centipoises} \times \sqrt{\frac{7.02}{(8.02 - \rho)\rho}}$$

where 7.02 and 8.02 are used when the floats in a two-float Viscorator (Fischer & Porter) are number 316 stainless steel having a specific gravity of 8.02.

Units such as the time-Engler, Redwood, degrees-Engler, API, and Barbey may be found in chemical handbooks or viscosimeter conversion charts.

REVIEW QUESTIONS AND PROBLEMS

7-10 Describe, with the aid of a neat diagram, any one of the following methods of determining the viscosity of a liquid: (a) concentric-cylinders method, (b) Stokes method, (c) Hagen-Poiseuille method, (d) torque method.

7-11 Verify that the following statement is true:

$$\text{Kinematic viscosity (centistokes)} = \frac{\text{absolute viscosity (centipoise)}}{\text{mass density}}$$

at the same temperature as the viscosity reading.

7-12 (a) Distinguish between seconds Saybolt Universal and the seconds Saybolt Furol.

(b) Describe, briefly and with the aid of a sketch, the operation of the Saybolt viscometer.

7-13 Convert a viscosity of 500 seconds Saybolt at 60°F to kinematic viscosity, in ft²/sec units.

7-14 The equation used with the Saybolt viscosimeter is

$$\mu = \rho \left[2.2 \times 10^{-3} t - \frac{1.8}{t} \right]$$

where μ is the viscosity, in poises, ρ is the mass density, in g/cm³, and t is the time, in seconds, for 60 cm³ of the liquid to run out of a specified orifice capillary of the viscosimeter having an ID of 0.0695 and a length of 0.483 in. If the time taken for 60 cm³ of an oil of specific gravity 0.92 to run out is 130 sec, compute the viscosity.

7-15 When a sphere of radius r cm sinks in a viscous liquid at a constant velocity of v cm/sec and μ is the absolute viscosity of the liquid, in poises, the resistance to the motion of the sphere is found to be

$$R = 6\mu r v \pi \quad \text{dynes}$$

Compute the viscosity of the liquid in which a sphere of diameter 0.0622 in. sinks 20 cm in 21.3 sec. The density of the liquid is 0.96 g/cm³ and that of the sphere is 7.9 g/cm³.

7-16 A laboratory viscometer of the Saybolt design is calibrated by two tests with liquids of known kinematic viscosity: $\nu_1 = 0.461$ stoke, $t_1 = 97$ sec; $\nu_2 = 0.18$ stoke, $t_2 = 46$ sec. Evaluate the constants K_1 and K_2 in the general equation $\nu = K_1 t + K_2/t$.

7-17 Describe briefly and with the aid of a diagram the design, operation, and construction of any continuous-reading or recording viscometer.

CHAPTER EIGHT

Fluid flow measurement

The book on the science of mechanics must precede the book of useful inventions.

LEONARDO DA VINCI

PRINCIPLES OF FLUID FLOW AND FLOW MEASUREMENT

Flow Measurement

Flow is defined as fluid in motion, where the term "fluid" includes liquids and gases. Flow measurement is very important in process plants, water treatment, and steam and gas production. Flowmetering was first used by the early Romans and Egyptians in their land-irrigation schemes for hydraulic and public utilities. Since then a number of famous scientists have been associated with flowmetering and fluid dynamics: Torricelli, Pascal, Leonardo da Vinci, Bernoulli, Stokes, Venturi, Reynolds, Von Karman, and Prandtl. Some of these names have already been mentioned in preceding sections of this text.

The term "flowmeter" refers to an instrument capable of measuring the quantity of fluid flowing in pipes and tubes. Weirs and open-channel flow-measuring elements used so frequently in water and sewage-treatment plants will be dealt with in a separate section.

There are two main classes of flowmeters. In the first class the rate of continuous flow is measured by means of a detecting element which produces a pressure-differential effect which is observable on a measuring device. This class of metering is termed the "inferential" or "head" class of meter because the flow may be deduced, indirectly, from the pressure-differential effect.

In the second class the fluid passes in successive quantities or displacements, either volumes or weights, filling and emptying in a cyclic manner containers of known capacities. The flow in this class of meter is deduced, directly, from this cyclic displacement movement. The discharge or flow rate is read on the dials incorporated in the body of the meter.

Class 1 *Inferential types of flowmeters*
Differential-pressure or head meters: Venturi tube, orifice plate, flow nozzle, Pitot tube (strictly a velocity meter)
Variable-area meters, Rotameters and Flowrators
Anemometers
Electrical meters

Class 2 *Displacement, volumetric, or quantity meters (mechanical and electrical):*

Piston   Spiral vane
Nutating disk   Bellows
Oscillating piston   Current
Rotary bucket

Flow of liquids. When a liquid flows through a passage such as a pipeline, it will be subjected to resistance due to friction and viscosity. If the average velocity of the fluid is very low, the fluid will flow in parallel lines along the sides of the pipe. In such a case the flow is said to be laminar, viscous, or streamline. If the velocity is increased beyond a certain critical value when eddy currents start to form, the laminar flow pattern is changed and the flow becomes turbulent.

Criterion of flow. The pattern of flow can be determined by evaluating the Reynolds number (Re), which is a term without dimension. The Reynolds number, used as a criterion of flow, takes into account the diameter of the pipe, mass density, velocity, and the dynamic viscosity of the fluid. The Reynolds number may be expressed as

$$\text{Re} = \frac{d\rho v}{\mu} \quad \text{or} \quad \text{Re} = \frac{dv}{\nu}$$

where d = pipe diameter, $[L]$
ρ = mass density of the fluid, $[M/L^3]$
v = velocity of the fluid, $[L/T]$
μ = dynamic viscosity, $[M/LT]$
ν = kinematic viscosity, $[L^2/T]$

Using dimensional analysis on the expressions,

$$\text{Re} = \frac{\rho \, dv}{\mu} = \frac{dv}{\nu}$$

$$\text{Re} = \frac{[ML^{-3}][L][LT^{-1}]}{[ML^{-1}T^{-1}]} = \frac{[L][LT^{-1}]}{[L^2T^{-1}]} = 1$$

Hence Reynolds number is nondimensional and is, as defined, just a number.

The critical value of the velocity occurs when the Reynolds number is equal to about 2,000, and is given by the expression $v_c = 2,000$. In practice it is found that:

1. If the Re value is less than 2,000, the flow is laminar, viscous, or streamline.
2. If the Re value is between 2,000 and 4,000, the flow is critical, i.e., in a transition phase, changing from laminar, viscous, or streamline to turbulent, or vice versa.
3. If the Re value is greater than 4,000, the flow is turbulent.

Figure 8-1 shows what the pattern of flow is like under viscous- and turbulent-flow conditions in a cross section of a pipeline. In viscous flow,

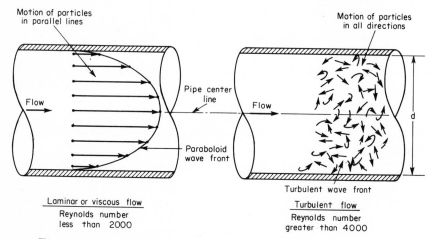

Fig. 8-1   Pattern of flow under viscous and turbulent conditions.

the velocity distribution takes the form of a paraboloid and the average velocity is half the maximum. Maximum velocity generally occurs at the center (Fig. 8-2). In turbulent flow, the velocity-distribution curve is flatter than in laminar flow.

Flow Measurement Fundamentals

Fluid friction. Fluids in motion are subjected to certain resistances which are assumed to be caused by friction, i.e., viscosity, which is the resistance to sliding between two adjacent layers of the fluid. Viscous resistance is a shear resistance and is probably due to overcoming the tension between the particles. This resistance of a fluid to tension occurs because of molecular attraction of the particles in the fluid.

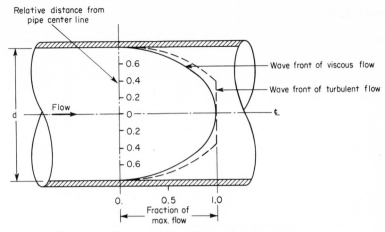

Fig. 8-2   Velocity distribution in viscous flow.

In practical experiments on flow measurements it is generally found that for steady viscous or streamline motion of a liquid, i.e., for velocities of less than the critical value, the frictional resistance is:

1. Proportional to the velocity
2. Proportional to the area of surface in contact
3. Independent of the pressure value
4. Greatly affected by temperature changes
5. Independent of the nature of the surface in contact

Point 5 infers that, when a liquid is flowing past a surface with a velocity of less than the critical velocity, a film of stationary liquid is formed over the surface. The resistance to flow in the rest of the pipe is caused by viscosity only.

When the flow is increased beyond the critical velocity, i.e., when turbulent flow occurs, frictional resistance is:

1. Proportional to the square of the velocity
2. Proportional to the mass density
3. Independent of pressure value
4. Independent of temperature effects which are negligible for small changes
5. Directly proportional to the area of surface in contact

Point 6 infers that the internal surface of the pipe is an important factor; i.e., the smoother the surface the lower is the frictional resistance.

Reynolds' Experiment on Flow through Circular Pipes

Osborne Reynolds carried out a number of experiments on the flow of fluids. An important one was performed to determine the loss of head or pressure in a pipe flow by measuring the fall of pressure over a known length of the pipe. From the fall in pressure, i, the slope of the hydraulic gradient is obtained.

$$i = \frac{h_L}{L} = \frac{\text{head loss between two sections of the pipe}}{\text{the distance between these sections}}$$

i.e., i = head loss per unit length of pipe. *Note:* The static head is the head of water due to the radial pressure of the liquid which acts outward in all directions.

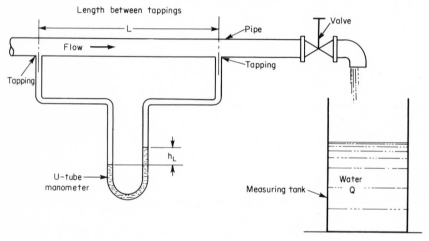

Fig. 8-3   Reynolds' experiment on flow.

The laboratory apparatus is set up as shown in Fig. 8-3. The velocity of the water in the pipe is obtained by timing the filling of a graduate with a stopwatch:

$$v = \frac{Q}{A}$$

where Q is volumetric flow per unit of time, and A is the internal area of the pipe. Tests are repeated for several velocities (by regulating the open position of the valve), and the corresponding values of h_L are recorded.

If a graph is plotted, the results are as indicated in Fig. 8-4. The graph indicates that a straight line exists up to a certain velocity; beyond this value the curve takes on an upward bend.   It is evident that the top portion of the curve follows an algebraic function of the type $i = kv^n$, where k and n are constants. In the straight-line portion of the graph, the value of n is unity. The values for n and k for the curved portion may be found by plotting log i or log (h_L/L) against log v.

Since $i = h_L/L = kv^n$, the logarithmic equation becomes

$$\log \frac{h_L}{L} = \log k + n \log v$$

Consider $v = 1$; then $\log v = 0$ and $\log (h_L/L) = \log k$. Hence, by referring to log tables, the value of k can be readily found. To find n, the equation

$$n = \frac{\log (h_L/L) - \log k}{\log v}$$

where $\log v \neq 0$, is used.

Fig. 8-4 Graph of head loss per unit length of pipe against velocity.

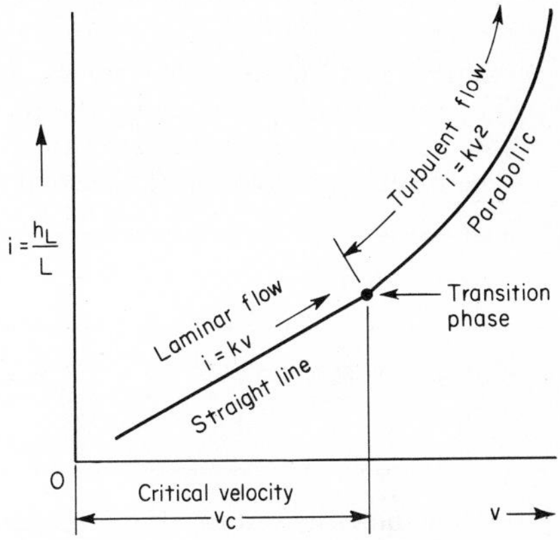

Now, if a new graph is constructed by plotting log v along the horizontal axis and log (h_L/L) along the vertical axis, the result will be similar to that shown in Fig. 8-5. The portion of the graph for which n is unity is the straight line AB. The remaining portion of the graph

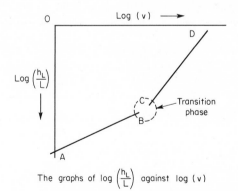

The graphs of log $\left(\frac{h_L}{L}\right)$ against log (v)

Fig. 8-5 The graphs of log (h_L/L) against log v.

appears as a straight line CD. The zone near the intersection of the two lines at C and B follows no defined law. This is because there is a transition phase, and viscous flow changes to turbulent or vice versa. The critical velocity occurs near the points C and B when Re = 2,000. The graph shows up two important points:

1. A viscous or laminar flow up to B
2. A turbulent flow for higher velocities beyond B

Example. Tests were performed on an 8-in. water pipe over a length of 8 ft. The velocity of flow through the pipe was regulated by means of a valve, and the corresponding head-loss values (using a U manometer) were recorded. The results are given in the accompanying table.

Test number	1	2	3	4	5
Velocity v, ft/sec	4.7	6.5	8.7	10.6	12.8
h_L/L	1.3×10^{-2}	2.5×10^{-2}	4.3×10^{-2}	6.3×10^{-2}	9.8×10^{-2}

Calculate the values of the constant k and n in the equation $h_L/L = kv^n$ and state whether the flow is viscous or turbulent.

Solution. The log values of v and h_L/L should be found and tabulated as in the accompanying table and the graph should be plotted.

Test number	1	2	3	4	5
$\log v$	0.672	0.813	0.940	1.025	1.108
$\log h_L/L$	-1.886	-1.601	-1.366	-1.200	-1.009

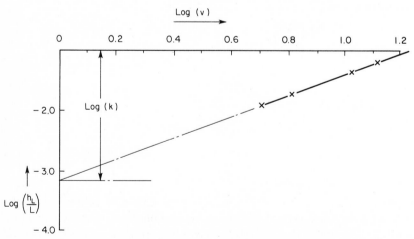

Fig. 8-6   The plot of log $(h_L/L) = \log k + n \log v$.

The graph will be as shown in Fig. 8-6. The calculations involved are the following:

When $\log v = 0$, $\quad \log k = \log \left(\dfrac{h_L}{L}\right)$

$$= -3.20 \quad \text{from the graph}$$

Looking up the antilog of 4.8, $k = 6.31 \times 10^{-4}$.

Now $\qquad n = \dfrac{\log (h_L/L) - \log k}{\log v} \qquad$ where $\log v \neq 0$

$$= \frac{-1.886 + 3.20}{0.672} = \frac{1.31}{0.672}$$

$$= 2.0 \quad \text{approx}$$

Therefore the general equation $(h_L/L) = kv^n$ now becomes $h_L/L = 6.31 \times 10^{-4} \times v^{2.0}$. In the term v^n, n is approximately equal to 2, which confirms the criterion discussed earlier for turbulent flow.

Color-band Method for Determining Critical Velocity

In addition to the method already described, the critical velocity may be found by allowing water to flow through a glass tube and injecting a thin stream of colored liquid (potassium permanganate solution) into the center of the stream. As long as the velocity is below the critical value the color band will remain in a straight line pattern along the center of the stream. As soon as the velocity exceeds the critical value, the colored band will be broken up because of turbulence and will mix with the water.

Loss of Head Due to Friction

The diagram in Fig. 8-7 shows two pressure gauges installed some distance apart in a pipeline. Because of friction there will be a head or

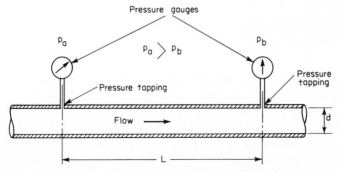

Fig. 8-7   Pressure loss in a length of pipe.

pressure loss between the two pressure locations. The pressure p_a will be greater than p_b because of the distance L that the fluid has to flow between the two gauges. Rational expressions for the loss of head or pressure due to friction are formulated in textbooks dealing specifically with mechanics of fluids, and they are reproduced here for reference purposes only. The head loss for laminar or viscous flow based on Poiseuille's equation is

Head loss (ft)

$$= \frac{32 \times \text{viscosity } \mu \times \text{length of pipe } L \text{ (ft)} \times \text{average velocity } v}{\text{weight density } w \times [\text{diameter } d \text{ (ft)}]^2}$$

$$h_L = \frac{32\mu L v}{w d^2} = \frac{32 \nu L v}{g d^2}$$

since

$$\nu = \frac{\mu}{\rho} = \frac{\mu}{w/g} = \frac{\mu g}{w}$$

$$\frac{\mu}{w} = \frac{\nu}{g}$$

The head-loss expression is usually written as a function of velocity head, and by rearrangement

$$h = \frac{64}{vd} \cdot \frac{L}{d} \cdot \frac{v^2}{2g} = \frac{64}{\text{Re}} \frac{L}{d} \frac{v^2}{2g}$$

For laminar or viscous flow in all pipes for all fluids the value of Darcy's friction factor f_L is

$$f_L = \frac{64}{\text{Re}}$$

where Re is the Reynolds number and its practical maximum for laminar flow is 2,000. Hence, the head loss

$$h_L = f \frac{L}{d} \frac{v^2}{2g}$$

Head loss for turbulent flow is given by the Darcy-Weisbach equation:

$$\text{Head loss (ft)} = \text{friction factor } f_t \times \frac{\text{length of pipe } L \text{ (ft)}}{\text{diameter } d} \times \text{velocity head } \frac{v^2}{2g}$$

$$h_L = f_t \frac{L}{d} \frac{v^2}{2g}$$

For turbulent flow a simple mathematical relation between the friction factor f_t and Reynolds number Re does not exist. The condition of the internal pipe walls and the degree of smoothness, a difficult quality to evaluate with reasonable accuracy, cause complex forms of turbulence and different values of f_t for the same Reynolds number. However, in actual head-loss computations, the values of f_t are selected from a set of curves found in most handbooks on fluid mechanics.

Velocity head. Consider water flowing from a tank under a constant head H. Let v be the velocity of the water, in feet per second, leaving at the orifice or opening near the bottom of the tank. Imagine a small quantity of water of weight w on the top surface. This quantity will have a potential energy equal to the product wH. Now this same quantity of water, when issuing through the circular opening, may be considered as having fallen through the height H. Potential energy is then converted to kinetic energy of the particle at the exit. This is shown in Fig. 8-8. If frictional losses for the moment are ignored then,

$$\text{Loss of potential energy} = \text{gain in kinetic energy}$$

or

$$wH = w\frac{v^2}{2g}$$

where g = gravitational acceleration.

Using dimensional analysis,

$$[F][L] = [F]\frac{[L^2/T^2]}{[L/T^2]} = [F][L]$$

By rearrangement

$$v = \sqrt{2gH} \qquad \text{or} \qquad H = \frac{v^2}{2g}$$

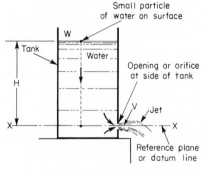

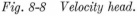

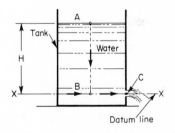

Fig. 8-8 *Velocity head.*   Fig. 8-9 *Analysis of energy levels.*

Bernoulli's Equation (Frictionless Flow)

Each particle of water in the tank system has the same total energy, regardless of position. This principle, known as the Bernoulli principle, is very useful in solving problems on the flow of liquids. (The derivation and application of the Bernoulli equation for fluid flow in pipes will be taken up later.) Bernoulli's principle on the conservation of energy may be written as follows: Let Z be the height of any particle of water considered above a chosen datum line or reference level.

Z = potential energy per pound of water (due to elevation of water particle)

$v^2/2g$ = kinetic energy per pound of water (due to velocity of water particle)

p/w = pressure energy per pound of water (due to pressure of water particle)

Then, according to Bernoulli's equation

$$\text{Total energy per pound of water} = Z + \frac{p}{w} + \frac{v^2}{2g} = \text{constant}$$

where w = the specific or weight density, i.e., lb/ft³
$\quad p$ = pressure, in psi, × 144 for fps units
$\quad v$ = velocity, ft/sec
$\quad Z$ = head, ft

Dimensionally

$$[L] + \frac{[F/L^2]}{[F/L^3]} + \frac{[L^2/T^2]}{[L/T^2]} = [L] + [L] + [L]$$

where F is the dimension for force, i.e., pound weight. Hence units are in feet head of water, i.e., in the dimension of $[L]$.

To go back to the tank, as shown in Fig. 8-9, consider the water flow through an orifice in the side of the tank with a velocity v under the static head H. Apply Bernoulli's energy equation to the points A, B, and C:

$$\text{Total energy at } A = \text{total energy at } B = \text{total energy at } C$$

Symbolically,

$$Z_a + \frac{p_a}{w} + \frac{v_a^2}{2g} = Z_b + \frac{p_b}{w} + \frac{v_b^2}{2g} = Z_c + \frac{p_c}{w} + \frac{v_c^2}{2g}$$

Applications of Bernoulli's principle may be observed in the laboratory aspirator, which serves as a useful vacuum pump, and also in the Venturi tube used in the simple up-draft carburetor of early car engines.

In the simple case of a liquid flow through a horizontal pipe or tube under conditions of no turbulence and negligible frictional losses, Bernoulli's equation may be written as

$$\frac{p_a}{w} + \frac{v_a^2}{2g} = \frac{p_b}{w} + \frac{v_b^2}{2g} = \text{constant}$$

where $Z_a = Z_b$, since the datum line is taken along the horizontal pipe centerline, and where the subscript a indicates conditions at a pipe section a–a and subscript b indicates conditions at a subsequent pipe section b–b.

To return to the tank problem, assume the line X–X to be the selected datum line through the center of the orifice opening and ignore atmospheric pressure, which is constant throughout. Then the equation yields

$$H + 0 + 0 = 0 + \frac{p_b}{w} + 0 = 0 + 0 + \frac{v_c^2}{2g}$$

Consider the arrangement shown in Fig. 8-10, which could be used for measuring the velocity at various sections across a river or open channel

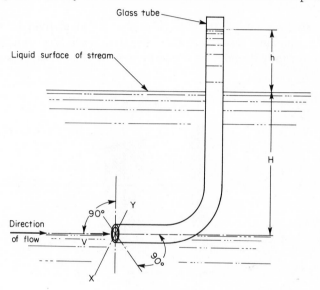

Fig. 8-10   The simple Pitot tube for measuring velocity of a stream flow.

in order to find the flow rate. Applying Bernoulli's energy equation to Y and X, which are respectively just inside and just outside the opening or mouth of the tube,

$$\text{Total energy at } Y = \text{total energy at } X$$

Then for steady conditions

$$\text{Stagnation pressure head} = H + h = H + \frac{v^2}{2g}$$

hence
$$h = \frac{v^2}{2g} \quad \text{or} \quad h = \frac{kv^2}{2g}$$

k is a correction coefficient depending upon the quality and precision of manufacture of the instrument. Correction for surface tension is another factor included in the correction factor. Hence $v = C\sqrt{2gh}$, where C is referred to as the Pitot-tube coefficient. The Pitot static tube used primarily in gas-flow measurements will be dealt with later on. Its construction and application will then be discussed in detail.

Obstructions. Any obstruction in the passage, any change of section, or any change in direction will interfere with steady flow conditions. Any one of the three causes eddy currents or transverse motion of the fluid particles, and the net effect is additional loss of energy due to friction.

Equation of Continuity

Consider an incompressible fluid (a perfect or ideal fluid in which no volumetric changes occur during a pressure variation) whose weight density is constant throughout the fluid and which is flowing steadily in a

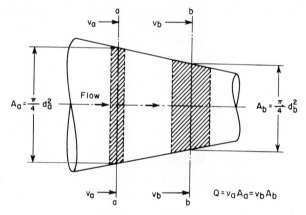

Fig. 8-11   Continuity of flow through a tapered pipe.

tapered pipe as shown in Fig. 8-11. For steady flow the rate of discharge is constant. For section a–a:

$$\text{Area} = A_a \qquad (\text{ft}^2)$$
$$\text{Velocity} = v_a \qquad (\text{ft/sec})$$

Hence

$$\text{Flow rate or discharge} = A_a v_a \qquad \text{ft}^3/\text{sec}$$

Since the same amount of fluid passes through section b–b

$$A_a v_a = A_b v_b = \text{rate of flow through the pipe}$$

The velocity at the narrow section b–b, shown in Fig. 8-11, is greater than that at a–a because the fluid particles must be pushed through the narrow section more quickly in order to maintain a constant flow rate.

Example. Consider water flowing through a pipe similar to that shown in Fig. 8-11. If the diameter at a–a is 12 in. and that at b–b is 6 in., calculate the velocity at each section if the constant flow rate is 10 ft³/sec. In liquid-flow measurement the weight density may be considered constant if pressure and temperature variations are insignificant.

Solution

$$Q \text{ (ft}^3/\text{sec)} = A_a \text{ (ft}^2\text{)} \times v_b \text{ (ft/sec)}$$

Using dimensional analysis,

$$\left[\frac{L^3}{T}\right] = [L^2]\left[\frac{L}{T}\right] = \left[\frac{L^3}{T}\right]$$
$$Q = A_a v_a = A_b v_b$$
$$10 \text{ ft}^3/\text{sec} = \frac{\pi}{4} d_a^2 \text{ ft}^2 \times v_a$$

$d_a = 12$ in. $= 1$ ft; hence

$$v_a = \frac{10 \times 4}{\pi}$$
$$= 13.3 \text{ ft/sec}$$

and
$$v_b = \frac{A_a}{A_b} v_a = \frac{d_a^2/4}{d_b^2/4} v_a$$
$$= \frac{d_a^2}{d_b^2} v_a$$
$$= \frac{1^2}{(\frac{1}{2})^2} v_a$$
$$= 4v_a = 4 \times 13.3$$
$$= 53.2 \text{ ft/sec}$$

$$\text{Mass-flow rate} = \rho A v$$

where ρ is the mass density.

$$\text{Weight-flow rate} = \omega A v$$

where ω is the weight density (or specific weight).

Rate of discharge or volume flow rate $Q =$
area of pipe $\times$ average velocity of flow

Gas Flow

In gas-flow problems the weight density is not constant, but varies with pressure and temperature, and it is necessary to use the gas-law equation $pV = RT$. R can be found from the equation

$$R = \frac{P}{wT} \qquad \text{or} \qquad R = \frac{PV}{T}$$

where P = absolute pressure
    T = temperature, degrees abs
    V = volume
    V_s = specific volume of a substance (volume per unit weight, or
        V_s = $1/w$, where w is the weight density)
The dimensions of R are

$$\frac{[FL^{-2}]}{[FL^{-3}](T)} = \frac{L}{T}$$

where T is the absolute temperature. Typical units in the engineering system are feet per degree Rankine or per degree Fahrenheit absolute. Values of R for some of the commonly used gases are given in Table 8-1.

Table 8-1   Reference data for some gases

Gas	Weight density at 68°F, lb/ft³	Gas constant R, ft/°R	Kinematic viscosity at 68°F and 1 atm, ft²/sec
Air	0.075	53.3	16.0×10^{-5}
Carbon dioxide	0.115	34.9	9.0×10^{-5}
Methane	0.042	96.2	19.3×10^{-5}
Nitrogen	0.073	55.1	17.0×10^{-5}
Oxygen	0.083	48.2	17.0×10^{-5}
Sulfur dioxide	0.170	23.6	5.6×10^{-5}

Example. A gas flows isothermally (at constant temperature) through a pipeline at the rate of 3 lb/sec. At one pipe section the diameter is 6 in., the pressure is 40 psia, and the temperature is 60°F. The gas constant R = 65 ft/°F abs. It is required to find the weight density w and the velocity v.

Solution. Applying the gas equation $w = P/RT$,

$$w = \frac{40 \times 144}{65(460 + 60)}$$
$$= 0.17 \text{ lb/ft}^3$$

Weight flow-rate = wAv

$$3 \text{ lb/sec} = (0.17 \text{ lb/ft}^3)(v \text{ ft/sec})\left(\frac{\pi}{4} \times \frac{1}{4}\text{ ft}^2\right)$$

Note: Units balance on both sides of the equation.

$$v = \frac{3 \times 16}{0.17\pi}$$
$$= 90 \text{ ft/sec}$$

Discharge through orifices and nozzles. Consider again the tank containing water with a hole or orifice in the side through which the water can flow out, as shown in Fig. 8-12. The quantity of water passing through

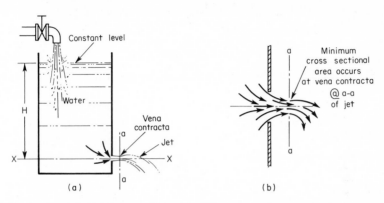

Fig. 8-12 (a) *Jet from orifice.* (b) *Magnified view at vena contracta.*

this orifice in a given interval of time will depend on the shape, size, and type of orifice. There will be a certain amount of frictional resistance at the sides or edge of the orifice. This resistance can be decreased by making the orifice sharp-edged, thereby reducing the contact area. The jet of water, in passing through the orifice, will contract in area as in the case of water from a tap or faucet. This contraction of area is caused by the water in the tank around the sides or edge of the orifice. The water, in flowing to the opening, will move in directions parallel to and perpendicular to the stream or jet.

The velocity in the perpendicular direction to the jet is destroyed on reaching the orifice, and instead there are lateral forces acting inward on the stream, causing the reduction of area. The section a–a of the jet at which the flow pattern first becomes parallel is called the *vena contracta.* The velocity at the vena contracta is now a maximum, and no further contraction in the stream occurs. In fact, the area appears to increase slightly on the downstream side of the vena contracta. The vena contracta is the determining factor when calculating flow through orifice plates, as will be seen later on.

Coefficient of contraction (C_c)

$$C_c = \frac{\text{area of jet at vena contracta}}{\text{area of orifice}}$$

This coefficient varies slightly with the head and the size, shape, and type of orifice. An average value for small, sharp-edged orifices may be taken as 0.65.

Coefficient of velocity (C_v)

$$C_v = \frac{\text{actual velocity at vena contracta}}{\text{theoretical value of velocity}}$$

If H is the head causing the flow and v_a is the actual velocity, then

$$C_v = \frac{v_a}{\sqrt{2gH}}$$

.The difference between the theoretical and actual velocities is caused by friction at the orifice edge and is very small for sharp-edged orifices. An average value for C_v is approximately 0.97, depending on the head, shape, and size of the orifice.

The coefficient C_v can readily be found experimentally. Consider the laboratory equipment shown set up in Fig. 8-13. Let the orifice in the

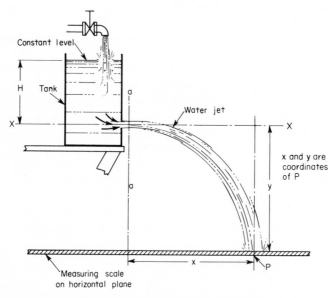

Fig. 8-13   Experiment to find C_v.

tank be parallel to the base, and keep the head constant by regulating the water tap. The horizontal (x) and vertical (y) ordinates of a point P in the jet can now be measured. The jet of water has a horizontal velocity of v but is acted upon by gravity g. Consider a particle of water in the jet at a–a and let t sec be the time for this particle to travel to point P. From simple dynamics

$$x = vt \qquad \text{and} \qquad y = \tfrac{1}{2}gt^2$$

By combining these two equations, the theoretical value of the velocity is obtained

$$v = \sqrt{\frac{gx^2}{2y}}$$

Hence

$$C_v = \frac{v}{\sqrt{2gH}} = \sqrt{\frac{gx^2/2y}{2gH}} = \frac{x}{2\sqrt{yH}}$$

Therefore, the value of C_v can be found from the final expression by measuring the distances x and y for a particular point in the jet and knowing the value of the height H. The coefficient of velocity can also be found by measuring the actual velocity of the jet by means of a simple Pitot tube.

Individually, the coefficients of velocity and contraction have little practical importance, whereas the coefficient of discharge is of major importance.

Coefficient of discharge (C_d)

$$C_d = \frac{\text{actual discharge}}{\text{theoretical discharge}}$$

Owing to resistance and friction, the actual discharge will be less than the theoretical calculated value. The coefficient of contraction can be determined by dividing the coefficient of discharge by the coefficient of velocity.

Differential-head Method of Flow Measurement

In flow measurement and metering, Bernoulli's equation as applied to incompressible fluid flow is initially written as

$$\Delta h = \frac{p_a - p_b}{w} = \frac{v_b^2 - v_a^2}{2g} + (Z_b - Z_a) + h_l$$

where Δh = head difference
h_l = head loss due to friction
which is derived from

$$Z_a + \frac{p_a}{w_a} + \frac{v_a^2}{2g} = Z_b + \frac{p_b}{w_b} + \frac{v_b^2}{2g}$$

This equation is true only if no external energies are added as from pumps, fans, or heat exchangers installed between the two sections a–a and b–b under investigation. In practice, when measuring a continuous flow, the pressure tappings are usually fairly close to each other so that h_l can be neglected. The development of Bernoulli's theorem for both compressible and incompressible fluids is given in Appendix B at the back of the book.

The largest and most useful group of flow-measuring devices is that which uses, as an indication of the quantity of flow, the difference in pressure resulting from a narrow constriction in the pipe through which the liquid is flowing. Such measuring instruments are based on the discoveries, in 1797, of the Italian Giovanni Venturi, who announced that fluids under pressure gain speed but lose head in passing through converging pipes and that the reverse is true for fluids flowing through diverging tubes.

The simple Venturi meter. Clemens Herschel was the first to put Venturi's principle into practice as a means of measuring flow. He made a series of tests with convergent-divergent tubes. He showed that the difference in pressure at the inlet and the contracted section or throat was related to the rate of flow. He called his instrument a *Venturi meter.*

Figure 8-14 shows the operation of a simple Venturi meter which is used to measure the flow velocity of liquids. (Later on, gas flow will be

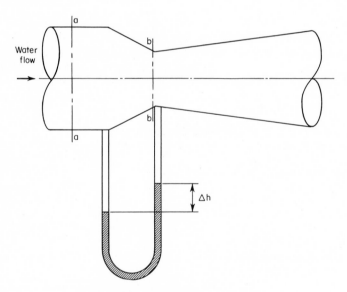

Fig. 8-14   Simple Venturi meter.

considered.) A liquid-filled U-tube manometer can be used to find the differential pressure or head, that is, $(p_a - p_b)/w$. For density effect see page 213. Let

A_a = area of pipe of inlet section a–a
A_b = area of constriction or the root section b–b

From the equation of continuity for steady flow

$$A_a v_a = A_b v_b$$

Hence
$$v_a = \frac{A_b}{A_a} v_b$$

$$= \left(\frac{d_b}{d_a}\right)^2 v_b$$

where d_a = internal pipe diameter at section a–a

d_b = diameter of constriction or throat diameter at section b–b

Bernoulli's equation can now be rewritten in the following way:

$$\frac{p_a - p_b}{w} = \frac{1}{2g}(v_b{}^2 - v_a{}^2) = \frac{1}{2g}\left(v_b{}^2 - \frac{A_b{}^2}{A_a{}^2}v_b\right) = \frac{v_b{}^2}{2g}\left[1 - \left(\frac{d_b}{d_a}\right)^4\right]$$

or
$$\frac{p_a - p_b}{w} = \frac{v_a{}^2}{2g}\left[\left(\frac{d_a}{d_b}\right)^4 - 1\right]$$

Summary. It is seen that the pressure drop between a–a and b–b is dependent upon the flow of the fluid and the ratio of the areas of the pipe to the area of the throat. If the differential pressure is known, then the rate of flow can be calculated from the equation

$$Q = A_a v_a = A_b v_b$$

The velocity through the throat is greatly increased at the expense of a decrease in pressure. This may be explained if one imagines that the particles of the fluid, in going through the narrow restriction, have to do so at a rapid rate. There is little time for them to push radially; they can push only in the forward direction of motion. One particle, in going through, is pushed by the one behind; the one behind fills a void left by the one in front. This accounts for the reduction in pressure and increase in speed at the throat or restriction. Consider the following problem.

Example. If the value of A_a is 10 times that of A_b (at the throat) and colored water is used in the manometer, calculate the velocity of v_a and that of v_b when the difference in levels is 6 in.

Solution. The velocity of flow at the throat or constriction is increased and the pressure is reduced sufficiently to cause the difference in levels of the liquid in the manometer or to show this difference by the reading on the corresponding pressure gauges.

1. Applying the equation of continuity:

$$A_a v_a = \frac{A_a}{10} v_b$$

$$v_b = 10 v_a$$

Hence
$$\frac{A_a}{A_b} = \frac{10}{1}$$

2. Applying Bernoulli's equation:

$$\Delta h = \frac{p_a - p_b}{w} = \frac{v_a{}^2}{2g}\left[\left(\frac{A_a}{A_b}\right)^2 - 1\right]$$

using dimensional analysis,

$$[L] = \frac{[F/L^2]}{[F/L^3]} = \frac{[L^2/T^2]}{[L/T^2]}$$

$$[L] = [L] = [L]$$

$$\Delta h = \frac{v_a{}^2}{2g}\left[\left(\frac{10}{1}\right)^2 - 1\right]$$

$$\frac{1}{2} = \frac{v_a{}^2}{2g}[100] \qquad \text{approx}$$

$$v_a = \sqrt{\frac{g}{100}}$$

$$v_a = 0.56 \text{ ft/sec} \qquad \text{Ans.}$$
$$v_b = 5.6 \text{ ft/sec} \qquad \text{Ans.}$$

It should be noted that these answers in the example are theoretical and that the true velocity will be less. The answers must be multiplied by the coefficient of discharge, which in the case of a Venturi meter is about 0.97. The design of Venturi tubes has been investigated very carefully, and standard dimensions have been determined. The student is referred to the publications of ASME, the British Standards Association, VdI in Germany, etc.

Orifice plate. The diagram in Fig. 8-15 shows a restriction orifice plate inserted in the pipeline. As before, the relation between pressure and velocity can be established from Bernoulli's equation

$$\frac{p_a}{w_a} + \frac{V_a{}^2}{2g} + Z_a = \frac{p_b}{w_a} + \frac{V_b{}^2}{2g} + Z_b$$

where p_a, p_b = static pressures, in psia, at a–a and b–b

$\quad v_a$, v_b = corresponding fluid velocities

$\quad Z_a$, Z_b = elevation of the pipe center lines at a–a and b–b

$\quad w_a$, w_b = respective weight densities of the fluid

$\quad A_a$, d_a = area and diameter at a–a

$\quad A_b$, d_b = area and diameter at b–b

$\quad g$ = gravitational acceleration

In general flowmetering practice the difference in level $Z_a - Z_b$ is insignificant even when vertical installations are considered. For incompressible flow it is assumed that there is no change in weight density; thus $w_a = w_b$. Hence, by rearrangement, the Bernoulli equation becomes

$$v_b{}^2 - v_a{}^2 = \frac{2g}{w}(p_a - p_b)$$

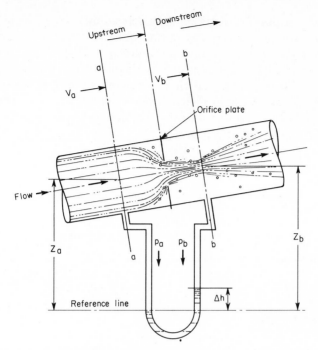

Fig. 8-15 Fluid flow through an orifice in a closed pipe.

Using dimensional analysis

$$\left[\frac{L^2}{T^2}\right] = \frac{[L/T^2]}{[F/L^3]}\left[\frac{F}{L^2}\right] = \left[\frac{L^2}{T^2}\right]$$

The volumetric flow rate Q (say, ft³/sec) from the equation of continuity gives

$$Q = A_b v_b = A_a v_a$$

Using dimensional analysis,

$$\left[\frac{L^3}{T}\right] = [L^2]\left[\frac{L}{T}\right] = \left[\frac{L^3}{T}\right]$$

The corresponding weight flow rate W (lb/sec) is

$$W = w A_b v_b$$

Using dimensional analysis,

$$\left[\frac{F}{T}\right] = \left[\frac{F}{L^3}\right][L^2]\left[\frac{L}{T}\right] = \left[\frac{F}{T}\right]$$

The area A_b shown in Fig. 8-15 is not an area that can be explicitly known. The point of minimum area, which occurs at the vena contracta, is located at a position along the pipe depending on the flow rate. In any practical scheme the pressure connections or taps for measuring the upstream and downstream pressures must be fixed at specified positions. The American Society of Mechanical Engineers (ASME), the American Gas Association (AGA), and the Instrument Society of America (ISA) have publications on fluid meters, their use and recommended practice, which should be consulted for correct selection.

From the equation of continuity

$$v_a = \frac{A_b}{A_a} v_b$$

The result of substituting this in the velocity equation is

$$v_b{}^2 \left[1 - \left(\frac{A_b}{A_a} \right)^2 \right] = \frac{2g}{w} (p_a - p_b)$$

This then yields an expression for the velocity v_b:

$$v_b = \frac{1}{\sqrt{1 - (A_b/A_a)^2}} \sqrt{\frac{2g}{w} (p_a - p_b)}$$

The flow-rate equation then becomes

$$Q = A_b K \sqrt{\frac{2g}{w} (p_a - p_b)}$$

where $\qquad K \text{ (flow coefficient)} = \dfrac{C}{\sqrt{1 - \beta^4}}$

$$C = \text{coefficient of discharge}$$

$$\beta = \frac{d_b}{d_a}$$

$$A_b = \frac{\pi}{4} d_b{}^2$$

The final equation for the flow rate becomes, for incompressible and ideal fluids,

$$Q = \frac{\pi d_b{}^2}{4} K \sqrt{\frac{2g}{w} (p_a - p_b)}$$

There are three generally accepted positions for the upstream and downstream taps for which this K coefficient has been established: (1) flange taps, where the holes are integral with the flange, (2) taps arranged $1D$ upstream and $D/2$ downstream, which are very close to being vena contracta taps, thus yielding a maximum pressure drop, and (3) pipe taps $2.5D$ upstream and $8D$ downstream, which give a pressure drop equal to the total loss of pressure; i.e., there is no further pressure recovery. The K coefficient for the three positions are tabulated in the

ASME handbook *Fluid Meters*. (Note: In Great Britain the coefficient of discharge has also been established for corner taps. See Fig. 8-19.)

Example. Water flowing through a 12-in.-diam pipe having a 6-in.-diam orifice causes a manometer gauge to indicate a differential pressure of 3.5 ft. The specific gravity of the manometer liquid is 1.25. The value of K is found to be 0.98. Calculate the flow rate, in cubic feet per second.

Solution. To find the differential pressure head, the principles of the differential gauge must be used. (For density effect, see p. 213.)

$$\frac{p_a - p_b}{w} = \Delta h = 1.25 \times 3.5 - 3.5 = 0.88 \text{ ft}$$

Hence

$$Q = \frac{\pi}{4} d_b^2 K \sqrt{\frac{2g(p_a - p_b)}{w}}$$

$$Q = \frac{\pi}{4} \left(\frac{6}{12}\right)^2 0.98 \sqrt{64.4 \times 0.88}$$

$$= \frac{\pi}{4} \times \frac{1}{4} \times 0.98 \times 7.54$$

$$= 1.5 \text{ ft}^3/\text{sec}$$

Orifice plates. The most common type of orifice plate consists of a thin plate of metal, circular in shape. Three forms, concentric, eccentric, and segmental (Fig. 8-16), are used. The concentric version has a small

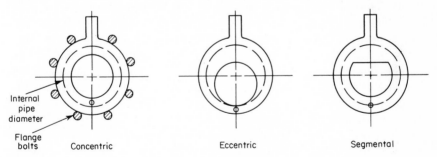

Fig. 8-16   Orifice plates.

central hole or orifice concentric with the circumference of the plate. Usually the design has to meet standard specifications conforming to ASI, ASME, or AGA recommendations. In the United Kingdom, the specifications are completely covered in British Standard Specifications No. 1042.

Figure 8-17 shows what occurs when an orifice plate is inserted in a fluid stream in a pipe. A liquid flow is considered because the glass piezometer tubes help to indicate the pressure from upstream to a downstream length of pipe. The pipe liquid will rise in these tubes until the pressure

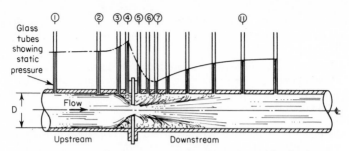

Fig. 8-17   Static-pressure gradient in orificed pipe.

due to the column of liquid in each tube is equal to the static pressure at that pipe section, as shown in Fig. 8-17. The column heights are then a measure of the pressure, and, by scanning the different values, the pattern of the pressure changes is observed as one proceeds along the pipe. At positions 1 and 2 no pressure change is significant. At 3 and 4, just before the orifice, there is a slight increase in pressure (owing to a back-pressure effect). The stream is then constrained to flow through the smaller area of the orifice, from which a jet issues. At sections 5 and 6 lower pressures are observed than at the upstream side because of the change in the stream-section area.

At the orifice or restriction, the velocity of the stream has increased a great deal and the pressure has fallen. The stream becomes a jet whose cross-sectional area decreases after leaving the orifice until it reaches a point, position 7, where it is a minimum and the velocity is a maximum. This, it will be recalled, is the location of the vena contracta and is due to the liquid being directed inward as it approaches the orifice and, because of inertia effects, persisting in this direction for a distance after it leaves the orifice. The static pressure at position 7 is a minimum, and this locates the distance of the vena contracta from the orifice plate. The distance between the vena contracta and the orifice plate varies with the ratio of orifice diameter to pipe diameter, that is, d/D. However, on the average, the distance is about one-half the pipe diameter. From the vena contracta the stream or jet section expands until it reaches the pipe diameter at 11.

Two very important facts are deduced from a study of this diagram. First, the downstream static pressure never recovers its upstream value. This is due in part to the velocity changes being accompanied by turbulence, which results in the dissipation of energy and increasing fluid friction. Both involve a pressure loss. The pressure-distribution curve gives the fraction of differential pressure across the orifice for various values of the ratio of orifice diameter to pipe diameter d/D. Using a typical value of $d/D = 0.6$, the percent of orifice head recovered (maximum recovery) is about 32% at a distance of just over 4 pipe diameters downstream. (One pipe diameter is the length of pipe equal to the internal diameter of the pipe D.) The percent loss works out at over 65 percent of the differential pressure across the orifice plate. It should be pointed out that, where pressure loss is important along a pipeline, careful consideration must be given to the selection of the detecting element.

The second important point demonstrated by the static pressure tubes along the pipeline on both sides of the orifice plate is that there appear to be a variety of positions at which to take pressure tappings or make connections to the measuring device or instrument. As already mentioned, there are three positions for which orifice coefficients are available.

A further development is the Dall orifice plate (Fig. 8-18a), which is similar in principle to the Dall flow nozzle. It has the advantage of a

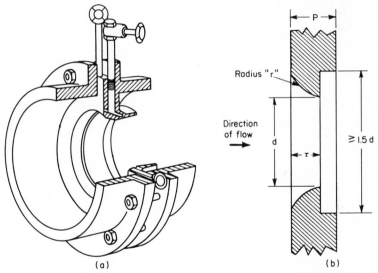

Fig. 8-18 (a) *A Dall short-insert tube.* (b) *Quarter-circle orifice plate.* [G. Kent (Canada) Ltd.]

very low net pressure loss, but it is unsuitable for fluids containing particles which might clog the small orifices.

When measuring highly viscous fluids such as bunker C oils, it may be desirable to use an orifice plate when the diameter of the pipe is in excess of 3 in., the maximum size for which variable-area meters are normally built. Under such conditions, however, the Reynolds number is below 10,000, so that large variations in flow will cause large variations in the orifice flow coefficient. This is due to the change in jet action in passing through the orifice plate. To overcome this, the use of an orifice plate with a rounded approach face was a possible solution, but there were certain difficulties in manufacture. However, after World War II a great deal of research work was done in this field by the oil companies. A design of orifice plate which gives reasonably good results for low Reynolds numbers is referred to as the quarter-circle orifice plate (Fig. 8-18*b*).

Nozzles. The flow nozzle is a design between the Venturi tube and the orifice plate, and it is used as a means of flow measurement. It is similar to a Venturi tube because of the curved form of approach, giving a gradual change of sectional area. The nozzle is cheaper than the Venturi tube in most industrial applications, but it is more expensive than the orifice plate. Figure 8-19*a* shows the ISA nozzle with corner tappings.

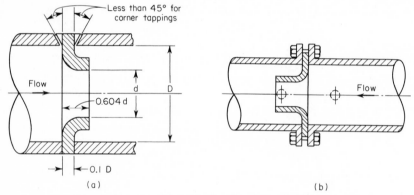

Fig. 8-19 (a) *ISA nozzle.* (b) *A typical flow nozzle.*

This is generally used when testing the discharge from compressors. The design shown in Fig. 8-19*b* is typical of an industrial style of nozzle with the pressure tappings placed about one pipe diameter upstream and the other in the vicinity of the nozzle outlet.

Flow nozzles are generally used for the measurement of high-velocity water or steam, where the pressure loss due to the use of an orifice plate would be excessive. In addition, for high-pressure fluids it is desirable that any primary measuring device be capable of being welded into the pipe, and the flow nozzle is the only type which can be. Nozzles are made by only one or two manufacturers, and therefore few published data are available on flow coefficients and pressure losses.

The Dall tube was designed by H. E. Dall of the George Kent Company. The tube is smaller and lighter than an equivalent short type of Venturi tube, and yet it gives far better differential-pressure recovery than the long type of Venturi tube. The Dall tube has a substantially lower pressure loss than any other known device. For these two reasons, the Dall tube is superior to any existing Venturi design, but it can be used only for fluids containing no particles which might clog the small open slot.

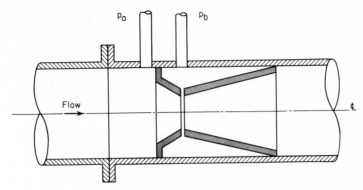

Fig. 8-20   Dall tube.

The Dall tube consists of a short length of parallel lead-in pipe followed by the converging upstream cone and the diverging downstream cone.

As shown in Fig. 8-20, in the Dall tube a circumferential slot or gap is formed between the smaller diameters of the two cones, which have a large included angle. It is at this slot that the lower pressure is measured. The effect of the abrupt change in contour of the flow results in adding a "streamline curvature" head to the differential head produced in accordance with the Bernoulli flow equation. In brief, the pressure at the throat is increased by a significant amount, and the discharge coefficient is therefore much below unity, i.e., in the region of 0.6 to 0.75. It is interesting to note that the slot is similar to the antistalling device on an aircraft, which prevents the breaking away of the airstream at high angles of incidence.

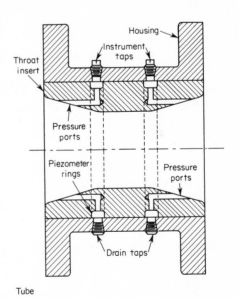

Fig. 8-21   Gentile flow tube.

The most recent addition to the designs of flow nozzles is the Gentile flow tube (Fig. 8-21), which is something like a Venturi tube. Instead of having the pressure tappings at right angles to the horizontal axis of the tube, however, it has them arranged like a double-ended Pitot, i.e., one facing upstream and one downstream. By this means the effect of static pressure is removed. A typical Gentile tube will have a coefficient of discharge of 0.93 and a pressure loss of 15 percent of the differential pressure. It has been constructed in sizes up to 72 in. The suppliers claim that the usual lengths of straight run upstream and downstream of the flow tube are not required unless there is a control valve on the upstream side.

Correction factors   *Compressible fluids.* For compressible fluids such as gases and vapors, the density does not remain constant when the pressure changes from P_a to P_b. As discussed in earlier sections, an adiabatic gas expansion is considered to take place; i.e., no heat flows from or to the fluid and no external work is done on or by the fluid. Hence, the expression developed in Appendix B can now be used:

$$Q = EA_bY \sqrt{\frac{2g\,\Delta P}{w_a}}$$

where Y is a constant referred to as the compressibility or expansion factor and $\Delta P = P_a - P_b$, the differential pressure. The actual value of this factor is a function of the gas specific heat ratio k, the β ratio of the orifice, that is, d/D, and v, the ratio of the upstream and downstream pressures. Although this expansion factor can be calculated from the theoretical considerations, it is generally established experimentally. The results are published in the form of tables and curves on fluid flow.

Supercompressibility. At low temperatures and high pressures a further correction factor has to be applied when measuring gases, because under such conditions they no longer obey the ideal-gas laws. This factor, generally designated Z, is called the supercompressibility factor, and, in fact, it is a correction to the weight density. Because of this it is more convenient to give the correction as

$$\frac{1}{\sqrt{Z}} = F_{pv}$$

where $1/Z = S$, a further variant used in certain cases. For the ideal gas Z and S are unity. For real gases Z varies between 0.5 and 1.5 or S varies between 2.0 and 0.67. Values of Z can be obtained from compressibility charts.

The critical temperature and pressure can be found in any suitable reference book, such as the *Chemical Handbook*, for all the constituents of the gas in question. The critical pressure and temperature can then be found by multiplying the volumetric fraction of each element in the gas by its respective critical pressure and temperature and adding each set of figures to obtain two totals which give the critical pressure and critical temperature of the mixture. For example, if the gas contains 50 percent hydrogen and the pressure is known to be 165 atmos abs and the temperature 278°K, the critical pressure is found to be 12.8 atmos and the critical temperature 33°K. By the law of partial pressure, hydrogen provides 0.5 × 12.8 atmos and 0.5 × 33°K. The same calculating is done for each of the gas constituents, and the pressures and temperatures so arrived at are totaled to give the critical pressure and temperature of the gas of mixed composition. The reduced pressure and temperature can now be calculated and the *Z* factor read from a compressibility chart.

$$\text{Reduced pressure } P_v = \frac{\text{actual pressure absolute}}{\text{critical pressure absolute}}$$

$$\text{Reduced temperature } T_v = \frac{\text{actual temperature absolute}}{\text{critical temperature absolute}}$$

Moisture. One further correction may have to be made in order to take care of the moisture content of the gas. The development of the formulas is given in all standard reference works on fluid flow.

Determining orifice size. If the reader has to determine the size of an orifice plate, he must have a great deal more information than can be conveniently contained in a textbook of this nature and must consult the standard works on the subject. On the North American continent the gas industry has developed a system which includes orifice plates of standard sizes, thus enabling a selection to be made by the use of a set of tables. It should be pointed out, however, that using a standard orifice plate under any given conditions in which flow is reduced to standard cubic feet based on 60°F and 14.73 psia (30 in. Hg) and saturated, a round figure for maximum flow is not necessarily obtainable for the chosen differential pressure.

As already noted, the following variations have to be considered: specific gravity due to changes in composition, pressure, temperature, supercompressibility, expansion factor, and Reynolds number. If each of these is assigned a factor, the flow formula can be written as

$$Q = C' \sqrt{hP_2}$$

where Q = cubic feet per hour measured at standard conditions

h = differential pressure, in. H_2O

P_2 = absolute downstream pressure, psi

$C' = CF_GF_TF_{PV}F_{e2}F_R$ = constant

F_G = specific-gravity factor

F_T = flowing-temperature factor

F_{PV} = superexpansibility factor

F_{e2} = expansion factor

F_R = Reynolds number factor

and C is the standard hourly natural-gas coefficient, which in addition to standard conditions, noted above, includes the following theoretical conditions: Reynolds number is infinite and the value of the differential pressure divided by the absolute pressure is zero. The value of this coefficient depends on the location of the differential-pressure taps and the diameter of orifice and pipe.

In Great Britain the standard reference work, published by the British Standards Institution, is *Flow Measurement*, B.S. 1042. The approach is a little different because the coefficient of discharge C_d is tabulated, rather than the orifice coefficient K used in North America. Also, instead of using β to designate the diameter ratio d/D, β^2 is used. β^2 is designated m.

The theoretical formula for flow as developed earlier uses consistent units, but in the industrial field certain inconsistent units are in common use. It is therefore desirable to modify the theoretical formula for practical use. The following formulas are taken from B.S. 1042. When the orifice diameter is known, the flow can be calculated as follows:

In pounds per hour
$$L = 359.1 C_d Z d^2 E \sqrt{h} \sqrt{w}$$

In imp. gallons per hour
$$G = 2{,}239 C_d Z d^2 E \sqrt{h} \sqrt{\frac{1}{w}}$$

In standard cubic feet per hour
$$Q = 7{,}859 C_d Z d^2 E \sqrt{h} \sqrt{\frac{P_1}{TP}} N$$

To find the orifice diameter when the rate of flow is known for corresponding units,

$$C_d Z m E = \frac{L}{359.1 D^2 \sqrt{h} \sqrt{w}}$$

$$C_d Z m E = \frac{G}{2{,}239 D^2 \sqrt{h}\, 1/\sqrt{w}}$$

$$C_d Z m E = \frac{Q}{7{,}859 D^2 \sqrt{h} \sqrt{P_1/T_\rho}\, N}$$

where C_d = coefficient of discharge

Z = a combined multiplier, the product of three separately specified multipliers for Reynolds number, pipe diameter D, and expansion factor y

$$m = \frac{d^2}{D^2} = \beta^2$$

$E = \dfrac{1}{\sqrt{1 - m^2}} = \dfrac{1}{\sqrt{1 - \beta^4}}$ called the "velocity of approach factor"

h = differential pressure, in. H_2O at 60°F (under air)

w = weight density, lb_f/ft^3, under working conditions at the position of the high-pressure tapping

P_1 = absolute pressure of gas or air, psia, measured at the position of the high-pressure tapping

T = absolute temperature of the gas or air (°F + 460) measured at the position of the high-pressure tapping

ρ = specific gravity of dry gas, relative to dry air at the same pressure and temperature (for air $\rho = 1$)

N = correction for water vapor in gas or air

Note that in measuring gas the orifice is designed for the mean conditions of pressure and temperature under which it is likely to operate, so that the scale on the instrument will under these conditions read in standard cubic feet, i.e., generally 30 in. Hg, 60°F, and saturated. The formulas above are worked out on this basis.

If the operating conditions vary from the design conditions, then certain corrections have to be made to the instrument readings. These can be found from the following formula:

$$\text{Correction factor } F = \sqrt{\frac{P_a T_d \rho_d}{P_d T_a \rho_a}}$$

where P_a, T_a, and ρ_a refer to actual operating conditions and P_d, T_d, and ρ_d refer to design operating conditions. As far as pressure and temperature are concerned it will be noted that we are only applying Boyle's and Charles' laws. Variations in moisture content may also have to be corrected for, but the effect is relatively small. If the reader should need to consider this correction, he would have to consult the standard reference works on flow measurement.

Pitot tube. Reviewing the earlier material on the operation of the Pitot tube, it will be recalled that, from Bernoulli's equation,

$$\frac{p_a}{w} + \frac{v_a^2}{2g} = \frac{p_b}{w} + \frac{v_b^2}{2g}$$

Now consider the effect of inserting the spherical object in a fluid stream as an obstruction to the flow. As shown in Fig. 8-22, the velocity will decrease along the center line until it reaches zero at the point where it impinges the object. A deceleration, it will be remembered, means an increase in pressure. p_a/w and p_b/w are denoted by the term "pressure head," and $v_a^2/2g$ and $v_b^2/2g$ by the term "velocity head." Therefore, it can be stated that the velocity head $v_b^2/2g$ (at the point of impact or stagnation point) has become converted to a pressure head p_x/w. This will be additional to the normal static pressure head p_s/w, and the sum of these two is equivalent to p_b/w. Symbolically,

$$\frac{p_b}{w} = \frac{p_x}{w} + \frac{p_s}{w}$$

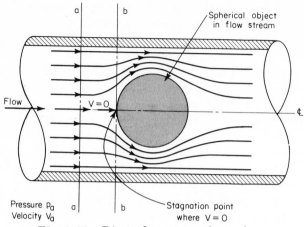

Fig. 8-22   Pitot tube—stagnation point.

From Bernoulli's equation, at the stagnation point where $v_b = 0$,

$$\frac{p_a}{w} + \frac{v_a{}^2}{2g} = \frac{p_b}{w}$$

hence
$$v_a = \sqrt{\frac{2g(p_b - p_a)}{w}}$$

If the object is now replaced by a tube having a small opening facing the direction of fluid flow as illustrated in Fig. 8-23, the velocity of flow can be

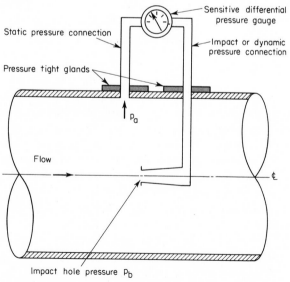

Fig. 8-23   Pitot tube.

measured. There is no flow through the tube, because velocity can be considered to be zero at the small impact hole. Instead, the velocity has produced the pressure head p_b/w at this point, and if a static pressure tapping is taken a little way upstream from the tube it will give p_a/w. If both pressure tappings are applied to a sensitive differential-pressure instrument (or U-tube manometer), a device for measuring the velocity of the fluid is obtained. Since g and w are known,

$$v_a = k(p_b - p_a)$$

where k is a combined constant.

It is important to measure the static pressure in the vicinity of the tube, and for this reason standard Pitot tubes are specified. Figure 8-24 shows

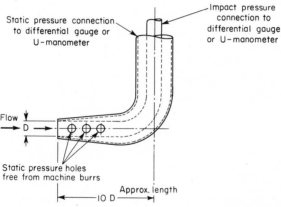

Fig. 8-24   Pitot static tube (sharp-ended head).

a popular design which is a combination of two concentric tubes used for airflow measurement. Here the static pressure is not measured by a piezometer but is measured close to the impact opening by means of small holes leading into the chamber formed by the inner and outer tubes. Pitot tubes of this design vary in size from $\frac{1}{8}$ to over 1 in. in diameter for large air ducts.

The main disadvantage of the Pitot static tube is that it can measure velocity at only one point at a time in the cross section of a pipe, duct, or tunnel. Now, the velocity of a fluid in a pipe, taken across the section, is not uniformly distributed; it varies from zero at the pipe wall to a maximum value near the pipe center line. In order to find the average velocity, it is necessary to make a traverse of the pipe or duct with the Pitot tube. The differential pressures at certain specified positions are carefully noted and recorded. Figure 8-25 indicates the positions and velocity readings in

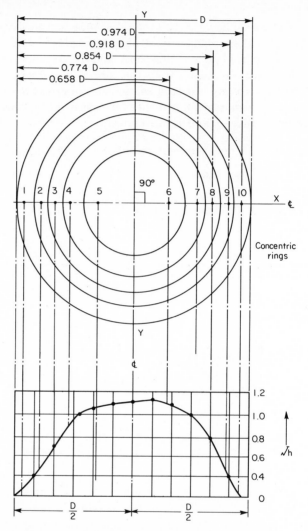

Fig. 8-25   Velocity gradient in a circular pipe.

a circular pipe. The pipe is considered as being divided into zones of equal area, and the velocity in each zone is found. Suppose five zones of equal area are required; this gives ten points on each diameter. These zones, or concentric rings of equal area, are formed by circles whose radii (r_1, r_2, r_3, r_4) are given by

$$r_1{}^2 = \frac{R^2}{5} \qquad r_2{}^2 = \frac{2R^2}{5} \qquad r_3{}^2 = \frac{3R^2}{5} \qquad r_4{}^2 = \frac{4R^2}{5}$$

where R is the radius of the pipe. The differential heads produced by the Pitot static tube when placed at points 1 to 10 are recorded. The points 1 to 10 are the points of the average radii of the annular zones from the pipe center line.

The readings are then repeated on a diameter at right angles to Y–Y, that is, along the X–X axis. This procedure is referred to in this case as method 1; an alternative method 2 is based on tests carried out at equidistant positions along the diameter of the pipe. The velocity curve or distribution $\sqrt{\Delta h}$ is plotted, and the values corresponding to points 1, 2, 3, etc., are read directly from the curve. In method 1 the average velocity can be found by finding the square root of the average velocity head. With method 1, for liquids,

$$V_{avg} = \sqrt{2gh_{avg}}$$

where h is expressed in feet head of the liquid being measured.

For gases,

$$V_{avg} = \sqrt{2gh_{avg}}$$

where h_{avg} is expressed in inches of water.

In method 2 the Pitot tube is placed from one side of the pipe to the other by equal increments. The velocity is then computed from each velocity head for each of these points and plotted on a graph. Plots of two traverses at right angles are made. The velocities at the points 1, 2, 3, . . . , 10 are read off and averaged.

For liquids $\qquad V_{local} = \sqrt{2gh_{local}}$

For gases $\qquad V_{local} = \dfrac{18.29}{\sqrt{w}} \sqrt{h_{local}}$

although, theoretically, $V = C\sqrt{2gh}$, where C is the coefficient of the instrument. The value of C is unity for values of Reynolds number exceeding 3,000.

The following are necessary precautions:

1. If results are to be accurate, the pipe or duct must not be helical. If a reasonable length of straight pipe is not available upstream of the Pitot tube, adequate straightening vanes must be installed.
2. The static and impact tubes must not be obstructed in any way, e.g., by incrustation.

The Pitot tube has the following advantages:

1. It produces no appreciable pressure loss.
2. It may be inserted through a small hole into the pipe or duct.

3. It is very useful for checking the flow of orifice plate, Venturi, or nozzle measuring elements.
4. It is used to plot a velocity distribution.
5. Its cost is low.
6. It is an exploratory device and rarely used permanently in industrial plants.

A limitation of the Pitot static tube is that the gas or liquid must be flowing at a high velocity in order to produce a noticeable differential. For example, an air velocity of approximately 50 ft/sec is necessary to set up a differential of 1 in. water head. For water a velocity of 5 ft/sec would set up a differential of 10 in. of water (¾ in. Hg approx).

In all types of Pitot tubes there is a chance of the axis of the head not being in alignment with the direction of the oncoming flow. An angle of yaw or misalignment up to 5° has little effect on the velocity values obtained; beyond 20° the error in the velocity determination is about 2 percent.

REVIEW QUESTIONS AND PROBLEMS

8-1 (a) Define the following terms in reference to flow measurement: laminar flow, critical velocity, and turbulent flow.
(b) Calculate the critical velocity, in feet per second, of a fluid flow in a 6-in.-ID pipe. The weight density of the fluid is 0.0764 lb/ft³, and the dynamic viscosity is 3.6×10^{-6} in the foot-pound units. Assume Re = 2,000.

8-2 (a) Why is the Reynolds number value important in fluid-flow calculations?
(b) Calculate the Reynolds number for the following flow conditions:
$v = 120$ ft/sec, $d = 8$ in., $w = 0.076$ lb/ft³, $\mu = 3.6 \times 10^{-6}$ fps units.
(c) Is the flow viscous or turbulent?

8-3 (a) Define the terms "viscous flow" and "turbulent flow."
(b) Show that the Reynolds number is a dimensionless term.
(c) Calculate the critical velocity for (1) fuel oil flowing through a 6-in. pipeline (kinematic viscosity at 60°F is 4.75×10^{-5} ft²/sec) and (2) water at the same temperature flowing through the same pipeline (kinematic viscosity at 60°F is 1.22×10^{-5} ft²/sec). *Hint:* Reynolds number = dv/ν (check units and dimensions).

8-4 Define the following terms: (a) head loss due to friction, (b) viscous and turbulent flow, (c) hydraulic gradient.

8-5   Calculate the type of flow occurring in a 12-in. pipeline when (a) water at 60°F having a kinematic viscosity of 1.217×10^{-5} ft²/sec and (b) fuel oil at 60°F having a kinematic viscosity of 220×10^{-5} ft²/sec flows at a velocity of 3.5 ft/sec.

8-6   (a) What do you understand by the term "critical velocity" of a flow in a pipeline?
(b) Describe briefly, with the aid of a diagram, a laboratory method of determining the head loss when water flows at known velocities through a horizontal pipe of uniform cross section.

8-7   Oil of absolute viscosity 0.002 lb sec/ft² and specific gravity 0.850 flows through 5,000 ft of 12-in. cast-iron pipe at the rate of 1.6 ft³/sec. Calculate the head loss in the pipe.

8-8   Benzene at 50°F and having a specific gravity of 0.90 flows through a horizontal 6-in.-diam pipe (commercial steel) at an average velocity of 11.0 ft/sec. If the friction factor $f = 1.6 \times 10^{-2}$, calculate the pressure drop, in pounds per square inch, in 200 ft of pipe length.

8-9   (a) What is meant by the "equation of continuity" in pipe-flow computations?
(b) A pipe 1 ft in diameter contracts gradually to 6 in. and then expands gradually to a 10-in.-diam section. If the average velocity in the 6-in. section is 18 ft/sec, calculate the average velocity at the other sections, assuming an incompressible fluid.

8-10   Water flows through a 2-in.-ID pipe at a rate of 6 lb$_f$/sec. Calculate the average velocity and the rate in U.S. gallons per minute.
Note: 1 imp. gallon = 10.00 lb H_2O at 62°F (277.4 in.³)
         1 U.S. gallon = 0.833 imp. gallon (231 in.³)

8-11   A gas flows isothermally through a pipe at the rate of 2 lb/sec. At one section the internal diameter is 6 in. and the absolute pressure reading is 30 psi. Calculate the average velocity if the temperature is 60°F and $R = 65$ ft/°R.

8-12   A pipe 8 in. in diameter expands to 14 in. Air flows through the pipe at a rate of 15 lb/min. At one section in the 8-in. pipe the gauge pressure is 40 psi and the temperature is 120°F. At one section in the 14-in.-pipe, the gauge reads 25 psi and the temperature 80°F. The barometric pressure is 30.0 in. Hg. Calculate the velocity in each pipe section. The value of R in the gas equation is equal to 53.3 ft/°F abs.

8-13   (a) What is meant by the term "velocity head"?
(b) State Bernoulli's principle on the conservation of energy for a steady liquid flow in a system.

8-14   Neglecting losses due to friction, calculate the velocity potential of a static head of 25 ft of water in a storage tank.

8-15 Water is flowing along a circular pipe with a speed of 24.0 ft/sec. (a) Express this as a velocity head, in feet of water. (b) What is the corresponding pressure, in pounds per square inch?

8-16 Water of weight density 62.3 lb/ft³ is flowing down a vertical tapering pipe 6 ft long, as shown in Fig. 8-26. The top of the pipe has a diameter of 4 in., the bottom a diameter of 2 in. If the quantity of water flowing is 300 gallons/min, calculate the difference in pressure, in pounds per square inch, between the top and bottom ends. Assume no frictional losses and that 1 gallon of water equals 10 lb.

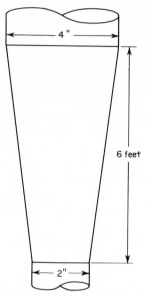

8-17 In Question 8-16 why is pressure p_1 less than p_2 and the velocity v_1 greater than v_2?

8-18 Describe briefly, with the aid of a diagram, the operation of measuring the velocity of a liquid flow in an open channel by means of a simple Pitot tube.

Fig. 8-26   Question 8-16.

8-19 The following observations were recorded during test runs on the calibration of a Pitot tube:

velocity v, ft/sec	1.86	3.92	4.20	7.80
head h, in. H₂O	0.76	1.73	3.50	14.40

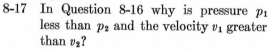

Plot, on graph paper, the velocity against the square root of the head and calculate the average value of the Pitot-tube coefficient for the units used during the tests.

8-20 Water flows through a circular horizontal pipe which is completely filled by the water. At point X the speed of the flow is 2 ft/sec, and at point Y the speed is 5 ft/sec. The cross-sectional area at X is 5 ft². Calculate (a) the cross-sectional area at Y and (b) the flow rate, in cubic feet per second, past X.

8-21 Define the following terms: (a) coefficient of contraction, (b) coefficient of velocity, (c) coefficient of discharge.

8-22 Briefly describe laboratory experiments to find the coefficient of discharge, velocity, and contraction.

8-23 In order to find the coefficient of velocity of a small circular sharp-edged orifice under low heads, the horizontal and vertical coordinates of the jet were measured when the water head above the center line of the orifice was 8.0 in. The horizontal ordinate of a certain point in the jet, from the vena contracta, was recorded as 32.5 in., while the vertical ordinate for the same point was 33.8 in. Compute the value for the coefficient of velocity.

8-24 The actual discharge through a sharp-edged circular orifice, 1 in. diameter, under a constant head of 4.00 ft is 3.24 ft³/min. Calculate the value for the coefficient of discharge.

8-25 Referring to the diagram for Prob. 8-25, the discharge equation for a rectangular orifice is given as

$$Q = 16\frac{2}{3}C_d B(H_2^{3/2} - H_1^{3/2})$$

If B, the width of the orifice, is 5.0 ft, $H_2 = 4.0$ ft, $H_1 = 2.0$ ft, and $C_d = 0.6$, calculate the rate of discharge, in cubic feet per second.

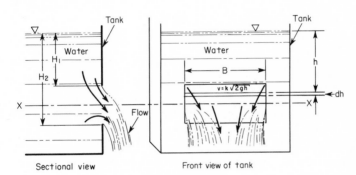

Prob. 8-25

8-26 (a) State Bernoulli's energy equation as applied to flow measurement for an incompressible fluid in a continuous system.

(b) State the dimension and typical units of each term in the equation of part (a).

8-27 A horizontally installed Venturi meter in a water pipeline has an enlarged area at one end of 2 ft² and a throat area of ¼ ft². Calculate the quantity, in cubic feet per second, of water going through the pipeline if the differential head is equivalent to 9 in. of water.

8-28 Given that Bernoulli's equation on energy for continuous flow for an incompressible fluid is

$$\frac{p_a - p_b}{w} = \frac{1}{2g}(v_b^2 - v_a^2) + (Z_b - Z_a) + h_l$$

Calculate the head loss of oil and direction of flow given the following information: A pipe carrying oil of specific gravity 0.87 changes in diameter from 6 in. at section A–A to 18 in. at section

B–B. Section A–A is 12 ft lower than section B–B, and the discharge is 5.2 ft³/sec. The pressures are 13.20 psi at A–A and 8.74 psi at B–B. See Fig. 8-27.

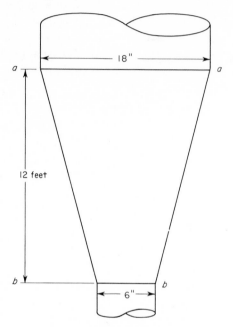

Fig. 8-27   Question 8-28.

8-29   (a) If the Bernoulli equation

$$\frac{p}{w} + \frac{v^2}{2g} + Z = \text{constant}$$

is considered to imply no change of energy, explain the significance of the terms as used in pipe-flow calculations.

(b) Show, with the aid of a labeled diagram, what measurements are essential in order to determine the flow rate with a Venturi meter installed at an inclined angle. Include the basic type of mercury manometer connections.

8-30   A horizontal pipe has a 4.0 in.² cross-sectional area. There is a constriction, like that of a Venturi, of the cross-sectional area of 1.0 in.² fitted in the pipeline. Gasoline (weight density 42 lb/ft³) flows with a speed of 6.0 ft/sec in the large pipe, where the pressure is 10.0 psi. Calculate (a) the speed and (b) the pressure in the constriction.

8-31   (a) Describe how the simple Venturi meter can be used for liquid-flow measurement.

(b) Using Bernoulli's equation as applied to a horizontal Venturi meter, show that

$$\Delta h = \frac{p_a - p_b}{w} = \frac{v_a^2}{2g}\left[\left(\frac{A_a}{A_b}\right)^2 - 1\right]$$

where the subscript a indicates conditions at the inlet section and the subscript b indicates conditions at the throat.

8-32   The difference of head registered in the two limbs of a mercury manometer (Fig. 8-14) with water above the mercury, when connected to a horizontal Venturi meter, is 7 in. The diameters of the pipe and throat are 6 and 3 in., respectively. Neglecting frictional losses and the effect of water column above the mercury, calculate the discharge through the meter.

8-33   Compare the operational and constructional features as well as the advantages and disadvantages of the industrial type of Venturi tube, Dall tube, and orifice plate. Compare the coefficients of discharge of each of these primary measuring elements.

8-34   An industrial type of Venturi tube has a discharge coefficient of 0.97, a throat diameter of 2.00 in., and a flow of 8,000 imp. gallons of water per hour having a differential of 50.0 in. H_2O. Calculate the flow with an orifice plate having a 20-in. diameter with a discharge coefficient of 0.60 if installed in the same pipeline and having the same differential.

8-35   (a) Describe, with the aid of neat diagrams, the construction and operation of (1) a Pitot static tube and (2) a manometer suitable for such a Pitot static tube when the differential is very small.
(b) List some of the merits and limitations of the industrial type of Pitot tube.
(c) A Pitot static tube used to measure the air velocity along a wind tunnel is connected to a manometer which indicates a head of 0.15 in. H_2O. Compute the air velocity if the Pitot coefficient unity and the specific or weight density for air is 0.075 lb/ft^3.
(d) Explain what method you would use to determine the average velocity of airflow through a large circular pipe and a large rectangular air duct.

8-36   During a set of Pitot-tube calibration tests with water flow, the following results were recorded:

Test	1	2	3	4	5
Velocity of water v, ft/sec	1.87	2.96	4.21	6.50	7.96
Head h, in. H_2O	0.76	1.72	3.50	9.11	14.39

Calculate the value of the constant for the Pitot tube when v is in feet per second and h is in inches.

8-37   (a) Describe, with the aid of a diagram, a typical ISA nozzle with corner tappings.

(b) Calculate the flow of air through a nozzle like that of part (a) having a discharge coefficient of 0.96 and diameter of 6.5 in. if the temperature of the air is 60°F. The upstream pressure is 10 in. water, and the differential is 4.4 in. of water.

DIFFERENTIAL PRESSURE OR HEAD METERS

Any differential-pressure instrument described in Chap. 5 would be suitable for use as a flowmeter. For example, the principle of the simple U-tube manometer or the industrial type has been used as the basis of many flow-measuring instruments. The ring-balance manometer is also useful to measure flow, particularly where low-pressure gases have to be metered. Then there is the basic metallic bellows, which can be readily adapted for flow measurement. In the normal industrial version two bellows back to back are used, as shown in Fig. 8-28. In the case of a

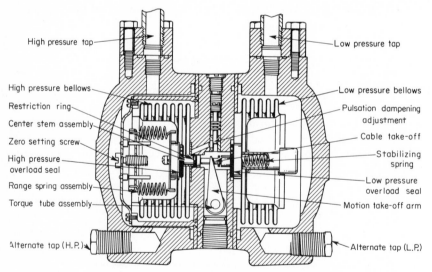

Fig. 8-28   Cutaway view of bellows-type flowmeter. (Honeywell Inc.)

diaphragm instrument, except for very low differential pressures, there is insufficient movement to operate an indicating pointer or the pen of a recorder. A force-balance transmitter, either electrical or pneumatic, is then used, as shown in Fig. 8-29.

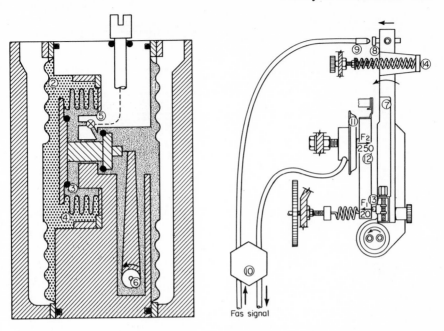

Fig. 8-29   Differential-pressure flowmeter and transmitter. (Honeywell Inc.)

U-tube Manometers

When U-tube instruments are used for flow measurement, the density effect and the square-law effect must be considered.

Density effect. Figure 8-30 shows a U-tube flowmeter with mercury filling, where each of the connecting tubes is filled with the fluid flowing through the orifice (or Venturi). The specific or weight density w_f of the fluid being metered cannot be neglected. If p_a and p_b are the pressures at the upstream and downstream tappings, the force-balance equation becomes

$$p_a + H_a w_f = p_b + H_b w_f + h_m w_m$$

but since

$$h_m = H_a - H_b$$

$$p_a - p_b = h_m w_m - w_f h_m = h_m(w_m - w_f)$$

From this expression it will be seen that weight density of the fluid appears in the term $w_m - w_f$ and has a reducing effect on the final differential reading h_m.

Example

Weight density of mercury at 60°F (w_m) = 0.488 lb/in.³. Weight density of water at 60°F (w_f) = 0.036 lb/in.³.

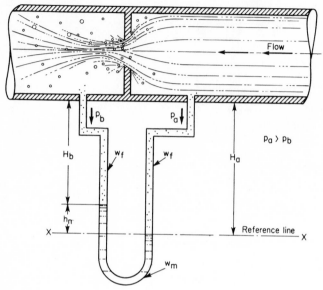

Fig. 8-30   U-tube flowmeter.

Therefore $\qquad$ $w_m - w_f = 0.488 - 0.036 = 0.452$

The error in the equivalent liquid columns using 0.488 lb/in.³ instead of 0.452 lb/in.³ is

$$\% \text{ error} = \frac{h_m w_m - h_m(w_m - w_f)}{h_m(w_m - w_f)} 100\% = \frac{w_f}{w_m - w_f} 100\%$$

$$= \frac{0.036}{0.452} 100\%$$

$$= 7\tfrac{1}{2}\% \qquad \text{approx}$$

It will be recalled when dealing with U-tube manometers that, for the arrangement shown in Fig. 8-33,

$$d = \frac{p_a - p_b}{w_m(1 + A_a/A_b)}$$

However, if there is a liquid above the mercury, the equation becomes

$$d = \frac{p_a - p_b}{(w_m - w_f)(1 + A_1/A_2)}$$

giving a modified value of d, the fall or rise of the float. The result shows the importance of considering the liquid columns and chambers in each of the connecting tubes to the manometer. In the case of "dry" meters with small filling capacity, e.g., bellows or diaphragm, the above density correction does not have to be made, because there is virtually no differential movement of the fluid in the two connecting lines.

Square-law effect. From Bernoulli's equation, the following expression was established:

$$v_b = \frac{1}{\sqrt{1 - (A_b/A_a)^2}} \sqrt{\frac{2g(p_a - p_b)}{w_f}} = \frac{1}{\sqrt{1 - (A_b/A_a)^2}} \sqrt{2gh}$$

and from this it will be seen that the flow is proportional to the square root of the differential produced.

Hence, if Q_1 is a flow rate having a differential of h_1 and Q_2 is another value at h_2 through the same pipe and orifice (or Venturi), then

$$\frac{Q_1}{Q_2} = \sqrt{\frac{h_2}{h_1}} \quad \text{and} \quad h_2 = \left(\frac{Q_1}{Q_2}\right)^2 h_1$$

For example, if $h_1 = 28$ in. H$_2$O, $Q_1 = 200,000$ lb/hr, and $Q_2 = 100,000$ lb/hr,

$$h_2 = \left(\frac{100,000}{200,000}\right)^2 \times 28 = 7.0 \text{ in. H}_2\text{O}$$

From this it will be seen that for half the flow there is only one-quarter of the differential. If now the flow becomes $Q_3 = 50,000$,

$$h_3 = \left(\frac{50,000}{200,000}\right)^2 \times 28 = 1.8 \text{ in. H}_2\text{O}$$

If h is plotted against Q, a parabolic curve results, as shown in Fig. 8-31. Now consider the actual instrument scale. If a standard linear magnifying device is used, the pointer or pen arm will have an angular movement θ directly proportional to the differential head, and since $Q^2 \propto h$, then $Q^2 \propto \theta$. If θ_{max} is the maximum pointer travel on a circular scale, then any other value will be found from the expression

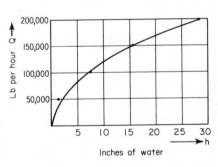

Fig. 8-31   *Square-law effect.*

$$\theta = \left(\frac{Q}{Q_{max}}\right)^2 \theta_{max}$$

For illustration purposes a typical industrial flow indicating scale having an angular span of 300° will be considered. If the previous values of the flow rate are taken, then

$$\theta_2 = \left(\frac{100,000}{200,000}\right)^2 \times 300° = 75°$$

$$\theta_3 = \left(\frac{50,000}{200,000}\right)^2 \times 300° = 1.9°$$

From these results it can be seen that the pointer moves only a quarter of the way round the circular scale for half the maximum flow, and for lower values the angular movement is very small. The results shown in Fig. 8-32a indicate the nonlinearity of the scale, having narrow increments

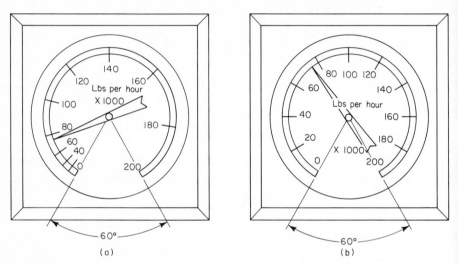

Fig. 8-32   (a) *Square-root scale.* (b) *Linear scale.*

at the low flow-rate values and gradually increasing as the flow increases. The scale is calibrated from the Q versus h curve.

Now compare this nonlinear scale with the linear one shown in Fig. 8-32b. From this comparison it will be seen that there is an equal division between the readings. This type of scale or chart is generally required, and for this reason many flowmeters are manufactured with a square-root compensation or correction device which results in the desired linearly divided scale. The relation of $Q \propto \sqrt{h}$ is corrected to read $Q \propto h$.

Methods of Square-root Compensation with U-tube Manometers

The methods of square-root compensation are numerous and beyond the scope of this text. However, a few of the common ones will be described briefly.

Mechanical methods; shaped mercury chamber. In this design, it is necessary to produce equal vertical movements of the float for corresponding changes of the flow so that all points may be referred to a linear scale. A downstream pressure chamber (Fig. 8-33) is shaped or

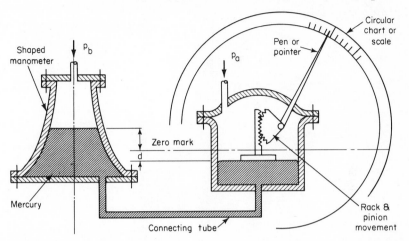

Fig. 8-33   Shaped mercury chamber. (The Foxboro Company Limited)

contoured to the form of a square-root law. The diagram illustrates the basic principle involved. From a study of this diagram, d, the depression of the level in the float chamber (connected to the upstream pressure), must be directly proportional to the flow rate Q in order to achieve a linear scale. The square root of the differential head $h + d$ must at all times be directly proportional to Q. These variables may be expressed by

$$\sqrt{h + d} = kQ \qquad \text{or} \qquad h + d = KQ^2$$

Also, the volume leaving the shaped manometer, at any time, will be the same as that entering the float chamber. If V is this volume and A_c is the cross-sectional area of the float chamber

$$d = \frac{V}{A_c}$$

If the shape or contour of the chamber is designed to take the form of the parabolic curve of Q versus h, then the square-root effect has been achieved.

Shaped bell-type measuring instrument. In this instrument, as shown in Fig. 8-34, the basic U-tube manometer takes a special design not unlike the inverted bell discussed earlier. The float chamber is provided with a hollow float whose internal surface is contoured to a curve of

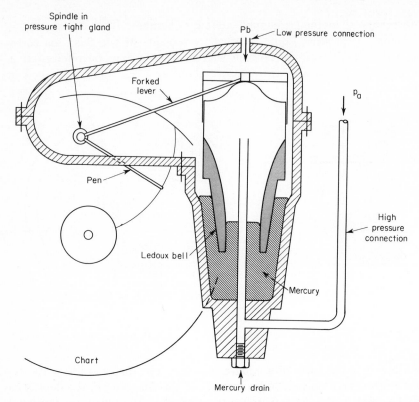

Spindle in
pressure tight gland

Pb — Low pressure connection

Forked
lever

p_a

Pen

High
pressure
connection

Ledoux bell

Mercury

Chart

Mercury drain

Fig. 8-34   Bell-type flowmeter. (Bailey Meter Company Limited)

parabolic or square-law shape. The mercury rises or falls in the inside of
the float as well as around the outside. The high pressure is connected to
the inside of the float, and the low pressure to the outside. The differential pressure will cause the float to rise in the mercury because the
internal pressure p_a is greater than p_b. At the same time the mercury level
inside the float will fall and the level on the outside will rise.

This process continues until equilibrium is reached, where the effective
weight or buoyancy of the bell just offsets the differential pressure. The
travel of the float will depend on the amount of mercury leaving the
interior of the float and entering the outside. The travel also depends on
the shape or contour of the internal surface of the float. If this is designed
to a parabolic curve, the travel of the float can be made to be substantially
linear for all points of the flowmetering range. This arrangement is
referred to as the Ledoux-bell type of flowmanometer. If design formulas
are required, A. Linford's book *Flow Measurement and Meters* should
be consulted.

Electrical methods. An example of this method is shown in Fig. 8-35. One side of the manometer is fitted with a unit having a large number (approximately 100) of vertical conducting rods arranged in a spiral

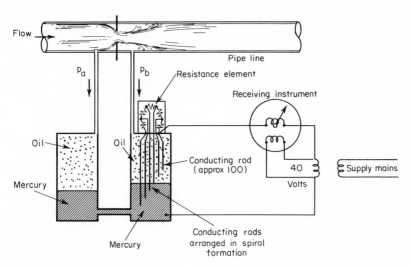

Fig. 8-35 Electrical manometer. (Republic Flow Meters Division of Rockwell)

form. These rods are connected to resistance elements at the top of the unit in such a way that they nearly form tappings from a continuous resistance. The rod lengths are carefully graduated so that the mercury falling or rising in the chamber, with flow-rate variations, breaks or makes contact with one rod after another. The circuit connection is made through the mercury and through the resistance assembly at the top of the unit. The level of the mercury controls the amount of resistance in the circuit because of its contact with the rods. If the contour of the spiral follows a parabolic curve, a means of compensating for the square-root effect is provided.

The oil, above the mercury in both limbs, results in the whole resistance unit being enclosed in oil, which protects the connecting rods from possible contamination from the fluid being metered. Consider the flow-rate equation:

$$Q = k \sqrt{p_a - p_b} = k_1 \sqrt{\Delta h} \qquad \text{hence } k_2 Q = \sqrt{\Delta h}$$

The conductance is measured in mhos, or the reciprocal of ohms, that is, $G = 1/R$, where R is the resistance in the element. One mho is defined as the conductance of a substance through which one ampere flows at a potential difference of one volt. Thus a wire with a resistance of 2 ohms will have a conductance of $\frac{1}{2}$ mho. The conductance G is made proportional to $\sqrt{\Delta h}$ by the parabolic contour of the conducting rods. Hence $\sqrt{\Delta h} = k_3 G$, and by substituting this in the earlier equation for $\sqrt{\Delta h}$,

$$k_2 Q = k_3 G$$

From which it is seen that conductance varies directly as the flow rate.

Flowmeters operating on this principle are electrical instruments with scales calibrated directly in flow units. Of course, it is essential to ensure that variations in circuit supply voltage do not effect changes in instrument readings. It should be observed that the circuit is suitable for distant metering or telemetering. Two leads are necessary between transmitter and receiving instruments, and transmission-line resistance does not influence the working of the system.

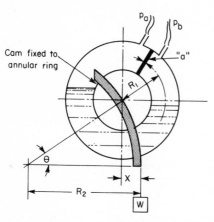

Fig. 8-36   Basic ring-balance meter.

The usual design of ring-balance meter used for flow measurement in Europe is shown in Fig. 8-36. The restoring weight W is suspended over a shaped cam surface. If a is the cross-sectional area of the partition in the annular tube upon which the differential pressure $p_a - p_b$ acts and R_1 is the radius from the fulcrum to the center of pressure, then x, the difference in the length of moment arms, is

$$x = R_2(1 - \cos \theta)$$

where θ is the angle of rotation from the horizontal. The moments acting about the fulcrum are

$$\text{Rotating moment} = \text{restoring moment}$$
$$(p_a - p_b)aR_1 = Wx$$
$$= WR_2(1 - \cos \theta)$$

where R_2 is the radius of the cam segment. Hence

$$\Delta p = \frac{W}{a}\frac{R_2}{R_1}(1 - \cos \theta) = K(1 - \cos \theta)$$

Since Q is proportional to $\sqrt{\Delta p}$, Q is also proportional to $\sqrt{1 - \cos \theta}$, because θ is the only other variable. If for maximum flow $\theta = 30°$, then $\sqrt{1 - \cos 30°} = 0.366$. Now half of this is 0.183, from which $\cos \theta = 0.965$. This gives θ nearly equal to 15°, which indicates that the rate of flow Q follows a linear relation (approximately) with the angle of rotation.

As mentioned earlier, there are various types of square-root compensators on the market and only a few have been described. Reference should be made to Rhodes' *Industrial Instruments for Measurement and Control* for other such devices.

Temperature and Pressure Compensation

The equation for compressible fluids such as gases was previously established as

$$Q = 7,859 C_d K d^2 E \sqrt{\frac{\Delta h p_a}{T S g}}$$

It will be observed-that both the pressure p_a and temperature T must remain fairly constant; otherwise, errors will occur and upset the instrument readings. If the variations are considered to be large and occurring sporadically, then automatic pressure and temperature compensation must be considered.

In the case of mechanical meters, pressure compensation may be achieved by taking a pressure tapping from the upstream side to a Bourdon tube. The free end of this Bourdon is linked to the mechanism operated by the float shaft or spindle which activates the recording pen or indicator. The deflection of the Bourdon tube with varying pressure adjusts, by way of the link, the multiplication value of the main operating mechanism and thereby corrects for pressure changes.

Temperature compensation could be carried out in the same way as for pressure, but in that case a temperature bulb and Bourdon tube would have to be installed in the pipeline. This would lead to a complicated design, particularly for mechanically operated flowmeters. However, both temperature and pressure compensation can be carried out by electronic means, which, of course, will increase the cost of the instrument. In earlier days of flow measurement, when no compensation devices were incorporated, the instrument was fitted with three pens to record flow, pressure, and temperature at the point of metering. In this way the entire operating conditions were present on one chart and any corrections to be applied were either calculated or referred to from data previously tabulated.

REVIEW QUESTIONS AND PROBLEMS

8-38 (a) Describe the importance of the density and square-root effects on the U type of manometer used for metering the flow of a liquid.

(b) In the ordinary straight type of U manometer $A_1 = 12.0$ in.^{2},

$A_2 = 2.6$ in.^{2}, and d, the depression level below the zero line $= 1.5$ in. Calculate the differential pressure if mercury and water are used in the manometer in (a) inches of mercury, (b) pounds per square inch, and (c) inches of water gauge. Use the expression

$$d = \frac{p_a - p_b}{(w_m - w_w)(1 + A_1/A_2)}$$

8-39   (a) What is meant by the expression a "dry" flowmeter?

(b) How would you use a metallic bellows differential-pressure gauge as a measuring device on a flowmeter?

(c) In part (b) would it be possible to extract the square-root effect? If not, why not?

8-40   (a) Compare the divisions of a nonlinear and linear scale or chart used for flowmetering.

(b) Why are the divisions on the nonlinear scale so closely spaced at the lower end of the scale?

8-41   What will be the difference in readings of a square-root scale and a linear scale of a flowmeter if the total scale range of both is 0 to 100,000 gallons/hr and the pointer, in each case, is at the midpoint of its maximum deflection?

8-42   By using the cam segment for square-root compensation on the ring balance used for flowmetering, calculate the value of the restoring weight W if $\Delta p = 4$ in. H$_2$O, $R_1 = 7$ in., $\theta = 30°$, $a = 1\frac{1}{2}$ in.^{2}, and $R_2 = 20$ in. The equation is

$$\Delta p = \frac{W}{a} \frac{R_2}{R_1} (1 - \cos \theta)$$

8-43   Describe, with the aid of a sketch, any one of the following methods for square-root compensation: (a) shaped mercury chamber, (b) Ledoux bell, (c) conducting-rods method, (d) cam-segment method, (e) any other method you know.

AREA METERS

Variable-area Meters

Variable-area flowmeters are frequently referred to as Rotameters or Flowrators, which, however, are trade names for the most commonly used patterns. The basic equation for flow through orifice, nozzle, and Venturi meter is

$$Q = AC_d \sqrt{2gh}$$

where A = throat or orifice area

C_d = coefficient of discharge

h = differential head

This equation indicates a possible alternative scheme, because if h is kept constant, A will vary linearly with Q. The area can be arranged to vary if a solid disk or sphere can be made to move inside a tapered or conical tube. A vertical tube of tapered form is used, the area gradually expanding from the bottom to the top. The fluid is permitted to flow in an upward direction, and in its stream a disk, free to move, floats in the fluid. A variable area or variable orifice is set up between the disk and the internal surface of the tube, and a pressure drop occurs across the lower and upper surface of the disk. The general arrangement of the float and tube is shown in Fig. 8-37.

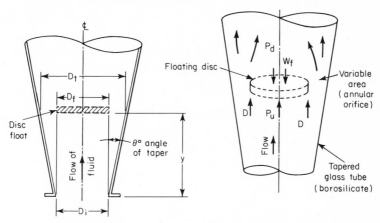

Fig. 8-37   Basic theory of variable-area meters.

When the float is at rest, for a certain flow rate, the forces acting on the disk are in equilibrium. Any change in the flow rate will upset the position of the float. The float will move up or down the tube, adjusting the variable area of the orifice because of the tapered shape of the tube. The movement continues until the pressure drop is again at its original value, and this occurs when the forces are in equilibrium once more. The position of the float is then a measure of the rate of flow. The following equations indicate the theory on which the operating principle is based. Referring to the previous figures, the forces acting on the float in the tube are:

1. The effective weight W_f of the float in the downward direction:

$$W_f\!\downarrow = V_f(w_f - w)$$

where V_f = the volume of the float

w_f = weight density of the float

w = weight density of the fluid

2. The total pressure

$$P_d\downarrow = p_b A_f$$

where p_b = pressure per unit area on top of the float

A_f = area of the float, or the projected area of a sphere if it is used as a float

3. The total pressure P_u acting in an upward direction on the lower surface of the float:

$$P_u\uparrow = p_a A_f$$

where p_a = pressure per unit area on the bottom of the float, or the projected area of a sphere if it is used as a float

4. There is a drag force D which has the effect of pulling the float upward. The value of the drag force will depend on the shape of the float and also upon whether the flow is turbulent or viscous. From the aerodynamics involved, it can be shown that

$$D\uparrow = C\mu VL$$

where C = constant depending on the float shape and nature of flow conditions

μ = absolute viscosity of the fluid

V = velocity of the fluid

L = a dimensional function equivalent to a length

$$[F] = \left[\frac{FT}{L^2}\right]\left[\frac{L}{T}\right][L] = [F]$$

Assuming conditions for turbulent flow with only the forces W_f, P_d, and P_u acting on the float, a simple approach can be given to an otherwise complex problem. When equilibrium is set up, it can be stated that the total downward forces are equal to the total upward force:

$$W_f + P_d = P_u$$

or, in terms of the other symbols,

$$V_f(w_f - w) + p_b A_f = p_a A_f$$

By rearrangement,

$$p_a - p_b = \frac{V_f}{A_f}(w_f - w)$$

In the basic equation

$$Q = AC_d\sqrt{2gh} \quad \text{or} \quad Q = AC_d\sqrt{2g\frac{p_a - p_b}{w}}$$

Hence
$$Q = AC_d \sqrt{2g \frac{V_f}{A_f} \frac{w_f - w}{w}}$$

Since the tube is tapered or conical in shape, from Fig. 8-37 it can be seen that:
$$D_t = D_i + 2y \tan \theta$$

where D_t = tube diameter at any distance y from the inlet
D_i = tube inlet diameter
θ = angle of taper
y = variable height of the float from the inlet

Now if D_f is the diameter of the float, the variable annular area through which the fluid flows is given by
$$A = \frac{\pi}{4} (D_t^2 - D_f^2)$$

For simplicity let $D_f \doteq D_i$ (normally D_f is slightly greater than D_i); then
$$A = \frac{\pi}{4} (D_t^2 - D_i^2)$$
$$= \frac{\pi}{4} [(D_i + 2y \tan \theta)^2 - D_i^2]$$

Hence
$$= \pi D_i \tan \theta y + \pi \tan^2 \theta y^2$$

The relation between A and y is nearly linear when the differences between the quantities $(D_i + 2y \tan \theta)$ and D_i are small, and this occurs when the angle of taper is fairly small. Therefore, $A = ky$, where k is a combined constant of the product π, and $\tan \theta$. Hence the equation
$$Q = kyC_d \sqrt{2g \frac{V_f}{A_f} \frac{w_f - w}{w}}$$

becomes $Q = Ky$, where K is the new combined constant. From the last equation it is noted that the flow rate and height of the float follow a straight-line relationship.

Weight-density Compensation

Of course, the weight density of the fluid being metered can vary with the temperature. If the above equation is differentiated with respect to w, the variable fluid density, and the result is equated to zero, a condition for immunity from weight-density variation will be obtained. It will be found that the weight density w_f for the float must be infinitely greater than that of the fluid. This result is not practicable, and therefore a compromise is made: the weight density of the material used for the float is several times the value of the fluid density. Thus a steel float is frequently used. When weight flow is being metered, $W = Qw$ or

$$W = kyC_d \sqrt{2g \frac{V_f}{A_f} (w_f - w)w}$$

If now this equation is differentiated with respect to w and the result is equated to zero, it is found that $w_f = 2w$. For liquids, this requirement is easily obtained by making the body of the float of either hollow or solid plastic material.

Viscous-flow Conditions

When the Reynolds number is less than 2,000, viscous-flow conditions exist and the force of viscous drag must be considered in the original function of L and the viscosity μ of the fluid. To reduce the effect of viscous drag force to a minimum in the equation $D = c\mu VL$, a reduction in L will decrease the drag force. Designing the float to the shapes shown in Fig. 8-38 will minimize the drag-force effect. In both cases, the effective

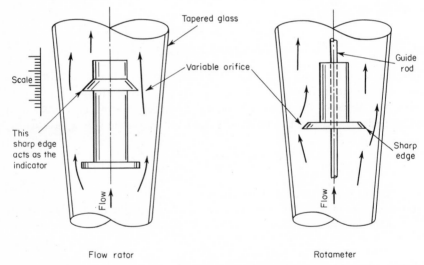

Fig. 8-38   Flowrator and Rotameter.

orifice portion of the float has to be reduced to a sharp-edged disk with a minimum length along the direction of flow.

Constructional Details of Rotameters

The fundamental feature of the Rotameter is the conically shaped glass tube, whose internal diameter must be manufactured to very close limits.

The glass is clear borosilicate, which is highly resistant to chemical action and thermal shock. The glass, for safety reasons, must stand very high pressures; otherwise, armor-plate-glass protection windows must enclose the meter.

Viscosity-immune floats require a guide, because the float disturbs the equilibrium of the fluid. The guide rod passes through the upper part of the tube, which has a glass scale. The end of the rod acts as an indicating pointer. The arrangement is shown in Fig. 8-39. For high working pressures, well beyond 500 psi, the float is enclosed in a metal tube. In the float is a magnet, and on the outside there is a magnetic coupling. As the float moves up and down, so will the pointer attached to the follower magnet. The pointer is fixed on a rotating unit in order to register the flow rate reading on a vertical scale.

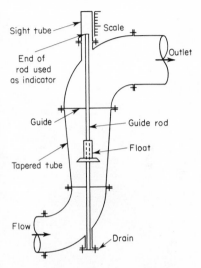

Fig. 8-39   Rotameter with viscosity-immune float.

Constructional Details of Flowrators

The float normally requires a guide; and to avoid the use of a central rod, the tapered glass tube is manufactured with vertical ribs molded in the glass. The ribs keep the float in a vertical and central position. Special armored glass tubes are manufactured for high working pressures. Metal-tube types with magnetic coupling are available. A magnet on a pivoted arm on the outside of the metering tube is designed to follow the movements of the float, which incorporates a magnet. The arm can also operate a pneumatic-bellows unit for automatic-control applications. Both the Rotameter and Flowrator may be used for telemetering and control applications by using electrical means of transmission.

Velocity Meters

It has already been seen that the Pitot tube is in fact a velocity meter, but there are other flowmeters falling in that classification which operate on a different principle. Chief among them are the propeller meter and the turbine meter. The propeller meter shown in Fig. 8-40 converts the liquid-velocity reaction into driving torque. When originally introduced, this type of meter was limited to relatively high velocities because, owing to

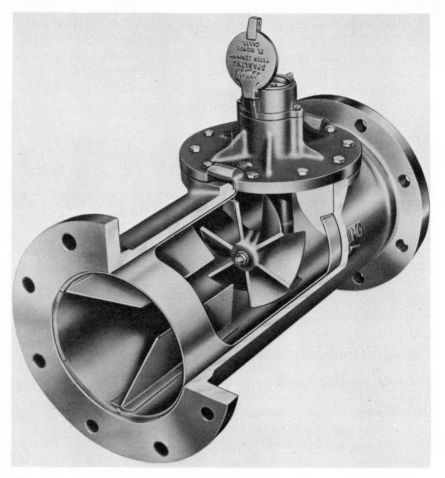

Fig. 8-40 Sparling propeller-type flowmeter. (Hersey-Sparling Meter Co.)

mechanical problems, accuracy fell off badly at low velocities. However, with improved bearing design this difficulty has been largely overcome and the use of the meter has been greatly extended. The meter has the advantage of causing a low pressure drop and has an almost unlimited overrange capacity. Sizes suitable for pipes up to 12 in. in diameter are available. By means of gearing, a digital readout of totalized flow is provided; i.e., a continuous local indication or record of flow rate is not possible. If, however, a continuous record is required, an electrical transducer, generally of the time-pulse type, can be fitted.

In the turbine meter the liquid enters the turbine rotor from both ends, passes through the wheels, and discharges through the space between the wheels. This is shown in Fig. 8-41a. The turbine meter otherwise has characteristics somewhat similar to those of the propeller meter, its accuracy falling off as the load drops. The pressure drop is high.

An adaptation of the turbine principle is used in the shunt-type meter, which is convenient for measuring relatively small quantities of liquids or gases, including steam, when only a totalized digital readout is required. This meter is built in sizes up to 3 in. It is shown in Fig. 8-41*b*. The opera-

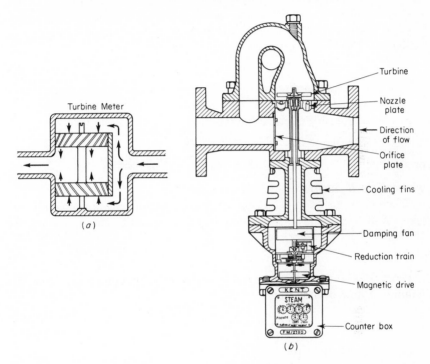

Fig. 8-41 (a) *Turbine meter.* (b) *Shunt-type turbine flowmeter.* [G. Kent (Canada) Ltd.]

tion of the shunt meter is based on the differential pressure generated by an orifice plate or other constriction to operate a differential-pressure-measuring device. The meter, as its name implies, is used to shunt a definite proportion of the total flow through a bypass, where the smaller discharge can be measured by means of a fan or turbine, the speed of rotation of the fan being reduced by damping. The torque T on the turbine is derived from the equation

$$T = K_1(p_1 - p_2) \tag{1}$$

where p_1 and p_2 are respectively the pressure upstream and downstream of the meter and K_1 is a constant.

The resisting torque is the sum of the following individual factors:

1. Mechanical frictional resistance
2. Resistance of the turbine rotating in the metered fluid
3. Resistance of the damping vanes rotating in the damping fluid

Mechanical frictional resistance is constant, and the design ensures that this force is as small as possible so that, within the working range of the meter, its effect is negligible. The meter is also so designed that the resistance of the turbine rotating in the metered fluid is small enough to be neglected. The resisting torque is

$$T_r = K_2 S^2 w_d \qquad (2)$$

where K_2 = a constant

S = revolutions of the turbine in unit time

w_d = density of the damping fluid

$$K_1(p_1 - p_2) = K_2 S^2 w_d$$

or
$$S = K_3 \sqrt{p_1 - p_2}\, \frac{1}{\sqrt{w_d}} \qquad (3)$$

where K_3 is a constant.

When the density w_d of the damping fluid is kept sensibly constant, the speed S of the turbine will be directly proportional to the square root of the differential pressure, i.e.,

$$S = K_4 \sqrt{p_1 - p_2} \qquad (4)$$

From the standard flow formula for differential-pressure flowmeters, the volume of flow in unit time

$$Q_1 = K \sqrt{p_1 - p_2}\, \frac{1}{\sqrt{w}} \qquad (5)$$

Hence, from the last two equations

$$S = K_5 Q_1 \sqrt{w}$$

where K_5 is a constant.

Similarly,
$$S = \frac{K_5 W}{\sqrt{w}}$$

where W is the weight of flow in unit time. When damping vanes are rotating in the metered fluid, since $w_d = w$, from Eq. (3)

$$S = K_3 \sqrt{p_1 - p_2}\, \frac{1}{\sqrt{w}}$$

and since, from Eq. (5)

$$Q_1 = K \sqrt{p_1 - p_2}\, \frac{1}{\sqrt{w}}$$
$$S = K_6 Q_1 \qquad (6)$$

that is, the meter will always read the actual volume passing regardless of the density.

With liquid damping, the reduction of the effective momentum of the turbine results in a corresponding reduction in the error of registration when the meter is measuring a pulsating flow. Of course, there is a practical limit to the speed and magnitude of the pulsations beyond which a registration error will occur.

Positive-displacement Meters

The most common water meter is the domestic pattern meter, which generally operates on the positive-displacement principle. The designs most usually employed are the nutating disk, the oscillating piston, and the vane type which are shown in Fig. 8-42a, b, and c. For larger quantities of liquid or gas the impeller type of meter is frequently used, the Connersville design being one of the best known. This meter, shown in Fig. 8-43, is not unlike a gear pump except that, in the place of gears, lobed impellers are used.

Another common gas meter is the bellows type. It is simply a diaphragm pump operated as a motor, and it is thus somewhat similar to the reciprocating-piston meter which was at one time used for the measurement of water, particularly the feed to boilers. It contains two bellows, each being alternately filled and emptied through passages controlled by slide valves, which are operated by the bellows. The sealed-drum meter (Fig. 8-44) is another gas meter often used to measure domestic-gas supplies.

Electromagnetic Flowmeter

The measurement of liquids containing suspended solids such as sewage or the feed to paper mills presented considerable problems until the advent of the electromagnetic flowmeter. As its name implies, it can be used to measure the flow of any flowing material which is electrically conductive. The meter can be regarded as a section of pipe which is lined with an insulating material. Two saddle coils are arranged opposite each other, and electrodes diametrically opposed are arranged flush with the inside of the lining. If the coils are energized, the moving liquid, as a length of conductor, cuts the lines of force, resulting in a generation of emf which is picked up by the electrodes. By suitable circuitry and amplification an electrical signal proportionate to flow can be obtained.

Figure 8-45 gives a general idea of the construction of such a meter. The principle on which the meter operates is that of the d-c generator. The generator rotor is replaced by the pipe between two magnetic poles. As the fluid flows through the magnetic field an emf is induced in it and can be

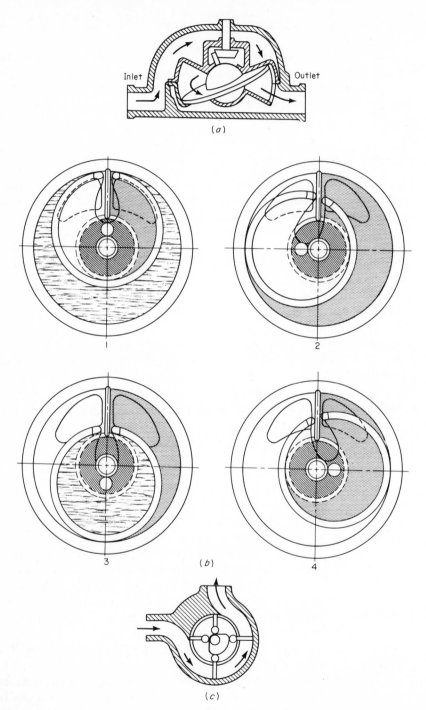

Fig. 8-42   (a) *Nutating-disk meter.* (b) *Oscillating-piston meter.* (c) *Vane-type meter.*

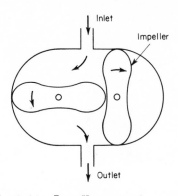

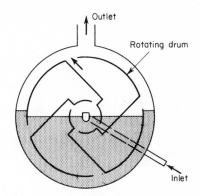

Fig. 8-43 Impeller meter for gas or liquid.

Fig. 8-44 Sealed-drum meter for gas.

picked up by the electrodes. This can be expressed mathematically as follows:

$$E = Blv \times 10^{-8}$$

where E = emf, volts

B = field strength, cgs units

l = conductor length, cm

v = velocity of conductor, cm/sec

In the case of the electromagnetic flowmeter, the flowing liquid represents the conductor and the internal diameter corresponds to the length l. If the field strength B is maintained constant, the only variable is v; hence the emf is proportional to the velocity.

The electromagnetic flowmeter has the advantage of causing no drop in the pressure of the fluid and having a very large range. It is not suitable for low velocities, the smallest range possible being 2 ft/sec for full scale or 1 ft/sec with the sacrifice of some accuracy. It is limited to the measurement of fluids having a conductivity in excess of 10 micromhos/cm. Of great importance is the fact that the readings are unaffected by variations in viscosity, density, temperature, pressure, or conductivity. The electrodes must, of course, be kept clean, and this can present a problem in the measurement of sewage, in which grease, a poor electrical conductor, may be present.

Mass-flow Measurement

In all the systems of flow measurement which have been described, it is the volume which is measured and not the weight. When weight flow is required, the volume has to be multiplied by the weight density of the particular fluid. With certain fluids, particularly gas, the weight density

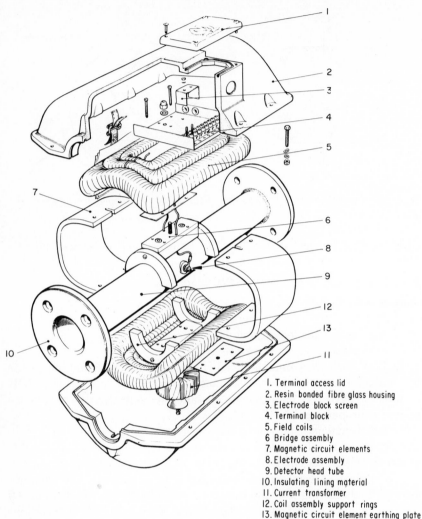

1. Terminal access lid
2. Resin bonded fibre glass housing
3. Electrode block screen
4. Terminal block
5. Field coils
6 Bridge assembly
7. Magnetic circuit elements
8. Electrode assembly
9. Detector head tube
10. Insulating lining material
11. Current transformer
12. Coil assembly support rings
13. Magnetic circuit element earthing plate

Fig. 8-45   Electromagnetic flowmeter. (Mawdsley's Ltd.)

does not remain constant, and so the volumetric measurement has to be corrected in order to obtain the volume of gas at some standard conditions. That is, when corrected to a standard density, one can refer to mass flow.

Normally these corrections are made with the aid of tables using average temperature and pressure readings. In the gas industry it is normal to record temperature and pressure at the same time as differential pressure so that these averages can be readily obtained. In many cases the variations are not sufficient to warrant any correction being applied, but that is not always true. For that reason there has arisen a demand for a mass flowmeter. The demand can, in part, be satisfied by obtaining electrical signals proportional to flow, temperature, and pressure. These are fed into a bridge circuit or analogue computer, and an output proportional to mass flow is obtained provided the weight density of the fluid has not altered appreciably. Nevertheless, this increases the number of components required, and accuracy suffers. A direct measurement of mass flow would be attractive, and several methods have been proposed. At least two of them have been tried out. For further details manufacturers' literature should be consulted.

REVIEW QUESTIONS AND PROBLEMS

8-44　(a) Describe the basic operation of a variable-area flowmeter.
(b) Sketch the graph of the position of the float against the flow rate.

8-45　(a) Discuss briefly the changes involved in instrument range and sensitivity if the solid spherical steel float of a variable-area flowmeter is replaced by a solid spherical plastic float.
(b) Calculate the mass of a spherical float of 1 cm diameter and of mass density $9 \, \text{g/cm}^3$ if the float is used in a tapered glass tube to indicate the flow rate of water.

8-46　The differential head across a particular float in a Flowrator used for metering water flow is found to be 12.0 in. water gauge, and the annular orifice area is $10.2 \, \text{in.}^2$. If the coefficient of discharge is 0.7, calculate the rate of flow, in cubic feet per second, of water at that instant.

8-47　(a) Discuss some of the constructional details of *either* a typical industrial type of Rotameter *or* Flowrator meter.
(b) In what way may the meter be made immune from weight-density and viscosity variations of the fluid being measured?

8-48　What principle is involved in the velocity meter? Name two types which have industrial importance.

8-49　When can an electromagnetic flowmeter be used and what are its advantages? Mention two processes in which this type of flowmeter has found extended use.

MEASUREMENT OF FLOW IN OPEN CHANNELS

Large volumes of liquid such as river water and sewage have to be measured in open channels. The devices used operate on the principle that, if a restriction of specified shape and form is placed in the path of the flow, a rise in upstream liquid level which is a function of the rate of flow through the restricted section will result. Such primary devices can be subdivided into *weirs* and *flumes*. Any primary measuring system, e.g., a float, static head, or bubbler system, can be used to ascertain the level.

The most commonly used weirs are the rectangular, the triangular or V notch, and the trapezoidal or Cipolletti weir. These are shown in Fig. 8-46a, b, and c. The rectangular weir will measure large flows, whereas the

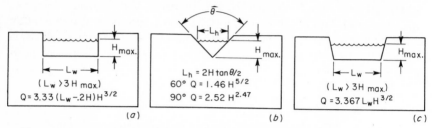

Fig. 8-46   (a) *Rectangular weir*, (b) *V-notch weir*, (c) *Cipolletti weir*.

V notch is more suitable for smaller flows below, say, 1 ft³/sec. The Cipolletti weir has characteristics similar to those of the rectangular weir, but it provides a rather simpler discharge formula. A view of a rectangular weir with end contractions is shown in Fig. 8-47, which also illustrates some of the technical terms associated with weir design. A suppressed weir has no end contractions, and the crest consequently extends the full width of the channel.

The theoretical formulas are arrived at by considering a layer of water at any depth y, where velocity $v = \sqrt{2gy}$.

$$\text{Flow } q = vA$$
$$dq = Lwv\,dy = Lw\sqrt{2gy}\,dy$$
$$\text{Total flow } q = Lw\sqrt{2g}$$
$$\int_0^H y^{\frac{1}{2}}\,dy = \tfrac{2}{3}\,Lw\sqrt{2gH^3}$$

A similar method can be used to arrive at the formulas for V notches and Cipolletti weirs. However, the true flow is less than the theoretical flow, and a discharge coefficient Cd has to be introduced for reasons like those that necessitate the use of a similar coefficient in connection with primary measuring devices used with head flowmeters in closed conduits. By introducing average flow coefficients, the following results are obtained:

Rectangular weir $q = 3.33(Lw - 0.2H)H^{\frac{3}{2}}$
60° V notch $q = 1.46H^{\frac{5}{2}}$
90° V notch $q = 2.52H^{2.47}$
Cipolletti weir $q = 3.367LwH^{\frac{3}{2}}$

In the case of the rectangular weir, double end contraction has been assumed; and to allow for this, $0.1H$ is subtracted for each end contraction from the length of the crest. Unfortunately, the coefficient of discharge is

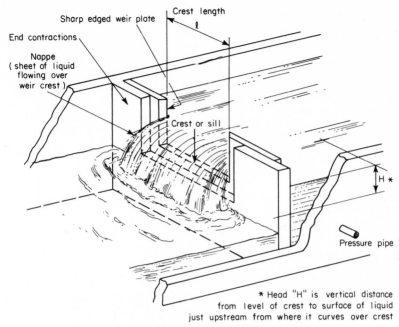

Fig. 8-47   Weir with double end contractions.

not constant but varies with the flow, so that for practical purposes the above formulas are of limited value. For this reason semiempirical formulas have been arrived at from a large number of experiments by British hydraulic engineers, and their use is recommended in cases where weirs are designed to British Standards specifications. Sometimes use may be made of the following approximate formulas for estimating purposes:

Rectangular weirs	$G = 2{,}160 L_w H^{3/2}$	imp. gallons/hr
	$= 1{,}800 L_w H^{3/2}$	U.S. gallons/hr
V notch	$G = 133.8 H \tan \dfrac{\theta}{2}$	imp. gallons/hr
	$= 111.5 H \tan \dfrac{\theta}{2}$	U.S. gallons/hr

where L_w is in feet, H is in inches, and G is in gallons.

Flumes

With flumes, the measuring section may be produced by a contraction of the side walls, by a hump in the channel bed, or by both side contractions and humps. However, the section most commonly in use is the Parshall flume, for which dimensions have been standardized. They are shown in Fig. 8-48.

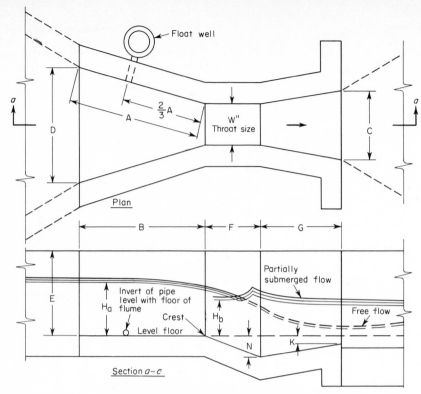

Fig. 8-48 Parshall flume dimensions.

W	A	⅔A	B	C	D	E	F	G	K	N	FLUME FLOW EXTREMES* MGD	
											MIN.	MAX.
0-3	1-6⅜	1-¼	1-6	0-7	0-10³⁄₁₆	2-0	0-6	1-0	0-1	0-2¼	0.02	1.23
0-6	2-⁷⁄₁₆	1-4⁵⁄₁₆	2-0	1-3½	1- 3⅝	2-0	1-0	2-0	0-3	0-4½	0.03	2.52
0-9	2-10⅝	1-11⅛	2-10	1-3	1-10⅝	2-6	1-0	1-6	0-3	0-4½	0.06	5.75
1-0	4-6	3-0	4- 4⅞	2-0	2- 9¼	3-0	2-0	3-0	0-3	0-9	0.07	10.41
1-6	4-9	3-2	4- 7⅞	2-6	3- 4⅜	3-0	2-0	3-0	0-3	0-9	0.10	15.90
2-0	5-0	3-4	4-10⅞	3-0	3-11½	3-0	2-0	3-0	0-3	0-9	0.27	21.39
3-0	5-6	3-8	5- 4¾	4-0	5- 1⅞	3-0	2-0	3-0	0-3	0-9	0.39	32.57
4-0	6-0	4-0	5-10⅝	5-0	6- 4¼	3-0	2-0	3-0	0-3	0-9	0.84	43.88
5-0	6-6	4-4	6- 4½	6-0	7- 6⅝	3-0	2-0	3-0	0-3	0-9	1.03	55.32
6-0	7-0	4-8	6-10⅜	7-0	8- 9	3-0	2-0	3-0	0-3	0-9	1.68	66.89
7-0	7-6	5-0	7- 4¼	8-0	9-11⅜	3-0	2-0	3-0	0-3	0-9	1.94	78.46
8-0	8-0	5-4	7-10⅛	9-0	11- 1¾	3-0	2-0	3-0	0-3	0-9	2.26	90.16

Dimensions in feet and inches.
   * Extreme minimum and maximum capacities of flume; the actual measuring range depends upon the type instrument selected and will lie within these extreme limits.

REVIEW QUESTIONS AND PROBLEMS

8-50   Describe with the aid of sketches the three common types of weir. Under what conditions would each be used?

8-51   Explain the terms "end contraction," "nappe," "suppressed weir."

8-52   What is the reason for using semiempirical equations to calculate flow over weirs rather than theoretical calculations to which a discharge coefficient is applied?

8-53   The theoretical formula for flow over a rectangular weir with double end contractions is given by

$$Q = \tfrac{2}{3}(Lw - 0.2H)\sqrt{2gH^3}$$

where all dimensions are in feet/per second units. The coefficient of discharge corresponding to $H = 20$ in. is 0.64. Calculate flow in U.S. gallons (imp. gallons) per hour when $Lw = 4$ ft and $H = 20$ in. Compare the result with that obtained by using the semiempirical formula

$$G = 177.5[147.9](Lw - 0.1H)H^{\frac{3}{2}}$$

where G is in U.S. gallons [imp. gallons], k is in inches, and Lw is in inches.

8-54   (a) For a triangular V-shaped flow weir in Fig. 8-49b with the notation indicated, show that the discharge equation is given by

$$Q = \tfrac{8}{15}C_d\sqrt{2g}\,H^{\frac{5}{2}}\tan\frac{\theta}{2}$$

where C_d is the coefficient of discharge.

(b) If $C_d = 0.6$ and for maximum flow $\theta = 90°$, show that

$$Q = 2.56H^{\frac{5}{2}}$$

Note: A V-shaped or rectangular weir can be considered as an orifice with an open top. Water flows over the weir. Weirs are used to measure the water discharge from channels, storage tanks, and reservoirs.

8-55   (a) For the rectangular weir in Fig. 8-46a show that

$$Q = \tfrac{2}{3}C_d\sqrt{2g}\,LH^{\frac{3}{2}}$$

where L is the length of the crest.

(b) Calculate the discharge of water over a rectangular weir with a crest length of 18 in. The head of water above the lower edge is 12 in. Assume a discharge coefficient of 0.60.

CHAPTER NINE

Temperature measurement

*If a man will begin with certainties he shall
end in doubts; but if he will be content to
begin with doubts he shall end in certainties.*

FRANCIS BACON

MECHANICAL SYSTEMS

Today, temperature is expressed in degrees tied to a limited number of
national and international scales, but the introduction of a temperature
scale is comparatively recent. Galileo was probably the first person to
consider temperature as a fundamental unit for which a scale had to be
provided. Even today, however, although the man in the street may think
he understands what it is, it is impossible to define temperature in every-
day language. It can most easily be considered as analogous to head in
hydraulics, because if a body A is at a higher temperature than body B
and the two are in contact, A will lose heat and its temperature will fall
while B will gain heat and its temperature will rise. (Heat, like water, will
not flow uphill.) The relative sizes, or other physical characteristics of A
and B, are irrelevant.

Today, two scales are in common use: the Fahrenheit scale, on which the
freezing point of water corresponds to 32° and its boiling point to 212°,
and the Celsius scale, which is gradually being adopted internationally, on
which these two points correspond to 0° and 100°. Before 1948 the Celsius
scale was referred to as the centigrade scale in Anglo-Saxon countries.
Formerly, the Reaumur scale was in use in certain industries, the two
fixed points for water being 0° and 80°. In physics, the corresponding
absolute scales, the Rankine and the Kelvin, are used. The zeros of these
scales, for practical purposes, can be regarded as −460°F and −273°C,
respectively. To determine absolute temperature on the Fahrenheit scale,
therefore, it is necessary to add 460°, and on the Celsius scale, 273°.
From the above it will be seen that

$$°C = \tfrac{5}{9}(°F - 32) \qquad \text{or} \qquad °F = \tfrac{9}{5}°C + 32$$

There is no doubt that, before Galileo's time, temperature indicators which were the forerunners of the Seger and Orton cones still in use today were available. All minerals when heated start to soften at a fairly definite temperature, and therefore the softening point is an indication of temperature. By combining different minerals, it is possible to produce a series of mixtures with different softening points which will cover a range of about 600 to 2000°C, in steps of about 25°C.

If the minerals are shaped into a small cone the softening point is observable when the cone starts to collapse. Seger and Orton cones are used in the ceramics industry and in isolated brickworks. The cones are given numbers; there are about 60 of them, each number corresponding to a fairly definite temperature. The lowest corresponds to 600°C and the highest to 2000°C.

It will be clear that a continuous indication or record of temperature conditions is not possible with such cones, and the use of the cones is therefore limited. When continuous indication or recording is required a large number of different systems are available. They can be broken down into the following general classifications.

1. Mechanical systems:
   Expansion of metals
   Expansion of fluids
2. Electrical systems:
   Resistance
   Thermocouple
   Total radiation
   Partial radiation
   Optical

Metal Expansion

All metals will expand when heated, and the amount of expansion will depend on the temperature and the coefficient of expansion. If, therefore, two strips of metal with dissimilar coefficients of expansion are bonded together, a distortion will occur on heating, as shown in Fig. 9-1. This is the basic operating principle of the common thermostat. For use as an industrial temperature indicator the bimetal strip is usually bent into a coil one end of which is

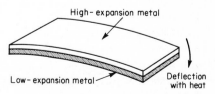

Fig. 9-1   Simple bimetallic strip.

fixed so that on expansion a rotary motion is automatically obtained, as shown in Fig. 9-2.

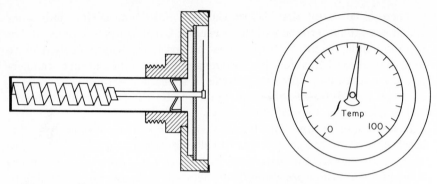

Fig. 9-2   Industrial temperature indicator with helical bimetal element.

Generally, one metal is Invar because of its low coefficient of expansion and the other metal is brass for low temperatures or a nickel alloy for higher temperatures. Bimetallic thermometers are very rugged and require virtually no maintenance. A range of −40 to 800°F can be covered and an overrange of about 50 percent can occur without causing damage. The speed of response is moderate. Very high accuracy is not claimed, being ±1 percent under ideal conditions of installation, but repeatability is usually consistent.

When it is satisfactory to have the indicator at the point of measurement, the bimetallic thermometer has much to recommend it. Its main disadvantage is that, owing to the necessity for enclosing the element in an outer sheath, the speed of response may be lower than that of other systems.

Fluid-expansion Thermometers

The simplest form of fluid-expansion thermometer is the glass-stem, mercury-filled thermometer such as that used for measuring air temperature and the clinical thermometer used for measuring body temperature. Each depends for its operation on the linear expansion or contraction of the mercury when heated or cooled. Some clinical thermometers may be advertised as "extra fast" but in fact may require one-minute insertion before an accurate reading can be obtained. This illustrates the fundamental difficulty involved in the measurement of temperature, namely, *lag.* One authority put it in a nutshell by saying that "we measure the temperature that *was* and not the temperature that *is.*"

In this type of thermometer the lag is caused mainly by the glass, which has a low thermal conductivity. Glass, however, is convenient because its transparency allows observation of the mercury column within. Nevertheless, glass has a number of peculiarities due to its structure, which alters over a period of time. Some of the changes take place immediately after manufacture, and they can be counteracted by careful annealing before calibration. The long-term changes, however, are unpredictable and can be dealt with only by checking the thermometer at regular intervals of, say, a year, against some standard and, if necessary, preparing a table of corrections from the readings obtained.

The volume of mercury contained in the stem when a reading is being taken is not negligible compared with that contained in the bulb, and therefore the depth of immersion is important. Glass thermometers are therefore made for either full or partial immersion. In the latter case the stem is marked with a line to show the required depth of immersion. If the thermometer is not immersed to the correct depth, an error in reading will occur. If a thermometer designed for full immersion is used for partial immersion, a correction can, in theory, be calculated from the equation

$$\text{Correction } x°C = 0.00016(t_1 - t_2)n$$

when calibration is in degrees Celsius, or

$$x°F = 0.00009(t_1 - t_2)n$$

when calibration is in degrees Fahrenheit. In these equations t_1 is the bulb temperature, t_2 is the average temperature of emergent stem, and n is the number of degrees exposed. However, it will be obvious that to arrive accurately at t_2 is most difficult. In any case, working to such a degree of accuracy is seldom, if ever, required.

Three features of construction are of interest:

Overload protection
Scale suppression
Retention of the level of the mercury column after the source of heat has been removed.

The first two are obtained by arranging enlargements in the capillary at the top and bottom into which the mercury can expand, and the last is obtained by means of a restriction between the bulb and the capillary. These three features are shown in Fig. 9-3.

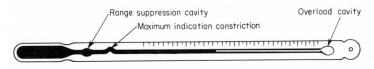

Fig. 9-3   Glass-stem thermometer.

The glass thermometer is used in industry, but it is usually protected from damage by a metal casing with a slot through which the mercury column can be observed. The bulb may also be protected. The glass thermometer is useful only where it is easily accessible for reading, and therefore its use is limited. Nevertheless, there is a range of "filled" systems operating on a similar expansion system which, as will be seen, overcomes this difficulty. The filled systems are divided by the Scientific Apparatus Manufacturers Association (SAMA) into the following classifications:

Class I   Liquid filled (but excluding mercury)
Class II   Vapor filled
Class III   Gas filled
Class V   Mercury filled.

The construction of all these systems follows the same general pattern, each system consisting of a bulb, a capillary tube, and a pressure-sensing device or spring which will be either a Bourdon tube or a bellows, as shown in Fig. 9-4. The liquid-filled systems, classes I and V, depend for

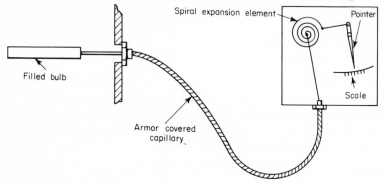

Fig. 9-4　Simple thermal system for industrial temperature measurement.

their operation on volumetric expansion of the liquid and give an almost linear response to temperature changes. The vapor-tension systems, class II, depend for their operation on vapor pressure, resulting in a nonlinear relationship, and the gas-expansion systems, class III, give a linear relationship because their operation is dictated by the ideal-gas laws. If these fundamental facts are remembered, there should be no difficulty in understanding how the equations applying to each system are developed.

In all temperature-measuring systems, sources of possible errors and means of overcoming the errors in part or whole have to be considered. In the case of filled systems, these errors have the following four causes:

Incorrect immersion
Changes in ambient temperature
Changes in barometric pressure
Difference in elevation between the bulb and the spring.

Table 9-1 summarizes certain characteristics of the filled systems.

Liquid-filled Systems, Classes I and V

Mercury filling, class V, is most frequently used. Such a system is regarded by many as the most satisfactory of all the filled systems. In class I, toluene has the advantage of a high coefficient of cubical expansion. Liquid-filled systems are not strictly constant-volume systems, because the filling expands and the change in volume has to be accommodated in the system. It is this change of volume which provides the pressure to operate the spring. The change in volume can be obtained from the expression

$$V = V_0(1 + Bt)$$

where V_0 = volume at the time of filling
$\quad\ \ V$ = new volume at temperature t
$\quad\ \ B$ = coefficient of cubical expansion

The following liquids are among those used in class I systems:

Liquid	Range
Xylene	−40 to +750°F (−40 to +400°C)
Ether	+70 to +195°F (+20 to + 90°C)
Alcohol	+155 to +260°F (+70 to +130°C)

Their use is not widespread because their thermal conductivity is much lower than that of mercury and the speed of response is therefore lower. Mercury has a conductivity nearly 50 times that of alcohol.

Large forces are available from the expansion of a liquid. Mercury is filled under considerable pressure in order to increase the range up to 1200°F (650°C) by raising the boiling point of the mercury. The lower limit is dictated by the freezing point of mercury, which is −40°F. This necessitates the use of very stiff Bourdons. Because of the high pressure and the affinity of mercury for all but ferrous metals, bulb, capillary, and Bourdon are made of steel.

By making the assumption that the liquid is maintained at constant volume, which is not strictly correct, an idea of the available pressure increment may be had. Assuming the liquid changes in temperature from 0 to 1°C, the effective volume increase v can be found as follows:

$$v = V(\alpha - \beta)$$

where V is the volume of liquid at 0°C and α and β are the coefficients of expansion of the liquid and the bulb envelope. To reduce the increased volume $V + v$ to the original volume V would require a pressure P, which can be obtained as follows:

$$P = \frac{1}{C}\frac{v}{V} = \frac{1}{C}(\alpha - \beta) \qquad \text{approx}$$

Table 9-1   Characteristics of classes of pressure-spring thermometers

Class	Liquid-filled — Class V, Mercury	Liquid-filled — Class I, Xylene	Vapor-pressure, Class II	Gas, Class III
Filling	Mercury under initial high spring pressure (note 2)	Xylene (or other hydrocarbon) under initial pressure	Volatile liquid (note 8)	Inert gas under moderate initial pressure
Scale	Uniform	Fairly uniform (note 5)	Progressive (note 9)	Uniform
Bulb volume	Medium, and varies inversely with length of range	Small	Medium (note 10)	Large, and varies with tube length
Minimum bulb length	3 to 5 in.	1 in.	2 in.	5 in.
Bulb material	Steel or stainless steel	Stainless steel, brass, Monel, or nickel	Brass, Monel, steel, silicon bronze, etc.	Brass, Monel, steel, silicon bronze, etc.
Average 63% response time (L) of average $\frac{7}{16}$-in.-diam bulb (note 1)				
With rapid circulation	In water 5 sec In air 60 sec	In water 6 sec In air 75 sec	In water 4 sec In air 50 sec	In water 7 sec In air 85 sec
With slow circulation	17 sec 600 sec	20 sec 750 sec	14 sec 500 sec	22 sec 850 sec
Maximum tube length	25 ft (note 3)	15 ft when uncompensated	250 ft (note 10)	300 ft (note 14)
Effects of temperature fluctuations along the capillary (tube error)	Vary with tube length and with area of capillary bore (note 4)	Vary with tube length (note 6)	None as long as bulb is hotter than tube (note 11)	Vary with tube length and inversely with bulb volume (note 15)
Can temperature fluctuations at spring be compensated?	Yes	Yes	Compensation unnecessary (note 11)	Yes
Effects of variations in atmospheric pressure (also altitude error)	Small (negligible in systems filled at high pressure)	Extremely small	Slight errors in lower end of range where actuating pressure is low	Slight errors at low working pressure only
Does different level of bulb and instrument affect calibration?	Yes	Yes, slightly (note 7)	Yes (note 12)	No
Lower limits of ranges	−38°C or −36°F	−100°C or −150°F	−180°C or −300°F (note 13)	−240°C or −400°F
Upper limits of ranges	540°C or 1000°F	400°C or 750°F	370°C or 700°F (note 13)	540°C or 1000°F
Usual maximum commercial length of one span	550 C° or 1000 F°	330 C° or 600 F°	160 C° or 250 F° (note 13)	550 C° or 810 F°
Usual minimum commercial length of one span	25 C° or 45 F°	22 C° or 40 F°	50 C° or 90 F° (note 13)	50 C° or 90 F°

From *Measurement and Control Handbook*, p. 30, Instruments Publishing Company. Reprinted by permission of the publisher.

Table 9-1 had to be compiled, in part, from information released for the first time by various qualified sources. No two sources agreed on all points.

1. For capillary bulbs, about 0.25 of the value of L for a $7/16$-in. bulb, plus a delayed start of about $0.1L$. All figures for L given in Table 9-1 are rounded averages of widely different values, especially for air.

2. Comparative advantages of the high-pressure mercury filling are ruggedness, durability, and permanent accuracy. A slight disadvantage is limited choice of bulb material.

3. 150 ft or more when "full compensation" is used. One method uses a gas-filled capillary alongside the mercury capillary, this body of gas actuating a second pressure spring, shifting the mercury mechanism to compensate for temperature fluctuations along the tube. In another method, the capillary tube is of high-expansion material and has running throughout its length a wire of low-expansion material, so that for a given change in temperature, the change in mercury volume is the same as that of the annular space it can occupy.

4. No effects when "full compensation" is embodied in the system.

5. Nonlinearity above 250°F is slight, and it is said to be the same in successive shipments of xylene accepted for fillings; therefore, printed recorder charts may be used.

6. Slight. Even with smallest standard bulb, change from ice to steam on 10-ft capillary is claimed to produce 1°F error in indicating bulb temperature. Some makers supply "full compensation" systems.

7. Lowest working pressure, at low end of usual range, is 300 psi; 10 ft head of xylene = 3.5 psi.

8. Characteristics of many volatile liquids being known, makers can supply proper filling for each range specified. It always is advisable to specify not only the range but the zone within the range where accuracy is most needed. The reason is that sensitivity increases with temperature.

9. A "progressive" scale is "closed" at its lower end and "open" at its upper end.

10. The capillary and spring for the usual ranges are completely filled with unvaporized liquid, with vapor generated only within the bulb. If bulb is excessively small or if tube is excessively long, low ambient temperature (reducing volume of liquid in tube and spring) would leave insufficient liquid in bulb where there must always be free surface.

11. In the usual arrangement, when any portion of the tube or spring is subjected to a higher temperature than that of the bulb, the pressure of the higher temperature is developed as long as any liquid is exposed to the hot spot. See text.

12. Considerably when working pressure differential is low. 10 ft water head = 4.33 psi. Assuming a high-Baumé hydrocarbon, we get about 3.5 psi for every 10 ft. Even more important is the total impairment of accuracy when bulb level is higher than spring and no liquid is left in bulb. Use of a transmission liquid sealed off from the active liquid by a bellows permits installing the bulb at a higher level than the spring. See text.

13. Liquids which will produce a vapor pressure sufficient to assure fair sensitivity at lower end of specified range are chosen. The upper end depends on liquid's critical temperature and pressure.

14. Fluid friction in the capillary is negligible, the medium being a gas, and the length limitation is imposed by the temperature errors. In plants provided with room-temperature control, longer tube lengths may be used. Some makers supply "full compensation."

15. The largest practicable volume of gas should be contained within the bulb, and therefore the longest length which the application can take should be specified, even where maker can supply "full compensation."

where C = compressibility of the liquid; for mercury $C = 3.71 \times 10^6$
per atmosphere
$\alpha = 18.2 \times 10^{-5}$
$\beta = 35.7 \times 10^{-6}$
whence $P = 40$ atm

Normally, regardless of the range, the Bourdon for a mercury-filled system is a standard size made from a flattened tube, while the volume of the bulb and the filling pressure are modified to produce the various ranges required. The greater the range the smaller the bulb.

Errors. An error will occur if the bulb is not totally immersed or, when a protective well is fitted, if the bulb has not been pushed down to the bottom of the well. Each part of the system—bulb, capillary, and Bourdon—behaves as a thermometer in its own right, so that changes in ambient temperature along the capillary or at the Bourdon will introduce an error. The error at the Bourdon is normally dealt with by means of a bimetallic compensator which will bias the spring movement in one direction or the other as the temperature rises or falls above or below the calibration temperature.

When the capillary exceeds 20 or 30 ft, the error is likely to be such that some form of compensation is required. The possible effect of changes in ambient temperature can be obtained as follows:

$$X = \frac{v_1 t_1}{V}$$

where X = error, degrees
V = volume of the bulb
v_1 = volume of capillary
t_1 = temperature change of capillary from calibrated value

Example
$V = 1$ in.^{3}
$v_1 = 0.4$ in.^{3} (100 ft of 0.2-in.-diam capillary)
$t_1 = 30°F$ (e.g., calibrated at 70°F and operating at either 40 or 100°F)
Therefore X becomes 12°F. With a range of 0 to 1000°F this represents an error of 1.2 percent, which is appreciable.

The importance of the ratio v_1/V will be obvious, but for maximum speed of response the bulb must be kept as small as possible. In any case, bulb size is virtually fixed for any given span because a standard spring is used for all ranges. On the other hand, a smaller-bore capillary can be used with a lower limit of 0.005 in. The speed of response, however, will be affected by the extra resistance to flow.

Full compensation can be obtained by running a second capillary from the bulb location, connecting the second capillary to its own Bourdon in the instrument case, and interlinking the second Bourdon with the main Bourdon. This is, of course, costly and involves further linkages which may add to the hysteresis of the system. A better method is to run an Invar wire down the center of the capillary in order to leave a small annular space around the Invar wire to accommodate the mercury. In this case the capillary is normally made of stainless steel.

Head errors have to be taken into account, particularly in the case of mercury because of its large weight density. In round figures, every foot difference in elevation between the bulb and the spring is equivalent to 6 psi. Bearing in mind the high filling pressure of the mercury, head error has to be considered only when the difference in elevation is considerable. The adjustment of the instrument is nearly always made on site, because the exact position of mounting is seldom known at the time an instrument is ordered. The effect of changes in barometric pressure can be neglected because of the high filling pressure used.

It has been noted that the Bourdon spring is standard for all ranges, so that the size of the bulb largely determines the range selected. Thus

$$\Delta V = V_b \phi R = \text{constant } K$$

where ΔV = Bourdon volume change, cm³
ϕ = differential expansivity between filling liquid and enclosing bulb, cm³/cm³ × °F
V_b = bulb volume, cm³
R = span, °F

By rearrangement,

$$V_b = \frac{K}{\phi R} = \frac{K_1}{R}$$

from which it can be seen that a large span requires a small bulb. K_1 will, to some extent, depend on the stiffness of the spring chosen; it varies from 65 to 200 as between different manufacturers.

The so-called dip effect with a mercury-in-steel system should be noted. If the temperature is increased suddenly, the bulb will momentarily expand faster than the mercury. This will cause the mercury to flow into the bulb, thus apparently indicating a sudden drop in temperature.

Class II, Vapor-filled System

This system is the most widely used of the filled systems because of its low cost. Its operation is based on Dalton's law, which states that the pressure of a saturated vapor depends only on its temperature. If a liquid which vaporizes easily is confined in a closed system, a vapor pressure is created at the surface of the liquid, i.e., at the interface level. The pressure will depend on the temperature. All liquids with free surfaces have molecules leaving and returning to the liquid continuously. If the temperature is increased, more molecules migrate permanently, and it is this action which causes an increase in pressure in the system. The amount of liquid in the bulb does not affect the vapor pressure provided some liquid is present. The relationship between vapor pressure and temperature is not linear, and a number of empirical formulas have been developed from experimental work. One of them is the following:

$$\log_{10} P = \frac{-0.05223a}{T} + b$$

where P = absolute pressure, mm Hg
     T = absolute temperature °K
and a and b are constants which have to be looked up for each liquid in a reference book such as the *Chemical Handbook*. From what has been said it will be evident that in order to measure the temperature with the bulb, the interface level must be kept in the bulb and the system has to be designed accordingly.

Class II group A designates the construction when the temperature of the bulb is higher than that of the rest of the system. Because the vapor condenses in the coolest part of the system, the capillary and spring must be filled with liquid and the bulb only partially filled so that the interface level remains in the bulb.

Class II group B designates the construction when the temperature to be measured is lower than that of the rest of the system. The vapor will then tend to condense in the bulb, and therefore the capillary and spring must contain no liquid, while the bulb will be about half-filled at ambient temperature.

Class II group C designates the construction when the temperature to be measured may be above or below that of the rest of the system. Clearly, it must be a combination of groups A and B, which necessitates a large bulb to accommodate the liquid from the capillary and spring when the bulb is at a lower temperature than the rest of the system. When the temperature crosses ambient, either going up or coming down, there will be considerable disturbance and a period when the pressure will not change, thus creating a lag in the system. Liquid will be migrating from the bulb into the capillary and spring, or vice versa.

This trouble can be overcome by a special design, class II group D, which employs a nonvolatile liquid which fills the capillary and spring and partly fills the bulb. A diaphragm is positioned above this buffer liquid, and the vaporizable liquid introduced above the diaphragm transmits its pressure, via the diaphragm, to the buffer-liquid-filled system.

The filling liquid for class II thermometers is partly decided by the range:

Sulfur dioxide	−30 to + 120°C
Ether	+10 to + 150°C
Alcohol	+65 to + 200°C

The nonuniform scale restricts the range which can be covered by any one instrument, because, if the spring is sufficiently sensitive to respond to the small pressure changes at the lower temperatures, it will be over-sensitive at the higher temperatures.

Theoretically, no ambient-temperature error should be involved with this class of thermometer. In practice, however, some possibility of error does exist because of the impossibility of excluding all traces of air from the system. There is, therefore, some limitation in the maximum length of capillary permissible.

Because the vapor pressures produced are relatively low, class II instruments have to use weak springs, and bellows are often substituted for Bourdons. For this reason it is practical to design the strength of spring to suit the range and span. For the same reason, a correction for barometer pressure should, in theory, be made. In practice, however, it never is, largely because of the extra cost. Also, head errors can be appreciable, but only in the case of class II A and class II D, or in the case of class II C when liquid is filling the capillary and spring, i.e., when the temperature of the bulb is above that of the rest of the system.

If the spring is above the bulb, the pressure within the spring equals the vapor pressure in the bulb minus the pressure due to the head of liquid in the capillary. In the same way, if the spring is below the bulb, the pressure within the spring equals the vapor pressure in the bulb plus the pressure due to the head of liquid in the capillary. The error E as percent of span can be found from

$$E = \frac{P_h}{\Delta P} \, 100\%$$

where P_h = liquid pressure, in psi, in capillary due to head
 ΔP = effective vapor-pressure change over the range
In order to be able to use convenient units, this can be rewritten

$$E = \frac{0.43hw}{\Delta P} \, 100\%$$

where h = head, in ft
 w = density, in g/cm³, which approximates specific gravity

Example. For the following example water is taken because vapor pressure can easily be obtained from steam tables. Range 300 to 500°F, that is, 200°F span.

At 500°F, vapor pressure = 680 psia
At 300°F, vapor pressure = 68 psia
        Difference ΔP = 612 psia

With bulb position 10 ft above or below the spring

$$E_{avg} = \frac{0.43 \times 10 \times 1 \times 100\%}{612}$$
$$= 0.7\%$$
$$= 1.4°F$$

In order to find the error at any point in the scale, the method of approach is the same. The pressure due to the head is added to or subtracted from the vapor pressure at the given temperature, and in the case of water the new boiling point can be found from the steam tables. The difference between this temperature and the selected point on the scale gives the error, in degrees.

Class III, Gas-filled Systems

The gas-filled system is assumed to operate in accordance with Boyle's and Charles' laws.[1] From this it can be stated that the absolute pressure varies directly as the absolute temperature if the volume remains constant. The scale is therefore linear. For convenience it can be expressed as follows:

$$P_t = P_0(1 + \beta t)$$

where P_t = absolute pressure at any temperature $t°C$
   P_0 = absolute pressure exerted by gas at 0°C
   β = coefficient of pressure increase = $\frac{1}{273}$
The pressure increment per degree rise in temperature is

$$\Delta P = \frac{P_0}{273}$$

Thus ΔP will depend on the pressure at 0°C, and the greater the filling pressure the greater this pressure increment will be. In general it is relatively small.

Immersion error can occur if the bulb is not completely immersed or if it is not pushed down into the well, when one is used. Error due to changes in barometric head occur, but they are normally negligible. Head errors are virtually absent because of the low weight density of the gases used. Errors due to changes in ambient temperature along the

[1] See pp. 53 and 54.

capillary are unavoidable, and although a second capillary and spring can be used, as in the case of liquid-filled systems, compensation is correct at only one bulb-temperature measurement. If the compensating spring is arranged to give full compensation at midscale, it will under-compensate above and overcompensate below that temperature. For that reason the bulb volume is usually made large relative to the capillary volume, 10:1 or more, which leads to a large bulb and a diminished speed of response. Therefore, relatively large spans or ranges must be used, and the final design is a compromise between maximum bulb size and allowable filling pressure. It must be remembered that gases depart from the ideal-gas laws at pressures higher than, say, 30 psi.

As in the case of the liquid-filled systems, each part of the system can be considered as a thermometer in its own right. Hence:

$$\underbrace{\frac{V_b P_1}{T b_1}}_{\text{bulb}} + \underbrace{\frac{V_c P_1}{T c_1}}_{\text{capillary}} + \underbrace{\frac{V_B P_1}{T B_1}}_{\text{spring}} = \frac{V_b P_2}{T b_2} + \frac{V_c P_2}{T c_2} + \frac{V_B P_2}{T B_2}$$

The error due to changes of temperature along the capillary is derived from the above on the assumption that the spring compensating is done by a bimetallic strip in the usual way. Error E as percent or range is

$$E = \frac{100 V_c \, \Delta T_c \, T_b{}^2}{(V_b T_c + V_c T_b) T_c R}$$

where T_c = mean capillary absolute temperature

ΔT_c = capillary temperature change from calibration temperature

R = span, °F

T_b = bulb temperature absolute (460 + °F)

From this the importance of the ratio of bulb volume to capillary volume is evident, as is the effect of the range span.

Example

    Bulb volume = 25 cm³
    Range span = 0 to 500°F
    Capillary bore = 0.012 in.
    Capillary length = 50 ft
    Calibration temperature = 80°F
    Capillary temperature change = ±50°F

From the above, capillary volume = 1.11 cm³. Assume temperature at center of range is 250°F.

$$E = \frac{100 \times 1.11 \times 50 \times 710 \times 710}{[(25 \times 540) + (1.11 \times 710)]540 \times 500}$$

$$= 0.73\% \text{ of range}$$

The gas most commonly used for filling is nitrogen, giving a range of −200 to +800°F (−90 to +450°C). The nitrogen thermometer is, in fact, used as a calibration standard.

REVIEW QUESTIONS AND PROBLEMS

9-1 (a) Describe the basic principle and operation of the bimetallic strip.

(b) Each of two pieces of metal, one iron and the other brass, has a length of 10 in. at 100°F. What will be the lengths at 1100°F if the coefficient of linear expansion for iron is 6.7×10^{-6} per °F and that for brass is 1.1×10^{-5} per °F?

9-2 (a) What are the desirable properties of a perfect thermometric fluid? Show to what extent mercury, alcohol, and air fulfill the conditions.

(b) What values on the Celsius scale are equivalent to temperatures of 185 and 0°F?

(c) What values on the Fahrenheit scale are equivalent to temperatures of 15 and −273°C?

(d) During a certain experiment on gases, the readings on a Celsius and a Fahrenheit thermometer were the same. What was the temperature?

9-3 (a) Define the coefficient of absolute expansion of a liquid.

(b) When full, a glass vessel contains 816.00 g of mercury at 0°C. The mass of mercury which fills it at 100°C is 803.21 g. The coefficient of absolute expansion of mercury is 0.00182 per °C. Calculate the coefficient of cubical expansion of glass.

9-4 A rod 1,000 cm long at 0°C is composed of two metal rods A and B joined end to end, the portions having coefficients of linear expansion 0.00003 and 0.00002, respectively. Calculate the lengths of the two portions A and B of the rod if the expansion is 3 cm at 80°C.

9-5 Describe some method for determining the relation between the pressure and temperature of a given mass of gas at constant volume.

9-6 (a) State Boyle's law.

(b) If 100 ft³ of gas in a container at 85.3 psig and at 27°C is permitted to expand to 1,000 ft³ at the same temperature, what is the new pressure, in psig?

9-7 (a) Describe briefly the laboratory method you would use to correct for the stem exposure of a mercury-filled thermometer.

(b) During a temperature-measurement test of a liquid, the average stem temperature is 85.5°C and the bulb temperature is 100.5°C. At the level of the liquid the reading on the scale is 20.0°C and the maximum scale reading is 120.0°C. Calculate the exposed-column correction if 1.6×10^{-4} per °C is the apparent coefficient of expansion of mercury in glass.

9-8 For the conditions given in the accompanying diagram by how much will the reading change if the thermometer is totally immersed? The apparent coefficient of expansion of mercury in glass is 1.6×10^4 per °C.

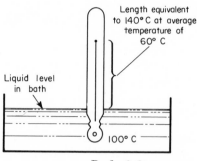

Prob. 9-8

9-9 (a) Distinguish between SAMA class I, II, III, and V thermal systems.

(b) State the fundamental principle governing the operation of class I, II, and III thermometers.

9-10 (a) Why is the relation of the volume of the bulb to that of the capillary so important in the liquid- and gas-expansion thermometers?

(b) If a liquid filled instrument has a range of 200 to 1200°F and the volume of the capillary is 0.4 in.³ and that of the bulb is 1.20 in.³, calculate the error in measurement due to a capillary change in temperature of 30°F.

(c) Express the error of part (b) as a percent of maximum scale and instrument span.

9-11 List five of the requirements for a liquid-filled thermometer. Describe, with the aid of a diagram, a typical "fully compensated" thermal system.

9-12 What are some of the requirements in the selection of a suitable liquid for a vapor-tension thermometer? Why is there a nonlinear graduation scale with this type of instrument? When will the capillary in a class II thermometer be full of liquid? What are some of the precautions to be taken with this type of thermometer? Consider elevation, position, and ambient-temperature changes.

9-13 Compute the filling pressure, in psig, at a temperature of 70°F in the design of a class III thermometer having a minimum temperature of 32°F and a maximum temperature of 1032°F with a corresponding pressure range of 500 psi for the measuring device.

9-14   A class I filled thermal system is calibrated to read correctly when the temperature surrounding the capillary is 70°F. The capillary is 100 ft long and has an internal diameter of 0.007 in. The volume of the bulb is 1.00 in.³. By how much will the reading at 70°F change if the temperature around 80 ft of the capillary drops to 10°F?

9-15   A class III filled system is to be so designed that a temperature change from 50 to 250°F will produce a change of 12 psi. Calculate the pressure in the system at 100°F. Assume the volume of the capillary is negligible in this case.

RESISTANCE THERMOMETERS

The operation of a resistance thermometer depends upon the variation with temperature of the resistance of an electrical conductor. The material is, in fact, subjected to a thermal strain, so that the phenomenon can be regarded as somewhat similar to that of the strain gauge. All metals possess this characteristic, but for industrial purposes the following requirements must be fulfilled:

1. The change in resistance per degree temperature change must be as large as possible.
2. The melting point must be as high as possible, or at least higher than the temperature to be measured.
3. The material must be of great purity so that results are repeatable.
4. The material must be reasonably easy to manufacture in order to minimize cost.

The heating effect of the current passing through the sensing element may limit the useful range as well as affecting accuracy. In the case of copper, the resistance change due to this heating effect may amount to as much as 0.47 per °C.

The three materials in normal use today are described in Table 9-2. The relationship between temperature and resistance takes the following form:

$$R_t = R_0(1 + at + bt^2 + ct^3 + nt^n)$$

where R_t = resistance at $t°$
   R_0 = resistance at some lower temperature, usually 0°C (32°F)
and a, b, and c are constants.

It will be noted that in all cases the maximum full-scale temperature is much below the melting point of the metal. This is due to the difficulty of preventing contamination at higher temperatures. Thus in the case of

Table 9-2   Resistance-thermometer metals

Material	Temperature coefficient of resistance, ohms/ohm°C at 0°C; range 0–100°C	Melting point, °C	Range limits
Platinum	0.00392	1773	−263–545°C (−442–1013°F)
Nickel	0.0063–0.0066	1455	−190–310°C (−310–590°F)
Copper	0.00425	1083	−40–125°C (−40–257°F)

platinum, a full scale above 600°C is not normally attainable, even though a metal-protecting sheath is provided, because above this temperature the sheath becomes slightly porous to gases.

How far the equation must be worked out depends on the range. For platinum two constants must be used if it is necessary to go up to 650°C. Three constants may be required for copper, although the relationship is nearly linear up to 120°C. In the case of nickel the relationship is definitely nonlinear and three constants are required for the common temperature range. Thus for a platinum element with $R_0 = 100$ ohms at 500°C the resistance at this temperature will be found to be 297.9 ohms; whereas if two constants are used, the value is 283.91 ohms. The difference of 4 percent is appreciable.

In most cases only the first constant a has to be considered. This is referred to as the temperature-resistance coefficient. It is defined as the ratio of change of resistance due to change in temperature of 1°C to resistance at 0°C; that is,

$$a = \frac{R_1 - R_2}{R_0} \qquad \text{per degree}$$

Resistance elements are frequently specified by their so-called fundamental interval, which is the difference in resistance between 0 and 100°C $(R_{100} - R_0)$. This appears in the well-known Callendar equation:

$$T = \frac{R_t - R_0}{R_{100} - R_0} 100 + \delta \left(\frac{T}{100} - 1 \right) \frac{T}{100}$$

where T = temperature of resistance winding, 0°C
R_t = resistance at temperature T, ohms
R_0 = resistance at 0°C, ohms
R_{100} = resistance at 100°C, ohms
δ = constant characteristic of each winding, approximately 1.5 for platinum

Table 9-3   Comparative figures on resistance vs. temperature for three metals
normally used for resistance thermometers

Metal	Ratios of resistances at following temperatures and 0°C, R_t/R_0											
	−200 °C	−100 °C	0 °C	100 °C	200 °C	300 °C	400 °C	500 °C	600 °C	700 °C	800 °C	900 °C
Copper	0.117	0.557	1.000	1.431	1.862	2.299	2.747	3.210	3.695	4.208	4.752	5.334
Nickel	...	...	1.000	1.663	2.501	3.611	4.847	5.398	5.882	6.327	6.751	7.156
Platinum	0.177	0.599	1.000	1.392	1.773	2.142	2.499	2.844	3.178	3.500	3.810	4.109

The constants R_0, R_{100}, and δ are determined by calibration at 0, 100, and 444.6°C, the boiling point of sulfur. Table 9-3 gives comparative figures on resistance vs. temperature for resistance thermometers.

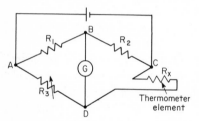

There are two common methods of obtaining a reading from a resistance thermometer: the deflectional method and the null-balance method. Both methods employ a bridge circuit supplied with current from an outside source. Figure 9-5 shows the bridge circuit in its simplest form; it can be used for either method.

Fig. 9-5   Simple bridge circuit for resistance thermometer.

Deflectional Method

At ambient temperature resistor R_3 is adjusted until there is no deflection on the galvanometer. The galvanometer reading, if directly sealed in temperature units will then be set by the zero adjustment to read ambient temperature. The voltage drop across R_1 and R_3 must be the same, i.e.,

$$IR_1 = I_3R_3$$

similarly,

$$IR_2 = I_3R_x$$

whence

$$I_3 = \frac{IR_1}{R_3} = \frac{IR_2}{R_x}$$

Therefore

$$\frac{R_1}{R_3} = \frac{R_2}{R_x}$$

$$R_x = \frac{R_3R_2}{R_1} \qquad \text{at balance} = R_b$$

For calibration purposes a fixed resistor R_z is fitted for range checking. When it is switched on, full-scale deflection should result. If it does not,

R_y is adjusted until the desired result is obtained. Readjustment will become necessary as the battery runs down.

As soon as R_x is heated, its resistance will change and a current will flow through the galvanometer. By the use of Kirchhoff's laws, or more rapidly by means of Thévenin's theory, it can be shown that

$$e = E \frac{R_x - R_b}{xR_x + y}$$

where e = emf across the galvanometer

E = emf from battery

$$x = \frac{R_b}{R_g} + \frac{R_2}{R_g} + \frac{R_3}{R_g} + \frac{R_b}{R_3} + 1$$

$$y = \frac{R_2 R_3}{R_g} + R_3 + R_b$$

The galvanometer can therefore be scaled directly in terms of temperature. In a fixed installation the battery will, of course, be replaced by a constant d-c supply. Further details of galvanometer design will be found in Chap. 12.

It will be noted that R_3 is in an arm of the bridge, so that any deterioration in resistance, e.g., a bad contact, will cause an error. It is therefore usual to make a slight rearrangement as included in Fig. 9-7.

Null-balance Method

In the null-balance method the resistance R_3 is continually so adjusted that there is no deflection of the galvanometer. To work out the answer for each new setting of the resistor would be tedious, and so in an industrial instrument the variable resistor is in the form of a slide wire carrying a pointer running over a scale which is calibrated in temperature.

A self-balancing potentiometer can, of course, be used when the voltage drop across the thermometer is balanced against the voltage drop across an accurately known standard resistance. The self-balancing potentiometer is dealt with in the section covering thermocouple pyrometry, the adaptation for resistance thermometry being shown in Fig. 9-6.

Fig. 9-6   Schematic of null-balance resistance thermometer. (Bristol Co., Bailey Meter Company Limited)

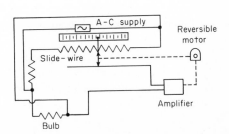

Errors

One of the advantages of a resistance thermometer is that the bulb can be located at a considerable distance from the indicating or recording instrument. However, when the distance is great, the resistance of the connecting leads has to be considered, because the instrument reads the total resistance between C and D. An error can therefore be introduced. Two methods of reducing or eliminating such an error are in common use.

The three-wire system. In the three-wire system (Fig. 9-7) the balancing resistor has been moved from R_3 and inserted between R_1 and R_2. Three wires of equal resistance are connected to the thermometer R_x as shown. At balance

$$\frac{R_1 + S_1}{R_2 + S_2} = \frac{R_3 + r}{R_x + r}$$

This gives complete compensation for error only when $R_3 = R_x$, but at other values the error is reduced to negligible proportions.

The four-wire system. In the four-wire system (Fig. 9-8) one pair of wires from each of the opposite ends of the bridge is brought to the thermometer resistance R_x. One pair is actually connected to the resistance,

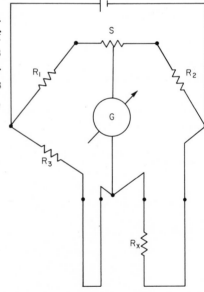

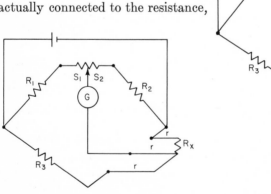

Fig. 9-7   *Three-wire system.*   Fig. 9-8   *Four-wire system.*

and the other two wires are looped at the thermometer. With this arrangement the same resistance is in each arm at all temperatures, and accurate compensation results.

Resistance systems, if correctly operated, are very accurate, and the platinum thermometer is often used as a calibrating standard. However, it is essential that the element be protected from contamination, because accuracy of results depends on the purity of the metal. For this reason, in nearly every case, the resistance element has to be protected by a sheath or well, and this results in an overall speed of response rather slower than that of other systems. For the various methods used in constructing the thermometer reference should be made to information published by the various manufacturers.

Temperature Measurement by Thermistor

A thermistor is one of the many semiconductors which are finding ever-increasing use. The resistance of a thermistor is solely a function of its absolute temperature, whether the source of heat is external, internal, or both. For this reason thermistors can be used not only for temperature measurement but also for temperature compensation as required by thermoelectric circuits.

In contradistinction to a resistance thermometer, the resistance of a thermistor decreases with temperature, i.e., the thermistor has a negative temperature resistance coefficient. This may be 3 to 5 percent/°C as compared with 0.4 percent/°C for a platinum thermometer. As an approximation,

$$R = R_0 e^{\frac{b}{T}}$$

where R = resistance at absolute temperature T
$\quad\ b$ = constant over small temperature interval
$\quad R_0$ = resistance at some standard temperature

Hence
$$\log_e R - \log_e R_0 = \frac{b}{T}$$

Thus T increases as R decreases. A thermistor may have a useful range of -100 to $400°C$.

A simple circuit for temperature measurement consists of a battery, resistor, thermistor, and microammeter. The thermistor can be at a great distance from the meter, and ordinary copper wire can be used for connection. A bridge circuit with the thermistor in one leg can also be employed. If the difference between two temperatures is required, two thermistors in different legs of the bridge can be employed. A very high degree of accuracy is possible.

If a very small voltage is applied to a thermistor, a small current will flow. It will not produce enough heat in the thermistor to raise the thermistor temperature appreciably above the ambient temperature. In this case Ohm's law will be followed. If, on the other hand, the voltage is gradually increased, the heat generated in the thermistor will eventually raise the thermistor temperature appreciably above the ambient temperature. The thermistor resistance will then decrease and more current will flow than if the resistance had remained constant. In this state the thermistor is used to measure temperature.

The voltage drop across a thermistor increases as the current increases until a maximum is reached beyond which the voltage drop decreases as the current increases, i.e., the negative-resistance characteristic exhibits itself. This characteristic of self-heat has led to the thermistor being used for many purposes other than for temperature measurement, e.g., measurement of flow, pressure, liquid level, and composition of gas, because its resistance changes whenever it is subject to anything that changes the rate at which heat is conducted away from it. One disadvantage of the thermistor for temperature measurement is that the temperature-resistance relationship is nonlinear.

Quartz Thermometer

Another recent development is the quartz thermometer. At the present time it is relatively expensive. It has a range of −40 to 440°C. Its operation is based on a quartz crystal resonator which has a precisely linear frequency-to-temperature relationship.

REVIEW QUESTIONS AND PROBLEMS

9-16   (a) Describe, with the aid of a diagram, the principle and operation of the resistance thermometer.

(b) In a resistance thermometer the bulb is made of copper wire. Its resistance at 20°C is 100 ohms. Compute the resistance value at −100°C and at 150°C.

9-17   At the time of balancing a Wheatstone bridge, R_1 = 200 ohms, R_2 = 400 ohms, and R_3 (the variable) = 300 ohms. What is the value of R_t?

9-18   (a) In the case of a platinum coil resistance thermometer why is it better not to exceed a measuring temperature of 500°C?

(b) Compute the resistance of the temperature-sensitive element at 0°C assuming a linear relation between resistance and temperature. The bridge shown in the accompanying diagram has

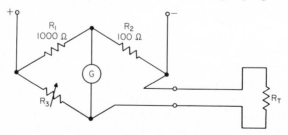

Prob. 9-18

$R_1 = 1,000$ ohms and $R_2 = 100$ ohms. It was balanced at 20°C and at 320°C with the values of the variable resistance R_3 of 30.0 and 90.0 ohms, respectively.

(c) Calculate the temperature coefficient of resistance of the element of part (b).

9-19 Make a very simple diagram of a "fully compensated" resistance thermometer.

THERMOELECTRICITY

The Seebeck effect. In 1821, Thomas Seebeck, a German scientist, took two dissimilar metal wires (e.g., copper and iron) and twisted the ends together so that there were two junctions, as shown in Fig. 9-9, the wires being separated except at the junctions. He observed that if one end was heated, an electromotive force (emf) was produced, causing a current to flow in the closed loop. The emf and current were found to vary with the temperature difference between the two junctions, that is, $T_2 - T_1$, as shown graphically in Fig. 9-10.

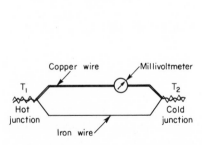

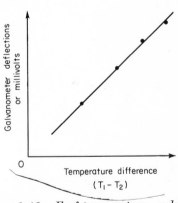

Fig. 9-9 The classical simple thermocouple circuit.

Fig. 9-10 Emf-temperature relationship in thermocouple.

The Peltier effect. Now consider what will happen if a simple thermocouple circuit has one of the wires cut and connected to a battery to pass an electric current, as shown in Fig. 9-11. Jean Peltier, a French

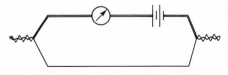

Fig. 9-11 The Peltier effect.

watchmaker, carried out this simple experiment in 1834 and observed that one of the junctions became warmer and the other cooler. In short, in Seebeck's work a temperature difference caused an electric current, whereas in Peltier's work a current was used to produce a temperature difference.

Little application was made of Peltier's work until the middle of the present century. If units comprising several banks of thermocouples are arranged in series and a direct current is passed through them, one bank is cooled while the other bank becomes heated. Obviously, the heating and cooling can be reversed by changing the direction of the current flow. Here we have an ideal system for a refrigeration or heating plant. This basic principle is used not only in industry but also in the medical field for heating or cooling components or organs.

The Thomson effect. The British scientist W. T. Thomson, who later became Lord Kelvin, deduced in 1854 that the Seebeck effect could be produced not only from dissimilar metals but also from the same metal wire or conductor if a temperature difference existed within that particular conductor. This cannot be demonstrated by experiment, because the current cannot be maintained. From this fact, the law of homogeneous metals deduces that the thermal emf from a thermocouple is independent of the temperature at intermediate points. The deduction arose from a consideration of thermodynamic equilibrium. Thomson, in fact, found in his experiment that if a current is flowing in a single wire which has a temperature gradient along it, heat is liberated when current is flowing from the hot end to the cold end and absorbed when the current is flowing from the cold end to the hot end.

Recent investigations have shown that electric currents arise between parts of the same conductor when varying degrees of stress exist without any difference in temperature. This provides the explanation of the hitherto mysterious corrosion of buried pipe lines. To cite an example, when a cold-formed pipe bend has been made in a straight pipe length and buried underground, an electric current may be generated between the bent or stressed section and the straight or unstressed portion. The return circuit could be through the surrounding soil, and metal could be removed from the pipe where the current left the pipeline to enter the soil. Techniques that are generally referred to as cathodic protection have been developed to protect the pipeline by minimizing this effect.

The Thermocouple

The arrangement of two dissimilar metals in the form of wires joined in the manner already described is called a thermocouple. The junction at the higher temperature is referred to as the "hot junction," that is, T_1, and that at the lower temperature as the "cold" or "reference junction."

The effective emf of the thermocouple, or the Seebeck effect, is the algebraic sum of the Peltier and Thomson emf's. If E is this effective emf, then from theoretical considerations:

$$E = c(T_1 - T_2) + k(T_1{}^2 - T_2{}^2)$$

where c and k are constants that depend on the metals used. An alternative form which is often used in the temperature measurements laboratory is

$$\log_{10} E = a \log_{10} T_1 + b$$

In this case T_2 is 0°C (32°F) and a and b are constants found experimentally.

It can be seen that if the effective emf E is to be a reliable measurement of the temperature of the hot junction, then it is important either to keep the cold-junction temperature (T_2) constant or to incorporate into the circuit some compensating device which will cancel out or nullify any change or variation in T_2. This matter will be taken up in more detail later on in the chapter. There are two important laws which should be discussed before considering actual arrangements of the thermocouple circuit.

The law of intermediate temperatures. If two junction temperatures of one circuit are taken as T_1 and T_2, then this circuit may be broken into two by using an intermediate temperature T_3 at the common junction. This law is best explained by the following illustration, and the numerical analysis is self-evident.

$$\left\{\begin{array}{l} \text{Let } T_1 = 212°\text{F} \\ \quad T_2 = 32°\text{F} \\ \text{Then suppose} \\ E_1 = 5.27 \\ \quad \text{millivolts (mv)} \end{array}\right\} = \left\{\begin{array}{l} \text{Let } T_1 = 112°\text{F} \\ \quad T_3 = 67°\text{F} \\ \text{Suppose it was} \\ \text{found that} \\ E_2 = 4.27 \text{ mv} \end{array}\right\} + \left\{\begin{array}{l} \text{Let } T_3 = 67°\text{F} \\ \quad T_2 = 32°\text{F} \\ \quad E_3 = 1.00 \text{ mv} \end{array}\right\}$$

By the law of intermediate temperatures, $E_1 = E_2 + E_3$; thus

$$5.27 \text{ mv} = 4.27 \text{ mv} + 1.00 \text{ mv}$$

Tables of thermoelectric emf's and temperature ranges are published in instrument handbooks and in publications available from instrument manufacturers. The tables are generally based on a cold-junction temperature of 0°C (32°F). If it should be necessary to refer to a cold-junction temperature other than 0°C (32°F), say, room temperature, then the law of intermediate temperatures makes possible a simple correction in the numerical analysis of the circuit.

The law of intermediate metals. Now consider the introduction of a third wire, XY, of different metallic composition into the loop circuit at the original cold junction (Fig. 9-12). The law of intermediate metals allows the circuit emf to remain unchanged provided both the new junctions, formed at X and Y as a result of the introduction of the third wire XY, remain at the same temperature as that of the original single junction. This law is very important in actual instrument practice because, in short, it means that, provided all the equipment for measuring the thermoelectric emf connected in the circuit at the cold junction end is maintained at the same temperature, the presence of any number of junctions of different metallic compositions will not influence the total emf in the circuit.

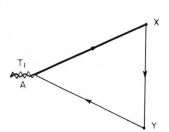

Fig. 9-12   The law of intermediate metals.

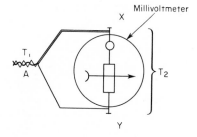

Fig. 9-13   The law of intermediate metals.

Instead of the wire XY a millivoltmeter can be inserted to measure the emf, as in Fig. 9-13. It is unimportant whether or not the millivoltmeter has brass terminals, copper internal connections with a copper coil, and a manganin (83 percent copper, 13 percent manganese, 4 percent nickel) resistor. These different metallic components will not affect the emf set up by the thermocouple as long as the temperature remains the same along the XY portion, which now becomes the new cold junction. It should be emphasized that if one or more of these metal connections differ in temperature from the others, additional emf's will be induced in the circuit and will cause errors in the final measurement.

Size of wire. The size of wires used in thermocouples is about No. 20 gauge for fast response and sensitivity. Heavy-gauge (No. 8 gauge) wires are used for higher temperatures, but at the expense of response and sensitivity.

Four main thermocouple combinations have found wide use in temperature measurement (Table 9-4). Chromel, 90 percent nickel and 10 percent chromium, forms the positive wire in the circuit. Alumel, 94 percent nickel, 2.5 percent manganese, 2 percent aluminum, 1 percent silicon, and 0.5 percent iron, forms the negative wire in the circuit. Platinum (pure) forms the negative wire, and the platinum-rhodium alloy forms the positive wire. Constantan, a typical analysis of which is 45 percent nickel and 55 percent copper, forms the negative wire in the loop circuit of a thermocouple.

Table 9-4   Thermocouple combinations

First wire	Second wire	Range, °F	Group
Platinum	Platinum, 10% rhodium	0–2700	Noble metals
Chromel	Alumel	0–2000	Base metals
Iron	Constantan	0–1600	Base metals
Copper	Constantan	−150–700	Base metals

The millivolts produced by a thermocouple are relatively low, as the following figures for degrees Fahrenheit show.

Combination	Average output, mv/°F
Platinum-rhodium	0.005
Chromel-alumel	0.023
Iron-constantan	0.03
Copper-constantan	0.025

Extension leads and compensating cable. When the measuring instrument is not directly adjacent to the thermocouple, the cold end of the thermocouple must be connected by extension leads to the instrument. These leads must have properties similar to those of the wires forming the thermocouple; otherwise, fresh thermocouples will be formed at the junctions. In the case of the base-metal thermocouples the extension leads are often composed of the same materials as the thermocouples and therefore form an "extension" of the thermocouple. However, in the case of noble-metal thermocouples it would be too expensive to use such extension wires, and therefore metals having thermoelectric properties similar to those of the thermocouple are used. These wires are then referred to as compensating leads or cable. Clearly, it is essential that in making the connections the correct wires must be joined together. If this is not done, fresh thermocouples will be formed. Incorrect connections frequently account for troubles experienced in operation.

Extension wires are relatively expensive and are generally heavy gauge in order to reduce resistance. This makes connections to terminals inconvenient, particularly to those of a multipoint switch. For this reason extension leads are sometimes taken to a junction box to which several thermocouples are connected. If the junction box is thermostatically controlled at a constant temperature, all wires can be run from there to the receivers in copper because an intermediate cold-junction point of constant temperature has been introduced.

In general, tables for thermocouples are based on a reference junction of 32°F (0°C). In most cases, however, the cold junction at the instrument will be at a higher temperature. Thus if this temperature is 75°F, the emf between 32°F and 75°F is in fact lost. This can be read directly from the table. In the case of iron-constantan the value will be found to be 1.2 2 mv.

Example. An iron-constantan thermocouple when heated gives an emf of 9.28 mv, with the cold junction at 75°F (24°C). To what emf does this correspond with a cold junction at 32°F (0°C)?

Solution. 9.28 mv + 1.22 mv = 10.5 mv. Tables based on 32°F can now be used, when it will be found that 10.5 mv corresponds to 385°F (195°C).

As with resistance thermometry, the temperature can be read using either the deflectional or null-balance (potentiometric) method.

Errors due to variation in cold (reference) junction temperature. Variation in cold-junction temperature causes an error whichever method of reading is used. Automatic cold-junction compensation can be provided by means of a bimetallic strip or bridge circuit.

Simple Deflection Type of Thermocouple Pyrometer

The fundamental arrangement of a deflection type of thermocouple pyrometer is shown in Fig. 9-14. The indicating instrument is a sensitive millivoltmeter which needs only a small current for the full-scale deflection. For details of moving-coil instruments see Chap. 12. The deflection is directly proportional to the emf of the thermocouple, which depends on the difference in temperature between the hot and cold junctions. It should be kept in mind that the emf from any thermocouple depends on the *difference* in temperature between the two junctions, and not on the temperature itself.

A galvanometer (millivoltmeter) is basically a low-torque instrument. The fundamental equation in engineering units is

$$\text{Torque} = \frac{B_g \, abn \, I}{9,810}$$

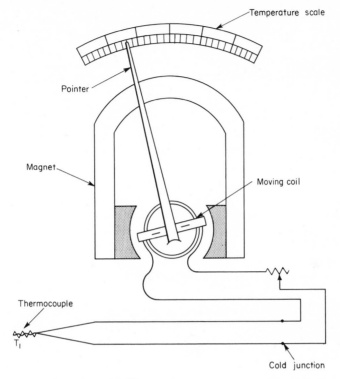

Fig. 9-14   Simple thermocouple pyrometer.

where B_g = flux density in air gap, lines
   ab = coil-sides area, cm²
   n = number of turns in coil
   I = current, amp

When a galvanometer is used as a deflectional instrument for temperature measurement, the minimum of current must be drawn in order to reduce the effects of variation in lead resistance caused by ambient-temperature changes. Therefore, a millivoltmeter used as an industrial pyrometer is a high-resistance and low-torque instrument.

   Errors due to variation of resistance of instrument coil with temperature. The coil of the galvanometer type of instrument used in thermocouple pyrometers is generally made from copper wire. The resistance of this coil will vary with temperature. For example,

$$R_t = R_{20}[1 + \alpha\,(t - 20)]$$

where R_t = resistance at $t°$
   R_{20} = resistance at 20°C, taken as the temperature at calibration
   α = 0.0043, the temperature coefficient of resistance of copper

A meter range of up to 0 to 20 mv should not have an error of more than ¼ percent of the reading for a change of 1°C in the ambient temperature.

Example. Referring to Fig. 9-15, the following values are given: thermocouple, iron-constantan; required range, 0 to 700°C (1292°F); lead resistance $R_l =$

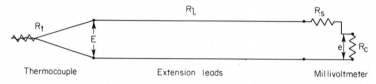

Fig. 9-15   *Errors due to ambient-temperature change.*

5 ohms (30-ft extension wire); thermocouple resistance $R_t = 1$ ohm; total external resistance = 6 ohms, excluding R_s series (swamp) resistor. Galvanometer movement:

$$e = 5 \text{ mv full scale}$$
$$\text{Coil resistance } R_c = 50 \text{ ohms at } 20°C \ (68°F)$$
$$\text{Current } I = 0.1 \text{ milliamperes (ma) for full scale}$$

Assume that external resistance does not change and that the millivoltmeter has automatic bridge compensation for cold junction which has been calibrated for 0°C with the case at 20°C (68°F). 700°C gives 39.2 mv. For correct reading the total circuit resistance must be

$$\frac{E}{I} = \frac{39.2 \text{ mv}}{0.1 \text{ ma}} = 392 \text{ ohms}$$

Series (swamp) resistor $R_s = 392 - R_c -$ external resistance
$$= 392 - 50 - 6$$
$$= 336 \text{ ohms}$$

If ambient temperature at instrument rises to 30°C (86°F) and 0.0043 is the temperature resistance coefficient of copper,

$$R_{30} = 50(1 + 0.0043 \times 10)$$
$$= 52.15 \text{ ohms}$$

i.e., an increase of 2.15 ohms.

Total new circuit resistance = 392 ohms + 2.15 ohms = 394.15 ohms

At full scale
$$I_{new} = \frac{39.2 \text{ mv}}{394.15 \text{ ohms}} = 0.0994 \text{ ma}$$

This represents an error of 0.6 percent.

If the millivoltmeter had a bimetallic-strip cold-junction compensation, which is mechanical and not electrical, the calculations will be somewhat different, because when the ambient increases from 20 − 30°C (68 − 86°F), the emf appearing at the instrument terminals will be reduced. Assume that calibration was made at 20°C; then for correct reading

$$\text{Emf at } 700°C = 39.2 - 1.0$$
$$= 38.2 \text{ mv}$$

When cold junction rises to 30°C,

$$\text{Emf at } 700°\text{C} = 38.2 \text{ mv} - 0.5 \text{ mv}$$
$$= 37.7 \text{ mv}$$

For 20°C total circuit resistance = 382 ohms. As before, coil resistance increases by 2.15 ohms when temperature rises to 30°C. However, with reduced emf total circuit resistance should be

$$\frac{37.7 \text{ mv}}{0.1 \text{ ma}} = 377 \text{ ohms for correct reading}$$

Adding the increase in coil resistance of 2.15 ohms, the new resistance is 379.15 ohms. Then at full scale

$$I_{\text{new}} = \frac{37.7 \text{ mv}}{379.15 \text{ ohms}} = 0.0995 \text{ ma}$$

This represents an error of 0.5 percent, so that the error is about the same whether automatic-bridge or bimetallic-strip cold-junction compensation is used.

Errors due to external resistance. External-resistance changes can also introduce errors which can be calculated similarly to those due to variation of resistance of the coil. Referring to Fig. 9-16, the external resistance comprises R_t and R_l. Of the two, R_l will normally be the greater. If E is the thermocouple emf, the voltage e appearing at the terminals of the meter is

$$e = E \frac{R_s + R_c}{R_s + R_c + R_t + R_l}$$

The current through the meter is

$$i = \frac{E}{R_s + R_c + R_t + R_l}$$

from which it will be seen that any variation in R_l will affect the readings of e. It is customary to mark the specified external resistance value on the instrument case. In some cases, particularly in the case of multipoint installations, the extension wire used can be limited to a short length connecting each thermocouple to a thermostatically controlled junction box; i.e., the cold junction can be maintained at a constant temperature. Under these circumstances copper wire can be used between the junction box and the instrument.

Bimetallic compensation. To compensate for the effect of temperature changes on the galvanometer control spring and coil resistance some meters are fitted with bimetallic devices to make the necessary mechanical correction, as shown in Fig. 9-17. When the ambient temperature changes and the electrical effect tends to move the pivoting coil in one direction, the bimetallic strip opposes this tendency. A meter is normally said to be temperature-compensated when a change of 10°F causes less than ¼ percent error in the instrument reading.

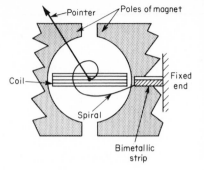

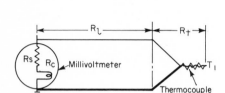

Fig. 9-16   External-resistance error   *Fig. 9-17   Bimetallic compensator.*
calculation.

The bimetallic strip consists of two metals of unlike expansion coefficients bonded together. If one end of the bimetallic strip is fixed and the other end is free, it will be found that the free end deflects with temperature variation owing to stresses set up by the unequal expansions. By knowing the values of the torque exerted by the spiral and strip, it is possible to arrange for a satisfactory compensation for any ambient-temperature variation. An instrument equipped with such a device is said to have case compensation.

The bimetallic strip can also be used to give cold-junction compensation in addition to spring-constant compensation. These two effects are opposed so that a combined coefficient α can be used. In the case of copper this coefficient is 0.00396 Ω per °C. By means of a bridge circuit it is also possible to effect automatic cold-junction compensation. For this purpose a resistance thermometer is inserted in one arm of the bridge circuit, which is fed by a constant d-c supply. With variations in ambient temperature, the bridge will be unbalanced, allowing current from the d-c supply to flow in one direction or the other and thus assisting or opposing the emf from the thermocouple and thereby compensating for variations in cold-junction temperature.

Potentiometer circuit. The potentiometer, as the name implies, is a device for measuring potential differences. The fundamental principle is the balancing of one voltage against another that opposes it. In the potentiometer the unknown emf which is to be measured is balanced against a voltage across a calibrated slide-wire. The basic circuit is shown in Fig. 9-18. The emf produced by the thermocouple is balanced against the voltage drop along the slide-wire S until the galvanometer reads zero, i.e., the circuit is in the null-balance position. The position of the contact arm is then a measure of the thermocouple emf and, in turn, the thermocouple temperature T_1. Since there is no flow of current in the circuit, variation in the resistance of extension wires does not have to be con-

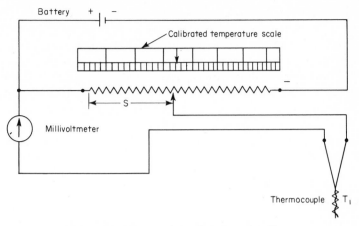

Fig. 9-18   Basic potentiometer circuit.

sidered. The potentiometer is therefore basically more accurate than a deflectional instrument.

To overcome emf variations in the supply from the battery, a standard cell (1.0184 volts) is introduced in the modified circuit which is basic for most temperature-indicating or recording instruments working on the null-balance principle. Such a modified arrangement of a simple null-balance potentiometer circuit is shown in Fig. 9-19. Now consider for

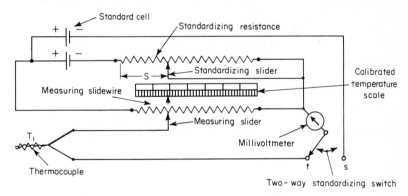

Fig. 9-19   Null-balance potentiometer circuit.

a moment the circuit with the switch in position S. The thermocouple is replaced by the standard cell as the emf source. The entire length of the slide-wire is now in the circuit, because the slide-wire is connected to the positive terminals of the battery and standard cell at one end and to the galvanometer at the other. The negative terminal of the standard cell is led directly to the opposite terminal of the galvanometer via the switch.

By adjusting the position of the standardizing resistance slider, the voltage of the battery is adjusted to equal and oppose that of the standard cell. Now, as long as the battery maintains this voltage, the thermocouple voltage can be read in terms of temperature, since the voltage across the entire measuring slide-wire remains constant.

When the thermocouple circuit is closed by rotating the two-way standardizing switch to position *t*, the standard cell is cut out of the circuit as shown. The measuring slider divides the slide-wire length so that some of the battery voltage is added to the thermocouple emf, and the total appears across the galvanometer. The remaining battery voltage is dropped by the rest of the standardizing slider. When the pointer of the galvanometer is at zero, these two voltages are equal and opposite and the slider-arm pointer indicates the temperature of the thermocouple.

The fundamental potentiometric circuit is also used for gas analysis and the measurement of pH, conductivity, and other process-plant variables. For this reason the reader is advised to learn the principle of the potentiometer thoroughly.

Automatic potentiometers (self-balancing). The position of the galvanometer pointer governs the amount and direction of the required correction

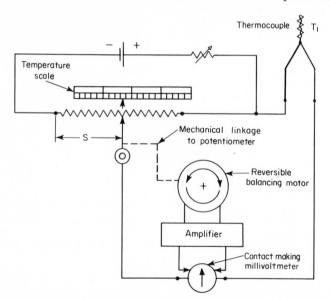

Fig. 9-20   Schematic arrangement of automatic potentiometer. (Bristol Co.)

to be applied to the potentiometer. The circuit shown in Fig. 9-20 is the arrangement used by the Bristol Company. There are a number of arrangements of automatic potentiometers, and it is suggested that the reader refer to publications of the various instrument manufacturers such as Honeywell, Foxboro, Bristol, and Leeds and Northrup. The reversible motor consists of two windings, one of which is supplied with line voltage. The other winding is referred to as the control winding. At a particular voltage in the control winding the motor remains stationary until there is a voltage change. The motor drives in one direction when the control voltage rises and in the reverse direction when the voltage falls. The basic balancing-motor characteristics are shown in Fig. 9-21.

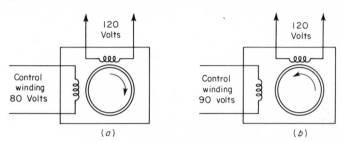

Fig. 9-21   Balancing motor.

Automatic standardization. Automatic standardization is often used with self-balancing potentiometers. At regular periods a changeover switch operated by the chart-driving mechanism or other timing device transfers for a short interval of time (10 sec) the balancing system from the potentiometer circuit to the standardizing circuit. The driving mechanism is also transferred from the slide-wire contact to the contact of the standardizing resistance in the battery circuit. Thus, any departure of the slide-wire current from the standard value is detected and corrected.

Typical plant installation. For industrial work the thermocouple pyrometer is constructed in a rugged manner in order to stand up to all conditions of operation. Figure 9-22 shows the two dissimilar metals

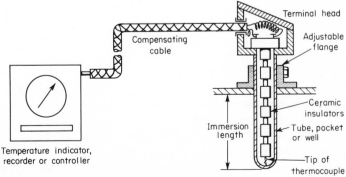

Fig. 9-22   Typical industrial thermocouple temperature-measuring system.

twisted together at one end to form the hot junction which touches the protecting sheath or well. The wires pass through ceramic insulators in the form of beads to the head containing the terminals. These terminals are connected to the indicator, recorder, or controller by means of extension leads or compensating cable.

Multipoint installations. Figure 9-23 shows the double-pole switch box for multipoint installation. Double-pole switching is logical, because two

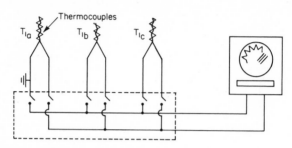

Fig. 9-23 Multipoint installation using double-pole switch box.

leads from the thermocouple are brought to the switch box. It should be stressed at this point that the contact resistances of the actual switches are of some importance. Any nonconducting film on the contacts is likely to cause trouble, because only a small voltage of the order 10^{-3} volts is available to penetrate the film.

Points of precaution when installing thermocouples:

1. Do not locate the thermocouple in a direct flame path.
2. Locate the thermocouple in an average-temperature zone.
3. Preferably locate the thermocouple where the hot junction can be seen from the furnace door.
4. Place the thermocouple in such a way that it is entirely immersed in the medium whose temperature is to be measured.
5. When connecting the thermocouple to extension leads or compensating cable, make sure that the correct wires are joined together.
6. Make sure that all connections are tight in order to avoid high-resistance contacts.
7. Avoid running wires parallel to or crossing closer than 1 ft to 110-volt (or higher) a-c supply lines, because induced currents will probably play havoc with instrument readings.
8. Carefully read the manufacturer's instructions to see that the best conditions exist for accurate results.

Materials for thermocouple pockets and wells. The following are some of the materials used for thermocouple pockets, which must be specified with care because of the high temperature and corrosive nature of many industrial applications.

Material	Limiting temp, °C (approx)
Brass	260
Copper	500
Steel and stainless steels	850
Nichrome	1000
Porcelain and fireclays	1250
Inconel	1200
Corundum (high aluminum content)	1600

Speed of response. Time is required for a temperature-measuring system to register any change in the temperature variable. This time factor is referred to as response. The time required to reach 63.2 percent of a step change is termed the time constant T, or lag coefficient, as depicted in Fig. 9-24. It is the time taken to register 63.2 percent of the change regardless of the magnitude of the change.

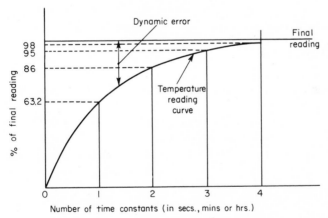

Fig. 9-24   Speed of thermostat response.

The effect of the pocket or well is to impede the transfer of heat to the sensing element, and this considerably reduces the speed of response. Agitation of the fluid around the sensing element will reduce the effect of static films and improve the speed of response. Thermocouples have a wide range, are fairly cheap, and permit long distances between them-selves and the receiving instrument.

REVIEW QUESTIONS AND PROBLEMS

9-20   Define the following: (a) Seebeck effect, (b) Peltier effect, (c) Thomson effect.

9-21   Discuss the importance of the laws of intermediate temperatures and intermediate metals as applied to a thermocouple circuit.

9-22   Write a brief account of thermoelectricity. Describe and explain, with the aid of a labeled diagram, how a thermoelectric emf of the order of 0.001 volt can be measured.

9-23   It was found experimentally that

$$\log_{10} E = a \log_{10} T_1 + b$$

and from a thermocouple system the following data were recorded: $E = 2.0$ volts when the hot junction was 900°F; $E = 4.0$ volts when the hot junction was 1150°F. Compute the values of the constants a and b and then the voltage when the hot-junction temperature is 1800°F.

9-24   Describe briefly the simple deflection-type thermocouple pyrometer and bimetallic-compensation device.

9-25   It was found during experiments with a copper-constantan thermocouple and by using the equation

$$E = c(T_1 - T_2) + k(T_1^2 - T_2^2)$$

that $C = 3.75 \times 10^{-2}$ mv/°C   and $k = 4.50 \times 10^{-5}$ mv/°C. $T_1 = 100$°C, and the cold junction T_2 is kept in ice. Compute the values of the two parts of the equation, and the resultant total of the emf, in millivolts.

9-26   Describe the operation of a typical self-balancing potentiometer used in industrial instrumentation.

9-27   (a) What is meant by the expression "standardization" as used in the simple null-balance potentiometer?
(b) Write brief notes on the possible error due to the variation of resistance both internally and externally of the simple millivolt-meter thermocouple circuit.
(c) What is the standard percentage error permitted in the case of part (b)?

9-28   The emf of an iron-constantan thermocouple was found to be 44.40 mv at 800°C with a cold-junction temperature of 0°C. If the cold-junction temperature changes to 15°C, what is now the corresponding emf? Assume a straight-line relationship between temperature and millivolts and the variation of emf with temperature as 6.0×10^{-2} mv/°C.

9-29   Describe the construction and operation of a moving-coil millivolt-meter as used for temperature measurement with a thermocouple.

9-30 Point out the advantages and disadvantages of the thermocouple as compared to the filled thermal systems. Consider such factors as distance to measuring instrument, speed of response, multipoint installation, accuracy, operating range, logging or computing possibilities, and relative expense and maintenance.

9-31 A platinum, platinum-rhodium thermocouple has an emf-temperature relationship given as

$$e = -3.23 \times 10^{-1} + 8.27 \times 10^{-3}T + 1.64 \times 10^{-6}T^2$$

where e is in millivolts and T is the temperature difference, in degrees Celsius, between hot and cold junctions.

(a) Calculate, to 5 significant figures, the emf value if the cold junction is at 30°C and the hot junction is at 1400°C.

(b) Calculate the minimum sensitivity, in microvolts, required to indicate a change of 1°C at 1400°C with a cold-junction temperature maintained at 30°C.

RADIATION PYROMETRY

Where temperatures are too high to enable a thermocouple or other temperature-sensing element to be used, other methods are available. All hot bodies emit radiant energy whose intensity bears a relation to the absolute temperature of the emitting surface. Radiation is a wave phenomenon analogous to light, and it occupies a definite place in the spectrum. Figure 9-25 shows the waveband with radiation expressed in

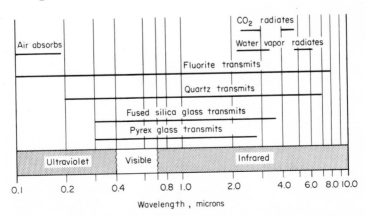

Fig. 9-25   Transmission band of materials.

microns. Sometimes centimeters are used, and more frequently used is the angstrom, which is 10^{-8} cm or 10^{-4} microns.

If there are two bodies A and B, A being the hotter, there will be a net transfer of energy from the hotter A to the colder B. If a number of bodies, all at the same temperature, are enclosed in a space impervious to heat, it is considered that each body radiates energy into the surrounding medium and continuously absorbs energy therefrom. Because there must be equilibrium, the two processes balance one another, so that the temperature of each body remains constant. This is generally referred to as the Prévost theory.

Consider the case of a fuel-fired furnace wherein the walls are at a lower temperature than the hot gases. A thermocouple placed in the hot-gas stream will receive heat by radiation from the walls, but since it is exposed to the heat of the hot gases and is therefore at a higher temperature than the walls, it will radiate more heat than it receives and hence will register a lower value than the true temperature of the gases. This phenomenon is most important when locating temperature-sensing devices of every sort in order to avoid measurement errors.

The Blackbody

In considering radiation the concept of the perfect blackbody has to be understood. It does not in fact exist, although something very near to it can be achieved.

1. A blackbody absorbs at all temperatures all radiation falling on it without reflecting or transmitting any.
2. A blackbody radiates more energy in a given time than any other body at the same temperature.

The blackbody is used as a reference standard against which other radiating bodies or surfaces are compared. Thus total emissivity of a body is the ratio

$$\frac{\text{Total radiation from a non-blackbody}}{\text{Total radiation from a blackbody}}$$

when the two bodies are of similar shape and are at the same temperature. Sometimes "emissive power" or "emittance" is used in place of "emissivity."

If two bodies of different temperature face each other, then there is a net transfer of radiant energy from the hotter to the colder body and the amount of energy transferred per unit of time is roughly proportional to the fourth power of the difference in the absolute temperature of the two objects. This fourth-power relationship is known as the Stefan-Boltzmann law. Radiant heat is a form of energy; its common units are the erg and the joule. The Stefan-Boltzmann law can thus be stated mathematically:

$$E = \delta T^4$$

where δ = Stefan's constant = 5.77×10^{-5} ergs/sec/cm^2/°K^4

T = absolute temperature of emitting surface, °K

and E, in ergs/cm^2/sec, is the emissivity of the body, in this case expressed as energy radiated from a unit area of the body's surface per second. It is sometimes referred to as radiant flux. Now from the Prévost theory it is known that the hotter body will lose heat to the colder body, which gives us

$$E_1 = \delta(T_1^4 - T_2^4)$$

If A is the area of the body, then the energy radiated is

$$W = A\delta\Sigma(T_1^4 - T_2^4)$$
$$= K(T_1^4 - T_2^4)$$

The emissivity factor Σ has been introduced because true blackbody conditions are never attained.

Where the British system of units is employed, this formula can be rewritten

$$Q = KA\left[\left(\frac{T_2}{100}\right)^4 - \left(\frac{T_1}{100}\right)^4\right]$$

where Q = radiant energy, Btu/hr

K = radiation constant 0.172

A = area, ft^2

T = temperature, °R

Temperature-measuring instruments which respond to all wavelengths and therefore operate according to the Stefan-Boltzmann law are referred to as *total-radiation pyrometers*. Another class of instrument utilizes only narrow bands of wavelength in the visible spectrum. Instruments of this class are referred to as *optical pyrometers*. A total-radiation pyrometer is therefore nonselective, whereas an optical pyrometer is selective. Another type is partly selective and can be referred to as a partial-radiation pyrometer. In connection with optical pyrometers two further laws have to be considered.

Wien's law. This can be written

$$E = B\lambda^{-5}e^{-B_1/\lambda T}$$

where E = intensity of blackbody radiation at any wavelength λ, cm

T = temperature, °K **or** R

e = base of natural logarithms

and B and B_1 are constants.

Planck's law

$$E = B\lambda^{-5} \frac{1}{e^{B_1/\lambda T} - 1}$$

In applying these laws to radiation pyrometry the wavelength λ can be selected at about 0.65 microns in the red portion of the spectrum, where the light is monochromatic or nearly so. Under these circumstances Wien's and Planck's law become virtually the same and can be rewritten

$$\log_e \frac{E^1}{B - \lambda^5} = \frac{B_1}{T} \quad \text{or} \quad T = \frac{-B_1}{\lambda \log_e (E/B\lambda^{-5})}$$

Thus if B and B_1 are known, T can be found by measuring E.

From a graph of Planck's law for several temperatures (Fig. 9-26) it is evident that the intensity of radiation varies appreciably with wave-

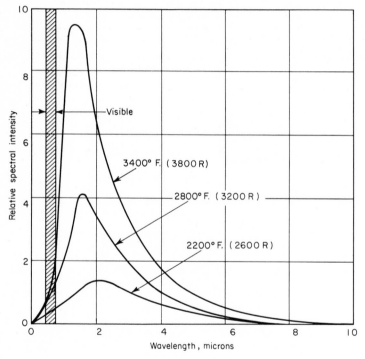

Fig. 9-26   *Spectral distribution of radiant energy.*

length. In addition, it should be noted that the point of maximum radiant intensity varies appreciably with wavelength and shifts to shorter wavelengths as the temperature increases. This phenomenon explains why, in heating, the color of a body changes from red through yellow to white, i.e., from 6500 to 4500 angstroms. A rough estimation of temperature from color can be obtained from Table 9-5. The point of maximum intensity is given by Wien's displacement law

$$\lambda_m T = 2,900$$

where λ_m is in microns and T is in degrees Kelvin.

Table 9-5   Temperature-color relationship

Color	Temp, °C	Temp, °F
Incipient red heat	500–550	930–1020
Dark red heat	650–750	1200–1380
Bright red heat	850–950	1500–1740
Yellowish red heat	1050–1150	1920–2100
Incipient white heat	1250–1350	2280–2460
White heat	1450–1550	2640–2820

The third type of instrument, which has been referred to as a partial-radiation pyrometer, operates on photoelectric principles. It possesses certain advantages over the total-radiation pyrometer, which is sensitive to smoke, water vapor, and CO_2. The partial-radiation pyrometer can be so arranged as to eliminate selectively part or all of the radiating effect of such constituents. It can, therefore, be effectively used to measure the roof temperature of a steel-melting furnace, where a total-radiation pyrometer is unsuitable owing to the radiating properties of water vapor and CO_2, which lead to very serious errors in reading.

Total-radiation Pyrometers

A typical total-radiation instrument is shown in Fig. 9-27. Radiation from source AB enters the pyrometer via aperature CD and is focused

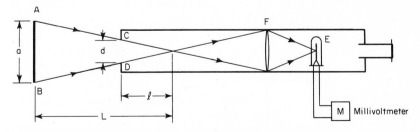

Fig. 9-27   Total-radiation pyrometer.

onto a small disk of blackened platinum E by means of lens F. In some models as in the one shown in Fig. 9-28, a concave mirror G is used for focusing purposes. This has the advantage that possible absorption of

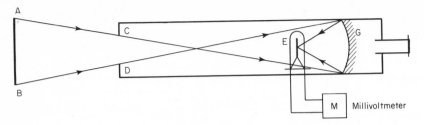

Fig. 9-28   Total-radiation pyrometer.

certain wavelengths by the lens is avoided. Fixed to the platinum disk are a number of thermocouples arranged in series to give a reasonable emf, and these are connected to a millivoltmeter. The radiation heats the disk and generates an emf which deflects the millivoltmeter pointer over a scale calibrated in degrees Fahrenheit or Celsius.

Certain precautions must be observed with the instrument:

1. The cold junction is usually designed to be quite close to the hot junction. For example, in the enclosed type of couple, the cold junction could be at the base pins which plug into a holder. The terminals of the latter are connected by copper cable to the indicator. The adjacent position of hot and cold junction ensures that both are equally, or very nearly equally, affected by any ambient-temperature change. The cold junction must be shielded, however, from radiation from the source, and conduction of heat from the housing to the couple can be reduced by filling the glass envelope with an inert gas.

In some designs the envelope is evacuated. The use of very fine thermocouple wire reduces conduction losses from the couple itself. Where excessive temperature rise of the pyrometer housing is likely to be encountered (e.g., near an open-hearth furnace of a steel plant), the housing should be enclosed in an asbestos-lined metal casing or in a water-cooled jacket.

If cold-junction compensation is necessary, a nickel resistance spool is sometimes connected as a shunt across the thermocouple leads at the cold-junction end. The variation of the resistance with ambient temperature is such that it is sufficient to compensate the thermocouple emf for cold-junction temperature change. In another design, a bimetallic compensator cuts off part of the incoming radiation if the temperature of the housing increases.

2. The distance between the source of radiation and the pyrometer is important, because the radiation must always be focused onto a receiving disk. There are two methods of ensuring this focus. In the first, the position of the lens or mirror may be so adjusted that, with varying distance of source from the mirror, the radiation is always focused onto the same

point. The diagram in Fig. 9-29 illustrates a Féry type of instrument. The concave mirror of highly polished stainless steel is adjustable by rack and pinion J and K. Two small mirrors M, inclined to one another, are placed near the receiving disk. Viewed through the eyepiece H, an image of the source is seen. When the instrument is correctly focused by adjusting the position of the concave mirror, the image will appear as a whole. When incorrectly focused, a split image will be seen.

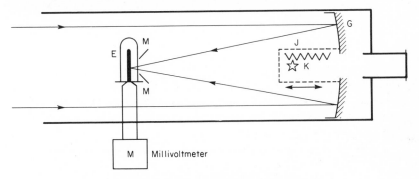

Fig. 9-29 Féry radiation pyrometer.

In the second method the position of the lens or mirror is fixed but the cone of radiation must always be such as to fill the aperture. This then becomes a secondary source, and provided it is completely covered, the radiation is always brought to the same focus. The instrument becomes independent, within limits, of the distance from the source, and it is termed a fixed-focus pyrometer. Referring to Fig. 9-27, from the geometry of the arrangement it can be seen that the relation between the distance L, the aperture diameter d, the distance l between the aperture and C, and the image diameter a is

$$L = \frac{al}{d}$$

If θ, the angular aperture, is known from the design,

$$l = \frac{d}{2 \sin (\theta/2)}$$

Hence
$$L = \frac{a}{2 \sin (\theta/2)}$$

The pyrometer geometry is usually so arranged that the diameter a of the source of radiation must be at least one-tenth of the distance L.

3. The atmosphere between the source and pyrometer should be kept clear of any absorbing media such as fumes or smoke likely to cause errors.

4. The lens and mirror must be kept clean, and the mirror in a highly polished condition.

5. Correction must be made when the source does not fulfil blackbody conditions.

6. The Stefan-Boltzmann law as regards the fourth power does not necessarily hold for every pyrometer. A truer statement would be $W = K[T_1^b - T_2^b]$, where b is an index which Burgess and Foote (National Bureau of Standards) found to vary from 3.28 to 4.26 for 22 or so tested instruments. The average was $\bar{x} = 3.89$. Therefore, the fourth-power law should not be used indiscriminately to extend an existing calibration.

Optical Pyrometers

As previously noted, radiant energy has wavelengths in the optical part of the spectrum, and the second class of pyrometer makes use of a single wavelength, or very narrow band of wavelengths, for measuring the temperature of a heated body. In a typical optical pyrometer (Fig. 9-30) the

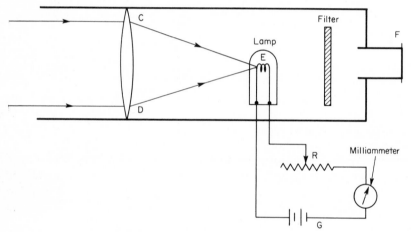

Fig. 9-30   Optical pyrometer.

radiation source is viewed through a telescope system consisting of an objective lens CD and eyepiece F. Inside the telescope is a small lamp heated by battery G. The current through E is adjustable by resistance R, and a milliammeter is connected in the heating circuit. A red optical filter is interposed between the eyepiece and lamp. On looking through the eyepiece, the source is seen as a bright circle, square, or other shape, and in the center of it is the image of the filament of the lamp.

The resistance R is adjusted until the brightness of the filament is equal to that of the radiation. When it is, the filament image appears to merge into the radiation image and present a uniform picture to the eye. This is indicated in Fig. 9-31. If the filament is not as bright as the source image, it appears dark against a lighter background (left diagram). If, on the other hand, the filament is brighter than the source image, it appears as a light band against a dark background (right diagram). The transition points between (a), (b), and (c) are very definite, and different technicians in the plant will record the same values within small limits of personal error. In some models, the whole instrument is portable and self-contained. The battery is located in the handle. The milliammeter, calibrated directly in degrees Celsius or Fahrenheit, is positioned just below the telescope section, where it is easily observable by the technician as he looks through the eyepiece.

 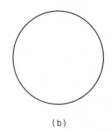 

(a) (b) (c)

Fig. 9-31   Filament images.

Lamps for optical pyrometers are generally not run at temperatures above 1400°C. In order to increase the usefulness of the instrument, an absorption screen can be placed in front of the objective of the telescope. The transmission factor for the screen is known, so that the fraction of the incident light which passes through it is also known. Thus, the instrument can be calibrated for a second range. Pyrometers of this kind having a range of 800 to 1250°C have an accuracy better than ±5°C, while those having a range of 1100 to 1900°C have an accuracy better than ±10°C.

International scale above the gold point, 1063°C. Temperatures on the international scale above 1063°C (1336°K) are based on the measurement of monochromatic visible radiation. The temperature is determined by means of the ratio of the intensity E_2 of monochromatic visible radiation of wavelength λ cm, emitted by a blackbody temperature t, to the intensity E_1 of radiation emitted by a blackbody at the gold point by means of the equation

$$\log_e \frac{E_2}{E_1} = \frac{C_2}{\lambda}\left(\frac{1}{1,336} - \frac{1}{t + 273}\right)$$

The constant C_2 is taken as 1.438 cm deg. The equation may be used provided $\lambda(t + 273)$ is less than 0.3 cm deg.

Partial-radiation Pyrometers

As the name implies, partial-radiation pyrometers are sensitive to radiation within a finite waveband. The sensitivity is inversely proportional to absolute temperature and wavelength. At 2000°K and at a wavelength of 0.65 microns in the visible red, a monochromatic receiver has a sensitivity 2.9 times that of a thermopile. This property and their high response speed make photocells suitable for use in partial-radiation pyrometers. A photocell has the further advantage that variations in emissivity do not introduce as large an error as they do with other radiation pyrometers. On the other hand, variations in ambient temperature introduce a greater error, and therefore in many cases partial-radiation pyrometers have to be water-jacketed.

Absorption by CO_2 and H_2O has no effect, and the error introduced by smoke is comparatively low. A typical unit is very similar to a total-radiation pyrometer except that the thermopile or thermocouple is replaced by the photocell. Depending on the use to which the instrument is to be put, various cell materials are used, two common ones being silicon and selenium. For further details manufacturers' literature should be consulted. (See also Photoelectricity, p. 379.)

REVIEW QUESTIONS AND PROBLEMS

9-33   By using the equation $E_1 = S(T_1^4 - T_2^4)$, if the temperature at maximum emissivity is 1700°C, determine the temperature at half the maximum emissivity. T_2 is observed to be 30°C.

9-34   Assuming that, in the equation $L = al/D$ for the radiation pyrometer, a is $\frac{1}{10}$ of L, compute the value of the aperature diameter D if $l = 5$ in.

9-35   Explain in detail the importance of blackbody conditions in high-temperature measurement.

9-36   An optical pyrometer is used to measure the temperature of a body with 80 percent blackbody emissivity. Applying the equation

$$\log_{10} \Sigma_\lambda = 9{,}560 \left(\frac{1}{T_c} - \frac{1}{T_0} \right)$$

if $T_0 = 1600$°C, what is the value of T_c, the true temperature?

9-37   Describe with the aid of a diagram the operation of the total-radiation pyrometer and a typical optical pyrometer.

9-38   Describe the photocell type of partial-radiation pyrometer and discuss its advantages and disadvantages.

CHAPTER TEN

The art and science of instrumentation

Measurement consists of information transfer with accompanying energy transfer. Energy cannot be drawn from a system without altering its behaviour—hence all measurements affect the quantity to be measured. Measurement is therefore a carefully balanced combination of applied physics (energy conversion) and applied mathematics (information transfer).*

Basic Functions of Instruments

A measuring instrument is simply a device for determining the value of a quantity, condition, physical variable, or phenomenon. Generally, the purpose served by an instrument is to ascertain the magnitude of some particular phenomenon under investigation. The value determined by the instrument is generally, but not necessarily, quantitative. The normal functions fulfilled by an industrial instrument come under one or more of the following headings:

Signaling-monitor. If the instrument is required only to indicate selected values of a measured quantity, then only a basic signal is necessary. For example, to check the air pumped into a tire at a gasoline station, the gauge could be designed to read "too low" or "too high" or, alternatively, it could be made to give an audible ring when the pressure is just right. A *monitor* is an instrument that is used to measure continuously or at intervals a quantity or condition that must be kept within a prescribed limit. An example is the oil gauge in an automobile.

Indicating-recording. An indicating instrument is provided with some kind of calibrated scale and pointer (indicator). The magnitude of the

---

* Peter K. Stein, "Measurement Engineering," vol. I, "Basic Principles," 3d ed., Stein Engineering Services, Inc., Phoenix, Ariz., 1964.

quantity is normally read on the scale to any subdivision or fraction within the limits of calibration and the human eye. A common example of an indicating instrument is a clock.

A recording instrument provides a written record, usually on paper, of the magnitude or value of the measured quantity against some other variable, usually time. The record is, in many ways, similar to a curve plotted on graph paper. Indicating and recording mechanisms may be actuated directly from the measuring system through a lever or linkage principle; examples are thermometers and pressure-gauge instruments. Alternatively, they are actuated indirectly by a servo-operated system in which the printing or recording pen is motor driven.

Registering-totalizing. This function of an instrument provides indication, by symbols of discrete increments or numbers, of the magnitude or value of some quantity or medium. The store cash register and domestic gas, water, and electric meters are typical examples of registering and totalizing operations. The readout presentation is digital, as opposed to the analogue presentation of the indicator or recorder.

Transmitting. The instrument is designed to transmit or convey information concerning the measured quantity to a remote point. The magnitude or value of the measured quantity is not necessarily important, but the transmission of data is, as in the case of the telephone.

Any combination of these functions may be found in an industrial measuring instrument, and no one function is more important than the others. One of the most important functions of an instrument is to control

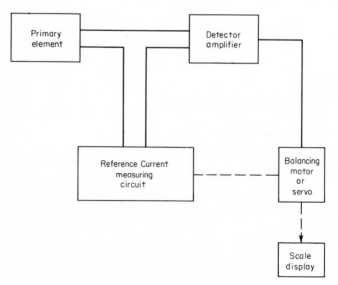

Fig. 10-1   Self-balancing indicating potentiometer.

the nature of the variable under measurement. The quality of control is frequently determined by the quality of measurement.

Readout and display. Normally, one must observe and record the physical parameters or process variables measured by the instruments. Readout and display systems do these jobs. Readout and display systems incorporate such indicating means as pointers, lights, and charts; they consist of the indicating and recording mechanism as well as the measuring circuit. The block diagram in Fig. 10-1 illustrates the function of display in an electronic self-balancing recording potentiometer.

Digital printout and computers. The use of digital printout mechanisms allows for the centralized recording of all variables on one information sheet. This means that the value of each variable appears on a sheet in actual numbers instead of as a line on a calibrated chart. The method makes it possible to combine the indicating, measuring, and control

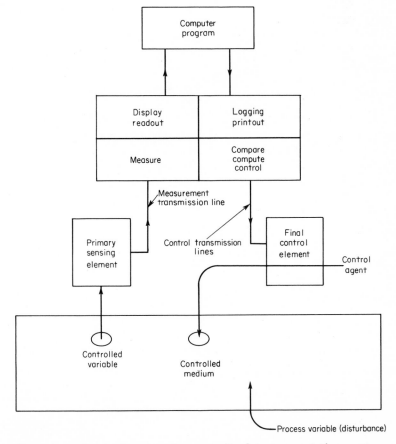

Fig. 10-2 Basic elements of a centralized instrumentation system.

systems so that the required rapid changes can be determined and incorporated into the process. In this way, complete centralization is achieved. The basic elements of such an instrumentation and control system are shown in block-diagram form in Fig. 10-2.

Least and Root-square Accuracy

In the specifications for industrial instruments it is often required to designate the overall accuracy of a measuring system. Many industrial instruments are not self-contained, but instead consist of separate units such as the primary sensing element (e.g., temperature bulb), secondary element (e.g., Bourdon-tube measuring unit), and manipulation element (e.g., scale and pointer components). These elements, as in a pressure-gauge transmitter-receiver system, may be obtained separately with accuracy limits specified for each element of the system. Let the accuracy of each unit be within $\pm a$, within $\pm b$, within $\pm c$, and so on. The least accuracy then becomes within $\pm (a + b + c + \cdots)$. The root-square accuracy becomes within $\pm \sqrt{a^2 + b^2 + c^2} + \cdots$. The root-square accuracy is more justifiable in an instrument system because it is not probable that all the units of the system will have the greatest static error at the same point at the same time.

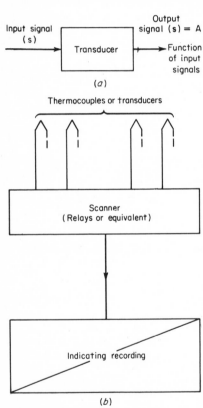

Fig. 10-3 (a) *Basic function of a transducer.* (b) *Scanning indicator-recorder.*

Data Transducers

Transducers might properly be considered the lifeline of instrumentation. Without them there would be little need for all the other apparatus normally associated with the functions of control and computation. Transducers are devices that can be actuated by waves from one or more transmission systems and that can supply related waves to one or more other transmission systems. The basic transducer function is shown in Fig. 10-3a.

On the input side, a transducer can convert a nonelectrical quantity into an electrical signal. An example is pressure-actuating a strain gauge type of transducer which then delivers an electrical output signal (which is a function of the input pressure) to an amplifier or "black box." On the other end of the black box an output transducer can change the electrical signal into a nonelectrical quantity, such as the position of a pointer on a meter. Almost any device capable of translating a physical variable into an electrical quantity may be used:

Bellows- or Bourdon-operated potentiometers, capacitors, and differential transformers
Thermocouples
Resistance thermometers
Thermistors
Strain gauges

Figure 10-3*b* is a block diagram of a basic scanning system consisting only of sampling, indicating, and recording functions. Electrical and electronic transducers for measurement applications are described more fully in Chap. 14.

Concept of Control Loop

The concept of a simple control loop can best be illustrated by means of Fig. 10-4, which shows the familiar shower-water control scheme. The

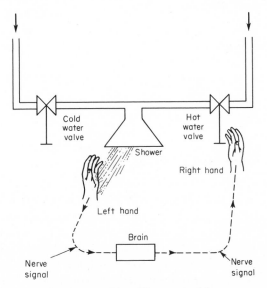

Fig. 10-4   Familiar control loop.

process is considered as the domestic shower water, and the controlled variable is the water temperature. The sensing element is the left hand, and the controller is the brain. In this case the final control element is the right-hand shower valve, with the measurement and control signals being the nerves. Figure 10-5 shows the shower-water process in block-diagram

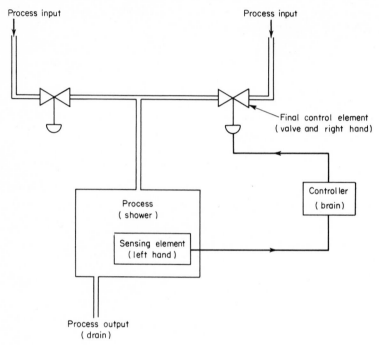

Fig. 10-5   Control loop in block-diagram form.

form. The application of the control loop to a typical industrial process is shown in the diagram, Fig. 10-6.

Fundamental Elements of Instruments

All instruments contain various component parts which perform prescribed functions in converting a variable quantity, parameter, or condition into a corresponding indication. The process of conversion in an instrument is necessary in order to change the measured variable, such as temperature, pressure, humidity, or chemical composition, into a more useful quantity, such as a corresponding displacement, pressure, force, or electrical impulse or potential. In most cases an industrial instrument ultimately converts the measured variable into a displacement.

Measuring means. The primary sensing element is the part of the instrument that first uses energy from the measured medium to produce a condition representing the value of the measured variable. The parts of a simple measuring and control scheme are shown in Fig. 10-7. The thermometer bulb is the primary sensing element, because it first converts

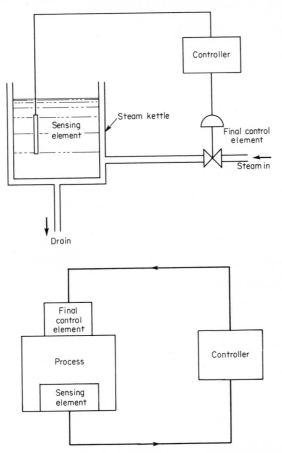

Fig. 10-6   Application of the control loop to a typical industrial process.

energy in the form of heat into a fluid displacement (expansion or contraction) within the thermal measuring system which, in turn, is proportional to the temperature at the bulb. Other parts of the measuring means are the capillary tubing, which connects the bulb to the recorder, and the spiral pressure element, which is inside the recorder case and which performs the functions of indicating and recording the temperature. There are many other types of measuring means available, such as thermocouple potentiometers, orifice-plate flowmeters, and pressure-level instruments, which are described in other chapters.

Controlling means. The controlling means consists of the controlling mechanism in the instrument, e.g., a simple electrical contact, and a power-operated final control element. In Fig. 10-7 the final control ele-

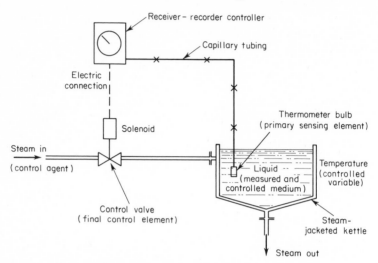

Fig. 10-7   A simple temperature-control system.

ment is the control valve on the steam line. In this case the valve is opened or closed by a solenoid power unit in accordance with the controller's electrical contact action.

Dynamic Characteristics

Two fundamental considerations in the evaluation of a measuring system are accuracy and speed of response. The important role of accuracy has already been described in this chapter, as well as in Chap. 1. Although response and lag are closely related to accuracy, the two are treated separately in order to clarify their meanings.

Response. Instruments rarely respond instantaneously to changes in the measured variable. On the contrary, they exhibit a characteristic sluggishness or slowness due to such properties as mass, thermal capacitance, or electrical capacitance. Industrial instruments invariably are used for measuring quantities that fluctuate with time. Dynamic and transient behavior of the instrument is just as important as static characteristics, which include accuracy, static error, reproducibility, drift, and sensitivity (Chap. 1).

The dynamic behavior of an instrument is determined by subjecting its primary sensing element to some known and predetermined variation in the measured quantity. The usual variations are:

1. Step change, in which the primary sensing element is subjected to an instantaneous and finite change in the measured variable. (Transient response)
2. Linear change, in which the primary sensing element is following a measured variable which is changing linearly with time. (Ramp change)
3. Sinusoidal change, which occurs when the primary sensing element follows a measured variable whose magnitude changes similarly to the change in a sinusoidal function. (Frequency response)

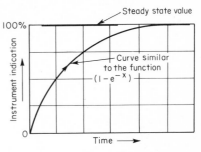

Figure 10-8 shows the three basic variations in response. It is not the intent to delve deeply into these basic response variations. Texts on the control fundamentals of industrial instrumentation describe these and other variations in great detail.

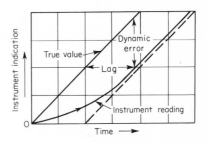

Speed of response—lag. Immediate and complete response to a change in a variable is an ideal which is not likely to be found in any physical measuring system. The response may vary in many cases, but generally it starts quickly and then takes time to complete its total effect in reaching a steady-state value. The time element involved is frequently referred to as *lag*, which is the falling behind of one physical condition with respect to

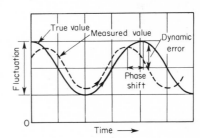

Fig. 10-8   Response curves.

another physical condition to which it is related. For example, a temperature change at the thermometer bulb shown in Fig. 10-7 would not be instantaneously detected. Heat energy must be transmitted through the bulb wall to the filling medium, causing an expansion of the fluid with consequent pressure rise which is transmitted to the receiving spiral pressure element. A lag occurs; it is the time interval between actual

occurrence of the temperature change and the registration of this change
by the indicating mechanism. The lag involves rate of heat transfer,
slight movement of the fluid, and the dynamics of the mechanical system.
In general, in any measuring system lag can occur at the primary element,
the transmission system, and the final measuring element.

Response of primary sensing elements. Because temperature is one of
the most important controlled variables in industrial processes, it is again
considered in relation to this topic. It should be stated, however, that the
conclusions reached apply generally to all other measuring means. To
revert to the bulb of the filled thermal system in Fig. 10-7, assume the
cylindrical element to be filled with a liquid or gas which expands or contracts with corresponding temperature changes. If the bulb is suddenly
immersed in the agitated bath maintained at 100°C, the temperature
readings plotted against time will appear as shown in Fig. 10-9. The curve

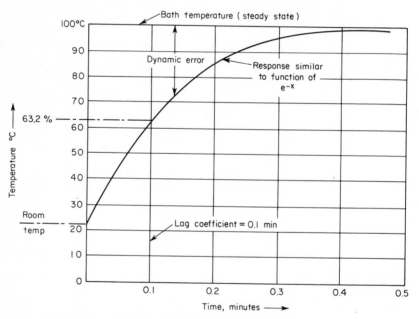

Fig. 10-9   Speed of response of temperature measurement.

is characteristic of an exponential function. Its initial portion is steep,
and it then flattens out gradually as it approaches the bath temperature
or steady-state equilibrium value with increase of time.

Lag coefficient. The lag coefficient is used to express the speed of
response of a bare primary element in terms of the time taken to attain
63.2 percent of the total change. In Fig. 10-9 the lag coefficient is equal to

0.13 min. In other fields it is often referred to as the time constant of the system. Compare pages 322 and 326.

Industrial Instrumentation

Meaning and purpose of instrumentation. Instrumentation may be defined as the art and science of applying measuring instruments and controlling devices to a system or process for the purpose of determining the identity or magnitude of certain varying physical or chemical quantities or phenomena. The purpose of instrumentation is the control of physical quantities or variables within specified quality limitations at maximum efficiency and minimum cost.

Modern instrumentation encompasses a large portion of the pure and applied sciences and includes the design, construction, and application of devices and systems to extend and supplement the human faculties used to sense, perceive, communicate, recall, compute, and control. The human senses, including those of sight, touch, taste, smell, hearing, and balance, are extended and refined by colored panel lights, surface-roughness gauges, pH meters, gas chromatographs, audiometers, and gyroscopic devices. Other instruments, such as wattmeters, magnetometers, and radiation counters, sense phenomena for which there is no corresponding human capability.

More specifically, instrumentation involves a system in which the detection, collection, storing, and processing of information and data may be used to make decisions or to respond to a command or to a feedback signal indicating a correction as a result of a decision. Signals generated by measuring instruments may be indicated, recorded, or transmitted to remote locations for input into computers, program analyzers, or automatic control equipment. Figure 10-10 shows the elements and functions of a simple feedback control loop.

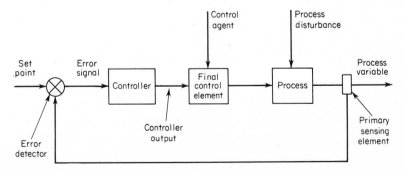

Fig. 10-10   Basic feedback control loop.

Process instrumentation. When measurements and instruments are used as a combined method or system for the measurement and control of industrial manufacturing, conversion, or treatment processes, the term *process instrumentation* is applied.

Automatic control. When the measuring and controlling instruments are so combined that measurements provide impulses or signals for remote automatic action, then the term *control system* is applied. A control system involves more than just the measurement and control of the changing characteristics of the substance being processed. The conditions constituting the process must also be measured and controlled. Moreover, the information about the measurements must be continuously available and the performance of control devices must be continuously monitored. The performance of control equipment can be monitored through the use of various techniques such as visual and audible alarm signals.

Open and closed loops. In the process industries, automatic control is justified by increased productivity, reduced costs, and more uniform quality. An automatic control system consists of five main parts: process, measuring means, error detector, controller, and final control element. These five elements of control can be interconnected in two ways, either in *open loop* or *closed loop*.

In open-loop control the output has no effect on the input. To cite a common example, if the domestic thermostat were installed outside on a cold day, the output (furnace heat) would have no effect on the input (outdoor temperature). If a condition such as the fuel Btu rating were to improve, the open-loop system would fail to control. Such an open-loop system is inherently stable because there is no self-excitation or regulation.

In a simple closed loop, if the thermostat is brought indoors, the output (furnace heat) will now affect the input (indoor temperature). This closed-loop thermostat system will continue to operate until the room temperature reaches the value set on the thermostat. In this closed-loop system, where there is feedback information from the output to the input, there is the possibility of instability through self-excitation. The advantages of closed-loop systems outweigh their disadvantages. Most texts on process control explain in great detail the theory and practice of control systems used in industry.

REVIEW QUESTIONS AND PROBLEMS

10-1   Describe the basic functions of an industrial instrument and a combination of these functions in any instrument you know.

10-2   (a) Define the terms instrumentation and control system.
(b) What are the basic elements of a centralized instrumentation system?

10-3   Sketch a simple block diagram of a heat-exchange control scheme and label the main measuring and control means used.

10-4   A transmitter, relay, and receiver are used in measuring a pressure at a remote point. The specified accuracies are transmitter, within ± 1.0 percent; relay, within ± 2.00 percent; receiver, within ± 2.00 percent. Compute the root-square accuracy of the system.

10-5   Define the terms and give examples in each case: (a) speed of response, (b) lag coefficient.

10-6   (a) Sketch the exponential curve of a step-change response.
(b) Given the expression for the speed of response of temperature measurement, $\theta/\theta_F = 100(1 - e^{-t/T})$, calculate the ratio when $t/T = 1$ and $e = 2.718 \cdots$, the natural logarithmic base.
(c) What is the value of the ratio in (b) when $t/T = 4$?

10-7   Describe the difference between an open-loop and a closed-loop control system.

10-8   Describe any industrial process that you know and give details of the automatic-control scheme involved. Support your information with the aid of block and flow diagrams.

10-9   When working in a measurements laboratory or when engaged in instrument practice, what are some of the habits, characteristics, and disciplines which should be acquired by the student early in his career?

CHAPTER ELEVEN

Applied electricity and measuring circuits

Give instruction to a wise man and he will be yet wiser.

PROVERBS

Electric Energy

Electric energy is produced by chemical cells (batteries), magnetic mechanisms (rotating generators), pressure-sensitive elements (piezo-electric crystals), light-sensitive cells, or temperature-sensitive elements (thermocouples). Electricity is a form of energy which may be compared with hydraulic energy. In its natural state electricity was no more than a scientific curiosity in the nineteenth century. However, as soon as methods were developed for converting vast amounts of natural energy into an electrical form and then, in turn, converting it into heat, light, or other useful form of energy, electricity became man's greatest aid to industrialization.

Hydraulic analogy. The comparison between hydraulic and electrical systems for conveying energy from one location to another is given in Fig. 11-1a and b. Electricity, in its fundamental nature, may be thought of as a medium by which energy can be conveniently conveyed from one location to another. It is the free electrons in the copper conductors shown in Fig. 11-1b which form the energy conveying means and which are the electrical equivalent of the hydraulic-fluid system.

Using the English system of units, the cubic foot or gallon is a suitable measure for a quantity of a hydraulic fluid. The rate of fluid flow in a pipeline is expressed in quantity per unit time, i.e., in cubic feet per second or gallons per hour. The pump supplies the force or pressure to the hydraulic fluid in order to cause it to flow. A pressure drop in a pipe flow is caused by a restriction (resistance), e.g., an orifice plate or partially opened valve.

In the case of an electric flow through a conductor, the conductor is a material having a very large number of free electrons per unit volume. For example, a cubic inch of copper contains about 1.4×10^{24} free electrons. Semiconductors—carbon, germanium, and silicon—have from 10^{15} to 10^{20} free electrons per cubic inch. The electric switch performs the same function as a valve in a hydraulic system; opening an electric switch is analogous to closing a hydraulic valve.

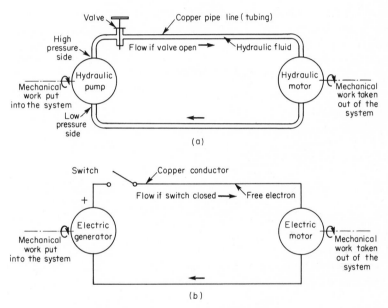

Fig. 11-1 (a) *Hydraulic system.* (b) *Analogous electric system.*

If the pressure developed by the pump increases, a condition when the pipe walls can no longer withstand the high pressure is reached. A burst or rupture occurs, allowing the fluid to escape. A similar condition occurs in an electric circuit. If pressure is applied to the insulating sheath or coating around a conductor, electrons can be torn free from their orbits. The breakdown depends upon the thickness of the pipe wall or the insulating sheath.

Quantity of electricity (Q). The coulomb is the fundamental unit of electric quantity. It refers to the number of charged particles (electrons). Physicists have calculated that a coulomb represents a quantity of 6.24×10^{18} electrons.

Example. If there are 2.80×10^{19} free electrons in a piece of copper wire, calculate the coulombs this represents.

Solution

$$Q = \frac{2.80 \times 10^{19}}{6.24 \times 10^{18}} = 4.49 \text{ coulombs}$$

Flow of electricity. In an electric circuit the term *current* (I) is used to refer to the rate of flow of the electric medium. Just as fluid flow can be measured in gallons per second so can electrical flow be measured in coulombs per second. One ampere (amp) is the rate of flow of the electrical medium when one coulomb of free electrons passes a certain point in a circuit in one second. "Amperes" and "coulombs per second" have the same meaning.

$$\text{Current (amp)} = \frac{\text{quantity (coulombs)}}{\text{time (sec)}}$$

$$I = \frac{Q}{t}$$

Example. If 120 coulombs passes a certain point in a circuit in half a minute, calculate the flow of current.

Solution

$$I = \frac{120 \text{ coulombs}}{30 \text{ sec}} = 4 \text{ amp}$$

Electric pressure. In order for a current to flow in an electric circuit, a pressure must be applied to the medium. In the case of the hydraulic system (Fig. 11-2) a potential difference is caused by the difference in

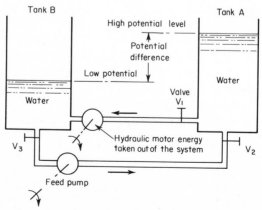

Fig. 11-2   Model to show potential difference in a hydraulic system.

pressure heads. When the valve V_1 is opened, the flow will be in the direction from tank A to tank B, that is, from a high potential to a lower potential or lower energy level. In the case of an electric circuit a similar condition may be considered as positive $(+)$ charge and negative $(-)$ charge. The term "charge" signifies a quantity of electrons with potential energy implied. There is an electric potential difference between the two points.

Potential difference (symbolized by V) may be expressed as the rise (or fall) in potential energy per unit quantity of electrons moved. *Voltage* is the measure of the potential-energy difference between two points in an electric circuit. The unit of voltage is the volt. The potential rise in the case of charging a battery is frequently called the electron-moving force, or *electromotive force*, abbreviated emf, and the symbol E is applied. The *terminal voltage* of a battery or generator when it delivers a current I is equal to the total emf E minus the potential drop (or voltage drop) in its internal resistance r. When current is being delivered, terminal voltage equals emf minus voltage drop in internal resistance: $V = E - Ir$.

Ohm's Law

The simplest direct-current (d-c) electric circuit consists of a battery, switch, conductors, and a resistance (resistor). The arrangement is shown in Fig. 11-3.

George Simon Ohm discovered, more than a century ago, that when the switch of such a simple circuit was closed the current remained steady provided the surrounding or ambient temperature of the conductor did not change. He discovered that by doubling the emf the current could be doubled and by trebling

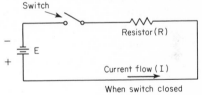

Fig. 11-3   A simple electric circuit.

the emf the current could be trebled. In short, he found that, for a given circuit, the ratio of the emf to the current remained a constant.

$$\frac{E \text{ (volts)}}{I \text{ (amp)}} = k$$

where k is a numerical constant.

It was also found that changing the resistance value resulted in a different value of the numerical constant. From test results Ohm concluded that the constant E/I ratio for a given circuit indicated a specific property of that circuit. For a given emf, the value of the constant increased as the current decreased. This constant represented an opposition of the circuit to the flow of current, and it was thus given the name *resistance.*

Resistance (*R*) in an electric circuit refers to the resistance to current flow. The unit is the ohm.

$$R \text{ (ohms)} = \frac{E \text{ (volts)}}{I \text{ (amp)}}$$

Example. Calculate the resistance of the filament in an optical pyrometer if a current of 120 ma flows through the circuit at 6.00 volts applied at the terminals.

Solution

$$R = \frac{6.00 \text{ volts}}{0.12 \text{ amp}} = 50 \text{ ohms}$$

The resistance of a unit length and cross section of conductor material is termed the *specific resistance* or *resistivity.* The specific resistance is indicated by the Greek letter ρ (rho). Since the mks (meter-kilogram-second) unit for both length and cross section is the meter, the mks standard conductor takes the form of a cube with each edge of its faces one meter in length. The resistivity of an electrical conducting material would be the resistance between opposite faces of a one-meter cube and would be expressed in ohms-meters.

In instrumentation work, resistivity is expressed in the foot unit of length and the mil (1.0×10^{-3} in.) as the unit of diameter. This practical unit of resistivity is expressed in ohms for a mil-foot conductor at a specified temperature (usually 20°C). Table 11-1 lists the resistivity of some common electrical conductors.

The area of a circle is $A = (\pi/4)d^2$, where d is the diameter. Since $\pi/4$ is a constant, the area is directly proportional to the square of the

Table 11-1   Resistivities of common conductors at 20°C

Conductors	ρ, ohms/cir mil-ft
Elements:	
Silver	9.7
Copper	10.3
Aluminum	17.0
Tungsten	33
Iron	72–84
Alloys:	
Brass	38–52
Chromel	625–655
Constantan (60% Cu, 40% Ni)	295
Nichrome (60% Ni, 12% Cr, 2% Mn, 26% Fe)	660

diameter. Because the majority of electrical conductors have a circular cross section, a new area unit is used. This is called the *circular mil* (cir mil) as opposed to the square mil. The circular mil is defined as the area of a circle whose diameter is exactly one mil. Hence $A = d^2$, where A is the area of a circle, in circular mils, and d is the diameter of the circle, in mils. The use of this circular measure avoids the possibility of error in multiplying d^2 by $\pi/4$.

Example. Calculate the cross-sectional area of a conductor, in circular mils, if the conductor diameter is 4 mils.

Solution

$$A = d^2 = 4^2 = 16 \text{ cir mils}$$

Calculation of resistance. The resistance of a conductor of uniform cross section is directly proportional to the resistivity and the length and inversely proportional to the cross-sectional area of the conductor. Symbolically,

$$R = \frac{\rho L}{d^2}$$

Example. The diameter, in mils, of an American wire gauge (AWG) No. 14 copper wire is 64.1. Calculate the resistance at 20°C of a 200-ft length of the wire.

Solution

$$\text{Diameter } d = 64.1 \text{ mils}$$
$$\text{Area } A = d^2 = 64.1 \times 64.1$$
$$= 4,109 \text{ cir mils}$$
$$\text{Resistance } R = \frac{\rho L}{d^2} = \frac{10.3 \times 200}{4,109}$$
$$\doteq 0.5 \text{ ohms}$$

Effect of Temperature on Resistance

It is found that, as a general rule, the resistivity of metallic conductors increases with temperature, whereas that of electrolytes, carbon, and insulators decreases with temperature. For common electrical conductors the equation is

$$R_t = R_0[1 + \alpha \, \Delta T + \beta(\Delta T)^2]$$

where R_t = resistance at any temperature T°C
$\quad\ R_0$ = resistance at 20°C
$\quad \Delta T$ = change in temperature, °C
and α and β are constants for the material. The constant β is so small that for narrow temperature ranges of, say, 0 to 150°C, it may be neglected.

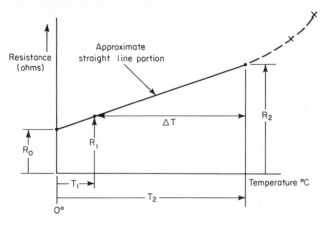

Fig. 11-4   The effect of temperature on resistance.

The equation then becomes

$$R_t = R_0(1 + \alpha \, \Delta T)$$

The graph is shown in Fig. 11-4. Values of α, which is called the temperature coefficient of resistance, are listed in Table 11-2.

Table 11-2   Temperature coefficient of resistance of common electric conductors at 20°C

Material	α, at 20°C
Silver.................	3.8×10^{-3}
Copper................	3.92×10^{-3}
Aluminum.............	4.0×10^{-3}
Tungsten..............	4.5×10^{-3}
Nickel................	6.0×10^{-3}
Constantan............	0.8×10^{-6}
Carbon................	5.0×10^{-4} (negative)

Example. The resistance of 1 mile of aluminum cable used on a transmission line is 0.26 ohm at 20°C. Calculate the resistance at 40°C.

Solution

$$R_t = 0.26[1 + 4.0 \times 10^{-3}(40 - 20)]$$
$$= 0.28 \text{ ohm}$$

The tungsten filament used in incandescent lamps and the heaters of some radio tubes provides a good example of *inrush current*. A 60-watt lamp operating on a 110-volt supply has a white-hot resistance of 220 ohms to limit the current through it to

$$I = \frac{E}{R} = \frac{110}{220} = 0.5 \text{ amp}$$

When the lamp is turned off, the cold resistance is about 20 ohms. Hence, at the instant that the lamp is turned on, before the filament has an opportunity to heat up, the inrush current will be

$$I = \frac{E}{R} = \frac{110}{20} = 5.5 \text{ amp}$$

To limit the initial surge on electronic and television equipment, nonlinear resistors, called *thermistors*, are used. A thermistor is a semiconductor whose electrical resistance decreases rapidly with increase of temperature. For example, the resistance may be of the order of 10^5 ohms at 20°C and only 10 ohms at 100°C. Some thermistors are used as sensitive temperature-measuring elements. A comparison between a linear resistor and a nonlinear resistor is given in Fig. 11-5a and b.

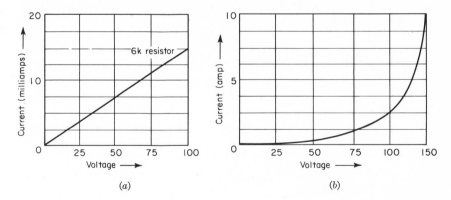

Fig. 11-5 (a) *A linear resistor.* (b) *A nonlinear resistor.*

A *ballast resistor* is one which takes advantage of a high positive temperature coefficient. As the voltage across the resistor is doubled, the accompanying increase in temperature practically doubles the resistance. This increase occurs with almost no increase in current. Frequently, this type of nonlinear resistor, called a *current regulator*, is useful to maintain a reasonably steady current during voltage variations. Further details on the characteristics of nonlinear resistors will be found in books on electronics.

Electric Power (P)

Power is the term for the rate of doing work in the mechanical sense. The watt is the unit of electric power; it is the rate of doing one joule of work in one second. Electrical power P, in watts, is the product of emf V, in volts, and the current I, in amperes.

$$P = VI$$
$$V = IR \qquad \text{Ohm's law}$$

Hence
$$P = I^2R = \frac{V^2}{R}$$

Example. The filament in an instrument panel lamp uses 0.5 amp when connected to a potential difference of 20.0 volts. Calculate the power rating.

Solution
$$
\begin{aligned}
P \text{ (watts)} &= V \text{ (volts)} \times I \text{ (amp)} \\
&= 20.0 \text{ volts} \times 0.5 \text{ amp} \\
&= 10.0 \text{ watts}
\end{aligned}
$$

The kilowatthour. If P is electric power, in watts, and t is time, in seconds, then the electrical work or energy is expressed in wattseconds. Now, if P is in kilowatts and t is in hours, the electric work or energy is expressed in kilowatthours. The kilowatthour is the practical unit of electric work or energy and is defined by the equation

$$\text{Work } W \text{ (kilowatthours)} = P \text{ (kilowatts)} \times t \text{ (hr)}$$

Conductance

Resistance is a measure of the ability of a circuit to oppose the flow of current. Conductance is a measure of the ability of an electric circuit to pass current. The letter symbol for conductance is usually G. The mho (ohm spelled backwards) is the basic unit for conductance and is the reciprocal of resistance:

$$G \text{ (mhos)} = \frac{1}{R \text{ (ohms)}}$$

Conductivity

The conductivity of a substance is the conductance of a unit length and unit cross-sectional area of that substance. Conductivity is denoted by the Greek letter σ (sigma) and is the reciprocal of resistivity:

$$\text{Conductivity } \sigma = \frac{1}{\text{resistivity } \rho}$$

The units are mhos per meter or mhos per mil-foot.

The arrangement in Fig. 11-6 shows a simple conductivity meter. Conductivity represents the ability of a substance to sustain one ampere of current at one volt potential. The applications of conductivity and conductance are found in pH, gas, and other analytical instruments discussed in later chapters.

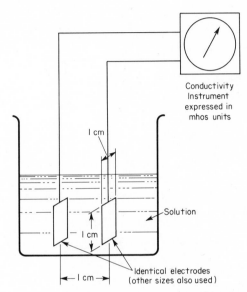

Fig. 11-6   Simple conductivity application.

Standard Graphic Symbols and Abbreviations

Some common abbreviations and prefixes used in electrical measurements are listed in Table 11-3. Selected standard graphic symbols used in instrument practice and drafting are given in Table 11-4.

Table 11-3   Some commonly used abbreviations

Prefix	Meaning	Abbreviation
Mega	One million, or 10^6	M
Kilo	One thousand, or 10^3	k
Milli	One thousandth, or 10^{-3}	m
Micro	One millionth, or 10^{-6}	μ (mu)
Micromicro or pico	10^{-12}	p

Example.   1   microfarad = 1 μf = 10^{-6} f;   1   micromicrofarad = 1 $\mu\mu$f = 10^{-12} f = 1 pf.

Table 11-4   Some standard graphic symbols

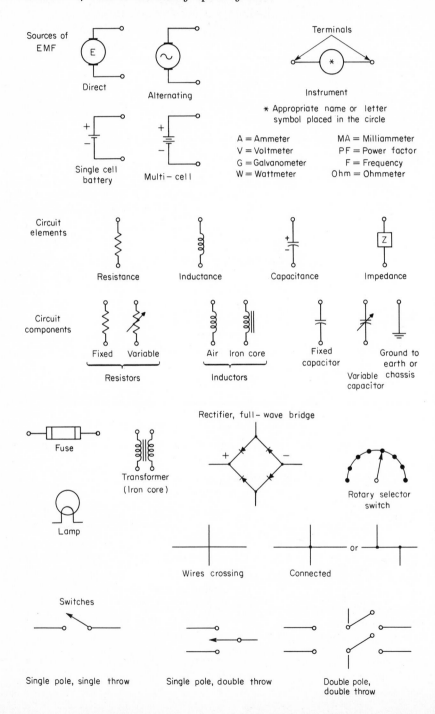

Sources of EMF

Direct

Alternating

Single cell battery

Multi–cell

Terminals

Instrument

* Appropriate name or letter symbol placed in the circle

A = Ammeter   MA = Milliammeter
V = Voltmeter   PF = Power factor
G = Galvanometer   F = Frequency
W = Wattmeter   Ohm = Ohmmeter

Circuit elements

Resistance   Inductance   Capacitance   Impedance

Circuit components

Fixed   Variable
Resistors

Air   Iron core
Inductors

Fixed capacitor

Variable capacitor

Ground to earth or chassis

Fuse

Transformer (Iron core)

Rectifier, full–wave bridge

Rotary selector switch

Lamp

Wires crossing   Connected   or

Switches

Single pole, single throw   Single pole, double throw   Double pole, double throw

REVIEW QUESTIONS AND PROBLEMS

11-1 What quantity of electricity passes through the filament of a lamp which burns for $1\frac{1}{2}$ hr and draws a current of 0.41 amp?

11-2 (a) State Ohm's law.

(b) Define voltage and ampere.

(c) Calculate the current drawn by an electric heater from a 120-volt supply if its resistance (when hot) is 30 ohms.

11-3 Calculate the resistance of 1,000 ft of copper wire having a diameter of 0.102 in.

11-4 Compute the resistivity of an alloy-metal conductor whose diameter, measured by a micrometer caliper, is 0.072 in. if the wire is 200 ft long and has a total resistance of 7.76 ohms.

11-5 (a) What is the effect of temperature on the commonly used electrical conductor over a narrow temperature range?

(b) Calculate the resistance of 1,000 ft of copper wire at 40°C given that specific resistance $\rho = 10.37$, the diameter $d = 32$ mils, and temperature coefficient of resistance α at 20°C $= 4.0 \times 10^{-3}$. Use the expression

$$R = \rho \frac{L}{d^2} [1 + \alpha(T_2 - T_1)]$$

11-6 Calculate the highest voltage that can be applied to a 5.0-kilohm 2.0-watt resistor.

11-7 (a) Distinguish between conductance and conductivity.

(b) If the total resistance of a circuit is 10 ohms, what is the conductance?

(c) The resistivity of commercial copper is 10.3 ohms/mil-ft. What is the conductivity?

Measuring Circuits with Direct Current

Measurement of current and voltage. The two instruments most frequently used to measure current and voltage in an electric circuit are the ammeter and the voltmeter, respectively. Details of their operation and construction are described in Chap. 12. Both instruments are direct reading; i.e., by reading the deflection of a pointer on each instrument scale, when the current is flowing, the amperage and voltage can be read simultaneously.

The ammeter has a very low internal resistance; and when it is placed in a circuit, it does not appreciably change the total resistance. The voltmeter has a very high internal resistance, and when it is connected

across a circuit, it does not appreciably change the total current flow.
The simple circuit diagram in Fig. 11-7 shows the ammeter A connected
in series with the circuit and the
voltmeter V connected across or in
parallel with the load R.

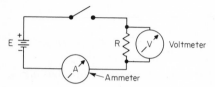

Series circuits. The circuit in Fig.
11-8 shows resistors connected in
series with the ammeter which may
be connected in series at any point
in the circuit. The ammeter reading
will be the same regardless of where
the ammeter is connected in the cir-

*Fig. 11-7 Measurement of am-
peres and volts in a simple circuit.*

cuit. Hence, from the circuit shown

$$I = I_1 = I_2 = I_3 \qquad \text{amp}$$

where I, I_1, I_2, and I_3 represent the current from the source which passes
through the resistors R_1, R_2, and R_3 in that order.

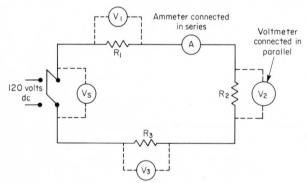

Fig. 11-8   A circuit showing resistors connected in series.

The resistance of the leads connecting the resistors is normally very
small and may be neglected. The total resistance R_T of the circuit is equal
to the sum of all the resistances:

$$R_T = R_1 + R_2 + R_3$$

The applied emf from the supply measured by the voltmeter V_s must be
equal to the sum of the potential drops measured by V_1, V_2, and V_3. Thus:

$$
\begin{aligned}
V_s &= V_1 + V_2 + V_3 \\
&= IR_1 + IR_2 + IR_3 \\
&= I(R_1 + R_2 + R_3) \\
&= IR_T
\end{aligned}
$$

Example. Calculate the current flow in a series circuit consisting of 30-, 20-, and 10-ohm resistors connected to a 120-volt source of emf.

Solution
$$R_T = R_1 + R_2 + R_3 = 30 + 20 + 10 = 60 \text{ ohms}$$
$$I = \frac{V}{R_T} = \frac{120 \text{ volts}}{60 \text{ ohms}} = 2 \text{ amp}$$

Parallel circuits. When two or more resistors are joined in parallel as shown in Fig. 11-9a, the effect is similar to water flow in a parallel branched pipework as shown in Fig. 11-9b. The pressure difference in the case of

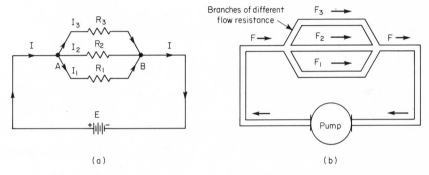

(a)   (b)

Fig. 11-9 (a) *Resistors in parallel.* (b) *Hydraulic analogy.*

water pipeline flow, or the potential drop in the electric circuit between A and B, will be the same for each branch of the network:

$$V = V_1 = V_2 = V_3$$
$$= I_1R_1 = I_2R_2 = I_3R_3$$

The total current that will flow from A to B is equal to the sum of the separate currents in each of the parallel branches of the network:

$$I = I_1 + I_2 + I_3$$

If the total resistance of the circuit is denoted by R_T, then

$$R_T = \frac{V}{I}$$
$$\frac{1}{R_T} = \frac{I}{V} = \frac{I_1 + I_2 + I_3}{V}$$
$$= \frac{I_1}{V_1} + \frac{I_2}{V_2} + \frac{I_3}{V_3}$$
$$= \frac{1}{R_1} + \frac{1}{R_2} + \frac{1}{R_3}$$

The characteristics of parallel circuits can be summarized as follows:

1. The voltage across all components in a parallel circuit is the same.
2. The total current is the sum of all the individual parallel-branch currents.

Example. The circuit diagram in Fig. 11-10 shows two resistors R_1 and R_2 in parallel and R_3 in series. If the d-c supply is 120 volts, calculate (a) the total resistance and (b) the circuit current.

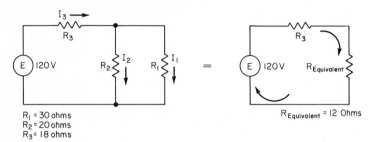

$R_1 = 30$ ohms
$R_2 = 20$ ohms
$R_3 = 18$ ohms

Fig. 11-10   Circuit diagram.

Solution. (a) To find the equivalent resistance for R_2 and R_1, which are in parallel,

$$\frac{1}{R_{equiv}} = \frac{1}{R_2} + \frac{1}{R_1}$$

$$R_{equiv} = \frac{R_2 \times R_1}{R_2 + R_1} = \frac{20 \times 30}{20 + 30} = 12 \text{ ohms}$$

The total resistance then becomes

$$R_T = R_3 + R_{equiv} = 18 + 12 = 30 \text{ ohms}$$

(b) $$I = \frac{V}{R_T} = \frac{120 \text{ volts}}{30 \text{ ohms}} = 4 \text{ amp}$$

The Wheatstone Bridge

A special type of resistance network (Fig. 11-11) is frequently used in instrument practice for determining the resistance of some unknown component. This network is called the Wheatstone bridge. The battery supplies a current to two paths, each having two resistors in series. A sensitive galvanometer, to indicate current flow, is connected between C and D. By using Kirchhoff's law, a relationship may be established among the four resistances.

Kirchhoff's laws are:

1. When two or more conductors meet, the total current flowing toward the junction is equal to the total current flowing away from it.

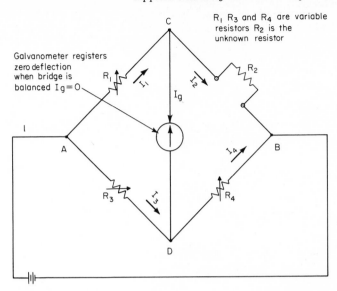

Fig. 11-11   The Wheatstone bridge measuring circuit.

2. In passing around and coming back to the starting point of any complete loop of a circuit the algebraic sum of the terms IR for the separate parts is equal to the resultant emf in that circuit.

By referring to the bridge circuit and applying the first law, the following may be written:

At A $\qquad\qquad\qquad I = I_1 + I_3$
At C $\qquad\qquad\qquad I_1 = I_g + I_2$
At D $\qquad\qquad\qquad I_4 = I_g + I_3$

By applying the second law for the circuit loop ACD,

$$I_1R_1 + I_gR_g = I_3R_3$$

Attention must be paid to the sign convention of the current. For circuit loop CBD:

$$I_2R_2 = I_4R_4 + I_gR_g$$

If the galvanometer indicates zero deflection, generally referred to as a null-balance position, then $I_g = 0$. The zero deflection is obtained by adjusting the variable resistances R_1, R_3, and R_4 until no current passes through the meter. Then $I_1 = I_2$.

For the circuit loop ACD $\qquad I_1R_1 = I_3R_3$
For the circuit loop CBD $\qquad I_2R_2 = I_4R_4$

Thus, when $I_g = 0$,

$$\frac{R_1}{R_2} = \frac{R_3}{R_4}$$

Hence

$$R_2 = R_1 \frac{R_4}{R_3}$$

The resistance under test (R_2) can be found by knowing the values of the other three resistances in the bridge circuit.

Example. A Wheatstone-bridge circuit similar to that shown in Fig. 11-11 is used to determine an unknown resistance R_2 and is balanced when $R_4 = 1,000$ ohms, $R_3 = 10$ ohms, and $R_1 = 160$ ohms. Calculate the value of R_2.

Solution

$$R_2 = R_1 \frac{R_4}{R_3} = 160 \frac{1,000}{10} = 16,000 \text{ ohms}$$

As long as the value of R_1 and the ratio of R_4 to R_3 are known, the value of R_2 (the unknown) can be readily found. Some commercial products are so constructed that the ratio of R_4 to R_3 is selected by a rotary switch. These ratios generally contain multiples of 10 from 0.00001 to 1,000. The values for R_1 can be adjusted by a system of rotary switches varying in resistance from 1 to 1,000 ohms and indicating the value on a dial.

The Potentiometer Circuit

One of the basic and important instruments used in electrical measurement is the potentiometer, which serves primarily to compare emf's. The fundamental principle is shown in Fig. 11-12. AB is a long, uniform, calibrated resistance wire with a scale for measuring length. A battery E sends a current, whose magnitude is controlled by the rheostat R_v, through the wire. A second cell E_s can be connected (by the switch in position S_1) between A and a flexible sliding contact C on the wire through the galvanometer. The emf E must be greater than E_s, but it need not be known. All the cells must be connected with the same polarity toward the connection A.

Two opposing factors control the current in the galvanometer G. Current through AB creates a voltage drop across AC with point C negative with respect to point A. Also, the cell E_s makes point D negative with respect to point A when switch S_1 is closed. Hence, for some point of the slider, voltage AC = voltage AD, and this occurs when the voltage CD = zero. At such a point the galvanometer indicates a null or zero reading, because $I_g = 0$.

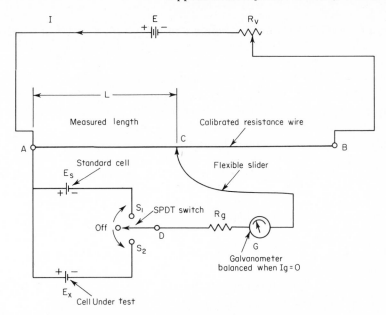

Fig. 11-12   Basic potentiometric measuring circuit.

By applying Kirchhoff's law to the loop $ACGE_sA$,

$$IrL_s + 0(R_g + R_e) = E_s$$

where r = resistance per unit length of AB

$\quad L_s$ = length AC corresponding to a null or zero reading on the galvanometer with E_s in the circuit

$\quad R_g$ = resistance of the galvanometer

$\quad R_e$ = internal resistance of the cell E_s

Hence $\qquad\qquad\qquad E_s = IrL_s$

The measuring procedure is simple. When switch S_1 is closed, the slider is moved until a zero reading is registered on the galvanometer, and L_s is noted. The procedure is repeated with S_1 open and S_2 closed. In this case, if L_x represents the length along AB for null-balance reading by the galvanometer, then the emf of the cell E_x under test is given by

$$\frac{E_x}{E_s} = \frac{IrL_x}{IrL_s} = \frac{L_x}{L_s}$$

or $\qquad\qquad\qquad E_x = E_s \frac{L_x}{L_s}$

At the balance position there is no current through the cell under test. I is the same in both tests, being controlled by R_v and E.

Standard cell. The standard cell is a primary cell, the emf of which is accurately known and which keeps a steady value with time provided that no appreciable power is drawn from the cell. There are a number of standard cells on the market; the Weston cell is one of them. This cell is a small H-shaped glass tube with mercury and a mercury-cadmium amalgam as electrodes and a saturated solution of cadmium sulfate as electrolyte. Mercurous sulfate is added as a depolarizing agent.

Certain precautions should be taken when using the standard cell. Never short-circuit the terminals of the cell, and never draw a current of more than one microampere from it. The emf of a standard cell is found to be

$$E = 1.0187[1 - 0.0004(\theta - 20)] \text{ volts}$$

where θ is the ambient or surrounding temperature of the cell on the centigrade scale.

Application of the potentiometer. The d-c potentiometer is used mainly for the calibration of electrical instruments. Large precision vernier potentiometers, together with standard resistors, standard cells, volt ratios, and a few standard indicating instruments, are generally kept in a laboratory or instrument workshop for standardizing purposes. This equipment can be used in conjunction with a converter for accurate measurement of alternating currents and voltages.

Inductance

In addition to the components of an electric circuit which resist the flow of current, there are those which resist a change in the current through the circuit. This property of an electrical component is called *inductance*. In about 1819, Hans Christian Oersted, a Danish physicist, showed that current flowing in a conductor produces a magnetic field. Michael Faraday, in England, and Joseph Henry, in the United States, showed that electric current and magnetic fields are closely related.

Mutual inductance. The circuit diagram in Fig. 11-13 shows a simple arrangement to illustrate mutual inductance. When the switch is closed, a current flows in the primary circuit. Magnetic lines of force are produced by the coil wound around the iron core. As the variable resistance is changed, the number of lines of magnetic force changes. This change causes a current to flow in the secondary circuit. The current in the secondary circuit flows in the direction which counteracts or opposes the effect of a change of current in the primary circuit. The voltage in the secondary circuit is called the *induced emf*. Its magnitude depends upon the rate of change of the primary current di/dt. This type of inductance is called *mutual inductance*.

Self-inductance. Consider the circuit diagram in Fig. 11-14. When the switch is first closed, the increasing magnetic flux produced by the rising

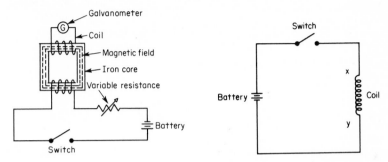

Fig. 11-13   Circuit showing mutual inductance.

Fig. 11-14   Circuit showing self-inductance.

current in the turn X of the coil will induce an emf in the turn Y. Since the increasing flux is due to the rising current, the induced emf will be in such a direction as to oppose the applied emf, so that the current cannot rise instantly. The induced emf is called a *counter emf* (cemf). H. L. Lenz, a famous physicist, reasoned that the process of induction must conform to the theory of conservation of energy, and in particular to the principle that reaction is equal and opposite to action.

Self-inductance can be defined as that property of an electric circuit that opposes any change in current in that circuit. The inductance of a circuit is responsible for a cemf being induced by a changing current and is in accordance with Faraday's law, namely, that the magnitude of the cemf is directly proportional to the rate of change of current.

The basic unit of inductance (L) is the henry. A circuit has an inductance of one henry when the current, changing at a rate of one ampere per second, induces a counter emf of one volt into that circuit. Symbolically, the inductance equation is

$$L = \frac{v_L}{di/dt}$$

where L is the inductance of a circuit, in henrys, v_L is the instantaneous cemf induced in that circuit, in volts, and di is the infinitesimal change in current, in amperes, during an infinitely small interval of time dt, in seconds. Hence di/dt represents the instantaneous change of current with respect to time.

Effect of inductance on current and voltage. Figure 11-15 shows a simple inductance and resistance in an LR circuit. The applied emf is equal to

$$E = v_R + v_L$$

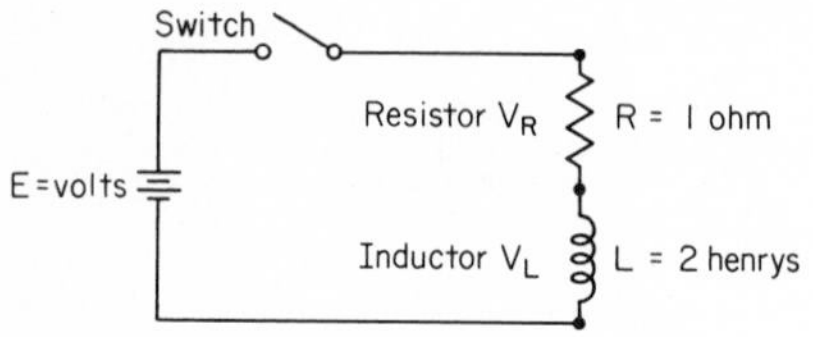

where v_R and v_L are the instantaneous values of the voltage across the resistor and inductor.

By definition

$$v_L = L \frac{di}{dt}$$

Fig. 11-15 A simple inductance-resistance or LR circuit.

Hence
$$E = iR + L \frac{di}{dt}$$

From this equation, when $\frac{di}{dt} = 0$, the current must be at a steady value I, hence

$$I = \frac{E}{R}$$

The relationship between the instantaneous current and time is shown in Fig. 11-16. If the switch is closed in a d-c circuit containing an inductance and resistance, time is required for the current to rise to a steady value. If the current could continue to rise at a constant rate, equal to its

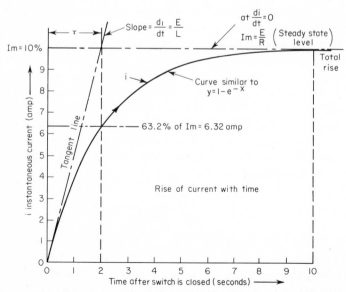

Fig. 11-16   Rise of current in a d-c circuit having inductance and resistance.

initial rate of rise, until it achieved the steady value indicated by the dotted line in Fig. 11-16, then we would have a convenient method for determining the time interval. This time interval is called the *time constant* of the *LR* circuit. The time constant is defined as the time required for the instantaneous current in an *LR* circuit to reach 63.2 percent of the steady state, or sustained level.

Voltage-time relationships. Figure 11-17 shows the relationship of instantaneous voltages across the inductance and resistance during the time the current rises to a steady-state level.

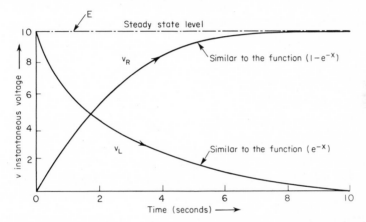

Fig. 11-17 Relationship of instantaneous voltages across inductance and resistance with time.

Inductances in series and in parallel. Inductances may be joined in series or in parallel, as shown in Figs. 11-18 and 11-19. When in series,

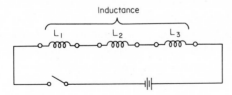

Fig. 11-18 Inductance in series.

the total inductance equals the sum of the individual inductances:

$$L_T = L_1 + L_2 + L_3$$

When in parallel, the reciprocal of the total inductance equals the sum of the reciprocals of the individual inductances:

$$\frac{1}{L_T} = \frac{1}{L_1} + \frac{1}{L_2} + \frac{1}{L_3}$$

Stored energy in an inductor. When an inductor is connected to a source emf, the energy supplied is stored in the magnetic field. The rising current forces the magnetic lines of force to expand against their natural characteristic of tending to become as short as possible. An analogy may be made to the countertorque built up when the elastic-band motor of a model airplane is wound. The work put into the elastic band is stored up and used to drive the propeller shaft. Energy stored by an inductance behaves in a similar way.

Since the rate of change of current is constant, the average value of the instantaneous current as it rises from zero to the maximum steady-state level is used. By a formal mathematical solution shown in the Appendix, the stored-energy equation is

$$W = \tfrac{1}{2}LI_m{}^2$$

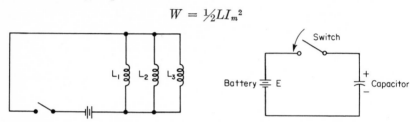

Fig. 11-19   Inductance in parallel.   *Fig. 11-20   Charging a capacitor without a current-limiting resistor.*

Capacitance

Inductance is the property of an electric circuit that resists a change in current; *capacitance* is the property which resists a change in voltage. The circuit component which contains capacitance is called a *capacitor* (Fig. 11-20). Essentially, a capacitor is an assembly of one or more pairs of conductors separated by insulators and used to retain an electric charge. The two conductors are called *electrodes* or *plates,* and the insulator, which may be solid, liquid, or gaseous, is referred to as the *dielectric.* The capacitor stores an electric charge under pressure in the same way a cylinder of compressed gas stores a charge of gas under pressure.

Referring to the circuit in Fig. 11-20, when the switch is closed, current begins to flow. It continues to flow until the voltage across the plates of the capacitor equals the battery voltage. When the capacitor voltage reaches this value, the current no longer flows in the circuit. The capacitor stores this charge. The symbol for capacitance is C, and the basic unit is the farad (f). A circuit has a capacitance of one farad when a charge of one coulomb is required to raise its potential by one volt.

$$\text{Capacitance } C = \frac{\text{coulombs } Q}{\text{potential difference } V}$$

where C is measured in farads.

The largest unit used in practice to express capacitance is the microfarad (μf):

$$1 \text{ microfarad} = 10^{-6} \text{ farad}$$

In many cases the microfarad is too large and the micromicrofarad ($\mu\mu$f) is used:

$$1 \text{ micromicrofarad} = 10^{-12} \text{ farad}$$

The micromicrofarad is also called a picofarad.

Charging a capacitor. Figure 11-21 shows a capacitor being charged through a current-limiting resistor. The effect of the resistor is to increase

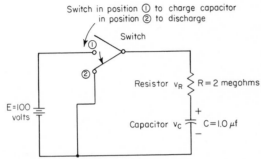

Fig. 11-21   An RC circuit charging a capacitor through a current-limiting resistor.

the time required to charge the capacitor. During the time that the switch is closed to complete the circuit, the sum of potential difference (PD) across the capacitor and the IR drop across the resistor must equal the applied emf:

$$E = v_c + iR$$

This current immediately begins to charge the capacitor, and the potential difference starts to build up across the plates of the capacitor.

In accordance with Kirchhoff's law, the IR drop across the resistor must decrease during the time that the PD builds up in the capacitor. The rate of rise of the instantaneous PD across the capacitor, dv_c/dt, depends on the preceding instantaneous current value. The instantaneous current depends on how much IR drop occurs across the resistance, and this, in turn, depends on how long the switch was closed.

The result of all this interdependence of the variables involved is the exponential rise of voltage across a capacitor as shown in Fig. 11-22. It should be noticed that the curve is similar to that established in the rise of current in an inductance of a d-c circuit as shown in Fig. 11-16.

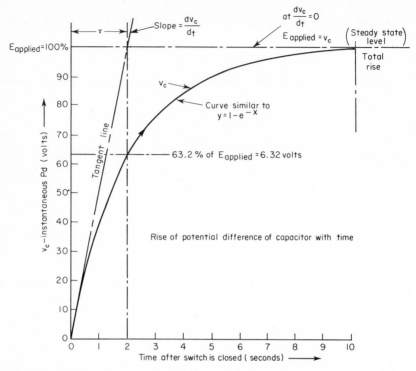

Fig. 11-22   Rise of potential difference across a capacitor of a d-c circuit having a resistance.

Discharging a capacitor. Figure 11-23 is the graph of the discharge of the capacitor in the same *RC* circuit. The capacitor-discharge curve has a shape similar to the charge curve; in fact, the two are almost mirror images.

Capacitors in series and parallel. When the capacitors are connected in series as shown in Fig. 11-24, the reciprocal of the total capacitance equals the sum of the reciprocal of the individual capacitances

$$\frac{1}{C_T} = \frac{1}{C_1} + \frac{1}{C_2} + \frac{1}{C_3}$$

These capacitors are put in series, since in a series circuit the total voltage becomes

$$V_T = V_1 + V_2 + V_3$$

Capacitors in series are frequently used to increase breakdown-voltage rating.

When the capacitors are connected in parallel, as shown in Fig. 11-25, the total capacitance equals the sum of the individual capacitances

$$C_T = C_1 + C_2 + C_3$$

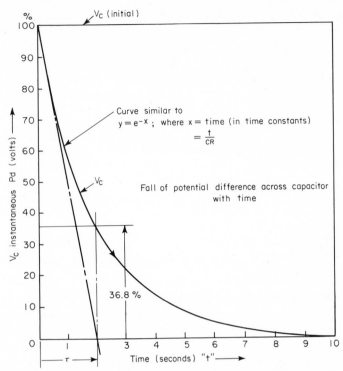

V_C (initial)

Curve similar to
$y = e^{-x}$; where $x =$ time (in time constants)
$= \dfrac{t}{CR}$

V_C

Fall of potential difference across capacitor
with time

36.8 %

*Fig. 11-23   Discharge of the same capacitor when switch is in position 2 of
RC circuit in Fig. 11-21.*

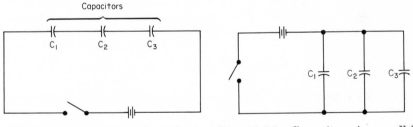

Fig. 11-24   Capacitors in series.   *Fig. 11-25   Capacitors in parallel.*

Simple *RC* Networks

The properties of capacitance are used in d-c circuits to oppose any instant
change in voltage across the circuit. This makes the capacitor useful for
smoothing out any fluctuations in the output from a pulsating source
of emf such as a rectifier. Resistance-capacitor networks have many
applications in instrumentation. The following are a few examples:

1. Precise timers for short intervals.
2. Suppressing a voltage surge with a capacitor.

3. Reset action in an electrical controller which is achieved in an *RC* circuit as shown in Fig. 11-26.

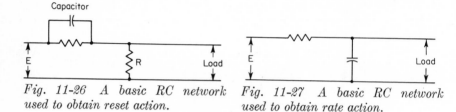

Fig. 11-26 A basic RC network used to obtain reset action.

Fig. 11-27 A basic RC network used to obtain rate action.

4. Rate action in an electrical controller which is achieved in an *RC* circuit as shown in Fig. 11-27.

REVIEW QUESTIONS AND PROBLEMS

11-8   (a) Explain the terms "series" and "parallel" in connection with electrical resistors in a circuit.

(b) Show that, if *n* similar conductors are arranged in series, the combined resistance is n^2 times as great as when they are arranged in parallel.

11-9   Resistors of 5, 10, and 15 ohms are arranged in parallel. Calculate their effective resistance.

11-10   Four cells, each of 1.5 volts emf and 2 ohms internal resistance, are used to pass a current through a single wire of 2 ohms resistance. The cells are arranged (a) all in series, (b) in two parallel groups of two in series, (c) all in parallel. Calculate the current in the wire in each case.

11-11   (a) Explain the theory of the Wheatstone bridge method for measurement of resistance.

(b) Figure 11-28 shows a slide-wire bridge which is based on the

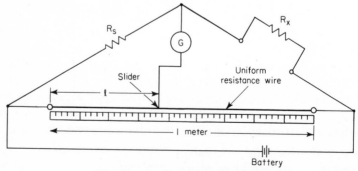

Fig. 11-28 A slide-wire bridge.

Wheatstone. The slide-wire is a uniform-resistance wire 1 m long. The standard resistor R_s = 20 ohms. Calculate the value of R_x if the bridge is balanced when the slide is 40 cm from the end that is connected to the standard resistor.

11-12 (a) Draw a diagram of a potentiometer and give the procedure for standardizing the potentiometer.

(b) How would you use a potentiometer to compare (1) two emf's and (2) two resistances? Explain the theory of the methods you describe. Give any example you know of to demonstrate the use of the potentiometer for calibration purposes.

11-13 A current of 0.1 amp enters a Wheatstone bridge consisting of three arms of 10 ohms each and one arm of 11 ohms. Calculate the current in the galvanometer if the galvanometer resistance is 100 ohms.

11-14 Define the terms (a) mutual inductance and (b) self-inductance. Sketch the graph of the instantaneous current-time relationship in an *LR* circuit and indicate the time constant for 63.2 percent of the steady-state value.

11-15 Calculate how long it will take for the instantaneous current in the *LR* circuit of Fig. 11-15 to rise to 5 amp.

11-16 If the current in a circuit is changing at the rate of 200 ma/sec and induces a cemf of 100 mv, calculate the inductance of the circuit.

11-17 A 20-henry inductance, whose resistance is 16 ohms, is connected through a switch to a 24-volt applied emf.

(a) What is the initial rate of rise of current when the switch is closed?

(b) Calculate the final steady-state current.

(c) How long does the current take to reach 63.2 percent of its steady-state value?

11-18 Describe briefly, with the aid of a graph and circuit diagrams, the charging and discharging characteristics of a capacitor using a current-limiting resistor and a two-way switch.

11-19 Explain why capacitors connected in series must all take the same charge.

11-20 A 0.01-μf capacitor and a 0.04-μf capacitor are connected first in series and then in parallel to a 500-volt source emf. Calculate (a) the total capacitance in each case, (b) the total charge in each case, (c) the charge and potential difference across each capacitor in each case.

11-21 (a) Describe any capacitor you know and give details of its construction, dielectric material, and application in instrumentation.

(b) Define the term "capacitance."

11-22 Calculate the amount of energy which is stored in a 500-$\mu\mu$f capacitor when it is charged to 15 kilovolts.

Alternating-current Circuits

Basic a-c theory. Nearly 90 percent of all generating stations in North America generate electricity as alternating current. One of the main reasons for the use of alternating current is that it can be readily increased or decreased in voltage without the use of any rotating machinery, and therefore the electric energy can be more economically and efficiently transmitted over long distances. There are many advantages to and applications for the use of alternating current in instrumentation. When a direct-current source is necessary, the alternating current is rectified into direct current by incorporating a suitable electrical or electronic device. In this section some of the fundamental characteristics of alternating currents and measuring circuits and the uses of alternating current in instrumentation will be discussed.

With an alternating current the voltage and current vary continuously between zero and maximum values. A comparison between an alternating current (assuming the form of a sine curve) and a direct current (straight line) is shown in Fig. 11-29. The emf and current of an a-c supply depend

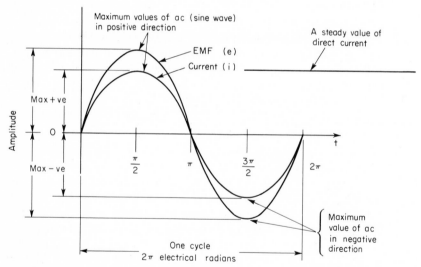

Fig. 11-29   A comparison of alternating and direct currents in a resistance circuit.

upon the rate at which the magnetic force lines are cut by a rotating coil in a magnetic field. Figure 11-30 shows a simple electric-wire conductor in the form of a loop or coil cutting a magnetic field.

Period and frequency. The period of an alternating emf or current is the time required for the emf or current to go through one complete cycle of

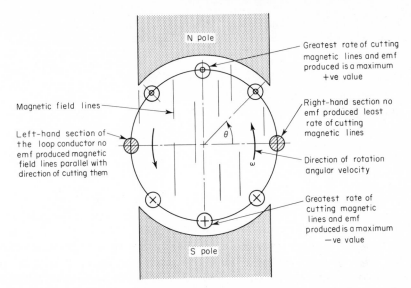

N pole

Greatest rate of cutting
magnetic lines and emf
produced is a maximum
+ve value

Magnetic field lines

Right-hand section no
emf produced least
rate of cutting
magnetic lines

Left-hand section of
the loop conductor no
emf produced magnetic
field lines parallel with
direction of cutting them

θ

ω

Direction of rotation
angular velocity

Greatest rate of
cutting magnetic
lines and emf
produced is a maximum
−ve value

S pole

Fig. 11-30   Variation of alternating emf and current through a cycle of rotation of the loop conductor in a magnetic field.

change:

$$1 \text{ cycle} = 360 \text{ electrical degrees} = 2\pi \text{ electrical radians}$$

The number of complete cycles per second of an alternating current is called the frequency, denoted by f. If, for example, an alternator has two poles, the emf and current generated will pass through one cycle once per revolution of the rotating coil. A 4-pole alternator will produce 2 cycles per revolution.

Frequency, or the cycles per second = number of pairs of poles ×
speed (revolutions per second)

In North America the usual a-c frequency is 60 cycles/sec.

The instantaneous values of the emf and current (assuming the waveform to be a sine curve) are

$$e \text{ (instantaneous voltage)} = E_{\max} \sin \omega t = E_{\max} \sin 2\pi f t$$
$$i \text{ (instantaneous current)} = I_{\max} \sin \omega t = I_{\max} \sin 2\pi f t$$

where f = frequency, cycles/sec
   $\omega = 2\pi f$ = angular velocity, electrical radians/sec
   t = time, sec, after the sine function passes its zero value in an increasing direction

The amplitude of the sine curve at any point indicates the instantaneous value of the emf or current at that instant.

Example. Establish an equation for the instantaneous emf of a 60-cycles/sec generator with a peak voltage of 180 volts. Calculate this value at $t = \frac{1}{100}$ sec.

Solution

$$e = E_m \sin 2\pi ft$$

but

$$2\pi f = 2 \times 3.14 \times 60 = 377 \text{ radians/sec}$$

Hence

$$e = 180 \sin 377t$$

at $t = \frac{1}{100}$ sec

$$e = 180 \sin 3.77$$

Recall that 2π radians $= 360°$, then

$$3.77 \text{ radians} = \frac{360}{2\pi} \times 3.77 = \frac{180 \times 3.77}{\pi} = 216.1°$$

$$e = 180 \sin 216.1° = 180 \times (-0.59) = -106 \text{ volts}$$

Effective or root-mean-square (rms) values. An alternating current fluctuates in intensity between a positive maximum and a numerically equal but negative maximum. Mathematically, the effective value of an a-c (sine-form) current is equivalent to 0.707 of its maximum value. A mathematical solution is given in the appendix. An alternating current is said to have an rms or effective value of one ampere if it develops heat in a resistance at the same rate as a steady direct current of one ampere.

$$\text{Effective emf } E = \frac{E_{\text{max}}}{\sqrt{2}} = 0.707 E_{\text{max}}$$

$$\text{Effective current } I = \frac{I_{\text{max}}}{\sqrt{2}} = 0.707 I_{\text{max}}$$

Alternating-current voltmeters and ammeters are calibrated to read effective values.

Example. Calculate the maximum values of the voltage and current in an a-c circuit if the voltmeter and ammeter register 120 volts and 4.0 amp, respectively.

Solution

$$I = 0.707 I_{\text{max}}$$

$$I_{\text{max}} = \frac{I}{0.707} = \frac{4}{0.707} = 5.65 \text{ amp}$$

Similarly,

$$E_{\text{max}} = \frac{E}{0.707} = \frac{120}{0.707} = 170 \text{ volts}$$

Characteristics of A-C Circuits

Pure-resistance circuit. A pure-resistance circuit is one containing no inductance or capacitance. In such a circuit the amperage and voltage are sine curves in phase, so that they reach their peak at the same time. This is shown in Fig. 11-29. When the voltage is zero, the current is zero; and when the voltage is a positive maximum, the current is also a positive maximum at the same instant. When this condition exists, the current is said to be in phase with the voltage.

Pure-resistance circuits can be dealt with as if they were d-c circuits. The usual laws apply if the effective values are used.

$$I \text{ (amp)} = \frac{E \text{ (volts)}}{R \text{ (ohms)}}$$
$$P \text{ (watts)} = E \text{ (volts)} \times I \text{ (amps)}$$

Examples of pure-resistance devices are radiant heaters, electric irons, and incandescent lamps.

A-C Circuits Containing Inductance

Inductance. Inductance, as described earlier, is a circuit property that is similar to resistance and analogous to the mechanical property of inertia. A circuit has an inductance of one henry if, when the current changes at the rate of one ampere per second, there is induced in it a counter emf of one volt. If there is no resistance in the circuit, any voltage drop that appears across the terminals of an inductor is due to the cemf induced in the coil by a changing current through it. A simple circuit having inductance is shown in Fig. 11-31.

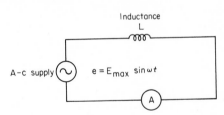

Fig. 11-31   Inductance in an a-c circuit.

According to Faraday's law of electromagnetic induction, the magnitude of the induced voltage at any instant is directly proportional to the rate of change of current. The instantaneous voltage that must appear across the inductor is then

$$v_L = L \frac{di}{dt}$$

now

$$i = I_{\max} \sin \omega t = I_{\max} \sin 2\pi f t$$

Differentiating both sides with respect to t,

$$\frac{di}{dt} = 2\pi f I_{\max} \cos 2\pi f t$$

hence, by substitution,

$$v_L = 2\pi f L I_{max} \cos \omega t$$

Thus the inductive voltage is represented by a cosine curve when the current is represented by a sine curve.

At the instant when a maximum positive voltage across the inductor is required, the current must be changing at the maximum rate in a positive direction. The maximum rate of change is indicated on the graph in Fig. 11-32, and this occurs when the slope di_L/dt is steepest. It should be noted

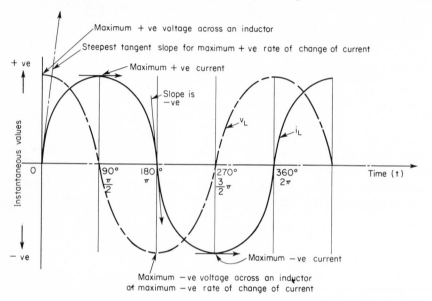

Fig. 11-32   Instantaneous values of v_L and i_L in an inductance circuit.

that the inductive voltage v_L is 90° ahead of the current in phase. Hence for a sine-wave voltage across an inductance, the current through the inductance must be a sine wave which lags the inductive voltage drop by 90°.

Inductive reactance. Since the inductor does not convert electric energy into heat as the ordinary resistor does, a term which describes the opposition to the flow of an alternating current is *inductive reactance*. Inductive reactance is the opposition set up by an inductance to the flow of alternating current. The symbol for inductive reactance is X_L, and

$$X_L = \frac{V_L}{I_L}$$

It should be noted that inductive reactance is a V/I ratio just as resistance is. For this reason the ohm is used as the unit of measurement of inductive reactance.

Thus an a-c circuit is said to have an inductive reactance of one ohm when an alternating current having an effective value of one ampere, when flowing through the inductor, sets up an inductive voltage drop with an effective value of one volt across the inductor.

$$1 \text{ ohm inductive reactance} = \frac{1 \text{ volt across inductor}}{1 \text{ amp through inductor}}$$

It was previously shown that

$$v_L = 2\pi f L I_{max} \cos 2\pi f t$$

and since $\qquad v_{L\,max} = 2\pi f L I_{max} \qquad$ at $t = 0$

the effective value of V_L is equated as

$$V_L = \frac{v_{L\,max}}{\sqrt{2}} = \frac{2\pi f L I_{max}}{\sqrt{2}} = 2\pi f L I_L$$

since $I_{max} = \sqrt{2}\,I_L$. Finally,

$$X_L = \frac{2\pi f L I_L}{I_L} = 2\pi f L = \omega L$$

From this result the inductive reactance is directly proportional to the inductance if the angular velocity of the generator or alternator producing the alternating current is held steady.

Resistance and inductance. In an a-c circuit with the inductance and resistance in series the current is the same in all parts. The conventional diagram of a circuit containing inductance and resistance is shown in Fig. 11-33. The resistance portion is shown physically separated from the

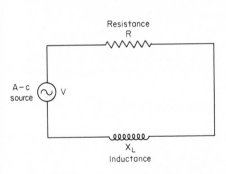

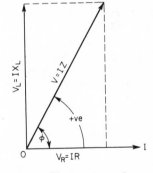

Fig. 11-33 An a-c circuit containing resistance and inductance.

Fig. 11-34 Vector or phase diagram corresponding to the a-c RL series circuit.

inductor, but in actual practice this is rarely so. The voltage and phase relations in an a-c circuit containing a pure inductor and pure resistor in series are shown in Fig. 11-34. Such a diagram is referred to as the vector or phase diagram.

The resistance drop IR is in phase with the current, the reference vector, which is laid off along the positive horizontal axis. The reactance drop IX_L leads the current by 90° and is laid along the positive vertical axis. The applied or impressed voltage V is the vector sum of IR and IX_L. The angle ϕ (phi) is called the *phase angle*.

Impedance. The joint effect of resistance and inductive reactance in an a-c circuit is known as *impedance*. It is denoted by the letter symbol Z. Impedance is defined as the total opposition to the flow of current in an a-c circuit. It is equal to the ratio of the effective voltage to the effective current and is expressed as

$$Z = \frac{V}{I}$$

Impedance, having a V/I ratio just as resistance has, has the ohm as its unit of measurement.

From the vector diagram, Fig. 11-34:

$$Z^2 = X_L{}^2 + R^2$$

The current in an a-c circuit containing inductance and resistance is given by

$$I = \frac{V}{Z} = \frac{V}{\sqrt{X_L{}^2 + R^2}}$$

An application of this equation offers a very direct method for measuring X_L and hence L. The current in an inductive circuit is measured when a known voltage is impressed. The resistance R is then measured and, if the frequency is known, the values of X_L and L can be calculated.

Example. An inductive circuit has a coil with a resistance of 10.0 ohms and inductance of 2.0 henrys connected to a 120-volt 60-cycles/sec a-c source. Calculate the value of the current.

Solution
Since

$$X_L = 2\pi f L = 2\pi \times 60 \times 2.0 \text{ ohms}$$
$$Z^2 = R^2 + X_L{}^2$$
$$Z = \sqrt{10^2 + (240\pi)^2} = 760 \text{ ohms}$$
$$I = \frac{V}{Z} = \frac{120 \text{ volts}}{760 \text{ ohms}} = 0.16 \text{ amp}$$

Capacitive reactance. The *capacitive reactance*, denoted by X_C, is the opposition set up by a capacitance to the flow of alternating current. It is defined as the ratio of the effective value of the capacitive drop in potential V_C to the effective value of the current.

$$X_C = \frac{V_C}{I}$$

An a-c circuit is said to have a capacitive reactance of one ohm when the effective value of one ampere sets up an alternating potential drop across the capacitor having an effective value of one volt.

From the defining equation for capacitance $v_C = q/C$, where q is the charge, in coulombs, and C is the capacitance, in farads,

$$v_C = \frac{1}{C} \int_0^t i \, dt = \frac{1}{C} \int_0^t I_{max} \sin 2\pi f t \, dt$$

$$v_C = - \frac{I_{max}}{2\pi f C} \cos 2\pi f t$$

The effective value of the voltage $V_C = I/2\pi f C$; hence

$$X_C = \frac{V_C}{I} = \frac{1}{2\pi f C} = \frac{1}{\omega C}$$

This capacitive reactance is in ohms, because it too follows the ratio V/I. The frequency f is measured in cycles per second and the capacitance C in farads. The capacitive reactance is inversely proportional to the product of the capacitance and frequency, or angular velocity of the alternator or generator.

The conventional wiring diagram for a resistance and capacitance in series in an a-c circuit is given in Fig. 11-35. The corresponding vector or

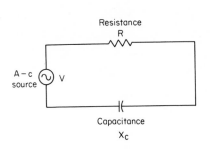

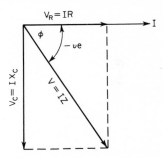

Fig. 11-35   An a-c circuit containing resistance and capacitance.

Fig. 11-36   Vector or phase diagram corresponding to the a-c RC series circuit.

phase diagram is given in Fig. 11-36. The capacitive drop IX_C lags the current by 90° and is laid along the negative vertical axis. The impressed voltage V is the vector sum of IR and IX_C. The angle ϕ, called the phase angle, is negative in this case.

Hydraulic analogy of capacitive reactance. The effect of a capacitor in a d-c circuit is to stop the flow of current. If an incandescent lamp is connected in series with a 10-μf capacitor and the circuit is connected to a

110-volt d-c supply, the lamp will not light up, because the circuit is open at the capacitor plates. The arrangement is shown in Fig. 11-37. If now the circuit is connected to an a-c supply line, the lamp will glow despite the fact that the circuit is open between the plates of the capacitor.

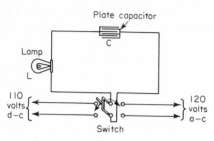

Fig. 11-37 Effect of a capacitor on an incandescent lamp in a d-c and a-c circuit.

The behavior of the capacitor has a hydraulic analogy, as shown in Fig. 11-38. The alternating current is similar to the back-and-forth or to-and-fro surging of water through a pipeline having a reciprocating pump. Water is pumped in one direction and then in the other. The tank C acts as a capacitor; the flexible, pressure-tight diaphragm stretched across the tank has the same effect as the capacitor dielectric. The capacity of the hydraulic capacitor tank depends upon the size of the tank and the elastic properties of the diaphragm.

The free-moving waterwheel (L), on which the surging flow does work, corresponds to the electric lamp in the electric circuit. When the current changes direction, the charges on the capacitor plates reverse. This causes

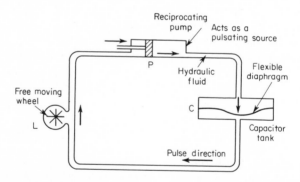

Fig. 11-38   Hydraulic analogy of a capacitor in an a-c circuit.

an oscillation of electron flow in the circuit depending upon the frequency of the a-c source. A 60-cycle/sec source will cause 120 pulse changes per second in the direction of current flow into and out of the capacitor.

Example. In an a-c circuit similar to that shown in Fig. 11-35 the capacitance is 30 μf, the voltage is 120 volts, 60 cycles/sec, and the resistance is 25 ohm. Calculate the value of current and phase angle.

Solution

$$X_C = \frac{1}{2\pi fC} = \frac{1}{2\pi \times 60 \times 30 \times 10^{-6}} = 88 \text{ ohms}$$

$$Z = \sqrt{R^2 + X_C^2} = \sqrt{25^2 + 88^2} = 91 \text{ ohms}$$

Hence $\quad I = \dfrac{V}{Z} = \dfrac{120 \text{ volts}}{91 \text{ ohms}} = 1.3 \text{ amp}$

$$\tan \phi = -\frac{88}{25} \quad \text{or} \quad \phi = \text{arc tan} \frac{-88 \text{ ohms}}{25 \text{ ohms}}$$

Hence $\quad \phi = -74.2°$

The negative sign indicates that the phase angle is below the reference vector *IR*.

Circuits containing resistance, inductance, and capacitance in series. Consider an ideal case of a series circuit (Fig. 11-39) containing pure resistance (without inductive or capacitive effects), pure inductance (without resistive or capacitive effects), and pure capacitance (without resistive or inductive effects). The corresponding voltage drop in such a circuit is shown in the vector, or phase, diagram of Fig. 11-40. In this circuit the inductive react-

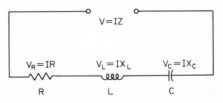

Fig. 11-39   The RLC series circuit.

ance is shown predominant over the capacitive reactance. The voltage V_R across the resistor is laid off in phase with the current. The voltage V_L across the inductive coil is 90° ahead of the current. The voltage V_C across

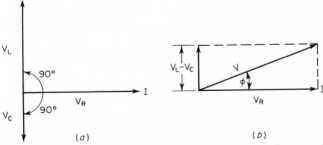

Fig. 11-40   (a) Pure resistance, pure capacitance, and pure inductance phase relation. (b) Final vector or phase diagram.

the capacitor lags the current by 90°. The net reactive voltage is $V_L - V_C$ and is designated by V_n in the phase diagram. Then

$$V_n = I(X_L - X_C)$$

The impedance Z is given by

$$Z = \sqrt{R^2 + (X_L - X_C)^2}$$
$$= \sqrt{R^2 + \left(2\pi fL - \frac{1}{2\pi fC}\right)^2}$$

Hence
$$I = \frac{V}{Z} = \frac{V}{\sqrt{R^2 + \left(2\pi fL - \frac{1}{2\pi fC}\right)^2}}$$

The ideal case does not exist in practice. The resistor usually contains more or less inductance, the inductor necessarily includes some resistance, and the capacitor may have losses to offer an appreciable equivalent resistance. However, the final phase diagram of the voltages in such a circuit can be reduced to one like that in Fig. 11-40.

The Choke Coil

A coil which is made up of a very large number of turns of heavy copper wire has little resistance in a d-c circuit, but, because of its high inductance, it offers a large impedance in an a-c circuit. By fitting the coil with a variable iron core, the impedance can easily be varied within a wide control limit. Such a device is very useful in instrumentation applications, where the coil acts as a "choke" without requiring a large expenditure of energy in the form of heat. The choke coil is useful for dimming lights for warning purposes on control panels.

Power in A-C Circuits

In d-c circuits the power is given by the product

$$W(\text{watts}) = V(\text{volts}) \times I(\text{amp})$$

In such circuits both the current and voltage are assumed to be steady and in phase. In a-c circuits this is not the case. During a quarter of the cycle, energy is supplied to the reactive component of the circuit, but this energy is returned to the source during the next quarter of the cycle. Therefore, no power is required to maintain the current in the part of the circuit which is purely reactive. All the power is used in the resistance portion of the circuit. From the vector diagram of Fig. 11-40

$$W = IV_R$$

but $V_R = V \cos \phi$; hence, $W = VI \cos \phi$

where W is the average power, in watts, when V is the effective value of the voltage, in volts, and I is the effective value of the current, in amperes. The angle ϕ is the angle of lag of the current behind the voltage.

Power factor. The quantity cos ϕ, called the *power factor* of the circuit, can vary from zero, for a purely reactive circuit, to unity for a pure resistance:

$$\cos \phi = \frac{IR}{IZ} = \frac{R}{Z}$$

Example. Compute the current in a circuit consisting of a coil inductor and a capacitor in series if the applied voltage is 110 volts, 60 cycles/sec. The inductance of the coil is 0.8 henry, and the resistance is 50.0 ohms. The capacitance of the capacitor is 8.0 μf. Also compute the power factor and power used in the circuit.

Solution

$$X_L = 2\pi f L = 2\pi \times 60 \times 0.8 = 300 \text{ ohms}$$

$$X_C = \frac{1}{2\pi f C} = \frac{1}{2\pi \times 60 \times 8.0 \times 10^{-6}} = 330 \text{ ohms}$$

$$Z = \sqrt{R^2 + (X_L - X_C)^2} = \sqrt{50^2 + (300 - 330)^2} = 58 \text{ ohms}$$

$$I = \frac{V}{Z} = \frac{110 \text{ volts}}{58 \text{ ohms}} = 1.9 \text{ amp}$$

$$\cos \phi = \frac{R}{Z} = \frac{50 \text{ ohms}}{58 \text{ ohms}} = 0.86$$

Hence

$$\text{Power factor} = 0.86$$
$$\text{Power used } W = VI \cos \phi$$
$$= 110 \text{ volts} \times 1.9 \text{ amp} \times 0.86$$
$$= 180 \text{ watts} \quad \text{mean value}$$

Alternatively, $W = I^2R$
$$= 1.9^2 \times 50 = 180 \text{ watts} \quad \text{mean value}$$

There are power losses in inductors other than the usual I^2R copper losses. Such losses are due to eddy currents and hysteresis in the core of the inductor. Hence the equivalent resistance of a coil may be greater than the ordinary or ohmic resistance as measured by the use of direct current.

Electrical Oscillations

Mechanical vibration may be set up in a body having inertia if a distortion produces a restoring force and the friction is not too great. A fairly heavy object suspended in air by a spring and set in motion is a good example of a mechanical vibration. Analogous conditions are necessary in an electric circuit for electrical oscillations to take place. A quantity or variable is in a state of oscillation while the value of that quantity or variable is continually changing so that it passes through maximum and minimum values. Just as inertia opposes change in mechanical motion, so inductance opposes change in the flow of electrons. The building up of a charge on the plates of a capacitor causes a restoring force on the electrons in the circuit. Resistance has the property of causing the electric energy to be converted to heat similarly to the way friction changes mechanical energy to heat. In order to produce electrical oscillations, it is necessary to have inductance, capacitance, and a minimum of resistance.

The frequency f of the oscillation is determined by the values of L and C. It is the frequency for which the impedance of the circuit is at a minimum, i.e., when the net reactance is zero. From the relation $X = X_L - X_C$

$$X = 2\pi f L - \frac{1}{2\pi f C} = 0$$

It follows that $\qquad f_r = \dfrac{1}{2\pi \sqrt{LC}}$

This frequency is called the resonant frequency.

Example. The frequency of oscillation in any circuit in which the resistance is small is given by

$$f = \frac{1}{2\pi \sqrt{LC}}$$

If the capacitance is 0.006 μf, the self-inductance is 80 microhenry (μh), and the incoming wave velocity is 3×10^{10} cm/sec, calculate the wavelength.

Solution

$$f = \frac{1}{2\pi \sqrt{6 \times 10^{-9} \times 8 \times 10^{-5}}}$$

$$= \frac{1}{2\pi \sqrt{48 \times 10^{-14}}} = 2.3 \times 10^5 \text{ cycles/sec}$$

Since $\qquad\qquad$ Velocity = wavelength $\times$ frequency

$$\text{Wavelength} = \frac{3 \times 10^{10}}{2.3 \times 10^5} \text{ cm}$$

$$= 1{,}300 \text{ m}$$

Series resonance. In the expression for a-c circuits containing resistance, inductance, and capacitance in series

$$I = \frac{E}{Z} = \frac{E}{\sqrt{R^2 + \left(2\pi f L - \dfrac{1}{2\pi f C}\right)^2}}$$

When the inductive reactance equals the capacitive reactance, the two will nullify each other and Z will equal R. A circuit in which such a condition exists is said to be in resonance with the applied voltage, and the current will then have its maximum value equal to E/R. Resonant circuits have great usefulness in power circuits, radio, and electronic equipment, and they are the basis of telecommunications. In the case of the radio, a particular frequency is tuned in by establishing a resonant circuit for that frequency. This is normally done by the use of a variable capacitor (condenser) to change the capacitive reactance of the circuit until resonance is established. Resonance occurs when

$$X_L = X_C$$

or

$$2\pi f L = \frac{1}{2\pi f C}$$

and

$$f_r = \frac{1}{2\pi \sqrt{LC}}$$

where f_r is the resonant frequency. Thus, by altering the value of C (or L), the circuit can be made resonant for any fixed frequency.

Example. Calculate the resonant frequency of a circuit containing a 0.005-μf capacitor in series with an inductance of 0.03 millihenrys (mh).

Solution. For a series resonance

$$f_r = \frac{1}{2\pi \sqrt{LC}}$$

$$= \frac{1}{6.28 \times \sqrt{3 \times 10^{-5} \times 5 \times 10^{-9}}}$$

$$= 410 \text{ kilocycles (kc)}$$

Parallel *RLC* Circuits

The computations involved in solving parallel a-c circuits are a little tedious, but they should present no difficulties. Figure 11-41 shows a typical parallel *RLC* arrangement, and the corresponding phase diagram is shown in Fig. 11-42. Since the two branches are in parallel, the same voltage is applied to each. The current and phase differences

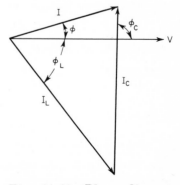

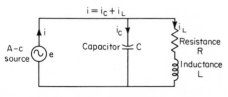

Fig. 11-41   A parallel RLC circuit.

Fig. 11-42   Phase diagram of RLC circuit.

in each branch are readily computed by the methods already described. The current drawn from the a-c source is found by adding the rms currents vectorially. The rms current is

$$I = I_C + I_L$$

But $\qquad I_L = \dfrac{V}{\sqrt{R^2 + \omega^2 L^2}} \qquad$ and $\qquad \tan \phi_L = \dfrac{\omega L}{R}$

where $\omega = 2\pi f$

Also, $\qquad I_C = V\omega C \qquad$ and $\qquad \phi_C = -\dfrac{\pi}{2} = -90°$

The total current I and phase difference between V and I can be found graphically by plotting the phase diagram to some convenient scale or by trigonometric methods. Since V is the quantity common to both branches, it is convenient to draw the phase representing V as the reference or horizontal vector. An inspection of the phase diagram (Fig. 11-42) shows that if I_C is reduced to a particular size, I will be in phase with V. If now I_L is fixed, this particular value of I_C results in minimum current being drawn from the a-c source or generator. A parallel circuit of this type is said to be antiresonant when V and I are in phase. For such a case, the necessary conditions when $\phi = 0°$ are

$$I = I_L \cos \phi_L \qquad I_C = I_L \sin \phi_L$$

An antiresonant circuit behaves like a very large pure resistance and the effective resistance becomes

$$R_{\text{eff}} = \frac{E}{I} = \frac{L}{RC}$$

Antiresonant circuits find extensive application in electronic equipment.

A-C Measuring Circuits

Only the fundamental a-c circuits which may be applied in instrument practice and measurement work will be mentioned in this section. Figure 11-43 shows the general form of an a-c bridge. The a-c bridge is similar to the Wheatstone bridge used in measuring circuits with d-c, the only difference being that the resistance symbols are replaced by impedance symbols. In order for the indicator to read zero or to be in the null-balance position, the voltage across its terminals must be zero. For this to be so, the voltage across the impedance Z_1 and Z_3 must be the same value in magnitude and phase.

$$V_1 = V_3 \qquad I_1 Z_1 = I_3 Z_3$$

But $\qquad I_1 = \dfrac{V}{Z_1 + Z_2} \qquad$ and $\qquad I_3 = \dfrac{V}{Z_3 + Z_4}$

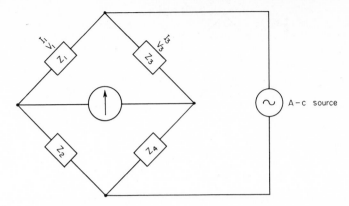

Fig. 11-43   Wheatstone bridge having impedance values in the a-c circuit.

For the bridge to balance,

$$\frac{VZ_1}{Z_1 + Z_2} = \frac{VZ_3}{Z_3 + Z_4}$$

Hence

$$Z_1Z_4 = Z_2Z_3$$

Capacitance measurement. By inserting a standard capacitor and an unknown capacitor in place of Z_2 and Z_4, and also by replacing Z_1 and Z_3 with resistances R_1 and R_3, respectively, the circuit in Fig. 11-44 can be

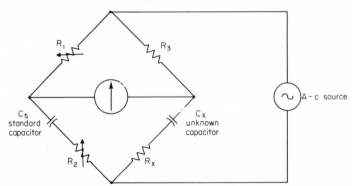

Fig. 11-44   Capacitance bridge measurement circuit.

used to compare capacitances. In this case

$$R_1R_x = R_2R_3$$

from which

$$R_x = \frac{R_2R_3}{R_1}$$

and

$$\frac{R_1}{\omega C_x} = \frac{R_3}{\omega C_s}$$

thus

$$C_x = \frac{C_sR_1}{R_3}$$

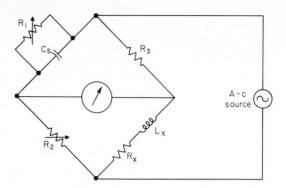

Fig. 11-45   The basic Maxwell bridge to measure inductance.

The Maxwell bridge. The Maxwell bridge circuit shown in Fig. 11-45 is used to balance the bridge by means of a standard capacitance for comparison purposes. In this case

$$R_x = \frac{R_2 R_3}{R_1} \qquad \text{and} \qquad L_x = C_s R_2 R_3$$

Example. A Maxwell bridge circuit similar to that shown in Fig. 11-45 balances when $C_s = 0.02 \times 10^{-6}$ farad, $R_1 = 500$ kilohms, $R_2 = 5.0$ kilohms, and $R_3 = 100$ kilohms. Calculate the resistance and inductance of the inductor under measurement.

Solution

$$R_x = \frac{R_2 R_3}{R_1} = \frac{5.0 \times 10^3 \times 1.0 \times 10^5}{5.0 \times 10^5} = 1,000 \text{ ohms}$$

$$L_x = C_s R_2 R_3 = 1.0 \times 10^{-8} \times 5.0 \times 10^3 \times 1.0 \times 10^5 = 5.0 \text{ henrys}$$

REVIEW QUESTIONS AND PROBLEMS

11-23   (a) Sketch the sine-wave form of an alternating current and voltage.

(b) Define period, frequency, and instantaneous current of an a-c source.

11-24   At what speed, in rpm, must the shaft of a six-pole 60-cycle/sec alternator be rotated?

11-25   Calculate the peak voltage of 120-volt 60-cycles/sec electrical supply.

11-26   An alternating voltage is expressed by the equation

$$e = 120 \sin 1,570t$$

Calculate (a) the frequency of the sine wave and (b) the instantaneous emf when $t = 0.005$ sec.

11-27   Calculate the maximum or peak value of a 6.0-amp alternating current.

11-28   An eight-pole alternator operates at 900 rpm and develops an emf having a sine curve with a maximum value of 300 volts. Calculate (a) the frequency, (b) the instantaneous emf value at $\frac{1}{720}$ sec, and (c) the effective or rms value of the emf.

11-29   (a) Define the term "capacitive reactance."
(b) A circuit containing a resistor of 25 ohms and capacitor of 30 μf in series is connected to a 120-volt a-c supply. Calculate the current and phase angle. Sketch the phase diagram.

11-30   (a) Define the term "inductive reactance."
(b) An inductor having an inductance of 0.14 henry and a resistance of 12.0 ohms is connected to a 110-volt 25-cycles/sec supply line. Compute the current in the inductor, the phase angle, and the power absorbed by the coil.

11-31   (a) Define impedance.
(b) An inductor has a resistance of 15 ohms and is connected to a 120-volt 60-cycles/sec source. A current of 5 amp passes through the inductor. Compute the inductance and the impedance.

11-32   Compute the impedance of a 60-cycles/sec a-c circuit containing an inductance of 0.7 henry in series with a capacitance of 40 μf. The resistance of the circuit is 50 ohms.

11-33   Draw vector diagrams on graph paper and solve the problems in Questions 11-31 and 11-32 graphically.

11-34   Compute the capacitive reactance of a 50-μf capacitor when an a-c current at 60 cycles/sec is impressed on it.

11-35   (a) Compute the current in a circuit containing an inductor and capacitor in series if the applied voltage is 110 volts, 60 cycles/sec. The inductance of the coil is specified as 0.8 henry and its resistance as 50.0 ohms; the capacitance of the capacitor is 8.0 μf.
(b) Compute the power used in the circuit.

11-36   (a) Define the term "power factor."
(b) Sketch a curve of instantaneous power against time in an a-c circuit of unity power factor. Sketch the curve in the case of a power factor of less than unity. Explain the significance of the negative parts of the curves.

11-37   (a) Define the nature and application of a choke coil.
(b) A choke coil draws a current of 5.0 amp from a 120-volt a-c source. A wattmeter connected to the coil reads 450 watts. Calculate the apparent power, the real power, and the power factor.

11-38   Describe the following electrical terms and cite analogous mechanical cases: (a) electrical oscillation and (b) resonant frequency.

11-39   Compute the resonant frequency of a circuit of negligible resistance containing an inductance of 40.0 mh and a capacitance of 600 $\mu\mu$f.

11-40   If the resonant frequency is 410 kc in a circuit containing an inductance of 0.03 mh, calculate the capacitance in series with it.

11-41   In a parallel RLC circuit similar to that shown in Fig. 11-41, if $R = 0.50$ ohms, $L = 3.00$ mh, and $C = 1.20$ μf, calculate (a) the effective resistance if the generator resistance is negligible and (b) the frequency of generator operation for the circuit to be antiresonant.

11-42   Draw the a-c bridge circuits (a) for comparing impedance values and (b) for comparing capacitance values.

11-43   The Maxwell bridge shown in Fig. 11-45 balances when $C_s = 0.01$ μf, $R_1 = 470$ kilohms, $R_2 = 5.0$ kilohms, and $R_3 = 100$ kilohms. Compute the value of the resistance and inductance of the inductor.

CHAPTER TWELVE

Fundamental electrical measuring instruments

Power is more certainly retained by wary measures than by daring counsels.

TACITUS

Basic Electrical Instruments

Electrical measuring instruments are actuated by an electric current or voltage, and the most common instruments are those designed to measure current, voltage, and power. There is, in addition, a wide variety of electrical instruments for measuring the less commonly required circuit variables such as impedance, resistance, frequency, inductance, capacitance, and power factor.

The instruments referred to may be classified as either industrial or laboratory instruments. The division is not clear-cut, but generally an industrial instrument should present information or readout data in a clear, comprehensible style. Also, an industrial instrument requires a minimum of skill from the user. Laboratory instruments usually demand a higher accuracy than industrial instruments and are maintained in ideal conditions for checking the calibration of industrial instruments.

Instruments for the measurement of current (ammeters), voltage (voltmeters), and power (wattmeters and watthour meters) can generally be classified as indicating, recording, or integrating or totalizing meters. Ammeters, voltmeters, and wattmeters are usually indicating instruments. A recording meter gives a continuous record of some electrical variable, normally by means of a pen on a moving chart in circular or strip form. An integrating meter measures a total amount over a period of time. A good example is the domestic watthour meter. The industrial ammeter, voltmeter, and wattmeter are designed to operate on either a magnetic effect or electromagnetic induction effect. For laboratory purposes the instruments may also be designed to operate on heating, chemical, or electrostatic effects.

Accuracy and precision. In actual instrument practice and measurement work the terms "accuracy" and "precision" have distinct meanings. Reference should be made to Chap. 1, in which these terms and others, such as standards, error, sensitivity, and techniques of calibration, are described. Because of the importance of accuracy and precision in electrical measurement it is advisable to review the meaning and application of the terms.

If two voltmeters of the same make and model are compared, it may be found that each has carefully ruled circular scales, knife-edge pointers, and probably mirror-backed scales to avoid parallax errors. The two meters may be read to the same precision. However, if the resistor in one meter becomes slightly defective, perhaps because of contamination, its readings will be subject to an error. The accuracies of the two instruments, although specified to be the same, may now actually be quite different, and whether this is so or not can be found only by comparison with a standard.

Accuracy is a matter of very careful measurement in terms of an accurately known standard. Precision, on the other hand, is essential in the detection of possible inaccuracies. Usually this detection is made during comparative test measurements. Although precision is a necessary prerequisite to accuracy, it does not necessarily guarantee it.

The permissible errors in indicating and other electrical instruments are laid down in recognized practices and standards, and must be adhered to. Precision-grade instruments are usually used for laboratory purposes and have permissible errors in the region of 0.3 percent. The permissible error is usually a percent of full-scale indication. For example, an instrument with 1 percent error could be 4 percent out at quarter-scale reading. For this reason multirange instruments are used.

Instruments for d-c Measurements

Most indicating instruments are designed to indicate the measured quantity or variable by means of a deflecting force. This force must be opposed by a controlling force for a steady-state reading to be achieved. The scale is normally an arc of a circle, and the controlling force is obtained from a specially designed spring which has a constant ratio of torque to angular displacement. Usually this controlling force is not sufficient, because in such an arrangement the inertia of the moving parts would tend to make the pointer oscillate about its steady-state position without coming to rest in a fairly short interval of time. A damping force must be introduced to prevent oscillation. However, if the damping force is too large, the indicator or pointer of the instrument responds very slowly and is said to be overdamped.

The ideal condition exists when the instrument reading reaches its final and steady deflection in the shortest possible time without overshoot. In this condition the instrument is said to be critically damped. Three curves showing the effect of damping upon the response of an instrument are given in Fig. 12-1. The damping force is proportional to the angular veloc-

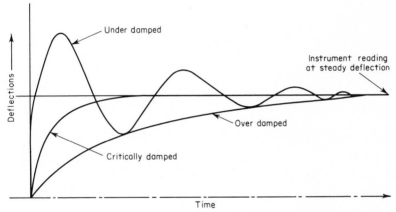

Fig. 12-1   Wave motions of instrument response.

ity of the moving system and does not in any way influence the final instrument reading.

In many ammeters and voltmeters damping is accomplished by winding the movable coil on a light frame of aluminum. The currents induced in this frame are quite effective in producing satisfactory damping. By careful design and manufacture the pointer is caused to reach its equilibrium or steady-state value very quickly with no noticeable oscillation. Various damping devices are available.

Galvanometers. The basic electrical instrument is the galvanometer, a device which measures very small electric currents. With highly accurate and precision techniques, readings of 1.0×10^{-11} can be detected and measured. The d'Arsonval, or permanent-magnet, moving-coil type of galvanometer has a very small control torque. The coil is suspended from a fine wire strip and, instead of a pointer, a small mirror attached to the coil reflects a spot of light onto a fixed, distant scale.

The basic schematic arrangement is shown in Fig. 12-2. Connections are made to the coil and to the terminals, which are marked t. The soft-iron cylinder core C and pole faces N and S are skillfully shaped to produce a radial magnetic field in the air gap, which has the virtue of being constant in magnitude and always parallel to the plane of the coil as the coil rotates. Under these conditions the instrument will have a scale with uniform graduations.

The action of the galvanometer depends upon the fact that a conductor carrying I amp in a magnetic field of flux density B webers/m^2 experiences a force of BIL newtons. L represents the length of the conductor or coil, in

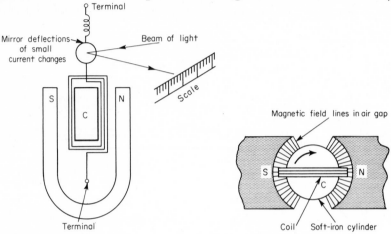

Fig. 12-2   Permanent-magnet moving-coil type of galvanometer.

meters. One newton is approximately equal to 0.225 lb$_f$. When a current is set up in a coil conductor suspended between the poles of a magnet, the coil is acted upon by a torque. This torque tends to turn the coil until the plane of the coil is perpendicular to the line joining its poles. The coil turns to the position in which the torque exerted on it by the magnet is just neutralized by the reaction of the twisted wire strip.

The torque exerted on the coil by the magnet is proportional to the current flowing through the coil. The reaction torque of the wire strip is proportional to the angular movement of the strip. These torques are equal in magnitude and opposite in sense; therefore, when the coil reaches its steady-state or equilibrium position, the angle through which the coil turns is proportional to the current. Symbolically,

$$I \propto \phi$$

where ϕ is the deflection of the coil, in angular degrees.

Figure 12-3 shows a typical arrangement of a portable commercial type of galvanometer. Usually, the spindle or pointer shaft holding the magnetic armature has an insert at the bottom end containing a jewel or similar bearing. This bearing rests on top of a hardened cone-shaped steel pivot. The scale of a galvanometer is usually in the form of a 100° arc marked with zero in the center and equal graduations on each side to indicate either the positive or negative sense of the current. It is basically an instrument for detecting, comparing, or measuring very low electric current and voltage.

Ballistic galvanometer. The ballistic galvanometer is designed to respond to a single short-time impulse. The impulse is measured by the

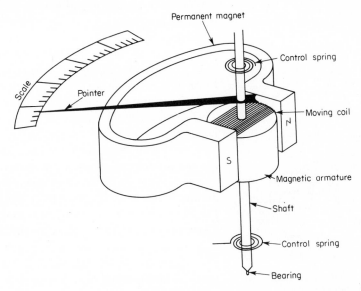

Fig. 12-3   Internal construction of a portable galvanometer.

first swing or deflection of the indicator. The period of the galvanometer is long enough the permit accurate observation of the maximum swing. The term "ballistic" is applied to this galvanometer because an impulse impressed upon the movement for a short period of time stores enough energy in the meter movement to carry its trajectory or transient motion. Under these conditions a deflection that is proportional to the charge is set up. This relationship is established from the fact that angular momentum $I\omega$ imparted to the coil is given by

$$\int I\,d\omega = \int T\,dt = k\int i\,dt$$

hence
$$I\omega = kQ$$

where I = moment of inertia of the coil
ω = angular speed imparted to the coil
T = torque produced by the current i
k = a constant
Q = total charge sent through the coil

As a result of its angular momentum, the coil deflects until its kinetic energy of rotation is transferred into the potential energy of the twisted-strip suspension. The deflection d produced in the instrument is proportional to the charge. Symbolically,

$$Q = kd$$

where k is the ballistic constant of the galvanometer. Ballistic galvanometers are frequently useful for the comparison of capacitors.

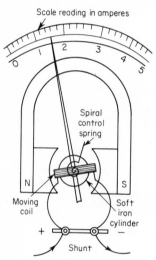

Scale reading in amperes

Spiral control spring

N S

Moving coil

Soft iron cylinder

Shunt

+ −

Fig. 12-4 Ammeter with low-resistance shunt.

Ammeters. An ammeter is connected in series with the circuit in which the current is to be measured. For this reason it must have a low resistance so that it does not alter the circuit current under measurement. The current-carrying capacity of the moving coil is very low. Consequently, such meters are generally used in conjunction with shunt resistors when used as ammeters.

A typical permanent-magnet moving-coil ammeter is shown in Fig. 12-4. Basically, the ammeter is a modified galvanometer. Consider the following case. A galvanometer having a resistance of 5.0 ohms is to be converted to an ammeter to read 5.0 amp full-scale deflection. A low resistance, called a *shunt*, is connected across the meter terminals. For full-scale deflection the galvanometer must carry just 0.002 amp. The shunt S must take the remainder, which is 4.998 amp. The potential difference across the meter is

$$V = IR = 0.002 \text{ amp} \times 5.0 \text{ ohms}$$
$$= 0.010 \text{ volt}$$

Hence the resistance of the shunt (R_s) can be calculated.

$$R_s = \frac{V}{I_s} = \frac{0.010 \text{ volt}}{4.998 \text{ amp}} = 0.002 \text{ ohm}$$

Since this resistance is so small, usually a small piece of heavy wire may be used.

In actual practice it is difficult to make the shunt resistance R_s exactly a certain value, particularly when the value is so small. In order to overcome this difficulty, a resistance slightly greater than that needed is connected to a comparatively large resistance r in series with the coil, and the value of resistance r is then adjusted to operate the meter to the desired range.

The circuit diagram is shown in Fig. 12-5*a*. Several ranges can be made available by the use of a number of removable shunts. Alternatively, the shunts can be used as shown in Fig. 12-5*b*. Connection is made to the posi-

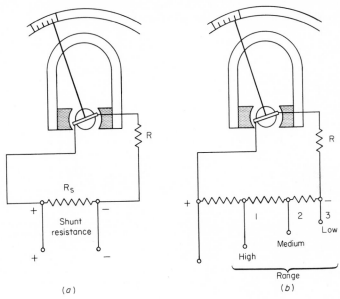

Fig. 12-5 Basic ammeter circuits.

tive terminal and to one of the three terminals marked high, medium, and low. With this arrangement, the shunt connections are permanent. Multi-range instruments are available with switch-selected ranges.

It is possible to obtain sensitive pointer or indicating instruments which have a full-scale deflection for 50 microamperes (μa). Laboratory instruments in which the coil is suspended on a taut phosphor-bronze strip are available. With such an instrument a full-scale deflection of 10 microamperes is obtainable.

Voltmeters. Voltmeters are connected across the voltage which is to be measured. They must have a high resistance so that a minimum of current is taken. A voltmeter is basically a low-range ammeter with a high-value resistor connected in series with it. For example, a 15-ma milliammeter, having a coil resistance of 5.0 ohms, may be fitted with a series resistor of 9,995 ohms in order to give a full-scale deflection for 150 volts, since

$$V = IR$$
$$= 15 \times 10^{-3} \text{ amp} \times (9,995 + 5) \text{ ohms}$$
$$= 150 \text{ volts}$$

Multiple ranges are readily obtained by means of tappings on the series resistor. The resistance of the voltmeter is

$$R = R_s + R_g$$

where R_s = resistance in series

R_g = resistance of galvanometer

The circuit diagram in Fig. 12-6 shows the use of resistors for voltmeter multipliers.

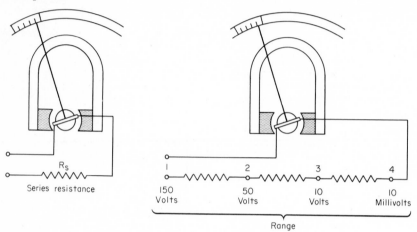

Fig. 12-6   Basic voltmeter circuits.

Example. Calculate the series resistance to be used with a galvanometer having full-scale deflection at 0.002 amp in order to use it as a voltmeter of range 0 to 200 volts.

Solution

$$R = \frac{V}{I}$$

$$= \frac{200 \text{ volts}}{0.002 \text{ amp}} = 100,000 \text{ ohms}$$

The voltmeter introduces two errors, namely, changing the current in the circuit and reducing the potential difference that is to be measured. In order to keep these errors as small as possible, the resistance of the voltmeter should be large in comparison with the resistance across which it is connected. This also ensures that the current taken by the voltmeter is small in comparison with that in the main circuit.

Ohmmeters and insulation test equipment. One of the most useful of test instruments is the ohmmeter, which measures resistance directly. A typical ohmmeter circuit is shown in Fig. 12-7, where T, T are test leads usually ending in metal tips or probes for making momentary contacts easily and R_s is a series resistor. The circuit is similar to that of a voltmeter with a self-contained power source E. The leads T, T are first short-circuited, permitting maximum current in G. This current is adjusted to a preset value with R_v. This value is marked zero ohms on the scale, and the R_v adjustment allows for small changes in E as the battery or cell ages. The test leads are then clipped to the resistor R_x to be measured, and the current decreases.

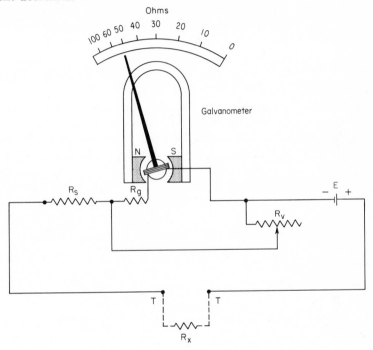

Fig. 12-7 Ohmmeter circuit.

By knowing the values of E, R_s, and R_g (the resistance of the galvanometer), the scale of the meter can be calibrated to read R_x directly. If the effect of R_v is neglected, the resistance of the meter is $R_s + R_g$ and the maximum current is $E/(R_s + R_g)$. This current will be cut in half if $R_x = R_s + R_g$, since the total resistance is then doubled. The midpoint of the scale is marked with the resistance of the meter. When the circuit is closed, there will always be some current unless R_x is very large. For this reason the scale is marked as infinite resistance with zero current indication. The scale is nonlinear, and for this reason ohmmeters may be subject to error. Multirange ohmmeters are manufactured. These instruments are valuable for testing continuity in a circuit and for obtaining the resistance values of circuit components.

The principle of the ohmmeter is used in many modern insulation-testing instruments, but voltages up to 1,000 volts are necessary. In some of the portable instruments the high voltage is obtained from a low-voltage battery by a transistor convertor, which is a fast-acting solid-state switch that rapidly reverses the battery connections and thereby produces an alternating voltage. This voltage is then transformed to a high level and rectified as a d-c output. Portable industrial instruments are limited to insulation resistances not exceeding 10,000 megohms.

Another form of ohmmeter uses a ratio meter movement having both a voltage and current coil. The steady deflection is proportional to the ratio of voltage to current, which is resistance. Small hand-driven generators are included with the instrument, when it is used for insulation testing, in order to give test voltages up to 1,000 volts.

Wattmeters. The wattmeter, as the name suggests, is an instrument for measuring electric power. It consists of two coils, one fixed and one movable, at right angles to each other. The fixed coil is made of heavy wire of low resistance and is connected in series with the load under test measurement. The movable coil is made of small wire and is connected in series with a multiplier of high resistance. This coil is connected in parallel with the load. The two coils are referred to as the current and voltage connections. The torque acting on the movable coil is proportional to both the current in the fixed coil and the voltage across the potential coil. Under these conditions the resultant indication of the meter is proportional to the product of the current and voltage, i.e., to the power of a d-c circuit. The equation for this is

$$W(\text{watts}) = I(\text{amp}) \times V(\text{volts})$$

A typical commercial wattmeter is shown in Fig. 12-8.

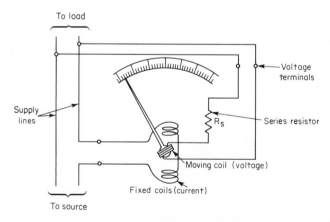

Fig. 12-8   Wattmeter circuit.

Watthour meter. The watthour meter measures the total amount of electric energy used during any given interval of time. A common example is the domestic type of meter used to indicate, by means of pointer positions on a set of dials, the amount of energy consumed. The basic circuit of the electrodynamometer type of meter is shown in Fig. 12-9. The meter

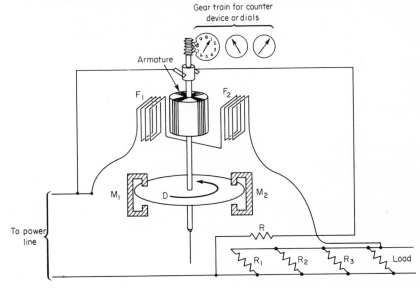

Fig. 12-9 Basic circuit of a watthour meter.

consists of a special type of miniature motor. It is so designed that its armature revolves at a speed that is proportional to the power used. This speed is achieved by having field coils F_1 and F_2 connected in series with the load. The armature is connected in parallel with the load through a resistor R.

The magnetic field of the armature is proportional to the voltage of the load. The resultant torque, being separately proportional to each of these fields, is dependent upon the product of the fields and hence on the product of current and voltage, or the power. Suitable counters with pointers and dials are geared to turn with the armature to indicate the watthours consumed by the load. The aluminum disk D attached to the bottom of the armature shaft rotates in the field of the magnets M_1 and M_2. The induced eddy currents act as a brake and also control the rate of rotation.

Instruments for A-C Measurements

Current and voltage measurements. A number of devices are capable of providing readings directly on the basis of alternating current. One such movement is the electrodynamometer movement, which will be described in later paragraphs. A less expensive instrument is the repulsion-type, moving–iron vane ammeter. Because of its lower cost it is used more extensively. Current passing through the fixed coil magnetizes two iron vanes positioned in the same plane. One of the vanes is fixed, and the other is attached to the movable indicator spindle.

The assembled arrangement ensures an identical magnetic effect upon the vanes despite the alternations of the current and its associated magnetic field. In this way the resultant repulsive force acts upon the vanes and repels the movable one from the fixed member, thus causing the pointer to indicate a deflection on the graduated scale. The amount of deflection is controlled by a spring which restricts the pointer and vane at a point where the magnetic and mechanical torques balance. The control spring returns the moving vane to its original position when the current ceases to flow through the instrument. A sectional view of the repulsion-type a-c meter for measuring either current or voltage is shown in Fig. 12-10.

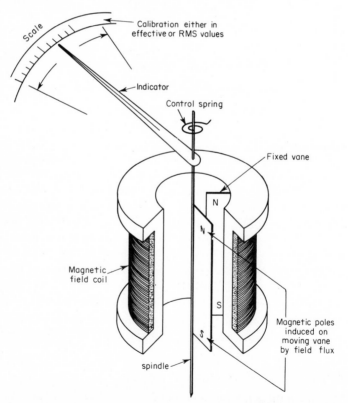

Fig. 12-10   Repulsion-type a-c meter for current and voltage measurements.

When the repulsion-type a-c meter is used to measure voltage, the minimum current drain is frequently sufficient to disturb the actual relationships in the circuit under test. Also, the effects of internal inductance limit the usefulness to power frequencies. For this reason, in radio and other communication systems, it is normal practice to convert alternating voltage to direct voltage by rectification and then to use a d-c voltmeter.

Rectifier instruments. Certain combinations of metals and semiconductors have the property of permitting the passage of an alternating current in one direction only. Copper-oxide rectifiers may be used with moving-coil instruments, and by this means they may be used for a-c measurements. A bridge rectifier circuit is shown in Fig. 12-11a. During

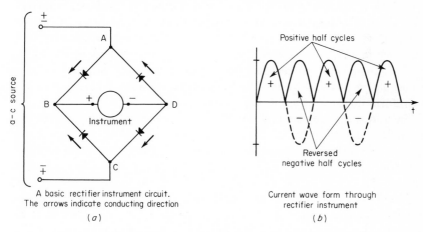

A basic rectifier instrument circuit.
The arrows indicate conducting direction

(*a*)

Current wave form through
rectifier instrument

(*b*)

Fig. 12-11   Rectifier instrument.

the positive half-cycle, the positive current direction is through rectifier *AB*, the instrument, and rectifier *DC*. During the negative half-cycle, the current direction is through *CB*, the instrument, and *DA*.

The corresponding waveform through the instrument is shown in Fig. 12-11b. The instrument registers the average value of the rectifier waveform and is calibrated in rms units on the basis that the form factor is equal to 1.11, where the form factor is referred to as the ratio of the rms value to the average value over a positive half-cycle, i.e.,

$$\text{Form factor} = \frac{E/\sqrt{2}}{2E/\pi} = \frac{\pi}{2\sqrt{2}} = 1.11$$

A simple type of copper-oxide rectifier makes use of a thin, semiconducting layer, formed on a metal backing, and another metal plate in contact with the surface of the semiconducting layer. Such an assembly is often referred to as a *rectifier block*. When an electrical potential is impressed across the two plates, current will flow through the unit more readily for one polarity than for the other. This property is due to the contact condition between the metal backing and the semiconducting layer, which also acts as a dielectric. At high frequencies, the effective capacitance, which is dependent on the area of the metal plates, bypasses the rectifying contact and greatly reduces the rectified direct current. The frequency range of uniform response is often extended by decreasing the area of the plates or by using crystal detectors. Rectifier-type instruments use selenium, doped germanium, and silicon PN crystal diode rectifiers. These are fully described in texts dealing with electrical and electronic techniques and equipment.

A perfect rectifier is yet to be designed. Generally speaking, most rectifiers have their limitations. Some are restricted in application, as in electronic circuits in which currents below 60 ma are to be registered. Nonlinearity of the scale frequently restricts the instrument in its voltage range. Generally, the rectifier instrument must only be used on truly sinusoidal waveforms where the form factor remains at 1:1.1; otherwise, waveform distortions set in and cause errors.

Vacuum-tube voltmeters. Of the various vacuum-tube instruments available on the market, the vacuum-tube voltmeter has the widest utility. The circuit arrangement may be designed for response to direct, rms, and peak voltage values. Generally, the scales of vacuum-tube voltmeters are calibrated in rms volts based, as previously mentioned, on truly sinusoidal waveform, and the readings are valid only if the input or applied signal is sinusoidal within the specified frequency range. If the instrument responds to the square of the rms value, the main requirement for accurate readings is that the harmonic content of the waveform be within the frequency range of the meter. Most vacuum-tube voltmeters incorporate a galvanometer or dynamometer type of indicator movement. Instruments that have a high degree of accuracy and precision and that give the value in the form of a digital readout have been developed.

Vacuum-tube voltmeters, as well as other a-c voltmeters, may be calibrated directly against a standardized a-c voltage source. Alternatively, calibration is performed by transfer-instrument methods, especially by using electrostatic voltmeters. Comparison with electrostatic meters yields an accuracy of ±1 percent up to 20,000 volts and a marginal lesser accuracy up to 60,000 volts.

Dynamometer wattmeter. The basic principle of the electrodynamometer was discussed when the operation of the watthour meter was described. The current in the circuit is passed through the fixed coil, and the voltage is applied to the moving coil through a series resistor. The deflection of the pointer on the instrument scale is proportional to the power in both a-c and d-c circuits. A wide range of switchboard and panel instruments using this principle is available. However, dynamometer wattmeters tend to read incorrectly at low-power-factor loads, and they must be especially designed to compensate for this shortcoming if they are used for low-power-factor work.

Induction wattmeter. When an alternating flux crosses a thin aluminum disk, an eddy current is induced in the disk. There is, however, no resulting torque on the disk. If now a second alternating flux having a time-phase displacement from the first is introduced, a second eddy current is induced. Each eddy current reacts with the other flux, resulting in a torque causing the disk to rotate. The most important application of this effect is the induction wattmeter, which is shown schematically in Fig. 12-12. The

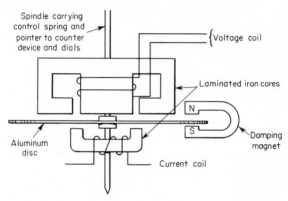

Fig. 12-12   Details of an induction wattmeter.

voltage is applied to the top coil, which is highly inductive, so that the portion of its flux crossing the disk is displaced 90° out of phase with the applied voltage. The other flux is received from the bottom coil, which carries the circuit current. The torque is proportional to $VI \cos \phi$, the total power value, and $\cos \phi$, the circuit power factor.

The induction wattmeter is normally recommended for a single-frequency source and will not operate on d-c.

Power-factor or phase meter. Power-factor meters indicate the power factor of an a-c circuit. They are similar in construction to an electrodynamometer wattmeter, with the exception that two moving coils are now fixed together at right angles. One moving coil takes the supply voltage through a resistor and the other through an inductor. No control spring is used. The torques on the moving coil are in opposition, and they reach a steady-state or equilibrium position at an angle equal to the power-factor angle. The reading is independent of current and voltage, but it is subject to frequency variations. Modified designs are used to measure power factors of balanced three-phase electrical systems.

Electrostatic voltmeters. Two parallel plates having a potential difference of V volts between them experience a force given by

$$F = \frac{AKV^2}{2d^2} \qquad \text{newtons}$$

where A = facing surface area of each plate, m^2
$\qquad d$ = distance of separation, m
$\qquad K = 8.85 \times 10^{-12}$

If, now, one plate is fixed and the other is held by a spring and its movement is displayed by an indicator or pointer, a simple form of electrostatic voltmeter is achieved. A commercial meter designed along these lines is manufactured to register voltages exceeding 500 kilovolts. Electrostatic voltmeters register true rms or effective voltages. They may be used on d-c and a-c circuits. They are normally used for high-voltage laboratory measurements.

REVIEW QUESTIONS AND PROBLEMS

12-1 Describe the three basic damping waveforms of response in an indicating instrument.

12-2 Describe, with the aid of a neat diagram, the basic operation and construction of either a laboratory or commercial type of galvanometer.

12-3 Explain the fundamental differences between a galvanometer, an ammeter, and a voltmeter. Include basic circuit diagrams to supplement your explanations. How are these instruments connected in a circuit?

12-4 A galvanometer indicates full-scale deflection by a current of 1.00 ma. If the resistance of the meter is 7.0 ohms, calculate the value the series resistance must be in order to measure voltages up to 50 volts.

12-5 A voltmeter of range 120 volts and resistance 9,600 ohms is connected in series with another voltmeter of range 150 volts and resistance 1,500 ohms. What are the readings when the meters are connected to a 125-volt supply?

12-6 Draw a diagram to show how a voltmeter may be provided with multiple range.

12-7 A millivoltmeter with a resistance of 0.80 ohm has a range of 24 mv. Explain how it could be converted into (a) a voltmeter with a range of 12 volts and (b) an ammeter with a range of 30 amp.

12-8   Describe, with the aid of a circuit diagram, the operation and calibration of an ohmmeter.

12-9   A galvanometer gives full-scale deflection for a current of 20.0 ma and has a resistance of 50.0 ohms. Determine the shunt and series resistors required to convert it to an ammeter of range 0 to 5 amp and a voltmeter of range 0 to 100 volts.

12-10   (a) Draw the waveform of a rectified a-c input.

(b) Describe in detail any rectifier instrument you know.

12-11   (a) Describe, with the aid of circuit diagrams, the action of any wattmeter and watthour meter you are familiar with.

(b) Calculate the cost of operating for 24 hr a lamp requiring 1.0 amp on a 100-volt line if the cost of electric energy is $0.05 per kilowatthour.

12-12   (a) Define the term "power factor."

(b) What are the power factor and true power of a load which has an impedance of 60 ohms with a 60° lag when connected to a 120-volt 60 cycle/sec source?

(c) Draw the phase diagram for part (b).

12-13   (a) Compare the operations of a dynamometer and induction-type wattmeter.

(b) A wattmeter shows a true power reading of 144 watts in an a-c circuit in which the effective or rms current is 2 amp. Calculate the resistance of this circuit.

12-14   (a) Describe the principles of operation and construction of any electrostatic voltmeter you know.

(b) With the aid of a diagram describe an instrument-transfer method for calibrating an a-c meter.

Circuit Devices

A few of the more important electrical and magnetic devices which are fundamental to industrial instrumentation will now be described.

Ordinary transformers. Alternating currents are used more widely than direct currents because of the simplicity with which the voltage can be increased or decreased. Voltage changes for alternating currents are achieved by means of a simple device, called a *transformer*, which consists of two coils of conducting wire, one around each side of a closed laminated iron core as shown in Fig. 12-13. Electric energy is supplied to one of the coils, referred to as the *primary coil*, and is delivered to the output or load from the other coil, referred to as the *secondary coil*. When the primary coil P is connected to a source of alternating emf, the current in the coil will set up an alternating magnetic flux in the laminated iron core. This magnetic flux will surge first in one direction and then in the other. The

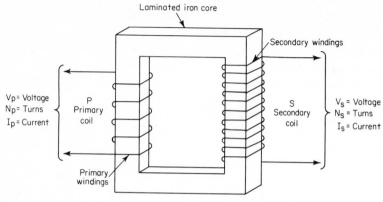

Fig. 12-13   A simple transformer.

alternating flux will cut the secondary coil S, causing an alternating emf, of strength dependent on the relative number of turns in the two coils, to be induced in it.

Since the rate of change of flux is nearly the same in the primary and secondary coils, it follows that the induced voltages are directly proportional to the numbers of turns in the coils:

$$\frac{\text{Primary voltage}}{\text{Secondary voltage}} = \frac{\text{total primary turns}}{\text{total secondary turns}}$$

Symbolically,
$$\frac{V_p}{V_s} = \frac{N_p}{N_s}$$

The use of transformers in the transmission of electric current over long distances is a matter of economy. A small current at high voltages requires only thin copper wires to transmit it. For the same rate of transmission of energy at low voltage, the current must be great, and stout copper leads are then necessary. The efficiency of a commercial transformer operating under favorable conditions is high, only a few percent less than ideal. Losses due to heat and eddy effects are usually small. Hence, the power input to the primary is nearly equal to the power output from the secondary.

$$\text{Power (watts)} = V_p I_p = V_s I_s \qquad \text{approx}$$

Hence
$$\frac{V_p}{V_s} = \frac{N_p}{N_s} = \frac{I_s}{I_p}$$

A transformer used to increase the voltage is called a step-up transformer. In a step-up transformer the increase in voltage is accompanied by a reduction in current. Conversely, in a step-down transformer a high voltage is applied to the primary winding and a lower voltage is obtained from the secondary winding. The decrease in voltage is accompanied by an increase in current.

Example. A step-down transformer at the end of a transmission line reduces the voltage from 2,400 to 120 volts at a receiving instrument. The power output is 0.9 kilowatts (kw), and the overall efficiency of the transformer is 92 percent. The primary, or high-tension, winding has 4,000 turns. Compute (a) the number of turns in the secondary or low-tension coil, (b) the power input, and (c) the current in the secondary coil.

Solution

$$\frac{V_p}{V_s} = \frac{N_p}{N_s}$$

$$\frac{2,400 \text{ volts}}{120 \text{ volts}} = \frac{4,000 \text{ turns}}{N_s}$$

$$N_s = 200 \text{ turns}$$

$$\text{Efficiency of transformer} = \frac{P_s}{P_p}$$

$$0.92 = \frac{900}{P_p} \text{ watts}$$

$$P_p = 980 \text{ watts}$$

$$I_s = \frac{900 \text{ watts}}{120 \text{ volts}} = 7.5 \text{ amp}$$

Small step-down transformers are widely used in instrumentation and control systems to operate danger alarms, buzzers, and thermostatic controls or with a-c/d-c rectifiers to operate electric relays or magnetic switches.

Differential transformers. A differential transformer is a very effective instrument for measuring small displacements. Figure 12-14 shows the

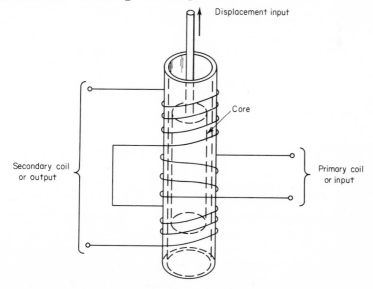

Fig. 12-14   Tubular-type differential transformer.

basic construction of a differential transformer. It has a primary or input winding on the central portion of a tube and half of the secondary or output winding on each end of the tube. The two halves of the secondary winding are wound in opposite directions. In this way the emfs induced in the two portions of the secondary winding oppose each other. Normally, a ferromagnetic core is inserted in the center of the tube. Its position determines the flux linkage with each coil. When the core is in the lower position, more flux links with the lower coil than with the upper coil, and the emf output will be 180° out of phase with the emf of the upper coil.

Similarly, when the core is in the upper position, more flux links with the upper coil than with the lower coil, and the net emf output will thus be in phase with the primary input emf. The polarity of the error signal depends on which side of center the core is located, and the magnitude of the error signal depends on how far the core is off center. When the output of this differential transformer is amplified and supplied to one phase of a two-phase motor, as illustrated in Fig. 12-15, the rotation of the motor will

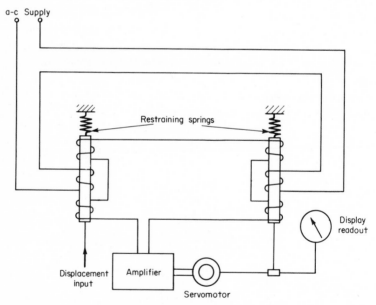

Fig. 12-15   Basic servo system to measure displacement by using differential transformers.

be determined by the position of the core. The motor moves the core of a similar type of differential transformer. In this transducer the output of the balancing transformer opposes the output of the input transformer, with the result that the motor will rotate until the outputs of the two transformers are equal. The indicator will register the displacement on a calibrated scale.

There are a variety of designs and constructions of differential transformers; another type is shown in Fig. 12-16. The transformer primary

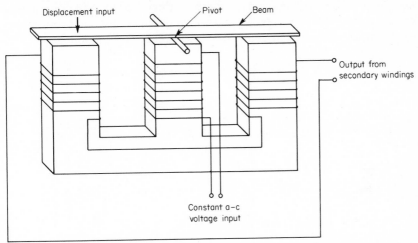

Fig. 12-16 E-shaped differential transformer.

winding is wound around the center leg of an E-shaped magnetic core, and the output windings are wound around the two outer legs of the core. The armature pivots about an axis in the center of the beam. When the armature is displaced, the reluctance (the ratio of magnetic force to magnetic flux) of the magnetic circuit through one half of the secondary winding is reduced and the reluctance of the magnetic circuit through the other half of the secondary winding is, at the same time, increased. The induced emfs in the two halves of the secondary winding oppose each other. The operation is similar in principle to that of the tubular type of transformer.

When high accuracy and sensitivity of displacement values are required, the differential transformer finds wide application. Displacements in fractions of microinches can be measured with such instruments. For this reason, differential transformers are useful component devices in control and servo systems.

Relays. The electric relay is an electromagnetic device by means of which contacts in one electric circuit are operated by a change in current in the same circuit or in some other circuit. The basic schematic arrangement of a simple electric relay is shown in Fig. 12-17. When the electromagnet M is energized by the passage of a current through it, the small soft-iron core disk or armature C is attracted toward the coil. The disk, attached to a lever, thus closes a second circuit. When no current flows through the electromagnet, the attraction or pull on C ceases and the control spring pulls the disk away and opens the controlled circuit.

This basic principle is used in electric protective relays to prevent dangerous conditions in electrical systems. Current relays, voltage relays, and power relays are designed to operate either against a high-limit control condition, in which case the controlled circuit is broken, or for a low-limit control condition, in which case the circuit closes again.

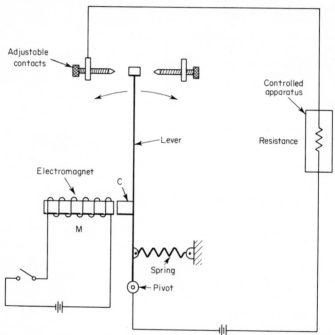

Fig. 12-17   A basic electric relay and control circuit.

REVIEW QUESTIONS AND PROBLEMS

12-15   Describe, with the aid of a neat sketch, the construction and operation of a transformer.

12-16   An instrument transformer operates on a primary of 720 turns and a secondary of 48 turns. The primary is connected to a 120 volt a-c supply. Calculate the voltage developed in the secondary.

12-17   The primary and secondary coils of a transformer used in an electrical control scheme have 500 and 2,500 turns respectively.
(a) If the primary is connected to a 110-volt a-c source, calculate the voltage across the secondary.

(b) If, now, the secondary coil is connected to the 110-volt line, calculate the voltage developed in the primary coil. Assume ideal conditions.

12-18 Explain the difference between step-up and step-down transformers and examples of their application in instrumentation.

12-19 A step-down transformer reduces a 2,400-volt a-c supply to 120 volts. The power output is 9.0 kw, and the overall efficiency of the transformer is 92 percent. The primary has 4,000 turns. Calculate (a) the number of turns in the secondary coil, (b) the power input, and (c) the current in the secondary.

12-20 With the aid of a sketch describe the operation of a differential transformer and its application to any control system you know.

12-21 Describe any on-off relay control schemes you are familiar with. Include a circuit diagram and describe briefly the principle of operation.

CHAPTER THIRTEEN

Basic electronics for instrumentation

To see what is general in what is particular and what is permanent in what is transitory is the aim of scientific thought.

ALFRED NORTH WHITEHEAD

Fundamentally, electronics is the study and science of freeing electrons from matter and of controlling their flow and direction in vacuum or gas-filled tubes, in conductors, or in semiconductors. This science probably began when Thomas A. Edison, in about 1883, invented the electric light bulb, which later on led to the development of the electronic tube and to other electronic instrumentation equipment which is used today. Basic concepts and examples of the uses of electronics will be described in this chapter. Owing to the wide scope of this science, some of these basic concepts will be described only briefly, but it is not the intention to ignore their importance, particularly in instrumentation applications.

Thermionic Emission

Free electrons exist in all matter. Their activity, however, can be stimulated by raising the temperature of the matter. With certain metals this results in the emission of large numbers of free electrons, which move at the urging influence of electric and magnetic fields. The mass of an electron is so infinitesimal (9.11×10^{-28} g) that electron inertia may safely be considered negligible. This progress of emission of large numbers of free electrons is called *thermionic emission* (Fig. 13-1). The higher the temperature the greater the number of electrons emitted. The emission is analogous to the escape of molecules from the surface of a liquid such as water.

A comparison of thermionic emission and the evaporation of a liquid or solid is interesting. In solids, the atoms are closely packed and the interatomic forces are so large that rarely does an atom acquire enough kinetic energy to break away from its location. In liquids the packing is not so close, and wandering molecules have enough energy to break the surface tension and escape, or evaporate.

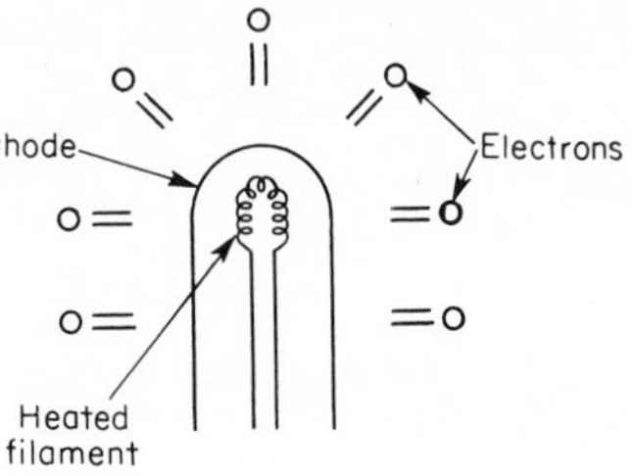

Fig. 13-1   Thermionic emission.

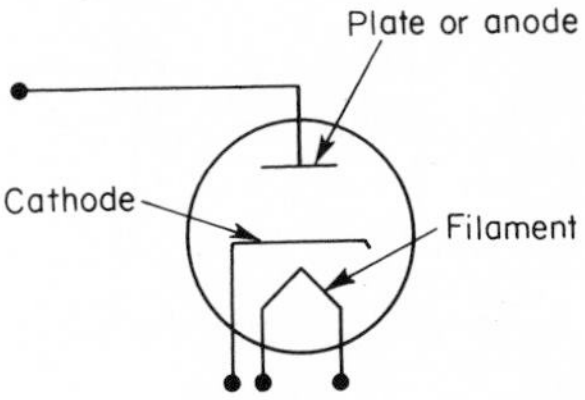

Fig. 13-2   Conventional arrangement of the elements of a diode.

Diode Operation

A simple two-element vacuum tube, called a *diode*, is shown in Fig. 13-2. It consists of an *anode*, or *plate*, and a *cathode*, or *filament*. The filament of the diode can be heated. When it is sufficiently heated, electrons are emitted from its surface. Operation of the diode depends on the emitted electrons.

Now, molecules evaporating from a water surface create vapor pressure above the liquid, which slows down further evaporation. Similarly, electrons emitted from a heated metallic surface form a kind of cloud or barrier around the emitter. This cloud has a high negative charge that tends to keep other electrons from being emitted. The charge builds up until an equilibrium of *space charge* is reached. At this point, no further emission takes place.

The positive charge applied to the *anode*, or plate, in an electronic tube will draw off some of the space charge to enable electron emission from the heated filament, or cathode, to continue. As the plate potential is increased, it becomes great enough to pull away the space charge as fast as electrons are being emitted from the cathode. When this condition is reached, there is a maximum current through the tube, called the *saturation current*.

At high operating temperatures, filaments would burn away rapidly if any oxygen were present. For this reason the emitter is operated either in a high vacuum or in some inert gas such as argon. Gas-filled tubes are frequently used as rectifiers and control devices in industrial instrumentation.

A-C Rectifiers

The circuit diagram in Fig. 13-3 shows how a diode can be used to rectify an alternating current. The original sine-wave alternating current and the unidirectional or rectified current are shown in Fig. 13-3. Since the

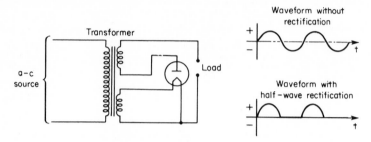

Fig. 13-3   Circuit and waveform of half-wave rectification.

plate is positive with respect to the cathode—the electron emitter—only during alternate half-cycles of the alternating current, there is current flow through the diode only during alternate half-cycles. Thus the current, although direct, is discontinuous. It is possible to make the direct current continuous by adding a second plate which is positive with respect to the cathode during the other half-cycles of the alternating current. The circuit for full-wave rectification is shown in Fig. 13-4.

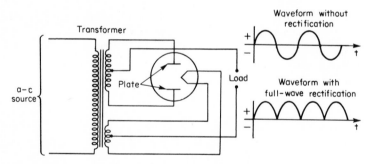

Fig. 13-4   Circuit and waveform of full-wave rectification.

Amplification; the Triode

Lee De Forest, an American physicist, in 1907 devised a method of controlling the action of a vacuum tube by adding a third element, which he called the *grid*. The grid, which is similar to a metal screen, is inserted between the filament and the plate and acts as a shutter to control the passage of electrons from the filament to the plate. If the grid is made negative, it repels the space-charge electrons and throttles down the filament-to-plate current. If the grid is made positive, it attracts electrons from the cathode, and this is undesirable.

The circuit diagram of Fig. 13-5 shows how the grid of a *triode*—the De Forest tube—can control large currents in the plate-load-filament

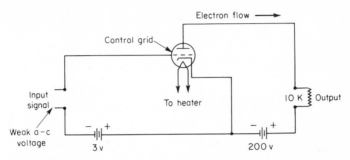

Fig. 13-5   Basic amplifier circuit showing function of the control grid in the plate-load-filament circuit.

circuit. Weak voltages on the grid effectively control the flow of relatively large currents in the plate-load circuit. One battery heats the filament, and another battery keeps a high positive potential on the plate. This function of controlling large plate currents with weak voltages applied to the grid is called *amplification*. Industrial electronic equipment and instrumentation control schemes actually operate on direct current developed by rectifier circuits similar to that shown in Fig. 13-4. Batteries or cells are shown symbolically in the circuit diagrams only for the sake of simplicity.

Voltage amplification. The voltage-amplification factor of a triode is defined as the ratio of the change in plate voltage to the change in grid voltage (in the opposite direction) such that the plate current remains constant. The voltage-amplification factor is represented by the Greek letter μ (mu). Symbolically,

$$\mu = \frac{\Delta E_p}{\Delta E_g} \qquad I_p \text{ constant}$$

where ΔE_p = incremental change in plate voltage
ΔE_g = incremental change in grid voltage
I_p = plate current

For example, an amplification factor of 20 means that if the grid voltage is changed by 1 volt, the effect on the plate current is the same as if the plate voltage were changed by 20 volts.

Characteristic curves of triodes. The amplification characteristics of a tube are normally presented in graphic form. The curves describe tube performance when the plate current is made to flow through resistances of various magnitudes. If the plate current I_p is plotted against the grid voltage I_g for a given set of values of plate voltages, a performance or

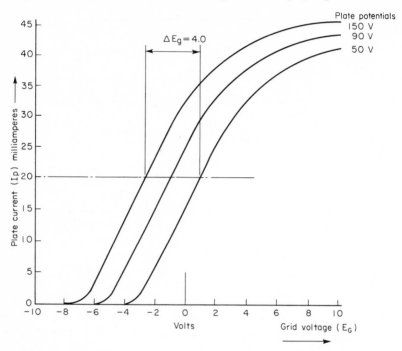

Fig. 13-6   Characteristic curves for a triode operated at three different plate potentials.

characteristic curve can be drawn. The family of characteristics is shown in Fig. 13-6. From these curves the following can be deduced:

1. As the grid is made more negative, the plate current decreases.
2. Small or incremental changes in grid voltage cause large changes in plate current.
3. The higher (the more positive) the plate voltages the greater the current flow.
4. When the grid is highly positive, the curves flatten out, which means that all the electrons leaving the filament are reaching the plate. This occurs when the slope $\Delta I_p / \Delta E_g$ is approaching a horizontal straight line.
5. Each plate potential has a certain value of grid bias (negative) for which all flow of electrons will stop. This value of E_g is referred to as the *cutoff point*.

Amplification factors determined by characteristic curves. The characteristic curve of a triode is an indicator of the triode performance as an amplifier as well as a rectifier. Consider the triode under a plate potential of 150 volts. The cutoff point is at $E_g = -8$ volts. If this tube is to amplify a weak a-c signal without any wave distortion, the signal can be applied to the grid along the line $E_g = -3$ volts, for this sets the center of the linear portion of the characteristic curve. The operation is shown in Fig. 13-7.

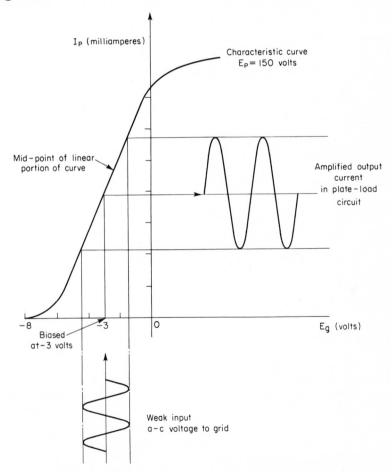

Fig. 13-7 Operation of a triode for undistorted amplification.

Referring to the family of characteristic curves for a typical triode in Fig. 13-6, consider the line of constant $I_p = 20$ ma across the linear portions of nearly all three curves. From the 150-volt plate potential to the 50-volt curve $\Delta E_p = 150 - 50 = 100$ volts. Between these same two curves, for a constant value of $I_p = 20$ ma, $\Delta E_g = 4.0$ volts (approximately). Given that $\mu = \Delta E_p / \Delta E_g$,

$$\mu = {}^{100}\!/_4 = 25$$

the voltage amplification factor of this triode.

Applications of Electron Tubes

Apart from current rectification and voltage and power amplification, electron tubes have other useful functions such as electrical response to light (photocells), conversion of electricity into radiation, and change of frequency in instrumentation and other electronic equipment. A few of these functions will be described briefly.

A variety of electronic tubes are available; each is designed to fulfill a certain purpose in complex control systems and circuits. Other components of such circuits include resistors, transformers, capacitors, switchgear, and inductors.

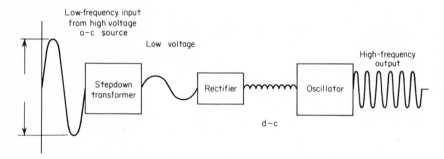

Fig. 13-8   Block diagram of frequency changer.

Frequency control. The block diagram in Fig. 13-8 shows the basic process of obtaining high frequency. Induction furnaces and dielectric heating equipment require high-frequency currents. Some radio sets require frequencies up to many millions of cycles per second.

Oscillation

The amplification of a vacuum tube can be changed by feeding a portion of the plate output signal back into the grid input. If this *feedback* is in phase with the signal already present at the input, it is called *positive feedback*. If the magnitude of the positive feedback is great enough, the signal becomes self-sustaining, thus forming an oscillator circuit. If, however, the feedback from the plate is 180° out of phase with the signal at the grid, it is called *negative feedback*. Although negative feedback causes a reduction in amplification, it is often used to increase the stability of the amplifier.

Photoelectricity

The photoelectric cell, or phototube, better known as the "electric eye," plays a very important part in control devices. Photoelectric cells are used in smoke-density meters, furnace-flame control, and level control of solids or liquids in storage tanks. They may also be used to count the items coming rapidly off a mass-production assembly line. The basic elements of a phototube are shown in Fig. 13-9. Certain compounds, e.g., selenium oxide, cesium oxide, and rubidium oxide, will emit electrons when exposed to light. This emission is similar to that of the thoriated-tungsten filament when heated. In the case of the phototube, the emission of electrons is approximately proportional to the intensity of light striking the light-sensitive coated cathode. Emission of electrons as a result of light is called the *photoelectric effect*. The cathode is normally constructed of copper in a semicircular shape, and it is coated with the light-sensitive oxide material. The anode is usually a wire running along the central axis of the tube.

A positive potential is applied to the anode and, when light strikes the cathode, electrons are emitted and attracted to the anode. As can be expected, the plate currents are very small indeed, about 15 microamperes. Because there is such a small current, only very sensitive relays are in the circuit. Alternatively, an amplifier is used to achieve currents of greater magnitude for control purposes in industrial equipment.

Transistor Fundamentals

Transistors are replacing electronic vacuum tubes in many measuring and control circuits used in instrumentation. Basically, a transistor can be used to amplify currents and to perform other functions usually performed by the thermionic tube.

Transistors are made of materials, called *semiconductors*, whose electrical conductivity lies between that of the insulators such as mica and the popular conductors such as copper. Germanium and silicon are two such substances. A comparison of the electrical resistance of some of the more commonly used conductors, semiconductors, and insulators is given in Fig. 13-10. The study of the physical properties and behavior of semiconductors is known as *solid-state physics*.

Germanium and silicon have a greater resistance to the flow of elec-

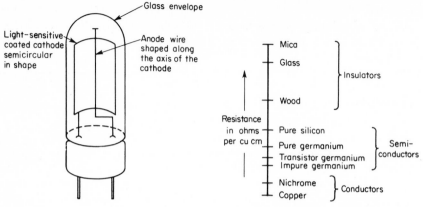

Fig. 13-9 Basic elements of a phototube.

Fig. 13-10 Comparison of the electrical resistances of some conductors, semiconductors, and insulators.

trons than conductive metals have, but the resistance is not as great as that of insulators. Adding small impurities causes an excess of electrons in these materials. One impurity makes the semiconductor electrically positive and another makes it negative. When a positive semiconductor is sandwiched between two negative semiconductors, the result is a transistor which performs like a thermionic tube. Such a transistor is referred to as an NPN type. Alternatively, when a negative semiconductor is sandwiched between two positive semiconductors, the result is referred to as a PNP type of transistor. The difference between these two types is in the direction of current flow through the transistor. The two basic

Fig. 13-11   Transistor symbols.

types of transistor are shown symbolically in Fig. 13-11. The advantages of transistors are:

1. They are small in size (about ⅜ by ¼ by ⅜ in.).
2. They have no delicate parts.
3. They consume very little power, and hence give off little heat.

These factors account for the advantages of using transistors instead of vacuum tubes in such devices as hearing aids, computers, and control mechanisms. Continued research work is being done in the field of solid-state physics to widen the applications of semiconductors.

REVIEW QUESTIONS AND PROBLEMS

13-1 What is meant by (a) thermionic emission, (b) space charge, and (c) rectification?

13-2 Describe, with the aid of diagrams, the operations and applications of (a) a diode and (b) an NPN transistor.

13-3 What is meant by the term "full-wave rectification"? Draw a circuit diagram to show how the rectification is obtained.

13-4 Define the following: (a) characteristic curve of triodes, (b) amplification, (c) voltage amplification factor.

13-5 From a set of characteristic curves of a triode at different plate potentials it was found that $E_p = 180 - 50$ volts and that, between these corresponding two curves for a constant I_p of 20 ma, $E_g = 6.0$ volts. Compute the voltage amplification of this tube.

13-6 (a) Define the terms "photoelectricity" and "phototube."
(b) Describe, with the aid of a circuit diagram, how a phototube or similar device can be used to measure and control the smoke density from a large industrial-plant furnace.

CHAPTER FOURTEEN

Electrical transducers

Precise measurement implies an attempt to measure the exact value and to discipline uncertainties.

J. SIMS

The Importance of Transducers

The field of automatic control and instrumentation requires the measurement of many different physical characteristics and phenomena. Without transducers, advances in the application of control and computation would have been impossible. Transducers have become convenient, economical, and highly efficient in operation by converting the various physical quantities or variables such as pressure, vacuum, temperature, humidity, flow, displacement, and acceleration into related electrical values, because such electrical values can readily be used for measuring, amplifying, transmitting, or controlling purposes.

Transducers, in a general sense, are devices that convert energy from one form to another. More specifically, they can be actuated by waves from one or more transmission systems or media and can supply related waves to one or more other transmission systems or media. The block diagram in Fig. 14-1 shows the input side of a transducer that can convert a nonelectrical quantity into a related electrical signal. The output signal can then be used for measuring and control-system purposes.

Energy Converters

Transducers. The action of transducers can be examined in terms of energy conversion. Any device which converts one form of energy into another form is basically a transducer. Examples are the telephone, which converts sound energy into an electrical signal; the thermocouple, which transforms heat energy into an equivalent electrical potential; the photocell, which converts light energy into electric current; the strain gauge, which converts tension or stress into electrical energy. In addition, there are a multitude of transducers which are designed to obtain electrical outputs from mechanical forms of energy input such as force, pressure, displacement, torque, and acceleration.

The term "transducer" can be applied in the reverse sense or direction. For example, the familiar loudspeaker converts electric energy into sound, and the simple solenoid in a relay component converts electric energy into mechanical motion. A typical arrangment of a transducer used to measure the angular velocity of an engine is shown in Fig. 14-2.

Actuators. Devices which convert or transform electric energy into another form of energy, as in the case of the solenoid, are frequently referred to as actuators, because

Variable under measurement

Input signal

Electrical or electronic transducer

Output signal as a function of input signal

Signal modified

Measuring instrument (receiver)

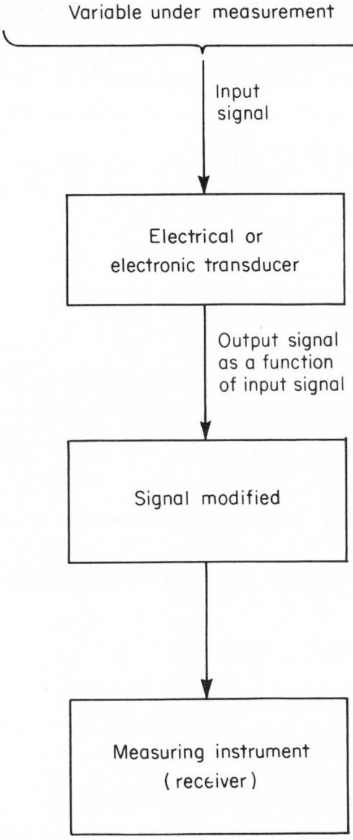

Fig. 14-1 Basic function of a transducer in a measuring system.

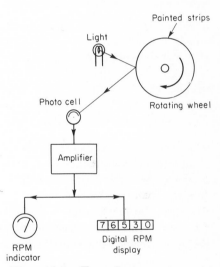

Fig. 14-2 Transducer system to measure rotational motion.

their immediate result is a positive physical action. An example is the familiar doorbell.

No process control system is complete without the final control element, which is the actuator. This device receives the output signal from a controller and converts it to a positive action to control a process. The final control element may, for example, actuate a valve, vary the speed of an electric motor, or open a furnace damper. In later paragraphs various principles and applications of transducers and actuators used in instrument practice and measuring systems will be described briefly.

Functions of Transducers in an Electronic System

In an electronic measuring system the transducer is the sensing or detecting element which converts the quantity which is being measured into a corresponding or related electrical quantity. The transducer detects or senses and then produces a signal which is modified or amplified to a proper level or form by a modifier. The receiving instrument provides a readout of the quantity which is being measured. The signal may also be received by a controller for control purposes. With the ever-expanding growth of knowledge in instrumentation technology, systems are planned to meet industrial needs. In a modern control room of any oil refinery or power plant transducers are employed to enable operators to monitor several variables at one control center.

Applications of Transducers

Selecting the most suitable transducer is the initial stage in designing an effective instrumentation system. However, to give a list of quantities that can be converted into an electrical output by a transducer would take too much space. It would have to include almost anything measurable, and measurements would range from pressure, temperature, and acceleration to heart sounds and the detection of nuclear radiation. The following are some of the transducers used in industry:

Mechanical. Strain-gauge type for force, weight, and pressure; flow gauges, accelerometers, and torque meters
Thermal. Electrical resistance thermometer, thermocouple
Optical. Photoconductive cells
Magnetic. Permeameters
Chemical. Humidity, moisture, pH, conductivity cells
Nuclear. Geiger tube, semiconductor detectors, ionization chambers

Electrical Measuring Principles on which Transducers May Operate

In instrument practice, transducers can be classified according to the basic electrical measuring principle involved in converting the varying quantity into a corresponding, closely related electrical variation. Some of the main electrical principles used in transducers and in measuring systems can be classified as follows:

1. Variable-resistance transducers:
   Pressure and strain gauges
   Resistance bulbs, thermistors, and thermoconductive thermometer elements

2. Voltage-divider transducers:
  Basic form of potentiometer position sensor
  Basic pressure-actuated voltage divider
3. Variable-capacitance transducers:
  High-frequency RC and LC sensing
  Reactance-tube type causing frequency modulation
4. Variable-inductance transducers:
  Linear-variable differential transformer for displacement
  Variable-reluctance pickup
5. Voltage-generating transducers:
  Piezoelectric pressure sensors
  Rotational-motion (rpm) tachometer
  Photovoltaic cell
  Thermocouple sensor element

Variable-resistance Transducers

The principle of the variable-resistance transducer is that the physical variable under measurement causes a resistance change in the sensing element.

Resistive-pressure transducers. In the case of pressure measurement the sensitive resistance element may take various forms, depending on the mechanical arrangement on which the applied pressure is caused to act. A bellows-operated unit coupled to a movable resistance contact is shown in Fig. 14-3. A sensitive diaphragm unit (Fig. 14-4) alters the

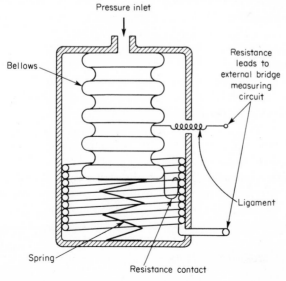

Fig. 14-3   Bellows-type pressure-sensitive resistance element. (Instrument Society of America)

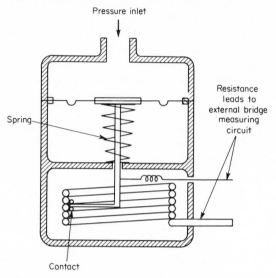

Pressure inlet

Resistance
leads to
external bridge
measuring
circuit

Spring

Contact

Fig. 14-4   Diaphragm-type pressure-sensitive resistance element. (Instrument Society of America)

resistance in the coil, and thus in the measuring circuit, according to the magnitude of the applied pressure. The familiar Bourdon tube and other pressure elements described in Chap. 5 are also examples of sensing elements that cause a change in resistance. The resistance change, when connected to a bridge measuring circuit, can then be taken as either a d-c or a-c signal to determine the pressure indication.

Metallic strain gauge. The strain gauge is a transducer employing electrical resistance variation to sense the strain or other results of force. It can be utilized as a very versatile detector for measuring weight, pressure, mechanical force, or displacement. In basic construction a bonded strain gauge (Fig. 14-5) is an electric conductor of fine wire looped back and forth on a flexible mounting plate, which is usually bonded or cemented to the member or test piece undergoing stress. The extension in length of the hairpin loops increases the effect of a stress applied in the direction of length. In short, a tensile stress would elongate the wire and thereby increase its length and decrease its cross-sectional area. The result would be an increase in its resistance, because the resistance R of a metallic conductor, at a constant temperature, varies directly with length L and inversely with cross-sectional area A. Symbolically,

$$R = \frac{kL}{A} \quad \text{ohms}$$

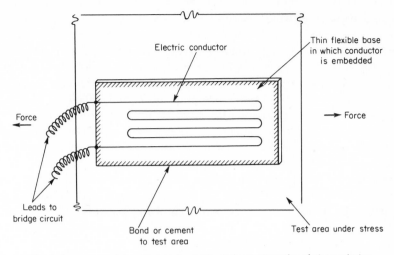

The strain gauge must be attached to permit maximum elongation of the conductor

Fig. 14-5   Application of a strain gauge.

where k is a constant depending upon the wire. With a good bond between the strain gauge and the test piece, either tensile or compressive strains can be measured. Generally, the current passed through the gauge is about 25 ma, the diameter of the conductor is about 0.001 in., and the resistance of the conductor is about 100 ohms.

Since a current flow through the strain-gauge element will have a heating effect which is proportional to the square of the current, any resulting change in resistance will have to be applied as a correction. One way to correct for the heating effect is to use a dummy gauge, in the opposite arm of the bridge circuit, which has the same current flowing through it. The schematic arrangement is shown in Fig. 14-6.

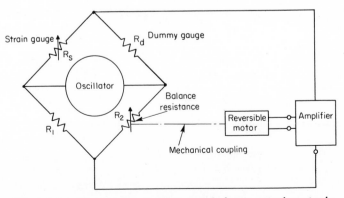

Fig. 14-6   A resistance bridge circuit for measuring strain.

The type of measuring device used to balance the bridge circuit, or to measure its unbalance, depends upon the required speed of response. For high-speed analysis, as used in research laboratories, an oscilloscope is used to measure the degree of unbalance, whereas in industrial applications a potentiometer is sufficient. Strain gauges are available in length from $\frac{1}{16}$ to $1\frac{1}{2}$ in. with a resistance range of 60 to 6,000 ohms. They are calibrated to determine strain due to tensile and compressive loads.

Semiconductor strain gauges. Strain-gauge sensitivity has been improved by using semiconductors. The flexible silicon strain gauge is a very practical device. It is as stable as the metallic type and has a higher output level. Semiconductor strain gauges can detect micro-inches of change in length per unit inch of length. A semiconductor element used in microstrain systems is shown in Fig. 14-7.

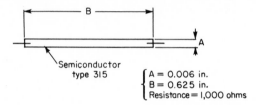

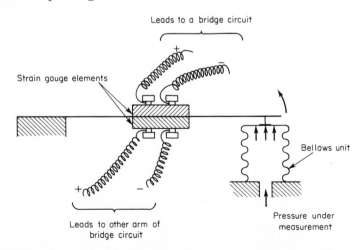

Fig. 14-7   *A semiconductor used in microstrain systems.*

Pressure-strain gauges. A means of detecting very small variations in pressure (Fig. 14-8) incorporates strain gauges cemented or bonded on both sides of a flexible cantilever. Each gauge will be in either compression or tension depending on the vertical motion of the bellows. In turn, the

Fig. 14-8   *An application of the strain gauge for pressure measurement.*

motion of the bellows depends on the pressure. Any slight pressure variation can be detected by the strain gauge bridge circuit and read on a suitable meter. The bellows–cantilever beam type of strain gauge device is suitable for measuring pressures from 0 to 50,000 psi.

Voltage-divider pressure transducer. A simple method of using the motion of a pressure-sensitive element such as a bellows or diaphragm is to actuate the arm of a potentiometer voltage divider. The moving arm of the voltage divider produces a voltage output proportional to the pressure variable, instead of a simple resistance variation. The voltage-divider potentiometer is suited to d-c indicating and recording systems which may not require amplification.

Variable-inductance Transducers

A simple device in which a change in inductance of a sensing element is produced by a pressure variation is shown in Fig. 14-9. In the *magnetic-*

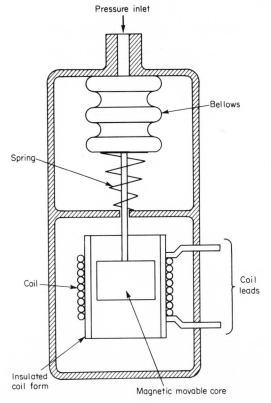

Fig. 14-9   Bellows-type pressure-sensitive inductance element. (Instrument Society of America)

pressure transducer the pressure acting inside the bellows causes a change in the position of the magnetic core and this, in turn, varies the inductance of a coil. The inductance change can then be made the basis of an electrical signal which can be connected to an a-c inductance-bridge circuit. A salient feature of the inductive type of transducer over the resistive type is that there are no moving contacts. This feature has an added advantage of providing continuous determination of the change in the variable, with no extra friction involved in the measuring system. An alternative design based on the principle of inductance variation is used to obtain a change in mutual inductance between two magnetically coupled coils instead of the self-inductance of one coil.

Variable-reluctance Transducers

When a change of an induced voltage is required, the transducer is sometimes referred to as a magnetic pickup or *variable-reluctance sensor*. A magnetic-pressure, reluctance type of transducer is shown in Fig. 14-10.

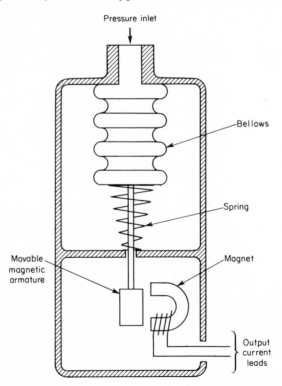

Fig. 14-10   Bellows-type pressure-sensitive reluctance-type element. (Instrument Society of America)

Variable-capacitance Transducers

Pressure changes can be detected by variation of capacitance. In one design the variation of capacitance is between a fixed plate and another plate free to move as the pressure changes. The energy-conversion unit of the transducer consists of a flexible diaphragm behind which are, in order, a dielectric material, a static plate, insulating material, and capacitor leads (Fig. 14-11). The pressure acting on the diaphragm

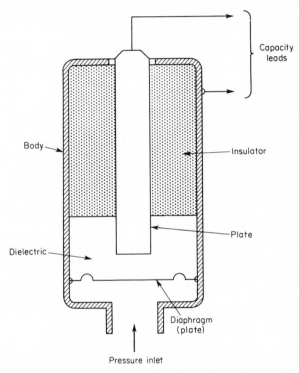

Fig. 14-11 Diaphragm-type pressure-sensitive capacitance element. (Instrument Society of America)

causes it to deflect. This results in a variation in the dielectric material, which, in turn, changes the capacitance of the unit. The final change then becomes a function of the pressure variations. The capacitance type of transducer, as in the case of a capacitance microphone, is basically a simple and inexpensive device. Unfortunately, the receiving instrument for the capacitive sensor unit requires a more complex measuring circuit than is needed for the other transducers. The reason for this is that when varying capacitance is made part of an a-c bridge to produce an a-c output signal, great care must be taken in the resistive and reactive balance process to prevent unwanted signal pickup in the high-impedance circuit. One important application of capacitance variation in instrument practice is to change the frequency of an oscillating circuit in a telemetering system. A telemetering system involves the transmission of measurements over very long distances, generally by electrical and electronic means, for indicating, recording, integrating, or control purposes.

Some of the disadvantages of capacitive-pressure transducers are, as mentioned, the high-impedance output, the necessity of being balanced resistively and reactively, and the fact that long leads tend to cause erratic signals. The main advantages have already been described.

Voltage-generating Transducers

Piezoelectric transducers. The deformation of various crystals, such as quartz, Rochelle salt, tourmaline, and barium titanate, creates electrical pressure proportional to the applied force or pressure. This action of generating a voltage by the application of a force or pressure is the principle used in the piezoelectric crystal transducer. A sectional view of a voltage-generating (piezoelectric) pressure transducer is shown in Fig. 14-12. Piezoelectric crystals are found in such devices as phonograph pickup cartridges and ceramic microphones.

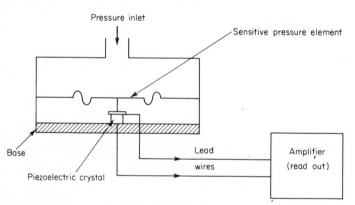

Fig. 14-12   Voltage-generating (piezoelectric) transducer in a pressure-measuring system.

In instrument practice, because of the high output voltage, amplitude, and frequency response, the piezoelectric crystal transducer is used in high-frequency accelerometers. As mentioned, the piezoelectric crystal is inherently a dynamic responding sensor and is not really suitable for steady-state conditions. The crystal sensing element has a high output impendance and low current output. This type of transducer is used with an a-c amplifier to increase the crystal output signal for readout purposes. Because it is a high-impedance measuring system, careful shielding is required, as is true of most high-impedance devices.

The main advantages of piezoelectric transducers are self-generating power, dynamic response, small size, and rugged construction. The disadvantages are the high-impedance output necessitating electronic-signal-conditioning systems, sensitivity to temperature variations, and, with long leads, the generation of noise.

Linear-variable Differential Transformer

In Chap. 12 the basic principle and operation of the differential transformer were described. This device may be designed to provide an electrical output which is linearly proportional to a mechanical displacement. The transducer is generally referred to as the linear-variable differential transformer (LVDT). As described in the preceding chapter, it is an electromechanical transducer of the variable-inductance type. To recapitulate, the basic principle, shown in the schematic diagram in Fig. 14-13*a*, is as follows: Three coils are wound on a cylindrical

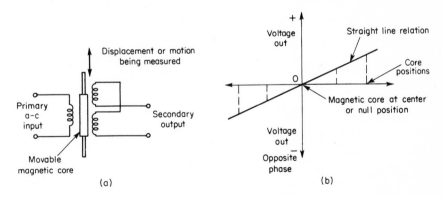

Fig. 14-13 (a) *Schematic diagram of a linear-variable-differential transformer.* (b) *Linear function of voltage output to position of magnetic core.*

coil form or tube. The center coil is the primary, which induces a voltage in each of two secondary coils, wound in opposite directions, on either side of it. The magnetic core is free to move axially inside the assembly as a result of a displacement.

When the primary coil is energized by alternating current, voltages are induced in the two secondary coils. Since these coils are connected in *series opposition*, the two voltages in the secondary circuit are opposite in phase. The resulting output of the transformer circuit is thus the difference between the two voltages. In the null, or balance, position the movable magnetic core is at a central point. If, now, the core is moved from the null position, owing to displacement variation, the voltage induced in the secondary coil will either increase or decrease according to the direction of the displacement change. In measuring systems, the transformer is designed to produce a differential-voltage output which varies linearly (Fig. 14-13b).

When the LVDT output is connected to an amplifier grid input, vacuum-tube voltmeter, or other high-impedance load, a high output voltage is required. For this reason, the secondary coil is wound with many turns to produce a large open-circuit voltage. Many differential transformers are actuated by direct current, because there is a built-in converter for changing the d-c to a-c excitation and there is a demodulator for supplying a d-c output. The entire device is compact, occupying only about half a cubic inch.

Applications. The linear-variable differential transformer can be used as a transducer to measure other variables having the characteristic of force, such as pressure, weight, or acceleration. A variety of designs, assemblies, and techniques are available to meet the demands of research and industry. To select one, the accelerometer is a good example which employs the LVDT.

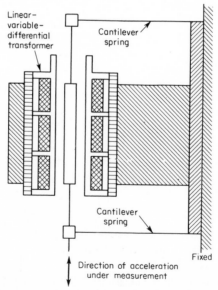

Fig. 14-14   A linear-variable differential transformer used to measure acceleration. (Schaevitz Engineering)

Accelerometer. In accordance with Newton's basic law of motion,

Force (F) = mass (m) × acceleration (a)

the elastic deformation of the sensitive measuring element, instead of being produced directly by an external force, may be a function of acceleration. Schaevitz Engineering manufactures the accelerometer shown in Fig. 14-14.

The secondary-circuit output signal, which can be picked up by any of the conventional measuring circuits described in this and preceding sections, is a function of the displacement of the movable magnetic core caused by acceleration. Accelerometers of the base-mounting type, capable of withstanding the extreme conditions of missile testing, operate on a similar principle.

REVIEW QUESTIONS AND PROBLEMS

14-1 Give examples of three common transducers and indicate the energy conversion in each case.

14-2 What is a strain gauge? Describe several applications and the basic theory of operation.

14-3 Identify three crystalline substances used in piezoelectric transducers. What is the energy conversion in such transducers?

14-4 Describe, by means of a simple diagram, a linear-variable differential transformer.

CHAPTER FIFTEEN

Humidity, dew point, and moisture measurement

The moderns have endeavored to subject the phenomena of nature to the laws of mathematics.

ISAAC NEWTON

Importance of Humidity Measurement

The moisture content of the atmosphere is of vital importance in many industrial processes, among them the manufacture of textiles, tobacco, paper, soap powders, chemical solvents, fertilizers, and wood products. Humidity measurement and control are necessary during many processes, e.g., the drying of chemicals such as benzene before chlorination. A major application of humidity measurement and control is in heating and air-conditioning systems.

Psychrometry is the name given to the study of the thermal dynamics of man's environmental atmosphere through the measurement of several variables, one of which is humidity.

Humidity of the atmosphere is a measure of the water vapor present in the air. It could be considered as the degree of dampness of the air. The problem of comfort during a hot, muggy day, referred to as a "humid day," is familiar to everyone.

Dry air is theoretically a mixture of gases that has a representative volumetric analysis, in percent, as given in Table 15-1. In practice, however, atmospheric air is never dry, because an important component of the normal air mixture is water vapor.

The *dew point* is that temperature at which the water vapor present in the air saturates the air and begins to condense; i.e., dew begins to form. If the temperature of the air is reduced below the dew point, the air remains saturated, although the partial pressure of the water vapor progressively decreases because of condensation.

Table 15-1   Composition of air

Gas	Volumetric analysis, %	Molecular fraction	Molecular weight
O_2	20.99	0.2099	32.00
N_2	78.03	0.7803	28.016
A	0.94	0.0094	39.944
CO_2	0.03	0.0003	44.003
H_2	0.01	0.0001	2.016
	100.00	1.000	

At night, after a very hot, humid day, the air cools, and it is possible for the humidity to reach 100 percent. Further cooling will cause the moisture to precipitate from the air. It is this condition that causes dew to form on anything left out at night. If the dew point is below 32°F (0°C), it is referred to as the *hoar-frost point*. The term "humidity" is also used to express the concentration of water vapor in gases.

Humidity Measurement

The amount of water vapor in the air may be expressed as relative humidity (a percent basis) or absolute humidity.

Relative humidity, %RH, Φ (phi). Relative humidity is defined as either (1) the ratio of the moisture content of the air to that which the air would have at the same temperature if saturated or (2) the ratio of actual water vapor pressure p_w in the air to the water vapor pressure in saturated air p_s at the same temperature. Since the perfect-gas laws are fairly accurate at the low pressures encountered with atmospheric air, the following equations hold true:

$$\text{RH} = \Phi = \frac{p_w}{p_s} = \frac{R_w T/v_s}{R_w T/v_w}$$
$$= \frac{v_s}{v_w} = \frac{\rho_w}{\rho_s} = \frac{W_w}{W_s}$$

where subscript w means water vapor and subscript s means saturated water vapor conditions. The symbols v_w and v_s indicate the respective specific volumes and ρ_w and ρ_s the respective mass densities. W_w and W_s are the corresponding weights. R_w is the specific gas constant for water vapor.

Dalton's law of partial pressures. If a liquid is allowed to evaporate into air at a pressure of, say, 76.00 cm Hg instead of into a vacuum, the rate of evaporation will be slower. However, the final saturated vapor pressure in air will be the same. From handbooks it can be found that the vapor pressure of water at 59°F (15°C) is 1.28 cm Hg. The resulting total pressure when the air is saturated will be 76.00 + 1.28 = 77.28 cm Hg. This illus-

what is referred to as Dalton's law of partial pressures, which is formally defined as follows: If two gases or vapors occupy a space, each exerts the same pressure that it would exert in that space if the other were absent. With this in mind, if the water vapor exerts a pressure p_w and if the pressure of the air is p_a, then the total pressure of the air is

$$p_{total} = p_w + p_a$$

Under such circumstances each part is said to exert a partial pressure, i.e., the pressure that each component would exert if it alone occupied the space. Symbolically,

$$\%\text{RH} = \frac{p_w}{p_s} \times 100\%$$

where p_w = partial pressure due to the water vapor in the air at any particular temperature

p_s = partial pressure due to the water vapor under saturated conditions at the same temperature

Absolute humidity. Absolute humidity is defined as the actual quantity of water present in a given volume of air. It is expressed either in grains of water per cubic foot of air or grams per cubic meter. Absolute humidity is not generally used in industrial process work. Relative humidity gives adequate information for indicating, recording, and process control purposes.

Specific humidity. Specific humidity is defined as the ratio of the mass of water vapor to the mass of dry air in a mixture. It is expressed either as grains of moisture per pound of dry air or pounds of moisture per pound of dry air. *Note:* 1 grain = $\frac{1}{7,000}$ lb. Specific humidity is used in North America, particularly in heating and air-conditioning computations. The graph in Fig. 15-1 indicates the maximum amount of water or moisture which can be held by air at various temperatures at a constant pressure of 29.92 in. Hg. Note that the relationship of moisture to temperature is not a linear function. As the temperature increases, the air can have a larger water vapor content.

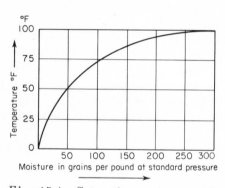

Fig. 15-1   Saturation moisture with temperature.

Methods for Measuring Relative Humidity

The first humidity sensor (a device which responds to a change in any controlled medium by a reproducible change of its properties) was built by Leonardo da Vinci in the fifteenth century. All he used was a piece of wool or cotton which increased in weight as it absorbed moisture from the atmosphere. Since then, hygromechanical elements have been made for humidity measurement and control. Modern requirements are speed, high sensitivity, and nonmechanical components. Electronic and dew-point sensors have been designed and manufactured to meet these requirements. Relative humidity can be measured by either of two basic instruments, namely, the hygrometer and the psychrometer.

Hygrometers

The hygrometer is a device which utilizes the physical or electrical change of certain materials as they absorb moisture.

Hygroscopic materials. The crystals of certain substances such as calcium chloride and lithium chloride have the property of absorbing water from or giving it up to the surrounding atmosphere until a state of equilibrium is reached. The degree of absorption depends upon the amount of water vapor present in the atmosphere, i.e. the relative humidity.

Chemical type of hygrometer. In accordance with the definition of relative humidity, the equation

$$\text{RH} = \frac{p_w}{p_s} = \frac{W_w}{W_s}$$

suggests a possible laboratory method for determining %RH by measuring the weight of water vapor actually present in a measured volume of air and then finding the weight necessary to saturate the same volume at the same temperature. In the operation of a simple chemical hygrometer a known quantity of air is first drawn through tubes containing a drying agent such as phosphorus pentoxide. These tubes are weighed before and after each test, and the difference in weight is equal to the water vapor absorbed. The same quantity of air is then passed through tubes containing glass wool which has sufficient water to saturate the air. In turn, the air passes through a second group of drying tubes which, as in the first case, are weighed before and after each test run. The difference in weight in the last test is the weight of water vapor required to saturate the air.

By using the equation

$$\%\text{RH} = \frac{W_w}{W_s} \times 100\%$$

with temperature constant, the percent of relative humidity can be computed. However, the procedure described, although quite interesting and academic, may be impractical for any modern industrial process, particularly if the humidity is fluctuating at frequent intervals.

Hair hygrometer. It has been found that human hair possesses the necessary property for changing its dimensions, particularly its length, with the variation in moisture content of the air. This type of hygrometer is the most common instrument for domestic use.

Psychrometers

Basically, the psychrometer is a device that registers the temperature difference between two primary sensing elements, one of them kept wet so that moisture is continuously being evaporated from its surface and the other kept dry.

Wet- and dry-bulb psychrometer. When water changes from liquid to vapor, heat is required (in the form of latent heat) to carry out the conversion. Provided the system is one in which heat is not readily able to reach the evaporating surface from the surroundings, the temperature of the surface will fall. This temperature drop is related to the water vapor pressure in the surrounding atmosphere.

By using the above facts it is possible to construct a humidity-measuring device known as the wet- and dry-bulb psychrometer. It consists of two identical thermometers, as shown in Fig. 15-2. The bulb of one ther-

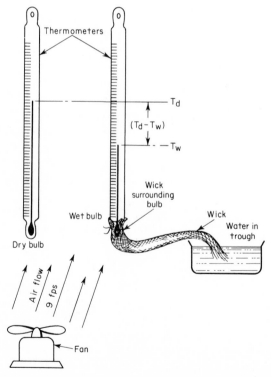

Fig. 15-2   The simple wet- and dry-bulb psychrometer.

mometer surrounded by a tight-fitting cotton wick dips into a bowl of water. This is referred to as the wet-bulb thermometer. Distilled or demineralized water should be used to avoid lime formation. The other thermometer, in an adjacent position, is referred to as the dry-bulb thermometer.

Dry-bulb temperature (DB or T_d) is the surrounding temperature taken without regard to humidity. It is the actual room or ambient temperature. Wet-bulb temperature (WB or T_w) is the minimum temperature attained by a thermometer with a wet-cloth-covered bulb in a 9 ft/sec airstream. The absolute or relative humidity can be readily determined from DB and WB readings by using a psychrometric chart.

The evaporation of water from the wick of the wet-bulb thermometer will reduce the temperature T_w below the dry-bulb temperature T_d by an amount which depends on the humidity of the air. The air can absorb so much water at a certain temperature and no more. Table 15-2 shows a range of RH values corresponding to T_d and T_w readings. If the tempera-

Table 15-2   Percent relative humidity

T_d, °F	\% RH when $T_d - T_w$, °F, is													
	1	2	3	4	5	6	7	8	9	10	11	12	13	14
30	89	78	67	56	46	36	26	16	6	0	0			
35	91	81	72	63	54	45	36	27	19	10	2	0		
40	92	83	75	68	60	52	45	37	29	22	15	7	0	0
45	93	86	78	71	64	57	51	44	38	31	25	18	12	6
50	93	87	81	74	67	61	55	49	43	38	32	27	21	16
55	94	88	82	76	70	65	59	54	49	43	38	33	28	23
60	94	89	83	78	73	68	63	58	53	48	43	39	34	30
65	95	90	85	80	74	70	66	61	56	52	48	44	39	35
70	95	90	86	81	77	72	68	64	59	55	51	48	44	40
75	96	91	86	82	78	74	70	66	62	58	54	51	47	44
80	96	91	87	83	79	75	72	68	64	61	57	54	50	47
85	96	92	88	84	80	76	73	70	66	63	59	56	53	50
90	96	92	89	85	81	78	74	71	68	65	61	58	55	52
95	96	93	89	85	82	80	75	72	69	66	63	60	57	54
100	96	93	89	86	83	80	77	73	70	68	65	62	59	56
102	96	93	89	86	83	80	77	74	71	69	65	62	59	57
104	96	93	90	86	83	80	77	74	71	69	65	63	60	58
106	96	93	90	87	83	80	77	74	72	69	66	63	60	58

tures are measured in degrees Celsius, they should then be converted to degrees Fahrenheit by using the equation

$$°F = \tfrac{9}{5}°C + 32$$

Consider the following example, in which the humidity-temperature tables are used.

Example. If the dry-bulb temperature is 80°F and the wet-bulb temperature is 70°F, determine, by means of Table 15-2, the relative humidity.

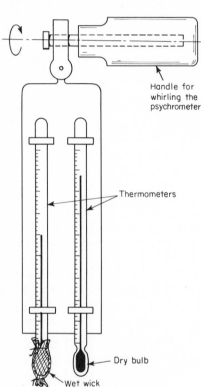

Solution $T_d - T_w = 80°F - 70°F$
$$= 10°F$$

From Table 15-2, at the intersection of the temperature difference $T_d - T_w = 10°F$ and $T_d = 80°F$, the RH value is 61 percent.

The sling or whirling psychrometer. The sling psychrometer (Fig. 15-3) consists of two mercury-in-glass thermometers securely fastened to a frame pivoted on a handle. The wet-bulb assembly with its cotton wick is so constructed that it cannot spill during operation. The frame is rotated at a specified rate by hand, and the movement of the thermometer bulbs through the air produces the required relative air velocity of about 9 ft/sec. The relative humidity can be found from the humidity chart when the wet- and dry-bulb temperatures have been read.

Fig. 15-3   The sling psychrometer.

Industrial Methods

Two-pen recorders. The thermometers used in humidity measurement need not be limited to the mercury-filled type, although mercury thermometers are more suitable for single-point installation. Mercury-in-steel thermometers have the advantage of incorporating devices for continuous display or recording purposes. These are common requirements of measuring systems when important process-plant data must be logged.

The humidity recorder has two pens which move over a chart graduated in degrees temperature. The pens record the wet-bulb temperature and dry-bulb temperature in different-colored inks. All that is required to determine the %RH is to note the T_d and $T_d - T_w$ values and then refer to the humidity-temperature tables or psychrometric chart. Figure 15-4

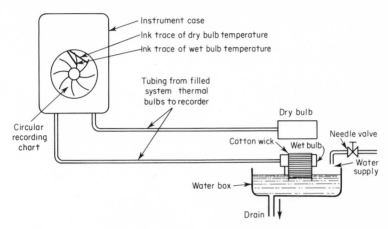

Fig. 15-4   Basic principle of humidity-measuring system.

shows the schematic arrangement of a humidity recorder using two separate identically filled system thermometers (thermal bulbs).

Electrical techniques. Electrical resistance thermometers and thermocouples also are used in the measurement of humidity. They have the advantages, apart from multipoint installation, of incorporating transmitting, recording, and controlling devices in the measuring system. The normal procedure of operation is to have the thermometers connected to one arm of a Wheatstone bridge and balanced at one temperature on the other arm. The wet and dry bulbs are switched in turn to the instrument and the temperatures are recorded. The relative humidity can then be found from the values in Table 15-2. In recording instruments the switching is performed automatically.

An instrument reading directly in terms of %RH is desirable, and an electrical resistance type of sensing element and double-bridge-circuit arrangement may be used for this purpose. In one circuit, the wet and dry bulbs form opposite arms. The out-of-balance current depends on the relative values of these two temperatures, i.e., T_d and T_w, and is a measure of the difference $T_d - T_w$. The second bridge measures the dry-bulb temperature T_d only, and the outputs from these two Wheatstone bridges are taken to a cross-coil type of galvanometer, one coil being affected by $T_d - T_w$ and the other by T_d. The steady position of the pointer indicates the relative humidity on a calibrated scale. The accuracy of such an instrument may be in the region of 3 percent. The general arrangement of the double-bridge circuit is shown in Fig. 15-5; the out-of-balance current is a measure of the RH.

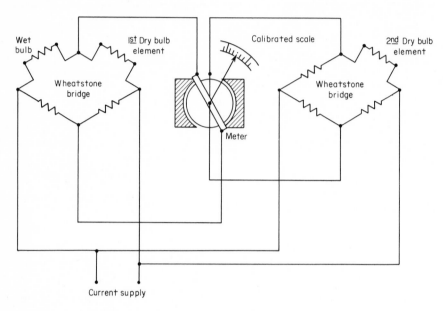

Fig. 15-5 Electrical resistance type of wet and dry bulb, direct-reading humidity instrument.

The use of transducers. Other electrical humidity devices and hygrometers use transducers which convert humidity or moisture variations into electrical resistance. A selection of systems incorporating transducers will be described briefly in this and subsequent sections. In one type of electrical hygrometer the amount of electric current depends upon the amount of moisture absorbed. The transducer is connected to the conventional bridge circuit; its resistance may be related to absolute or relative humidity.

Honeywell offers a relative-humidity sensor consisting of gold-leaf electrode grids applied to an insulating plate. A humidity-sensitive film is applied to the plate. This film carries an alternating measuring current between the electrodes. The resistance of the film is a function of the amount of active salt (LiCl) in the film and of the ambient RH. Single sensors can be used in bridge networks for control, or composite sensors of two to ten individual elements can be used in more elaborate circuits to give direct readout of RH.

Generally, many fabrics have a high value of electrical resistance (low conductivity) when they are dry and a much lower value when moist. This difference in resistance is thus a measure of moisture left in the material. The measurement may be made by passing the fabric or similar hygroscopic material between probes or rollers, making contact with the material under observation. Figure 15-6 shows a schematic arrangement of such a moisture meter.

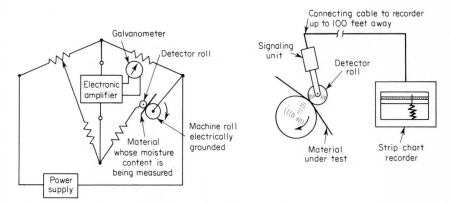

Fig. 15-6   An industrial moisture meter circuit. A small electric current passes from the detector roll through the material whose moisture content is being measured to the ground machine roll. The resistance of the material is used as the unknown resistance in the Wheatstone bridge circuit. The potentiometer in the recorder is calibrated in moisture-content values. (Honeywell, Inc.)

Dew-point instruments. The dew point, as mentioned earlier in this chapter, is defined as the temperature at which the partial pressure of water vapor in the atmosphere or other gas equals the saturation vapor pressure. The dew point is also referred to as the temperature to which the medium must be reduced for water to commence condensing from it.

There are a variety of different dew-point-measuring devices on the market, of which the Foxboro Dewcel hygrometer is one. The dew-point-measuring system consists of a humidity-sensitive cell, a power unit for furnishing the proper current to the Dewcel element, and a recorder, indicator, or controller with scales normally calibrated in dew-point temperature. The principle of operation is, briefly, as follows. Moisture determination by the element is based on the fact that, for every water vapor pressure in contact with a saturated salt solution, there is an equilibrium temperature at which this solution neither absorbs moisture from nor gives up moisture to the surrounding atmosphere. Below this equilibrium temperature the salt solution absorbs moisture. Above this temperature, the saturated salt solution dries out until only dry crystals remain.

The actual Dewcel element consists of a tube on which is wound a glass tape impregnated with lithium chloride. Over this glass tape is wound, in turn, a pair of gold wires parallel to but not touching each other. A 25-volt a-c supply is connected to these wires. Current can pass between the wires but only through the lithium chloride solution in the tape. If there is an increase in the relative humidity, it must be accompanied by an increase in the partial pressure of the water vapor in the atmosphere, and this becomes greater than the vapor pressure of the lithium chloride solution. The result is that water vapor condenses into the solution and dilutes it. The resistance is reduced and an increased current flows between the two wires. This produces an increased heating effect, which raises the temperature of a sensitive element (normally an electrical resistance element) inside the tube on which the tape is wound. The temperature detected is used as a measure of dew-point temperature, absolute humidity, or vapor pressure. Figure 15-7 shows a simple arrangement of the Dewcel measuring system.

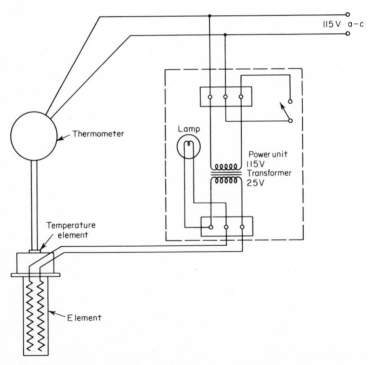

Fig. 15-7   Schematic diagram of a Foxboro "Dewcel" hygrometer. (The Foxboro Company Limited)

Electrolytic hygrometer. Beckman Instruments manufactures an electrolytic hygrometer which provides an efficient and practical means for detecting traces of water in gases. In one design the cell consists of a tube with a pair of closely spaced platinum wires wound in a double helix on its inner surface. In the space between the wires is a film of phosphorous pentoxide, and a d-c voltage is applied to the unit.

A sample of gas containing moisture is passed through the cell. The moisture is absorbed by the phosphorous pentoxide and electrolyzed into hydrogen and oxygen ions. The result is an electrolysis current with a magnitude that is proportional to the mass rate of flow of moisture into the meter. The rate of flow of the gas sample is kept constant by means of a flow controller in the sample line after the cell.

The instrument can be calibrated in parts of water per million parts of gas. The hygrometer is also an accurate analyzer for measuring dew point of gases. A typical arrangement of an electrolytic hygrometer measuring system is shown in Fig. 15-8.

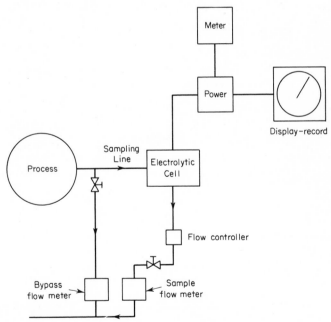

Fig. 15-8 An electrolytic hygrometer measuring system. (Beckman Instruments Inc.)

The Psychrometric Chart

The Carrier Psychrometric Chart, Fig. 15-9, gives the relation between the variables that measure humidity, such as wet- and dry-bulb tempera-

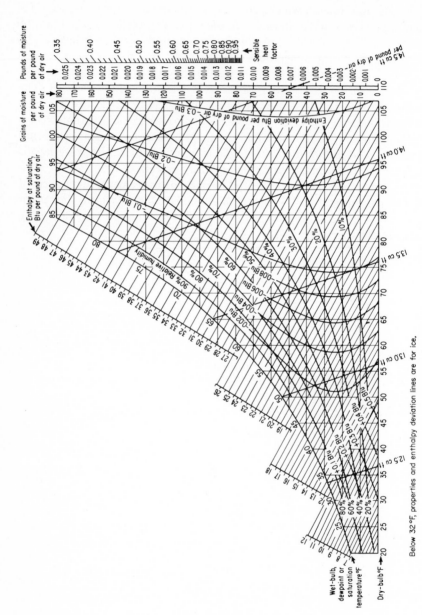

Fig. 15-9 Psychrometric chart. (Carrier Corporation)

Below 32°F, properties and enthalpy deviation lines are for ice.

tures, dew point, %RH, and grains of moisture per pound of dry air at a specified atmospheric pressure. If some of the variables are known, the chart can be used to determine the others.

Example. If the wet-bulb temperature WB (saturation or dew-point temperature) is 60°F and the dry-bulb temperature DB is 70°F, determine the %RH, dew point, and grains of moisture per pound of dry air.

Solution. First locate the point of intersection on the chart of the vertical line representing 70°F DB and the oblique line representing 60°F WB. From this point all the other values are read. By interpolating between the humidity lines on the 70°F DB line, read RH equal to 56 percent, follow the horizontal line left to the saturation curve, and read the dew point equal to 53.6°F. Follow the horizontal line to the right, and read the grains of moisture per pound of dry air, that is, 61.4 grains.

REVIEW QUESTIONS AND PROBLEMS

15-1 Define the following terms: (a) dew point, (b) relative humidity, (c) specific humidity, (d) partial water vapor pressure, and (e) dry- and wet-bulb temperatures.

15-2 If the partial pressure of water vapor in the atmosphere is found to be 12.5 mm Hg at 68°F and the saturation pressure is 17.5 mm Hg, calculate the percent relative humidity.

15-3 If the weight of vapor at saturation conditions is 1.9×10^{-3} lb/ft³ of air, compute the corresponding weight of the water vapor at a relative humidity of 0.72.

15-4 (a) Why should the water supply used in industrial psychrometers be at the ambient temperature?
(b) Why is it that at higher temperatures the atmosphere will have a larger moisture content than at lower temperatures?
(c) Plot a graph to show temperature against moisture content.

15-5 If the wet-bulb or saturation temperature is 60°F and the dry-bulb temperature is 70°F, find the percent relative humidity. Reference should be made to psychrometric tables or chart.

15-6 Discuss the importance of humidity measurement and control in any industrial process you know.

15-7 Describe, briefly, the construction and operation of a wet- and dry-bulb hygrometer.

15-8 (a) What does a psychrometric chart describe?
(b) What is the function of the hygroscopic film or coating on a dew-point-sensing element?
(c) What is the difference between a hygrometer and a psychrometer?

15-9   As a future instrument technologist, make a brief technical report on two different types of direct-reading relative-humidity instruments available on the market. Explain their relative merits.

15-10   Describe the operation and construction of any electronic relative-humidity or dew-point sensor.

15-11   The temperature in a room is 80°F, and the relative humidity is 30 percent. Calculate (a) the partial pressure of the steam and the dew point, (b) the density of each component, and (c) the specific humidity. The barometer reading is 29.92 mm Hg. Reference should be made to steam tables.

CHAPTER SIXTEEN

Electrochemical measurements

The scientific principles required in engineering are relatively few, but they must be well known. The difficulties usually encountered are in their application.

JOHN PERRY

THE MEASUREMENT OF pH, SOLUTION POTENTIAL, AND CONDUCTIVITY

In this section are described the basic principles and applications of sensing elements and instruments used in the measurement of pH, solution oxidation-reduction potential (abbreviated redox), and electrical conductivity. The success of many research and industrial projects—chemical, medical, and bacteriological processes—depends on the accurate measurement and control of acidity or alkalinity.

pH Measurement

The degree of acidity or alkalinity is denoted by using a scale, referred to as the pH scale, of the common logarithms of the numerical values of hydrogen-ion concentration. That is, the pH is the exponent or power of the logarithm base 10. A detailed explanation and derivation of the pH scale is given in a later paragraph in this section. Before one can readily accept the pH scale and its application, the basic chemistry involved must be understood.

Chemical fundamentals. Elements exist either in a pure state or in chemical combinations, called *compounds*, with other elements. An example of a compound is sodium chloride. Each element is composed of minute particles called atoms, which differ in weight from the atoms of other elements. For example, an atom of oxygen weighs approximately 16 times as much as an atom of hydrogen. The atomic weight of any element is determined by using carbon 12 as a reference standard.

Atoms normally exist not in a free state, but in combination with other atoms of the same or of different elements. The basic combination of two or more atoms is referred to as a molecule. A molecule of hydrogen contains two hydrogen atoms. One molecule of water is a combination of two hydrogen atoms with one oxygen atom, which can be shown in chemical symbols as the molecular equation

$$2H_2 + O_2 \rightleftharpoons 2H_2O$$

The molecular weight of a compound is the sum of the atomic weights of all the elements that are combined to form the basic molecule. Consider the case of water, which has a molecular weight of

$$(2 \times 1.008) + 16 = 18.016$$

where the atomic weight of hydrogen is 1.008.

In spite of their infinitesimal size, atoms themselves consist of smaller particles: a nucleus and orbiting electrons. An electron possesses a negative electrical charge, and each kind of atom has a definite number of electrons. The atom also has an equal number of positive particles, called protons, in the nucleus; and the protons maintain electrical neutrality.

Atoms can combine to form molecules in two ways. Covalent bonding involves the sharing of outer-orbit electrons among the constituent atoms of a molecule. In this type of bonding, every electron pair corresponds to a single valence bond. Electrovalent bonding involves the outright transfer of one or more electrons from one atom to another. This type of atomic interaction is called *electrovalent* because of the electrostatic nature of the binding force. Molecules which have been formed in this way will separate into the component atoms when subjected to certain influences. The molecules, when breaking apart, tend to group together in such a way that no voids or gaps occur in the configuration of their outer electron orbits.

Ionization. Ionization of the electrovalent type of molecule often occurs. To cause ionization, the molecule must be subjected to the proper influences such as a very high temperature, a strong electric charge, combustion, or dissolution in a solvent such as water. An atom which loses electrons is positively charged, and an atom which accepts electrons is negatively charged. These electrically charged groups are referred to as *ions*. Their formation is called ionization. A positive ion, in solution, is attracted to a cathode, which is a negatively charged electrode. A negative ion, in solution, is attracted to an anode, which is a positively charged electrode.

By way of explanation, sulfuric acid is made from sulfur trioxide and water as indicated by the equation

$$H_2O + SO_3 \rightleftharpoons H_2SO_4$$

Now, when sulfuric acid is dissolved in water, it ionizes to form hydrogen ions, indicated by the positive sign, and sulfate ions, indicated by the negative sign. Using chemical symbols, the reaction is written

$$H_2SO_4 \rightleftharpoons 2H^+ + SO_4^{--}$$

During the ionizing phase, each hydrogen atom loses one electron, thus becoming positively charged. The sulfate group acquires or gains one electron from each of the two hydrogen atoms, thus becoming negatively charged.

Many compounds, however, do not ionize when dissolved in water. Sucrose dissolves in water, but its molecules remain whole and electrically neutral. Compounds such as sucrose are formed by covalent bonding of the atoms.

Acids, bases, and salts. Acids, bases, and salts ionize when dissolved in water. The solutions they form are called *electrolytes* or *electrolytic solutions*. Ionization also occurs when chemicals are dissolved in liquids other than water, but this aspect of ionization will not be dealt with here. Ionization is a continuous process and, in the case of a water solution of sulfuric acid, hydrogen and sulfate ions are constantly recombining to form acid molecules. Acid molecules, in turn, are constantly breaking down into ions. Under steady-state conditions, this reaction continues until the number of molecules being formed equals the number being ionized. The number of ions in a solution at equilibrium depends upon three very important factors:

1. The nature of the dissolved compound is important, because chemical compounds do not yield the same number of ions. Electrolytes are highly ionized, whereas nonelectrolytes may contain only a few ions in solution.
2. The concentration of the dissolved compound is important, because the total number of ions in a solution is not in direct proportion to the quantity of compound in it. Doubling the amount of electrolytic chemical in a solution does not double the number of ions present in solution.
3. The temperature of the solution influences the number of ions in the solution. In general, the number of ions in a solution at equilibrium increases as the temperature increases.

The pH scale. The Danish biochemist, Sven Sorenson, in 1909, suggested the use of the pH scale as a measure of the hydrogen-ion concentration in a solution. He wrote in French, using the p from the word *puissance*, meaning power in the mathematical sense. The H stands for H^+ ion. He indicated that the logarithm of the number of gram equivalents of hydrogen could be adopted to express hydrogen-ion concentration. It should be recalled that the logarithm of a number is the power to which the base 10 must be raised in order to equal the number. Expressed mathematically,

$$\log_{10} 1,000 = 3$$

because, by definition, $10^3 = 1,000$.

In most solutions the hydrogen-ion concentration is a fraction, and the logarithm for it is a negative number. Sorenson proposed a new symbol to avoid the negative sign. He suggested the symbol pH to mean the negative of the logarithm (or the logarithm of the reciprocal) of the hydrogen-ion concentration. Mathematically, the expression is

$$pH = -\log_{10}[H^+] = \log \frac{1}{[H^+]}$$

$$[H^+] = 10^{-pH}$$

where the brackets indicate concentration of the things they enclose. For example, the hydrogen-ion concentration of pure water at 25°C is 0.0000001, or 1.0×10^{-7}. The pH value of water becomes

$$pH = -\log_{10}[H^+] = \frac{1}{\log_{10} 10^7} = \frac{1}{7}$$

Thus the pH value for water is 7.

The hydrogen-ion concentration of ammonium hydroxide is 0.0000000000231, and the pH of ammonium hydroxide is

$$\frac{1}{\log_{10} (2.31 \times 10^{+11})} = \frac{1}{11.364}$$

or 11.364.

A comparison of pH and acidity of some common materials is given in Table 16-1, which is taken from the Bristol Product Data No. Q 1310-2, *A primer on pH*, issued by the Bristol Company.

Effect of temperature on pH. Hydrogen ion concentration generally increases with temperature, but the relation is not linear. The pH-temperature coefficient varies with the material. Acid solutions normally have small temperature coefficients and alkaline solutions normally have large pH-temperature coefficients, since the H^+ ion of alkaline solutions comes from water and water has a relatively high pH-temperature coefficient. For example, the pH value of pure water at 25°C is 7.00, whereas at 100°C it becomes 6.09.

Methods for Measuring pH

Two distinct methods are used to measure or determine the pH of a solution; they are the color effect and the electrode method. The color effect is based on the change of color of indicators over small ranges of the pH

Table 16-1   *Comparison of pH and acidity of common materials*

Acidity (Normality of free H$^+$ ion)		pH	Approximate pH of common materials
0.00000000000001	10^{-14}	14.0	— Sodium hydroxide (1.0 N)
0.0000000000001	10^{-13}	13.0	— Sodium hydroxide (0.1 N)
0.000000000001	10^{-12}	12.0	— Lime (saturated solution) — Copper cyanide plating bath — Household ammonia (10%)
0.00000000001	10^{-11}	11.0	— Ammonium hydroxide (0.1 N) — Washing soda (1%) — Milk of magnesia
0.0000000001	10^{-10}	10.0	— Soap solutions — Very alkaline natural soil
0.000000001	10^{-9}	9.0	— Borax solutions (0.1 to 10%)
0.00000001	10^{-8}	8.0	— Seawater — Baking soda (1%) — Fresh eggs — Human blood plasma
0.0000001	10^{-7}	7.0	— Theoretically pure water — Fresh milk
0.000001	10^{-6}	6.0	— Corn — Distilled water after standing in air — Nickel plating bath
0.00001	10^{-5}	5.0	— Molasses — Boric acid (0.1 N) — Hydrochloric acid (0.00001 N)
0.0001	10^{-4}	4.0	— Beer — Tomatoes — Very acid natural soil — Orange juice — Wines
0.001	10^{-3}	3.0	— Pickles — Fruit jellies — Grapefruit juice — Vinegar (4% acetic acid) — Ginger ale
0.01	10^{-2}	2.0	— Alum (0.1 N) — Lemon juice — Hydrochloric acid (0.01 N) — Gastric (stomach) fluids — Lime juice — Phosphoric acid (0.1 N)
0.1	10^{-1}	1.0	— Sulfuric acid (0.1 N) — Hydrochloric acid (0.1 N)
1.0	10^{-0}	0.0	— Sulfuric acid (1.0 N) — Hydrochloric acid (1.0 N) — Hydrochloric acid (10.0 N)
10.0	10^{+1}	−1.0	

Bases (pH 14.0 – 7.0)

Acids (pH 7.0 – −1.0)

Source : The Bristol Co.

scale. The method using the color effect is quite satisfactory when an accuracy not exceeding 0.2 pH is required. No instruments are involved and therefore no details are necessary. The electrode method permits continuous recording and control of the pH of a flowing chemical solution or process. The pH instrument is based on the fact that a solution containing hydrogen ions will determine the potential of a suitable electrode immersed in the solution. The potential produced is a measure of the hydrogen-ion concentration and, in turn, the pH value of the solution.

Electrode elements. The electrodes form part of a closed electrical circuit which includes the solution whose pH is being measured and also the measuring instrument. The positive electrode produces a change in voltage proportional to the hydrogen-ion concentration of the solution in which it is immersed. The other electrode remains at a constant voltage. The common sensing electrode is the glass silver chloride electrode, the silver–silver chloride electrode being used as the reference electrode.

A schematic arrangement of the circuit used for pH measurement is shown in Fig. 16-1. The voltage produced by the two electrodes is applied

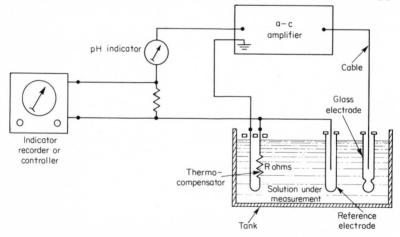

Fig. 16-1   Simple circuit diagram for pH measurement.

as the input to a null-balance millivolt potentiometer similar to that described in connection with thermocouples. Incorporated in the circuit is a temperature-compensating resistor which is immersed in the chemical solution or process. Its resistance change with solution temperature corrects the pH measurement for the operating temperature.

The silver–silver chloride (reference) electrode is made up of silver, silver chloride, and a solution of potassium chloride. The silver–silver chloride internals have a high stability in high-temperature solutions.

The potential of this half-cell is determined by the concentration of the potassium chloride solution.

The measuring or sensitive electrodes used with the reference electrode are as follows: (1) the glass electrode, (2) the hydrogen electrode, (3) the quinhydrone electrode, and (4) the antimony electrode. The glass electrode is used widely because it covers practically all ranges of pH, and it will be discussed here. The general theory of its operation is based on the fact that, when two solutions of different hydrogen-ion concentration are separated by a thin membrane of glass, an electrical potential which is a function of the difference in solution concentrations is set up.

If the pH of one of the solutions is known, the pH of the other solution can be found by measuring the difference in potential. The glass electrode has a high electrical resistance, of the order of 10^9 ohms, which may not be easily detected on millivolt meters of low sensitivity. For this reason, special potentiometers which incorporate vacuum-tube amplifying are an aid in detecting the unbalance. Figure 16-2 shows the general details of

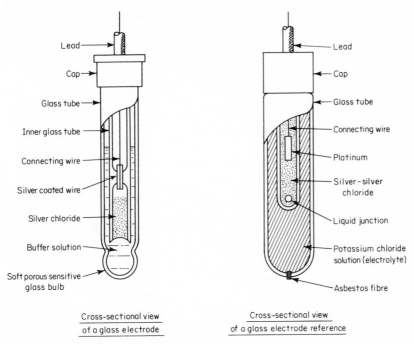

Lead	Lead
Cap	Cap
Glass tube	Glass tube
Inner glass tube	Connecting wire
Connecting wire	Platinum
Silver coated wire	Silver-silver chloride
Silver chloride	Liquid junction
Buffer solution	Potassium chloride solution (electrolyte)
Soft porous sensitive glass bulb	Asbestos fibre

Cross-sectional view
of a glass electrode

Cross-sectional view
of a glass electrode reference

Fig. 16-2   General details of glass electrodes.

typical glass electrodes. When the instrument is required for continuous-recording purposes, the null type of recording potentiometer is used. The instrument is graduated from 0 to 14 in order to cover the pH range.

Solid-state pH meter. Measurement of the pH of plant processes may not have been used in the past as often as it could have been used, the main reason being the difficulty in maintaining a high resistance between the reference probe and the glass electrode. The glass electrode and part of the meter circuit must be insulated from the ground by at least 1.0×10^5 megohms. However, even moderate humidity can cause the formation of a water film and thus lower the resistance. Fumes and dust can also lower the resistance.

The glass electrode gives the most accurate measurement of pH. Other electrodes, particularly the antimony electrode, have been used, but they have disadvantages which outweigh both the fragility and resistance disadvantages of the glass electrode. When using solid-state electronics, a point to keep in mind is the advantage of placing the pH meter or its high-resistance circuit with the electrode. The inaccessibility of the solid-state circuits has been found acceptable also because they require little maintenance and no periodic adjustment. The circuit diagram of a solid-state pH meter is shown in Fig. 16-3.

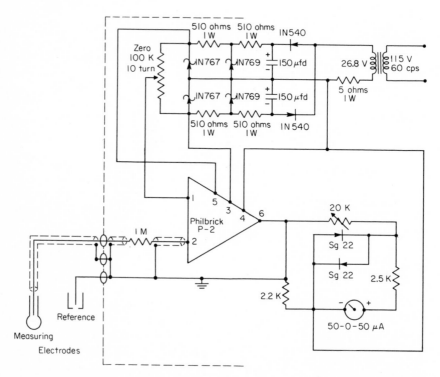

Fig. 16-3   Circuit diagram of solid-state pH meter. (Rohm & Haas of Canada Limited)

Control equipment. High-impedance d-c power amplifiers, instead of deflectional instruments, are required for pH measurement, because the measuring instrument must not draw any appreciable current from the electrodes. Any current flow tends to cause polarization at the electrodes, which immediately disturbs the accuracy of measurement. Pneumatic and electrical control equipment which is available for thermocouple potentiometric control circuits can also be used to serve pH control schemes. A typical control scheme is shown in Fig. 16-4.

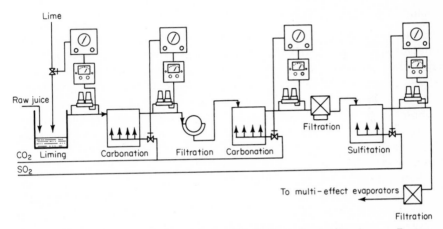

Fig. 16-4 Beet sugar refining; simplified flow sheet. (Beckman Instruments Inc.)

Application notes. The instrument engineer and technician should not attempt to use an electrode element for pH beyond its calibrated scale. If a pH-measuring system is properly selected and its installation is in accordance with recommended instrument and engineering practice, the measurement will be accurate and reliable. Owing to the high-resistance circuit normally employed in pH-measuring instruments, installation in atmosphere containing large quantities of moisture, dust, and corrosive gases must be avoided. When installation in a contaminated atmosphere is unavoidable, every precaution should be taken to protect the measuring system.

No pH-measuring or control system can operate properly unless the solution is of a homogenous nature. Careful consideration must be given to the design of the mechanical mixing equipment involved. In general, measuring electrodes when first put into service undergo a slight change over a period of time. For this reason they must be checked frequently until they stabilize. The change is caused by the glass absorbing some of the chemical solution; also, the glass itself is very slowly dissolved. If the process liquid contaminates the probes by coating them with sludge or scum, they should be washed with tap water. On no account should distilled water be used, because it destroys the effectiveness of the electrode elements.

The installation and operations instructions booklet supplied with the pH equipment should be carefully read by all concerned with equipment application. Important precautions in the use of the equipment should be displayed for the attention of personnel.

Solution-potential Measurement

Oxidation-reduction (redox) potential measurement is similar to pH measurement in that both are associated with ions in solution. As described in earlier paragraphs, these ions, all electrically charged, have either a deficiency or excess of electrons and are termed positive or negative ions, respectively. Oxidation-reduction is generally characterized by a transfer of electrons between the reactants. Oxidation involves a loss of an electron or electrons, or an increase in positive charge. The presence of oxygen is not necessarily required. Reduction involves a gain of an electron or electrons, or a reduced positive charge.

Platinum-calomel electrodes. The elements used are usually the platinum and calomel electrodes. Other types of electrodes can be used for special applications. The elements are immersed in the solution. An electrical potential, depending upon the relative concentrations of oxidized and reduced ions, will result as electrical output signals. The potential developed indicates the equilibrium between the tendency of oxidized ions to acquire electrons from the metal electrode and thereby become reduced and the tendency for the reduced ions to give up electrons to the electrode. In many industrial processes redox measurement is the most reliable means by which the process can be controlled. It may not be the only one that can be used, but it should certainly be considered along with other measurements.

Conductivity Measurement

Redox and pH measurements depend on the properties of certain ions. Conductivity is influenced by all ions in solution. Conductance, as described in the section dealing with applied electricity and measuring circuits, is measured in mhos, which is the reciprocal of ohms. It should be recalled that one mho is defined as the conductance of a material through which one ampere flows at a potential difference of one volt.

Conductivity cells. Conductivity was referred to as the mhos measured between two electrodes exactly one centimeter square and separated by exactly one centimeter in a solution at a particular temperature. Electrodes are, however, manufactured larger or smaller than 1 cm square and separated by more than 1 cm. The relationship between such cells and the 1-cm² standard is referred to as the constant. The conductivity of the solution is then equivalent to the measured conductance times the cell constant.

A Wheatstone bridge circuit, as described and illustrated in the section dealing with measuring circuits, is the basis of operation of the measuring instrument. The instrument is used in conjunction with a means of compensating for temperature variations. The Bailey Meter Company manufactures a range of electrolytic-conductivity cells.

To retain the specified accuracy and sensitivity of the measuring system, the cells should be installed in locations free of mechanical vibration, corrosive gases, dust, and excessive humidity. Solution conductivity is very important in the pH measurement of boiler feed water, acids, and the condensate from evaporators. Conductivity cells are also used as the basis of some systems for regulating the level of liquids in storage tanks by operating the discharge pumps.

REVIEW QUESTIONS AND PROBLEMS

16-1   Define (a) ionization, (b) reference and measuring electrodes.

16-2   Describe Sorenson's method of establishing a pH scale.

16-3   Compute the pH value of a solution having a hydrogen-ion concentration of 2.3×10^{-11}.

16-4   With the aid of a schematic diagram describe the operation of an industrial pH-measuring and -control installation.

16-5   (a) Describe some of the applications of pH, redox, and conductivity-measuring instruments.

   (b) Sketch, in block diagrams, any measuring and control systems involving one of the instruments of part (a).

   (c) Mention some of the installation instructions, operating instructions, and precautions to be taken with each instrument mentioned in part (a) in order to retain the specified accuracy and sensitivity of the readings.

CHEMICAL COMPOSITION ANALYSIS

Theory of Chemical Composition Measurement

As stated in the first part of this chapter, all matter is comprised of a systematic arrangement of atoms consisting of neutrons, protons, and electrons. Neutrons and protons comprise the nuclei of atoms, and each nucleus is surrounded by orbiting electrons. The protons in this nucleus are positively charged, and the electrons are negatively charged. There will be a sufficient number of electrons in each atom to neutralize the positive charge on the nucleus. The total number of neutrons plus protons determines the atomic weight. Atoms combine to form molecules by sharing electrons. All combinations of atoms in a molecule of matter can be represented by a definite system of electron energy states. These energy states can best be understood by observing the results of interaction between the matter and an external source of energy, which may be of the following types:

(1) Electromagnetic radiation
(2) Chemical affinity
(3) Electrical or magnetic fields
(4) Thermal or mechanical energy

By measuring the results of this interaction between the matter under test and the applied energy state, it is possible to learn much about the chemical composition of the matter. It is beyond the scope of this book to elaborate further on the underlying theories involved, and only the more common applications and types of measuring equipment will be discussed.

Applications in Industry

Chemical-composition analysis is vitally important in nearly all of the continuous-process industries, and particularly so in the petrochemical industries. Incoming raw materials may be sampled to assure compliance with required chemical specifications or to optimize the yield and minimize production costs. In-process analysis is normally necessary at various stages to ensure that there will not be excessive waste at the end of the production process owing to failure to meet the final-product specification. Many analyzing instruments are now available to make continuous on-line measurements and thereby permit a fast response to the control mechanism which will adjust the appropriate input to bring the process back into control. This type of continuous analysis obviously permits much greater product through-put with less wastage than is possible with the more conventional batch-analysis technique.

Chemical-composition analysis is also employed to assure public health and safety, as in the case of municipal water-treatment and sewage-disposal plants and industrial plants emitting toxic liquids or gases. The objective in all cases is to determine what chemical elements are present or how much of one or more of several known elements are present. The former is referred to as qualitative analysis, the latter as quantitative analysis.

Methods of Analysis and Measurement

Emission spectrometry. Spectrometry is the science of measurement of wavelength position within a spectrum. If we regard the electrons in an atom as possessing definite energy levels of differing values, then when an electron passes from one level to another under an external influence, there will be either emission or absorption of energy according to the direction of change. A change from higher to lower levels is accompanied by emission of energy, and one from the lower to the higher levels by an absorption of energy. The necessary preliminary to radiation emission is that an atom must be raised to an energy level above that of the passive or unexcited state. This may conveniently be done by heating the substance in a flame or by subjecting it to a d-c arc, an a-c arc, or a spark-discharge process.

A prism spectrometer in its basic form is depicted in Fig. 16-5. It consists of an entrance slit to pass a narrow beam of light, a system of

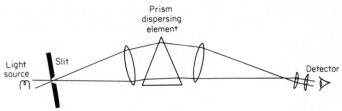

Fig. 16-5 Basic prism spectrometer.

optical lenses which form an image of the entrance slit on the detector, a dispersing element such as a prism, and a detector, which may be the human eye, a photographic film, or a photoelectric cell or similar device. The emission spectrometer includes the basic prism spectrometer plus a source of thermal excitation and a device for measuring the amount of radiation produced at each of the emitted wavelengths.

Both qualitative and quantitative measurements of the chemical elements in even very small samples of matter may be obtained by thermally exciting (heating) the sample to produce emitted radiation which is passed through the narrow slit. This radiation is collimated and dispersed by the prism to produce a spectrum of slit images according to wavelength in the focal plane of the spectrograph. The image densities are then measured with a densitometer and compared with the density recordings from known samples.

Mass spectrometry. In mass spectrometry the material to be studied is subjected to an ionizing process and the resulting ions are physically separated according to mass by electromagnetic means, so that a mass spectrum is produced. Quantitative and qualitative analyses are accomplished by comparing the spectrum of the unknown sample with the spectra of known materials. The ionizing process may be performed in several ways. When gaseous materials are analyzed, electron bombardment of the gas in an evacuated chamber is the normal practice. A direct emission of ions can be obtained from some solid materials, by covering a heated filament with a thin layer of the material.

Another method is to produce two electrodes of the material under test and create a high-voltage spark between them, thereby producing ions of the material. The positive ions are accelerated by a potential difference between a system of electrodes and are collimated or focused by their passage through slits in the electrodes. The ions are then separated according to mass and collected on an electrode to produce a small current which is proportional to the intensity of the beam. This current is amplified and fed to a measuring instrument. By varying the accelerating voltage or the magnetic field, ions of each mass present can be brought to the collector and a mass spectrum can be obtained. Mass spectrometers are particularly well suited for analyzing liquid and gaseous samples. Another important application is in leak detection, such as the testing of vessels and connected tubing which must be absolutely impervious to leakage under pressure or vacuum conditions. In such applications, helium is usually used as the tracer gas and the mass spectrometer is sensitized to detect only helium.

Ultraviolet-absorption spectrometry. Many materials absorb ultraviolet radiation quite readily, and the concentration of these materials in an unknown mixture can be determined by observing the patterns of absorption vs. wavelength. The absorbance of a substance is directly proportional to the concentration of the material which causes the absorption. Thus each hydrocarbon has a characteristic absorption spectrum which differs in some degree from the spectra of other hydrocarbons.

The basic ultraviolet analyzer consists of a radiation source, optical filters, sample cell, detector, and output meter. A transmission measurement is made by calculating the ratio of the reading of the output with the cell filled to the reading with the cell empty. The concentration can be calculated from the known absorptivity of the substance or can be obtained by comparison with known samples. The schematic layout of an industrial ultraviolet analyzer is depicted in Fig. 16-6. The ultraviolet source may be a mercury, hydrogen, xenon, or sodium arc or a tungsten lamp, depending upon the wavelength and other requirements.

Ultraviolet analyzers are well suited to many industrial applications requiring continuous analysis. They are relatively simple, accurate, and highly sensitive to many gases and liquids. They cannot be used for the analysis of mixtures of metals, because metals are completely opaque to ultraviolet radiation. Materials that absorb ultraviolet and hence can be quantitatively determined by this method include many organic and inorganic materials such as nitrates, halogens, unsaturated hydrocarbons, ketones, benzene compounds, naphthalenes, and anthraquinones.

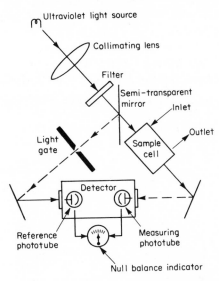

Fig. 16-6   Schematic of industrial ultraviolet analyzer.

Infrared-absorption spectrometry. In absorption spectrometry, suitable radiations of particular wavelength in the appropriate region of the spectrum are employed. An infrared analyzer responds to the absorption of infrared radiation. When light is passed through a light-transmitting solid or fluid, absorption of radiant energy takes place, depending on the chemical identity of the absorbing medium. The number of molecules per unit volume (concentration) and the length of light path within the medium (thickness traversed) influence the amount of absorption in terms of the ratio between incident and transmitted light. Thus each hydrocarbon has a characteristic absorption spectrum, so that a graph of wavelength versus percentage absorption (transmission) enables the hydrocarbon to be identified. The fundamental laws which govern the relationships between the variables were formulated by Lambert and Beer.

In operation, first the proper wavelength must be selected from an examination of the spectrum of each component. Then by setting the instrument successively at each of these wavelengths and comparing the absorption of the unknown with that of a set of standards of known concentrations, the amounts of each component can be determined.

The basic components of an infrared absorption spectroscope are:

1. A source of infrared radiation, one such being the Nernst filament. This is a tubular element of rare-earth oxides heated by an electric current and operating at 1800° to 2000°C.
2. A detector that is sensitive to infrared radiation, a commonly used one being the vacuum thermopile.
3. An amplifier to enable a record to be obtained.
4. A comparison cell having infrared-transparent windows and located between the source and the detector through which the sample passes.

A sample single-beam infrared spectrometer is shown in Fig. 16-7.

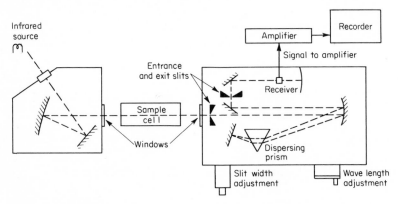

Fig. 16-7   Simple single-beam infrared spectrometer.

Infrared spectrometry is useful in the qualitative and quantitative analysis of a number of organic gases and liquids. Oxygen, hydrogen, nitrogen, chlorine, and all other elemental diatonic gases, as well as the inert gases, do not absorb infrared radiation and therefore cannot be measured by this method.

Gas chromatography. The name chromatography is somewhat misleading, but it originated with a discovery by Tswett in 1906. In his experiments he found that when a solution of mixed colored pigments was allowed to filter through a column of firmly packed pulverized calcium carbonate, the individual pigments passed down the column at different rates and so could be separated into distinctive color bands. The result was called a *chromatogram*. A modern variation of this is to be found in *paper chromatography*, in which compounds in solution migrate at different speeds across a sheet of porous paper.

Gas chromatography is a method of separating mixtures of gases by passing a sample mixture and a carrier gas, usually helium, through a column packed with a suitable fractionating agent. During the passage through the column, the fractionating agent causes the various components to be retained for different periods of time. When there is a suitable detection device in the stream leaving the column, the times of emergence and quantities of the various components can be determined. For a given column and fractionating agent with constant carrier pressure, carrier flow rate, and column and detector temperature the retention times are all held constant. Therefore, the time that elapses between sample injection and component detection will serve to identify that particular component.

The basic block diagram of a chromatograph is shown in Fig. 16-8. It comprises four major components: the sample-introduction units, the

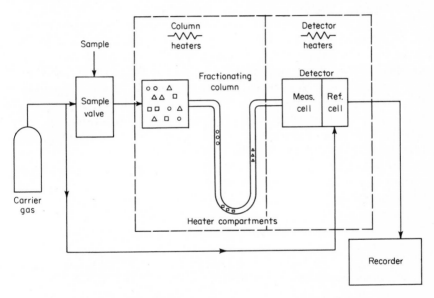

Fig. 16-8   Block diagram of a chromatograph.

fractionating column, a detector, and a recording device. The fractionating column, the heart of the system, is usually constructed from a copper or stainless-steel tube about $\frac{1}{4}$ in. in diameter and from 1 to 50 ft long. Adsorption columns are packed with a fine-mesh material such as charcoal, silica gel, or activated alumina. Partition-type columns are packed with an inert material such as fire brick or diatomaceous earth and coated with a nonvolatile liquid called a partitioner.

The capillary column is quite different in structure; it comprises tubes with an inside diameter of 0.01 in. and a length of 150 to 1,000 ft coiled into a compact helix. The sample introduced into such a column must be kept small in size, but the column is highly selective and has a relatively high speed of response—as fast as a few seconds compared to many minutes for adsorption and partition-type columns.

Detectors may be of several types. Differential thermal-conductivity cells are the most popular, since they are relatively inexpensive, sensitive, and stable. They may comprise either matched resistance wires or thermistors arranged in a bridge circuit. Other types are the hydrogen-flame ionization detector, argon ionization detector, and catalytic combustion detector. The detector causes a recording instrument to indicate a concentration curve or peak for each component of the mixture. The qualitative identification is made by the retention time, which is the elapsed time from injection of the sample to detection. The quantitative or concentration measurement is based on the magnitude of the peak.

Chemical reaction products measurement. Chemical composition can be determined by promoting a desired chemical reaction and then measuring the reaction products. Several types of instruments are available for this purpose. The most commonly used one is the impregnated-tape type, in which a reagent-treated paper on a fabric tape is suspended in the stream of fluid or gas to be analyzed. The reaction impregnant is selected to produce some distinguishable effect measurable by color, opacity, electrical conductance, or fluorescence. Concentrations ranging from fractions of a part per million up to several percent can be measured by this technique. Devices of this type are frequently used in combustion-control applications to monitor smoke and exhaust gases and in air-pollution control to determine the type of dusts, aerosols, and corrosive or toxic gases present.

Suitable instruments must be employed to measure the distinguishing characteristic of the reaction product, which in turn is a measure of the concentration of the isolated component. If the reaction product causes a change in color, the measurements are made colorimetrically; if it causes a dilute suspension to form in a liquid, then the measurements are made nephelometrically. A colorimeter is a photosensitive device which can detect and measure color differences. A nephelometer is similar in many respects, but it measures the light diffraction from particles suspended in solution and thus indicates the degree of turbidity.

Concentration can also be determined by measuring the change in electrolytic conductance. An important application of this technique is found in dissolved-oxygen analyzers which are used to automatically and continuously measure the oxygen concentration in high-purity water, such as that used as feedwater to high-pressure steam generators. Since the instrument detects minute traces of oxygen (as low as 1 part per billion), it can monitor oxygen removal, which is essential in order to minimize corrosion in the steam-generating plant.

A schematic diagram of a dissolved-oxygen analyzer is given in Fig. 16-9. The sample at a constant flow rate and pressure enters the resin

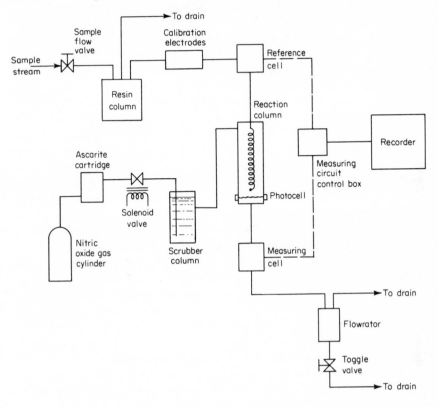

Fig. 16-9   Schematic diagram of a dissolved-oxygen analyzer.

column, which removes metallic cations present and replaces them with hydrogen ions. The outflow from the resin column flows to the reference cell, where its electrical conductivity is measured, and then into the reaction column. Nitric oxide flows from its cylinder through an ascarite cartridge and scrubber; these remove traces of acid nitrogen compounds which would produce false oxygen readings. The nitric oxide flows into the reaction column, where it joins the sample and reacts chemically with it.

The sample then flows into the analyzing cell, where its electrical conductivity is measured. The analyzer output signal is the difference in conductivity between the sample in the reference cell and that in the analyzing cell. A temperature-compensating network corrects the differential-conductivity measurement for any temperature variation of the sample, and this corrected reading can be fed to a recording instrument. The differential conductivity is quantitatively proportional to the amount of dissolved oxygen in the sample, so a continuous record of the dissolved-oxygen content is thereby obtained.

Thermal-conductivity gas analysis. This is the most common method of gas analysis because of its simplicity, reliability, relative speed, and easy adaptation to continuous recording and control. It is based on the fact that various gases differ considerably in their ability to conduct heat. The gas analyzer employs a hot wire mounted in a chamber containing the gas. The hot wire is maintained at an elevated temperature with respect to the cell walls by passing an electric current through it. An equilibrium temperature is attained by the wire when its electric power input is equalized by all thermal losses from it.

By proper design it is possible to minimize all heat loss except that due to gaseous conduction. Under these circumstances, the temperature rise of the wire is inversely related to the thermal conductivity of the gas confined within the cell. The hot wire is made of material, such as platinum, having a high temperature coefficient of resistance, and it is therefore possible to measure changes in the equilibrium temperature merely by measuring the change in resistance of the wire.

A Wheatstone bridge is normally used to measure this resistance change. In practice, it is preferable to use two hot-wire cells in adjacent arms of a Wheatstone bridge, one of the cells containing a reference gas and the other containing the gas to be analyzed. Thus the bridge responds to the difference in temperature rise of the two hot wires.

This type of analyzer is particularly suited to applications involving mixtures of two gases, such as air with oxygen, carbon dioxide or sulfur dioxide or helium and nitrogen mixed with oxygen, carbon dioxide, or hydrogen. It is possible but often difficult, to utilize this technique to analyze complex mixtures of several gases. An important application is in the measurement of combustibles in the products of combustion. The thermal-conductivity oxygen in the products of combustion can also be measured by this system, but some combustible gas, for example, hydrogen, has to be added in order to turn the oxygen to water. Table 16-2 gives a summary of the above methods of analysis and their possible applications.

Oxygen analyzers. The measurement of oxygen content in the products of combustion is an important guide to the economical operation of heating plants and steam-power plants, as well as in other applications. A number of techniques have been developed, including the thermal-conductivity method previously mentioned. More common, however, are

Table 16-2 Chemical composition analysis; methods and applications

Method	General applications: analysis of	Specific applications: to determine presence or quantity of	Limitations	Sampling requirements
Colorimetry	Gases, liquids, vapors, solutions, slurries, and solids	A color in dyestuffs, pigments, paints, etc.	Sensitivity approximates that of human eye	Sample may be liquid or solid; in case of paint may be wet or dry
Emission spectrometry	Gases, vapors, liquids, solutions, suspensions, slurries, solids	Most elemental constituents or any sample, particularly analyses of minerals, metals, and alloys	Can be used to identify 70 elements	Sample must be contained in arc or spark source
Mass spectrometry	Gases, vapors, liquids, solutions, and some solids	Atoms, molecules, and free radicals; to detect helium tracer gas in leak-detection systems	Mass resolution obtained at expense of selectivity	Sample admitted to system at very low pressure
Infrared spectrometry	Gases, vapors, liquids, solutions, and thin-film solids	Any heteroatomic molecule	Sensitivity affected by presence of interfering substances	0.1 to 0.5 ft³/min of clean, dust-free, and condensate-free sample
Ultraviolet spectrometry	Gases, vapors, liquids, solutions, and sometimes thin-film solids	Aromatic and other double-bonded organic materials such as acetone, benzene, carbon disulfide, halogenated hydrocarbons, Cl_2, ozone, NO_2, SO_2, and many biological materials		Laboratory instruments accommodate samples of 10 to 100 cm³, depending on length of sample cell; not usually employed for continuous sampling
Thermal conductivity	Gases and vapors	H_2, CO_2, acetone, Cl_2, He, H_2, SO_2, H_2S in air	Usually limited to binary systems	Sample must be clean, dry, non-corrosive, and free of suspended particles
Chromatography	Gases, liquids, vapors, solutions	Ethylene, isobutane in hydrocarbon compounds	Generally limited to separation of components with boiling points within 50°C of each other	Carrier gas must be inert to the sample and free of impurities. Liquid samples are volatilized before injection. Flow rate and temperature must be maintained constant

the paramagnetic oxygen analyzers, which depend for their operation on the fact that oxygen is unique among gases in being strongly attracted into a magnetic field. Most gases are diamagnetic; i.e., they are repelled by a magnetic field. For a paramagnetic gas the force of attraction is inversely proportional to the absolute temperature. The number of molecules per unit volume is also inversely proportional to the absolute temperature and is directly proportional to the partial pressure of the gas at a standard temperature.

Smoke-density measurement. The measurement of smoke density is important in all large heating-plant installations because of the growing concern over air pollution. All large municipalities now have strict regulations governing the density of smoke ejected to the atmosphere and the time during which smoke of a given density can be ejected.

The simplest method of measurement is by visual comparison with the Ringelmann scale, which is nothing more than a series of six colored squares ranging from white (0) through increasingly darker shades of gray to solid black (5). This technique is obviously not satisfactory for continuous measurement, but it is in general use by air-pollution inspection authorities.

For large plants, however, an automatic, continuous sampling system is necessary, and such a system generally utilizes a lamp and photocell located on opposite sides of the stack. As smoke flows up the stack, it obscures the light in proportion to its density. The photocell measures the intensity of the light being transmitted through the smoke and converts this to a proportional electrical signal which can be recorded or used to energize an alarm device.

REVIEW QUESTIONS AND PROBLEMS

16-6 (a) Can mixtures of metals be analyzed by ultraviolet spectrometry?
(b) Why or why not?

16-7 Can oxygen be detected by infrared spectrometry?

16-8 Describe one unique property of oxygen which is the basis for its identification and quantitative measurement in several commercial analyzers.

16-9 Name the carrier gas most commonly employed in a chromatograph.

16-10 What is a Ringelmann chart?

Glossary

The terms in this glossary have been selected because they have, through use, become standard language in instrumentation technology; the definitions have been selected for their clarity. Many of the terms have been taken from the lists compiled by the Terminology Committee of the Instruments and Regulator Division of the American Society of Mechanical Engineers, while others come from various publications of the Instrument Society of America, American Institute of Electrical Engineers, American Society for Testing Materials, British Standards Institution, and the Society of Instrument Technology. The range of terms selected is not meant to be comprehensive or complete, but it has been intentionally extended beyond the scope of a first-year text on measurement fundamentals for industrial instrumentation in order to encourage the reader to view instrumentation with a more discerning eye.

Aberration. The failure of a lens to bring all rays of light to an exact focal point' thus causing colored fringes.

Absolute humidity. Water-vapor content expressed directly as the mass or weight of water present in a specified unit volume of air or gas.

Absolute measurement. One which is not relative but independent. A measurement in terms of the fundamental standards of mass, length, and time.

Absolute pressure. The pressure of a liquid or gas measured in relation to a perfect vacuum (zero pressure).

Absolute viscosity. The tangential force per unit area of either of two horizontal planes at unit distance apart, one of which is fixed while the other moves with unit velocity, the space between the two planes being filled with the substance under test.

Absolute zero. The temperature at which the molecular motion that constitutes heat ceases and at which an ideal gas, kept at constant volume, would exert no pressure. This temperature is $-273.15°C$ or $-459.67°F$.

Absorption. The solution of gases in liquids (sometimes by solids).

Absorption curve. A graph in which the intensity of the transmitted radiation is plotted as a function of the thickness of the material medium.

Accuracy. In measurement, the degree of correctness with which a measuring device yields the "true value" of a measured quantity. The true value refers to an accepted standard such as the standard meter or volt. It is assumed that a true value always exists even though it may be impossible to determine.

Accuracy of an indicated or recorded value. The ratio of the difference between the indicated or recorded value and the true value, usually expressed in percent of reading or percent of full-scale reading.

Action. Generally, in reference to a controller or regulator, the form of signal used to regulate the final control element to effect control. Types of action are on-off, proportional, reset, and rate.

Adsorption. A concentration of a substance on a surface, e.g., molecules of a gas or of a dissolved or suspended substance on the surface of a solid.

Altimeter. An instrument that measures the elevation above a given datum plane.

Ambient conditions. The conditions of temperature, humidity, pressure, vibration, etc., existing in the medium that surrounds an instrument.

Ambient temperature. The temperature surrounding the object under consideration.

Ammeter. An instrument that indicates the magnitude of flow of an electric current in a circuit. It is provided with a scale usually graduated in amperes, milliamperes, or microamperes.

Amplification. The process of obtaining an output signal that is greater than the input signal through auxiliary power controlled by the input signal.

Amplification factor. The ratio of the change in plate voltage to the change in control grid voltage required to hold the plate current of a vacuum tube constant.

Amplifier. A device whose output is an enlarged reproduction of the essential features of an input wave and which draws power from a source other than the input signal.

Amplitude. The greatest distance through which a vibrating body moves from the midpoint.

Amplitude modulation. Modulation in which the amplitude of the carrier is the characteristic varied.

Analogue computer. A device or apparatus that converts mathematically expressed variables into mechanical or electrical equivalents. Quantities are represented without explicit use of a language as distinguished from a digital computer, which represents the quantities by the use of a language such as digits.

Analysis. The evaluation of the identity and/or the concentration of the constituents or components.

Anemometer. An instrument for measuring the velocity of the wind.

Anode. An electrode of a tube (or cell) through which the principal stream of electrons leaves the interelectrode space.

Aperiodically damped. Attaining constancy or steady change without any oscillation.

Armature. That part of the moving member of an instrument upon which the magnetic flux reacts to provide deflecting torque.

Attenuation. The amount of decrease of the amplitude of a signal as it passes through any part of a control unit or system.

Attenuator. A device designed to cause a loss in energy in a system without bringing in any appreciable distortion.

Audio. Pertaining to frequencies of audible sound waves taken as 20 to 20,000 cycles/sec.

Automatic control. The operation in which the value of a controlled condition is compared with a desired value and corrective action, dependent on the difference, is taken without human intervention.

Automatic controller. A device or equipment that measures the value of a variable and operates to correct or limit deviation from a selected reference. It includes means for both measurement and control.

Automatic control system. Any operable combination of one or more automatic controllers connected in closed loops with one or more processes.

Automation. In mass-production manufacturing, the technique of using self-directing, self-regulating, and self-correcting equipment and machines instead of human labor and control.

Backlash. In gears, the amount by which the width of a tooth exceeds the thickness of the engaging tooth on the pitch circle.

Bandwidth. The range of frequency within which performance, with respect to some variable characteristic, falls within specified limits.

Bar. The unit of absolute pressure in cgs system equivalent to 10^6 dynes/cm^2.

Bellows. A pressure-sensing element consisting of a convoluted metal cylinder close at one end, which a differential pressure causes to expand or contract.

Bimetallic element. A temperature-sensitive-element device consisting of two or more metal alloys mechanically bound so that, owing to differential expansion, the bimetal bends in a particular direction when heated.

Binary cell. An information-storing element existing in one or the other of two stable states.

Blackbody. A theoretical concept of a body which absorbs at all temperatures all radiation falling on it without reflecting or transmitting any and which radiates more energy in a given time than any other body at the same temperature.

Bolometer. An extremely sensitive instrument for measuring heat radiation using resistance thermometry.

Bourdon gauge. A pressure-sensing element that consists of a curved tube having a flattened elliptical cross section which is closed at one end. A pressure applied to the inside of the tube tends to straighten the tube.

Bridge circuit. An electrical network in which the value of an unknown component is obtained by balancing one circuit against another. It normally consists of four resistances connected in a diamond form with a current-detecting device connected between two opposite corners of the diamond.

Burden of an instrument. The volt-amperes consumed by the instrument, generally specified for "normal" voltage and current conditions.

Calibration. The act or process of making adjustments or markings on a scale so that the readings of an instrument conform to an accepted and certified standard. The act of checking readings by comparison with an accepted and certified standard. The errors or corrections revealed by such comparisons are normally plotted on a curve.

Calibration instrument. One that is used to determine, generally after comparison with a standard, the point locations at which scale graduations should be placed to correspond to a series of values of the quantity or variable which the instrument being calibrated is to measure.

Capacitance. That property of an electric circuit which opposes any changes in the potential difference.

Capacitance meter. In electricity, an instrument for measuring capacitance. If the scale is graduated in microfarads, the instrument is usually designated as a microfaradmeter.

Capacity. The measure of the maximum quantity of energy or material which can be stored within the confines of a stated piece of equipment or vessel. It is measured in units of quantity.

Cascade control. In an automatic control system the resetting of the set point of a secondary controller by the output of a primary controller.

Cathode-ray oscillograph. An oscillograph in which a photographic or other record is produced by means of the electron beam of a cathode-ray tube.

Cathode-ray oscilloscope. An oscilloscope which uses a cathode-ray tube as the indicating device.

Cathode-ray tube. An electron-beam tube in which the beam can be focused to a section on a surface and varied in position and intensity to produce a visible pattern.

Choke coil. An inductor inserted in a circuit to offer large impedance to an alternating current.

Chopper. A device to interrupt a continuous current or flux. It is mainly used in electronic circuits to convert a d-c signal to an a-c signal.

Closed loop (feedback control system). A combination of control units in which the controlled quantity is measured and compared with a standard representing the desired performance. Any deviation from the standard is fed back into the control system in such a way as to reduce this deviation.

Collimator. A tube containing a convex achromatic lens at one end and an adjustable slit at the other, the slit being at the focus of the lens. Entering light rays leave as a parallel beam of light.

Command. An input which is established or varied by means external to and independent of the feedback control system.

Comparator. In computers, a circuit which compares two signals and supplies an indication of agreement or disagreement.

Compensation. Provision of a supplemental device to counteract known sources of error.

Compressibility. The rate of decrease of volume per unit volume with the application of hydrostatic pressure.

Compressibility factor. The ratio of the actual volume of a given mass of gas to the volume which it could have at the same temperature and pressure if it were an ideal gas.

Computer. A machine used for carrying out mathematical calculations automatically.

Conduction of heat. The transfer of heat from one part of a body or system to another part in direct contact with it, the heat energy being transmitted from molecule to molecule.

Continuous process. A process in which, for extended periods, proportional components or materials are fed in uninterruptedly at one point or points while products uninterruptedly leave at another point or other points.

Control agent. See *Manipulated variable.*

Control elements. The portion of the feedback control system which is required to influence the manipulated variable with the actuating signal.

Controlled medium. That process, energy, or material in which a variable is controlled.

Controlled variable. That quantity or condition of the controlled system which is directly measured and controlled.

Controller. A device which automatically executes a control function by comparing the measured variable with the desired result and adjusting the input in such a way as to bring the process or function into line with the established control point.

Controlling means. Those elements or units of an automatic controller which are involved in producing a corrective action.

Control-point setting. See *Set point.*

Control system. An assembly of control equipment coordinated to perform a planned set of control functions.

Corrective action. The variation of the manipulated variable produced by the controlling means.

Coupling. That connecting means through which signals or actions directly related to two or more closed-loop automatic controllers are combined to achieve a control function beyond the capabilities of independent automatic controllers.

The association of two circuits in such a way that power may be transferred from one to the other.

Crystal oscillator. A generator of alternating-current energy the frequency of which is determined by the mechanical properties of a piezoelectric circuit.

Curie. A unit of radioactivity: the quantity of any radioactive nuclide in which the number of disintegrations per second is 3.700×10^{10}.

Current amplification. The ratio of the current produced in the output circuit of an amplifier to the current supplied to the input circuit.

Cybernetics. The theory of communications and control mechanisms in living beings and machines. Feedback-control techniques applicable both to living organisms and to machines.

Cycle. The complete sequence of values of a periodic quantity which occur during a period.

Damping. Decrease in the amplitude of an oscillation or wave motion with time.

Damping factor of an instrument. The ratio of the deviations of the indicator following an abrupt change in the measurand in two consecutive swings from the position of equilibrium, the greater deviation being divided by the lesser.

D'Arsonval movement. The mechanism of a permanent-magnet moving-coil instrument.

Dead band. The range of values through which the measured variable may be varied without initiating effective response.

Dead time. Any definite delay, measured in units of time, between two related actions.

Dead zone. The largest range of values of the variable under measurement to which the instrument will not respond effectively.

Decibel. The unit used to compare levels of intensity. Intensities I_1 and I_2 are said to differ by x decibels (db), where $x = 10 \log_{10} (I_2/I_1)$.

Decibel meter. An instrument for measuring, in decibels, the electrical power level of an audio-frequency alternating current above or below an arbitrary reference level.

Derivative action. Action in which there is a predetermined relation between a time derivative of the controlled variable and the position of a final control element. See *Rate action.*

Desired value. See *Set point.*

Deviation. The difference between the instantaneous value of the controlled variable and the set point.

Dial. A disk or plate, suitably marked, which serves to indicate angular position of a needle or pointer.

Differential analyzer. A mechanical or electrical computing device of the analogue type suited for solving differential equations.

Differential pressure. The difference in pressure between two pressure sources, measured relative to one another.

Differential-pressure cell (d/P cell). A device for measuring the difference between two pressures, using diaphragms, bellows, or similar means. These cells are used to measure certain variables such as flow or liquid level.

Differential-pressure gauge. A gauge using two independent containers each connected to a different applied-pressure source. A single pointer over the dial indicates the difference in pressure between the two pressure sources.

Diffusion. Flow of a constituent of a single-phase mixture relative to the flow of another constituent or other constituents.

Digital counter. A counter in which numerical information is represented by means of combinations of numbers.

Diode. A two-electrode device consisting of an anode and a cathode.

Displacement. Change of position.

Display. Visual presentation of a signal.

Distance-velocity lag. See *Dead time.*

Dither. A signal of controlled amplitude and frequency applied to a servomotor operating a transfer valve such that the valve is consistently in a state of "quiver" and cannot stick at its null position.

Dose meter. Any instrument or device which measures radiation dose rate.

Drift. Gradual departure of instrument output from the calibrated value. The deviation of the instrument indication with respect to time from an initial value when the measured variable and ambient conditions are kept constant.

Droop. See *Offset.*

Dynamic response. The behavior of an output in response to a changing input.

Eddy current. Current induced in the body or unit of a conducting mass by a variation of magnetic flux.

Effective value. The square root of the average of the squares of the instantaneous values of the quantity taken throughout one cycle.

Efficiency. The ratio of the useful output of the quantity to its total input.

Elastic chamber. The container or chamber within which a pressure medium is confined. It may be a single flat or currugated diaphragm, a Bourdon tube, a bellows, a piston moving against a spring, or a combination of any of these.

Electric controller. A device or combination of devices which serves to govern the electric power delivered to the equipment to which it is connected.

Electric hygrometer. An instrument for registering by electrical means the humidity of the ambient atmosphere.

Electric tachometer. An instrument for measuring rotational speed by electrical means.

Electric telemeter. Equipment used to detect or measure a variable occurring at a remote location. An electrical signal is transmitted to the indicating or recording location and there translated into identifiable terms.

Electric thermometer. An instrument which uses electrical means to measure temperature.

Electric transducer. A transducer in which all the waves or signals concerned are electric.

Electrode. A conducting element that performs one or more of the functions of emitting, collecting, or controlling by an electric field the movements of electrons or ions.

Electrodynamic instrument. An instrument which depends for its operation on the reaction between the current in one or more movable coils and the current in one or more fixed coils.

Electromagnetic oscillograph. An oscillograph in which the record is produced by means of a mechanical motion derived from electromagnetic forces.

Electromechanical transducer. A transducer for receiving waves or signals from an electric system and delivering waves or signals to a mechanical system, or vice versa.

Electron. An elementary particle of rest mass equal to 9.107×10^{-28} g and charge equal to 4.802×10^{-10} statcoulomb. Its charge may be either positive or negative. The positive electron is usually called a positron; the negative electron is sometimes called the negatron. Most often the term "electron" means the negative electron.

Electron-beam instrument. An instrument which depends for its operation on the deflection of a beam of electrons by an electric or magnetic field or both.

Electron-beam tube. An electron tube the performance of which depends on the formation and control of one or more electron beams.

Electron tube. An electron device in which conduction by electrons takes place through a vacuum or gaseous medium within a gas-tight envelope.

Electron volt. The increase in energy of an electron when passing through a potential rise of 1 volt. (1 electron volt = 1.6×10^{-12} ergs, approx.)

Electrostatic instrument. An instrument which depends for its operation on the forces of attraction and repulsion between bodies charged with electricity.

Electro-thermic instrument. An instrument which depends for its operation on the heating effect of a current or currents.

Emissivity. The ratio of the rate of emission of radiant energy by an opaque polished portion of a material, due to temperature alone, to the rate of emission by the same area of a blackbody at the same temperature. The rate at which the surface of a solid or a liquid emits electrons when additional energy is imparted to the free electrons in the material by the action of heat, light, or other radiant energy or by the impact of other electrons on the surface.

End device. The final system element that responds quantitatively to the variable function and performs the final measurement operation. An end device performs the final conversion of measurement to an indication, record, or the initiation of control.

End-scale value of an instrument. The value of the actuating electrical quantity which corresponds to end-scale indication. When the zero is not at the end or at the electrical center of the scale, the higher of the two values is taken.

Equivalent network. A network which, under certain conditions or use, may replace another network for simulation.

Error. The difference between the indicated value and the true value of the measured variable. When the indicated value is higher than the true value, the sign of the error is positive.

Error signal. A measurement of the error between the set point and the controlled variable signals by means of an automatic control device.

Feedback. The returning of a portion of the output signal to the input of a control system or transmission system in order to compare the two signals or to amplify or stabilize the output signal.

Feedback control system. A control system which tends to maintain a prescribed relationship of one system variable to another by comparing functions of these variables and using the difference as a means of control.

Feedback signal. A signal responsive to the value of the controlled variable. The signal is returned to the input of the system and compared with the reference signal to obtain an actuating signal which returns the controlled variable to the desired value.

Filter. Any one of many kinds of devices that selectively permit some kinds of matter or energy to pass through them.

Final control element. That portion of the controlling means which directly changes the value of the manipulated variable.

Flame photometer. A device with which spectral emission from a solution sprayed into a flame source is analyzed to determine the composition of the solution.

Flip-flop. An electronic circuit having two stable states and ordinarily two input terminals (or input signals) each of which corresponds to one of the two states. The circuit remains in one state until caused to change to the other state by application of the corresponding signal.

Floating action. Action in which there is a predetermined relation between the deviation and the rate of motion of a final control element.

Flow diagram. A graphical representation of a sequence of operations.

Fluid. A substance which is continually deformed under any finite shearing stress as long as the stress is maintained. Specifically a liquid or gas.

Fluidity. The rate at which a fluid is continuously deformed by a shearing stress; the reciprocal of viscosity.

Foot-candle. A unit of illumination: the illuminance on a surface one square foot in area on which there is a uniformly distributed flux of one lumen or the illuminance at a surface all points of which are at a distance of one foot from a uniform source of one candle.

Foot-lambert. A unit of luminance equal to the value of $1/\pi$ candle per square foot or to the uniform luminance of a perfectly diffusing surface emitting or reflecting light at the rate of one lumen per square foot.

Free impedance. The impedance at the input of a transducer when the impedance of the load is made zero.

Frequency. The number of times a cycling quantity repeats itself per unit of time; usually expressed as cycles per second.

Frequency response. Two relations between sets of inputs and the corresponding outputs. One relates frequencies to the output-input amplitude ratio; the other to phase difference between output and input.

Frequency-response analysis. A method of systematically analyzing process-control problems, based on introducing cyclic inputs to a system and measuring the resulting output signals at various frequencies.

Full-scale deflection (FSD). The maximum reading on a measuring indicator or recorder. Percentage accuracy generally refers to *FSD*.

Full-scale value. The largest value of the actuating quantity which can be indicated on the scale or, in the case of an instrument having its zero between the ends of the scale, the arithmetic sum of the values of the actuating quantity corresponding to the two ends of the scale.

Full-wave rectifier. A combination of rectifier elements so arranged that the output current is unidirectional for every instantaneous value and either polarity of an applied a-c voltage.

Fundamental units. A small number of units of mass, length, and time from which other units of measure are derived.

Gain. Ratio of output to input of any section of a control system. If a signal gets smaller, it is said to be attenuated; if it gets larger, it is said to be amplified.

Galvanometer. An instrument for indicating or measuring a small electric current or a function of the current by means of a mechanical motion derived from electromagnetic or electrodynamic forces which are set up as a result of the current flow.

Gamma ray. A quantum of electromagnetic radiation emitted by a nucleus, each such photon being emitted as a result of a quantum transition between two energy levels of the nucleus. Sometimes, loosely, an X-ray photon of high energy, exceeding about 10^4 electron volt.

Gauge. A device or instrument, containing the primary measuring element, applied to the point of measurement.

Gauge pressure. The pressure of a fluid measured relative to the local atmospheric pressure.

Gaussmeter. A magnetometer provided with a scale graduated in gauss or kilogauss.

Geiger counter. An instrument used for the detection of ionizing radiations, chiefly alpha, beta, and gamma rays; also capable of registering individual photons.

Getter. A material which is included in a vacuum system for the purpose of absorbing or adsorbing the residual gas.

Graduation. A division or mark on an instrument to indicate degree or quantity.

Graphic panel. A control panel which pictorially displays and indicates the relative position and function of measuring and control points to process equipment. The panel represents a total plant operation.

Grid. An electrode having one or more openings for the passage of electrons or ions.

Ground. An electrically conducting connection, accidental or intentional, to the earth or to some other conducting body at zero potential with respect to earth.

Gyroscope. A wheel or disk mounted to spin rapidly about an axis and free to rotate about one or both of two axes perpendicular to each other and to the axis of spin. The spinning gyroscope either offers resistance, depending upon its angular momentum, to any torque which would tend to change the direction of the spin axis or, if free, changes its spin axis in a direction perpendicular both to the torque and to the original spin axis.

Half-wave rectifier. A rectifier which delivers unidirectional output current only during the half-cycle when the applied alternating-current voltage is of the polarity at which the rectifier has low resistance. During the opposite half-cycle, the rectifier passes no current; hence, a half-wave rectifier rectifies only one-half of the alternating-current wave.

Harmonics. A sinusoidal quantity having a frequency which is an integral multiple of the fundamental frequency. For example, a wave the frequency of which is twice the fundamental frequency is called the second harmonic.

Head. Pressure resulting from gravitational forces on liquids. Measured in terms of the depth below a free surface of the liquid, which is the reference zero head.

Heterodyne conversion transducer. A conversion transducer in which the output frequency is the sum or difference of the input frequency and an integral multiple of a local oscillator frequency.

Hot-wire instrument. An electrothermic instrument which depends for its operation on the heating effect of a wire carrying a current.

Hunting. The undesirable oscillation of an automatic control system such that the controlled variable swings on both sides of the predetermined reference value without seeming to approach it.

Hydraulic gauge. A gauge specifically designed for use at high pressures and where water or a noncorrosive liquid is the pressure-transmitting medium.

Hydrophone. An electroacoustic transducer which responds to water-borne sound waves and transmits equivalent electrical signals.

Hydrostatic-head gauge. A gauge using one or more elastic chambers and differing from the ordinary types of pressure gauge only in the graduation of the scale. The scale is normally graduated to indicate, in feet or meters, the head of water or other liquid.

Hygroscopic. Descriptive of material which readily absorbs and retains moisture.

Hysteresis. The lagging of effect behind cause, a phenomenon occurring in induced magnetism but chiefly in the elastic and magnetic behavior of materials. When a body is stressed, the strain lags behind; i.e., the strain for a given value of stress is greater when the stress is decreasing than when it is increasing. On removing the stress completely, a residual strain remains. Flexibility and loose fits in linkage and backlash in gearing are some of the causes of hysteresis in instruments.

Ideal gas. A gas which obeys Boyle's law and has zero heat of free expansion.

Immersion length. The portion of a thermometer immersed in a fluid under temperature test by the thermometer.

Immiscible. Incapable of being mixed to form a homogeneous substance; usually said of liquids such as oil and water.

Impedance. The complex ratio of a force-like quantity (force, pressure, voltage, temperature, or electric field strength) to a corresponding related velocity-like quantity (velocity, volume velocity, current, heat flow, or magnetic field strength).

Impulse. A force acting during a very short time.

Impulse-type telemeter. A telemeter which employs intermittent electric impulses as the translating means.

Incompressibility flow. Fluid flow under conditions such that fluid density remains substantially constant.

Independent variable. A variable external to the measuring system, e.g., ambient temperature, pressure.

Indicating instrument. An instrument in which only the present value of the quantity measured is visually indicated.

Inductance. The property of an electric circuit which tends to oppose change of current in the circuit.

Induction instrument. An instrument which depends for its operation on the reaction between a magnetic flux set up by one or more currents in fixed windings and electric currents set up by electromagnetic induction in movable conducting parts.

Inductive coupling. The association of one circuit with another by means of inductance common to both.

Inertia. The property of any object which causes it to resist change in its state of motion.

Instruction. Information which, when correctly coded and introduced as a unit into a digital computer, causes the computer to perform one or more of its operations.

Instrument. A device or mechanism for measuring the value of a variable quantity under observation; for extending or replacing the perceptual, communicative, manipulative, or intellectual abilities of man. Generally, a device incorporating measuring, controlling, indicating, recording, and, in some cases, operating abilities.

Instrumentation. The science and technology of applying the combination of instruments and control equipment used in the operation of a system or manufacturing process.

Integral action. A control action which produces a corrective signal proportional to the length of time the controlled variable has been away from the set point. Same as *Reset action.*

Integrator. A device or mechanism which continually totalizes or adds up the value of a quantity (for a given time) in digits.

Ion. Any electrically charged particle of molecular, atomic, or nuclear size.

Ionization. The process whereby a neutral atom or molecule is split into positive or negative ions.

Ionizing radiation. Any electromagnetic radiation capable of producing ions, directly or indirectly, in its passage through matter.

Isentropic. Without any change in the entropy.

Isothermal. Without any change in temperature.

Isotope. One of several different nuclides having the same number of protons in their nuclei and hence the same atomic number but differing in the number of neutrons and hence in mass number.

Jet. The exhaust stream or rapid flow of fluid from a small orifice, opening, or nozzle.

Jewels. The recessed bearings in which the pivots of an instrument turn.

Kelvin temperature scale. A thermodynamic absolute-temperature scale having as its zero the absolute zero of temperature ($-273°C$).

Kinematic viscosity. The ratio of absolute viscosity to the mass density of the fluid.

Lag. Any deviation from instantaneously complete response to an input signal. Refers to delay, and is expressed in seconds or minutes. Lag is caused by various conditions singly or jointly such as capacitance, inertia, resistance, or dead time.

Lambert. A unit of luminance equal to $1/\pi$ candle per square centimeter and, therefore, equal to the uniform luminance of a perfectly diffusing surface emitting or reflecting light at the rate of one lumen per square centimeter.

Laminar boundary layer. That portion of the boundary layer in which the motion approximates streamline flow and the Reynolds number is less than 2,000.

Limit of error of an instrument. The maximum error thoughout the scale under specified conditions.

Limit switch. A switch which is operated by some part or motion of a power-driven machine or equipment to change the electrical circuit associated with the machine or equipment.

Lineal scale length. The circumferential distance traveled by the indicating pointer or pen in moving from one end of the scale to the other.

Linear. A term applied to the relationship between two quantities such that a change in one quantity is exactly proportional to the associated change in the other quantity.

Linearity. The degree to which the calibration curve of a device matches or conforms to a straight line. The linearity error is generally the greatest deviation from the best straight line that can be drawn through the measured calibration points.

Load circuit. The circuit through which the main power current flows.

Logger. An instrument which automatically scans a series of conditions such as temperature and pressure and records or logs such readings on a chart, usually with respect to time. A digital logger records numerical values.

Logic (computer). The manner in which the basic computer elements are connected to provide the reasoning and decision-making activity of the computer.

Longitudinal wave. A wave in which the direction of displacement at each point of the medium is normal to the wavefront.

Lumen. The unit of luminous flux; it is equal to the flux through a unit solid angle (steradian) from a uniform point source of one candle at a unit distance away.

Mach number. The ratio of the velocity of an object to that of sound in the medium being considered.

Magnetic amplifier. A device, similar in construction and appearance to a transformer, used to perform the amplifying functions of electronic tubes or transistors in some application. A device using saturable reactors.

Magnetic field. A state of the medium in which moving electrified bodies are subject to forces by virtue of both their electrification and motion.

Magnetic head. A transducer for converting electric variations into magnetic variations for storage on magnetic media, for reconverting energy so stored into electric energy, or for erasing such stored energy.

Magnetic tape. A magnetic recording medium having a width greater than approximately 10 times the thickness. The tape may be coated or homogeneous.

Magnetometer. An instrument used for measuring the intensity or direction, or both, of a magnetic field.

Magnification. The magnitude of an output signal or optical image divided by the magnitude of the input signal or image.

Manipulated variable. That quantity or condition of the control agent which is varied by the automatic controller in order to affect the value of the measured (controlled) variable. For example, when heating water with a steam jacket, the flow of steam is referred to as the manipulated variable.

Manometer. A gauge used for measuring pressures of gases or vapors, generally with a liquid filling.

Manual controller. A controller having all its basic functions performed by devices which are operated by hand.

Mass. The amount of matter contained in an object and measured by the inertia of the object.

Mass density. Measured as mass per unit volume, for example, grams mass per cubic centimeter.

Mass number. The total number of nucleons (protons and neutrons) in the nucleus of an atom or nuclide.

Mass spectrometer. An instrument used for separating the ions of a mixture by means of the effects of magnetic or electric fields on moving ions. The separation depends on differences in the ratios of mass to change of the component ions.

Measurand. A physical quantity, condition, or property which is to be measured.

Measured variable. See *Controlled variable.*

Measurement system. A system consisting of one or more measurement devices interconnected to perform a complete measurement from the first operation to the end result.

Memory. Any device into which information can be introduced and then extracted at some later time.

Metrology. The science of precise and accurate measurement using highly scientific disciplines and techniques.

Microbar. A unit of pressure equivalent to one dyne per square centimeter.

Microcurie. One-millionth of a curie.

Micron. A unit of length equal to 10^{-6} m.

Mil. A unit of linear measurement equal to 0.001 in.; a unit of angular measurement.

Millibar. A common unit of pressure used in weather records equal to a thousandth of a bar or 1.0×10^3 dynes/cm². A bar is 1.0×10^6 dynes/cm².

Millimeter of mercury. A unit of pressure equivalent to $\frac{1}{760}$ of the pressure exerted by a column of mercury 760 mm high at 0°C under standard gravity of 980.665 cm/sec².

Moderator control. Control of a nuclear reactor by adjusting the position or quantity of the moderator in such a way as to change the fraction of neutrons that, before leaking out or being captured, are slowed to speeds at which they can excite fission in the fuel used.

Modulation. The process whereby some characteristic of a wave is varied in accordance with another wave.

Modulus of elasticity. The ratio of stress to strain within the elastic range of a material.

Molecule. The smallest piece into which a substance can be broken without losing its chemical properties and identity.

Moment of force. The effectiveness of a force to cause rotation about an axis. Measured by multiplying the magnitude of the force by the perpendicular distance from the line of action of the force to the axis of rotation.

Moment of inertia. A measure of the resistance offered by a body to angular acceleration by virtue of the mass of the body.

Monitor. An instrument used to measure continuously or at intervals a variable condition that must be kept within prescribed limits. It scans a number of measuring points and indicates which have wandered too far from the desired values.

Multiple action. Motion in which two or more controller actions are combined.

Multirange. Capable of being used for measuring two or more ranges.

Negative feedback. Feedback which results in decreasing the amplification effect.

Neper. A unit used to describe the scalar ratio of two currents or two voltages, the number of nepers being the natural logarithm of such a ratio.

Network analyzer. A set of electric-circuit elements which can be readily connected to form models of electric networks. Each model thus formed may be used to infer the electrical quantities at various points on the prototype system from corresponding measurements on the model.

Neutral zone. A predetermined range of values of the controlled variable in which no change of position of the final control element occurs.

Newtonian material. A material which when subjected to shear stress undergoes deformation in which the ratio of shear rate (flow) to shear stress (force) is constant.

Noise. Meaningless stray signals in a control system which interfere with reception.

Non-Newtonian material. A material which when subjected to a shear stress undergoes deformation in which the ratio of shear rate (flow) to shear stress (force) is not constant.

Nozzle. A duct of changing cross section in which fluid velocity is increased. The shape is usually converging-diverging.

Nucleus. The positively charged core of an atom, consisting of positively charged protons and neutral neutrons, with which is associated practically the entire mass of the atom.

Nutation. The oscillation of the axis of a rotating object.

Obscuration. The fraction of the incident radiation which is removed in traversing a distance through smoke.

Offset. The steady-state difference or deviation between the control point and the value or the controlled variable corresponding to the set point. Offset is normally caused by load changes.

Ohmmeter. A direct-reading instrument for measuring electrical resistance. It is provided with a scale that is normally graduated in either ohms or megohms.

On-off control action. Action that occurs when a final control element is moved from one of two fixed positions to the other and vice versa with a small change of the controlled variable.

Open-loop control system. A control system in which the controlled quantity is allowed to vary in accordance with the inherent characteristics of the control system and with the controlled power equipment for any given adjustment of the controller. No comparison is made between the actual value and the desired value of a process vari able.

Operand. In computer work a word on which an operation is to be performed.

Operating-pressure range. Stated high and low values of pneumatic pressure required to produce full-range operation when applied to a pneumatic intelligence-transmission system, a pneumatic motor operator, or a positioning relay.

Optical density. The common logarithm of the ratio of the incident radiation to the transmitted radiation.

Optical pyrometer. A temperature-measuring instrument consisting of a standardized comparison source of illumination and some convenient arrangement for matching this source, either in brightness or in color, against the source whose temperature is to be measured. The comparison is normally made by the eye.

Optimization. Theoretical analysis of a system including all characteristics of the process such as thermal lags, capacity of tanks and towers, and lengths and sizes of pipes and similar equipment. The analysis is made, normally with the aid of frequency-response curves, in order to obtain the most desirable instrumentation and control scheme.

Orifice. An aperture in a plate used in connection with flowmetering usually symmetrical and often circular and of a diameter large in comparison with the thickness of the plate.

Oscillator circuit. A circuit containing both inductance and capacitance, so that voltage impulse will produce a current which periodically reverses.

Oscilloscope. An instrument which makes visible the instantaneous values of one or more rapidly varying quantities as a function of time or of another electrical or mechanical quantity.

Oscilloscope tube. A cathode-ray tube used to produce a visible pattern, which is the graphical representation of electrical signals, by variations of the position of the focused spot or spots in accordance with those signals.

Overshoot. The amount by which a changing process variable exceeds the desired or steady value as changes occur in a system. The amount of overtravel of the indicator beyond its steady value.

Parallax. In instrumentation, the optical phenomenon responsible for errors in reading when the eye is not directly in line with a pointer whose tip is not in the same plane as the instrument scale.

Parametric variation. The change in system properties, such as resistance, magnification, or area, which may affect the performance or operation of the feedback control system.

Partial pressure. The pressure of a given component of a gaseous mixture.

Pentode. A five-electrode electron tube containing an anode, a cathode, a control electrode, and two additional electrodes that are normally grids.

Percent error of an instrument. The difference between the percent registration of an instrument and 100 percent.

Period of an instrument. The time interval between two consecutive transits of the pointer or indicating means of an undamped instrument in the same direction through the rest position following an abrupt change in the measurand.

pH. The measure of effective acidity or alkalinity of solutions based on the concentration of hydrogen ions. pH values less than 7 are considered acidic, pH values greater than 7 are considered basic. At 7, the solution is said to be neutral.

Phase angle. In electricity, the difference between the phase relationship of current and voltage expressed as the angle between the vectors of current and voltage.

Phase meter. A meter for measuring the difference in phase between two alternating quantities of the same frequency.

Phase shift. A time difference between the input and output signal of a control unit or system.

Phosphorescence. Emission of radiation by a substance as a result of previous absorption of radiation of shorter wavelength. The emission may continue for a considerable time after cessation of the exciting irradiation, in contrast to fluorescence.

Photoelectric cell. A device the electrical properties of which undergo a change when it is exposed to light.

Photoelectric effect. The ejection of bound electrons from a system by photons incident upon it in such a way that the whole energy of a photon is absorbed for each electron ejected.

Photoelectric pyrometer. An instrument, based on a phototube, which measures the temperature of a hot object by measuring the intensity of energy radiated by the object.

Photon. A quantum of electromagnetic radiation.

Phototube. An electron tube having an electrode that emits electrons when irradiated.

Pickup. A device that converts a sound or other form of intelligence into corresponding electrical signals, such as a microphone, a television camera, or a phonograph pickup. The minimum voltage, current, or power to actuate a relay. Interference from a nearby circuit or system.

Piezoelectric. The property of certain crystals to set up an electric charge or potential difference when subjected to a mechanical strain or, conversely, to produce a mechanical force when subjected to an electric field.

Pinion. A gear with a small number of teeth. Of two gears that run together, the one with the smaller number of teeth is termed the pinion.

Pirani gauge. A bolometric vacuum gauge which depends for its operation on the thermal conduction of the gas present. Pressure is measured as a function of the resistance of a heated filament.

Pitot static tube. A parallel or coaxial combination of a Pitot tube and a static tube, used in measuring fluid flow.

Pitot tube. A cylindrical tube with an open end pointed perpendicularly upstream, used in measuring impact pressure of flowing fluids.

Polarography. A method of chemical analysis based on comparative measurements of current-voltage curves under conditions which ensure concentration polarization of one electrode and constant potential at the other electrode.

Positioning action. Movement in which there is a predetermined relation between value of the controlled variable and position of a final control element.

Potentiometer. A device for measuring an unknown electromotive force or potential difference by balancing it, wholly or in part, by a known potential difference produced by the flow of known currents in a network of circuits of known electrical constants. In order to measure process-control variables by means of a potentiometer, variables such as flow, temperature, humidity, pressure, and level must first be translated into electrical signals that vary proportionally with changes in the variable.

Power factor. The ratio of active power to apparent power.

Power-factor meter. A meter designed for measuring power factor.

Precession. A change in the orientation of the axis of a spinning body such as a gyroscope or projectile.

Precision. The degree of reproducibility among several independent measurements of the same true value under specified conditions. Quality or exactness. A measure of the precision of a representation is the number of distinguishable alternatives from which it was selected.

Pressure. Force per unit area.

Pressure, dynamic. The pressure exerted by a moving fluid and striking at a point causing the fluid to come to rest.

Pressure gauge. An instrument or gauge designed to indicate and having a scale graduated to show pressure measurements above atmospheric only.

Pressure, static. The pressure exerted by a fluid at rest and indicated on a pressure gauge.

Pressure vacuum gauge. A gauge designed to indicate pressures below atmospheric.

Primary detector. The first system element that responds quantitatively to the measurand and performs the initial measurement operation. A primary detector performs the initial conversion or control of measurement energy and does include such components as transformers, resistors, or amplifiers when they are used as auxiliary means.

Primary element. That portion of the measuring means which first either utilizes or transforms energy from the controlled medium to produce an effect which is a function of change in the value of the controlled variable.

Process. The collective functions performed in and by the equipment in which a variable is to be controlled.

Program control. A control system whereby the set point is automatically varied during definite time intervals in order to make the process variable vary according to some prescribed sequence or manner.

Proportional action. An action in which there is a continuous linear relation between the value of the controlled variable and the position of a final control element. Produces an output signal proportional to the magnitude of the input signal. In a control system proportional action produces a value correction proportional to the deviation of the controlled variable from set point.

Proportional band. The amount or magnitude of deviation of the controlled variable from set point required to move the final control element through the full range expressed as a percentage of span.

Proportional plus derivative action. Combined proportional-position action and derivative action.

Proportional plus reset action. Combined proportional-position action and reset action.

Pulse. A variation of a quantity whose value is normally constant; characterized by a rise and fall and of finite deviation.

Purging. Elimination of an undesirable gas or material from an enclosure by displacing it with an acceptable gas or material.

Pyrometer. A thermometer of any design usable at relatively high temperature, usually above 1000°F.

Q factor. A rating, applied to coils, capacitors, and resonant circuits, equal to reactance divided by resistance. The ratio of energy stored to energy dissipated per cycle in any mechanical or electrical system.

Q meter. A meter for measuring the quality factor Q of a circuit or component.

Quantization. A process in which the range of values of a wave is divided into a finite number of subranges each of which is represented by an assigned, or quantized, value that is a small value within the subrange.

Radar. The use of radio waves, automatically retransmitted or reflected, to gain information concerning a distant object.

Radiation. The emission and propagation of energy through space or a material medium in the form of waves such as electromagnetic waves. Corpuscular emission, such as alpha and beta radiation, or rays of mixed or unknown type, such as cosmic rays.

Radiation pyrometer. An instrument in which the radiant energy from the object or source to be measured is utilized in the measurement of the temperature of the object. The radiant energy within wide or narrow wavelength bands filling a definite solid angle impinges upon a suitable detector. This detector is normally a thermocouple or thermopile, a bolometer responsive to heating effect of the radiant energy, or a photosensitive device connected to a sensitive electrical instrument calibrated in degrees of temperature.

Radioactivity. The intensity of emission from a specimen undergoing spontaneous nuclear disintegration.

Radioisotope. A radioactive isotope of an element.

Rangeability. The relationship between the range and the minimum quantity that can be measured.

Range of an instrument. The limits between which an instrument measures, e.g., from 100 to 200 psi.

Rate action. A control action in which there is a continuous linear relation between rate of change of the controlled variable and position of a final control element. Produces a faster corrective action than proportional action alone. Frequently called derivative action, although strictly it refers to first derivative only.

Rate time. The amount of time, usually expressed in minutes, by which proportional action is advanced by the addition of rate action.

Reactance. The component of the impedance of an electric circuit, not due to resistance, which opposes the flow of an alternating current. The reactance is the algebraic sum of that due to inductance in the circuit with value, in ohms, equal to the product 2π, the frequency, in cycles, and the inductance, in henrys, and that due to the capacitance in the circuit with a value, in ohms, equal to the reciprocal of the product 2π, the frequency, in cycles, and the capacitance, in farads.

Readability. The smallest fraction of a division to which the index can be read with ease either by estimation or by use of a vernier. The readability is expressed in divisions.

Recorded value. The value recorded by the marking device on a chart with reference to the division lines marked on the chart.

Rectifier. A device used for converting an alternating current into a continuous or direct current.

Reference junction. The junction of a thermocouple which is at a known or reference temperature.

Register of a meter. That part of a meter which registers the revolutions of the rotor or the number of impulses received from or transmitted to a meter in terms of units of electric energy or other quantity under measurement.

Relative humidity. The ratio of the actual partial pressure of water vapor in air to the partial pressure at saturation at the same ambient temperature.

Relay. A device, normally electromechanical in operation, generally operated by a change in one low-powered electric circuit and thereby controlling one or more other electric circuits.

Repeatability. See *Reproducibility.*

Reproducibility. The closeness with which a measuring instrument repeats indications when measuring identical values of the measured variable under the same conditions. Normally expressed as a percentage of the span of the instrument.

Reset rate. The number of times per minute that the effect of the proportional-position action upon the final control element is repeated by the proportional-speed floating action. Expressed as the number of times proportional response is repeated or duplicated in one minute.

Resistance. Opposition to flow; measured in units of potential change required to produce unit change in flow.

Resistance thermometer. An electrical thermometer which operates by measuring the electrical resistance of a resistor, the resistance of which is known as a function of its temperature.

Resistivity. The resistance of a material expressed in ohms per unit length and unit cross section.

Resistor. A device which conducts electricity but converts part of the electric energy into heat.

Resonance. The condition when the frequency of a small periodic force applied to a system capable of oscillation approaches the natural frequency of the system.

Response. The quantitative expression of the output of a device or system as a function of the input under explicitly specified conditions.

Response time of an instrument. The time required, after an abrupt change has occurred in the measured quantity to a new constant value, until the indicator has first come to an apparent rest in its new position. The time required for the instrument to reach a specified percentage of the total change that it will make as a result of a step change in the measured variable.

Responsiveness. The ability of an instrument to follow changes in value of a measured quantity.

Rheology. The study of the deformation and flow of matter, used in connection with viscosity measurement.

Rheopexy. The thickening caused by flow and lost on standing. The term is used in connection with viscosity.

Rheostat. A resistor which is provided with means for readily adjusting its resistance.

Ringelmann number. A number that describes observed smoke intensity by a comparison with a chart of white through gray to black on which white is 0 and black is 5. Each chart step represents 20 percent change in smoke density. The Ringelmann number can be regarded as percent obscuration.

Roentgen. The quantity of X or gamma radiation such that the associated corpuscular emission per 0.001293 g of air produces, in air, ions carrying one electrostatic unit of quantity of electricity of either sign.

Roentgen rays. X rays.

Rutherford. A unit of measure of radioactivity, named after Lord Rutherford, equal to 10^{-6} radioactive disintegrations per second.

Sampling action. The action that occurs when the difference between the set point and the value of the controlled variable is measured and correction is made at intermittent intervals.

Scale factor. The factor by which the number of scale divisions indicated or recorded by an instrument should be multiplied to compute the value of the measurand. In analogue computing, a proportionality factor which relates the magnitude of a variable to its representation within a computer.

Scanner. An instrument which automatically checks a number of measuring points for the purpose of collecting information or data.

Screen grid. A grid placed between a control grid and an anode of a vacuum tube, usually maintained at a fixed positive potential, for the purpose of reducing the electrostatic influence of the anode in the space between the screen grid and the cathode.

Sector. The large oscillating gear or segment in a pressure gauge which is actuated by the elastic chamber. It meshes with the pinion to actuate the indicating pointer.

Self-operated controller. A controller in which all the power necessary to operate the final control element is derived from the controlled medium through the primary element.

Self-regulation. An inherent characteristic of a process which aids in limiting deviation of the controlled variable.

Sensing element. The part of a transducer which is in contact with the medium being measured and which responds to changes in the medium. Frequently referred to as the *sensor*.

Sensitivity. The ratio of change of output to change of input. The least signal input capable of causing an output signal having desired characteristics.

Servomechanism. A closed-loop system in which the error deviation from a desired value is automatically corrected to zero and in which mechanical position is usually the controlled variable.

Set point. The position to which the control-point-setting mechanism is located or set and which is the same as the desired value of the controlled variable.

Signal. An action used to convey information.

Significant numbers of digits. A set of digits from consecutive columns beginning with the most important or significant digit different from zero and ending with the least significant digit whose value is known or assumed to be relevant.

Sine wave. A wave made up of instantaneous values which are the product of a constant and the sine of an angle having values varying linearly.

Span of an instrument. The difference between the highest and lowest scale values of an instrument. On instruments starting at zero, the span is equal to the range.

Stability. That characteristic or attribute of a system which enables the system to develop restoring forces equal to or greater than the disturbing forces so as to restore a state of equilibrium.

Stability (dynamic). That property of a physical system having positive damping which allows eventual asymptotic approach to constancy of response when the input becomes constant.

Stability (static). Constancy of static and dynamic calibration despite changes of environmental and internal condition.

Stable. Showing no tendency to undergo any spontaneous change.

Standard cell. A cell used as a standard of electromotive force.

Straightening vanes. A device placed between a flow-measuring unit and a flow-disturbing fitting to establish normal, long-pipe flow conditions.

Strain gauge. An element (wire) which measures a force by using the principle that electrical resistance varies in proportion to tension or compression applied to the element.

Suppressed range. A range of an instrument which does not include zero. The degree of suppression is expressed by the ratio of the value at the lower end of the scale to the span.

Suppressed zero. An indicating or recording instrument in which the zero position is below the limit of travel of the indicating means.

Synchroscope. An instrument for indicating whether two periodic quantities are sychronous.

System error. The ideal value minus the value of the ultimately controlled variable.

Systems engineering. Control engineering studies in which a process and all the elements affecting a process are considered for automatic control operation.

Telemetering. Transmission of measurements over long distances generally by electric or electronic means for indicating, recording, or integrating information.

Temperature. The relative hotness or coldness of a body as determined by the ability of the body to transfer heat to its surroundings. There is a temperature difference between two bodies if, when they are placed in thermal contact, heat is transferred from one body to the other. The body which loses heat is said to be at the higher temperature.

Temperature, Celsius. Temperature as measured on the Celsius scale, on which the freezing point of water is 0° and the boiling point is 100°. Also called the centigrade scale.

Temperature coefficient of resistance. The change in resistivity of an electrical conductor for each unit change in temperature.

Temperature, Fahrenheit. Temperature as measured on the Fahrenheit scale, on which the freezing point of water is 32° and the boiling point is 212°.

Temperature, international. Temperature as measured on a scale, established by international agreement, which covers the range from the boiling point of oxygen to the highest temperatures of incandescent bodies and flames. The scale is based on six fixed points and upon specified interpolation formulas.

Temperature, Kelvin. Temperature as measured on a scale based on the laws of thermodynamics and known as a thermodynamic scale. On this scale the ice point and the steam point are separated by 100°. The zero of this scale is the absolute zero, which is approximately 273.16°K below the ice point.

Temperature, Rankine. Temperature as measured on a scale, based on absolute zero of the Fahrenheit scale, on which the freezing and boiling points of water are separated by 180°. The ice point is approximately 491.67°F.

Test. To ascertain the performance characteristics of a meter or instrument while the device is functioning under controlled conditions.

Theodolite. An optical device for measuring horizontal and vertical angles with high precision.

Thermal radiation. Electromagnetic radiation whereby a body loses heat to its surroundings.

Thermionic emission. Electron or ion emission due to the temperature of the emitter.

Thermistor. A resistor or semiconductor whose resistance varies with temperature (generally in an inverse ratio) in a definite desired manner. Used to measure temperature and to compensate for temperature variation in circuits as a nonlinear circuit element.

Thermocouple. A means of measuring temperature consisting basically of a pair of end-joined dissimilar conductors in which an electromotive force is developed by thermoelectric effects when the two junctions are at different temperatures.

Thermocouple instrument. An electrothermic instrument in which one or more thermojunctions are heated directly or indirectly by an electric current or currents and supply a direct current which flows though the coil of a suitable *d-c* device such as one of the permanent-magnet moving-coil type.

Thermometer. An instrument for the measurement of temperature.

Thermopile. A group of thermocouples connected in series usually to a device used either to measure radiant energy or as a source of electric energy.

Thermostat. A temperature-operated unit that receives its energy by thermal conduction or convection from the source being controlled.

Thixotropy. The rate of change of viscosity with time. Certain liquids possess the property of increasing in viscosity with the passage of time when the liquid is left undisturbed. When the liquid is agitated, the viscosity returns to its original value.

Thyratron. A hot-cathode gas tube in which one or more control electrodes initiate, but do not limit, the anode current except under certain operating conditions.

Time constant. The time required for a varying quantity to reach $1/e$, or approximately 63.2 percent, of its total change.

Tolerance. The amount of permissible deviation of a machine part from a specified dimension. The numerical difference between the largest and smallest permissible limits for any specific dimension in order to provide a clearance.

Torr. Suggested international standard term to replace the English term millimeter of mercury when referring to low absolute pressures, i.e., high vacuums.

Torricellian vacuum. Space, containing mercury vapor, which is produced at the top of a column of mercury when a long tube sealed at one end is filled with mercury and inverted in a basin of mercury. The mercury falls in the tube until it is balanced by the atmospheric pressure.

Transducer. A device capable of being actuated by waves or signals from one or more transmission systems or media and of supplying related waves or signals to one or more other transmission systems or media. An electromechanical device which converts a physical quantity being measured, such as temperature or pressure, to a proportional electrical output.

Transfer lag. That part of the transmission characteristic, exclusive of dead time, which modifies the time-amplitude relationship of a signal and thus delays the full manifestation of its influence.

Transient motion. The motion of a system other than steady-state vibration.

Transistor. A small semiconductor amplifying device which performs the same functions as a vacuum tube.

Triode. A three-electrode electron tube containing an anode, a cathode, and a control electrode.

Turbulent flow. Fluid flow in which the velocity of the fluid medium varies in time in both direction and magnitude.

Two-position action. Action, such as open-shut or on-off, in which a final control element is moved from one of two fixed positions to the other.

Ultrasonic detector. A device for detecting high-frequency pressure waves above the limit of audibility.

Ultrasonic generator. A device used for the production of sound waves in the ultrasonic range.

Ultrasonics (supersonics). The study of sound in the frequency range above about 15 kilocycles/sec.

Ultraviolet. Electromagnetic radiation, of wavelength from about 136 to 4,000 angstroms, extending from the visible spectrum at the violet end up to low-frequency X-rays.

Unit sensitivity of an instrument. The change in the measured quantity required to cause a motion of one scale division on the instrument.

Vacuum. Space in which there are no molecules or atoms. A perfect vacuum is unobtainable, since every material which surrounds a space has a definite vapor pressure. The term is used for any gaseous space at pressures below atmospheric.

Vacuum gauge. A manometer for measuring pressure below 760 mm Hg.

Van de Graaf generator. An electrostatic generator which employs a system of conveyor belt and spray points to charge an insulated electrode to a high potential.

Vapor. Substance in the gaseous state which may be liquefied by increasing the pressure without altering the temperature. A gas below its critical temperature.

Var. The unit of reactive power, the product of current and voltage and the sine of the phase angle.

Variable. A process condition, such as temperature, pressure, level, flow, or humidity, which is susceptible to change and which can be measured, altered, and controlled.

Varmeter. An instrument for measuring reactive power.

Vector quantity. A quantity which requires for description both direction and magnitude.

Velocity. Rate of motion in a given direction; measured as length per unit time.

Vena contracta. The smallest cross section of a fluid jet which issues from a freely discharging aperture or orifice or is formed inside a pipe owing to a constriction.

Venturi meter. A constriction meter in which the constriction takes the form of a Venturi tube.

Venturi tube. A short tube of varying cross section usually cone-shaped and having a convergent-divergent shape. The flow through the venturi causes a pressure drop in the smallest section, the amount of the drop being a function of the velocity of flow.

Vernier. A device for measuring subdivisions of a scale.

Viscometer. An instrument for measuring viscosity.

Viscosity. The property whereby a fluid tends to resist relative motion within itself.

Viscosity, kinematic. The ratio of the coefficient of viscosity to the density of a fluid.

Voltage divider. A network consisting of impedance elements connected in series to which a voltage is applied and from which one or more voltages can be obtained across any portion of the network.

Voltage-range multiplier. A special type of series resistor installed externally to a voltmeter and used to extend the range of the voltmeter.

Volt-ampere meter. An instrument used for measuring the apparent power in an alternating-current circuit. It is provided with a scale graduated in volt-amperes or in kilovolt-amperes.

Voltmeter. An instrument for measuring voltage.

Watt. The energy expended per second by an unvarying electric current of one ampere flowing through a conductor the ends of which are maintained at a potential difference of one volt. The power, in watts, is given by the product of current, in amperes, and the potential difference, in volts.

Wattmeter. An instrument for measuring the magnitude of the active power in an electric circuit. The scale provided is usually graduated in watts, kilowatts, or megawatts.

Wave. A physical activity in a medium such that at any point in the medium some of the associated quantities vary with time and at any instant of time vary with position.

Waveband. A term applied to a recognized section or division of the radio spectrum. For example, the intermediate waveband generally includes wavelengths between 100 and 600 m.

Weight. The force of attraction between the earth and a given mass.

Weight density. Weight per unit volume e.g., pounds weight per cubic inch.

Well. A receptacle or container sealed at one end and adapted to receive a temperature-sensitive element. A pressure-tight receptacle containing the sealing or filling liquid of a manometer.

Wheatstone bridge. A four-arm electric circuit all arms of which are predominately resistive. A divided electric circuit used for measurement of resistances.

X Rays. Penetrating electromagnetic radiation of wavelengths very much smaller than those of visible light, of the order of 5×10^{-7} to 5×10^{-10} cm, and usually produced by bombarding a metallic target with fast electrons in a vacuum.

X-ray spectrum. The characteristic frequencies of X rays emitted by an element bombarded by cathode rays.

Young's modulus. The ratio of the stress on a cross section of a stretched wire or a rod under tension to the longitudinal strain on the wire or rod.

Zero. Nought; the starting point of a scale or a stationary position neither positive nor negative.

References and suggestions for further reading

American Petroleum Institute (API), *Manual on Installation of Refinery Instruments and Control Systems*, Parts 1 and 2, New York, 1965. *Guide for Inspection of Refinery Equipment;* chap. 15, "Instruments and Control Equipment," New York, 1962.

ASME, *Fluid Meters: Their Theory and Application*, 5th ed., 1959.

Baird, D. C., *Experimentation: An Introduction to Measurement Theory and Experiment Design*, Prentice-Hall, Inc., Englewood Cliffs, N.J., 1962.

Barr, G., *Monograph of Viscometry*, Oxford University Press, London, 1931.

Bartholomew, Davis, *Electrical Measurements and Instrumentation*, Allyn and Bacon, Inc., Boston, 1963.

Beckman Instruments Corporation, *Industrial pH Handbook*.

Bingham, E. C., *Fluidity and Plasticity*, McGraw-Hill Book Company, New York, 1922.

Bonsall, R. B., *Basic Chromatography*, Honeywell Inc., Philadelphia.

Bridgeman, P. W., *Dimensional Analysis*, Yale University Press, New Haven, Conn., 1922.

Bristol Company, *A Primer on pH; Humidity Measurement*, Product Data Publication.

British Standards Institute, *Flow Measurement*, B.S. 1042.

Carroll, G. C., *Industrial Process Measuring Instruments*, McGraw-Hill Book Company, New York, 1962.

Considine, D. M. (ed.), *Process Instruments and Controls Handbook*, McGraw-Hill Book Company, New York, 1957.

Dunn and Barker, *Electrical Measurements Manual*, Prentice-Hall, Inc., Englewood Cliffs, N.J., 1955.

Dushman, S., *Scientific Foundations and Problems of Vacuum Techniques*, John Wiley & Sons, Inc., New York, 1949.

Eckman, Donald P., *Industrial Instrumentation*, John Wiley & Sons, Inc., New York, 1961.

Elonka and Parsons, *Standard Instrumentation Questions and Answers*, vol. 1, McGraw-Hill Book Company, New York, 1962.

Evershed & Vignoles Ltd., London, *Electronic Noflote Pump Control*.

Feather, Norman, *The Physics of Mass, Length and Time*, Edinburgh University Press, Edinburgh, 1962.

Fischer and Porter Co., *Fischer Governor Leveltrol for Specific Gravity Measurement*.

Foxboro Company, *pH Dynatrol*.

Fribance, A. E., *Industrial Instrumentation Fundamentals*, McGraw-Hill Book Company, New York, 1962.

Guthrie, Andrew, *Vacuum Technology*, John Wiley & Sons, Inc., New York, 1963.

Guthrie and Wakerling, *Vacuum Equipment and Techniques*, McGraw-Hill Book Company, New York, 1949.

Handbook of Measurement and Control, 2d ed., Part Two, "Instruments and Automation," The Instruments Publishing Company Inc., Pittsburgh, Pa., December, 1954.

Harris and Hemmerling, *Introductory Applied Physics*, 2d ed., McGraw-Hill Book Company, New York, 1963.

Industrial Nucleonics Corporation, *Level Control—Radiosotopes*.

Instrument Manual, 3d ed., United Trade Press, London, 1960.

Ipsen, D.C., *Units, Dimensions, and Dimensionless Numbers*, McGraw-Hill Book Company, New York, 1960.

Jackson, Herbert W., *Introduction of Electric Circuits*, Prentice-Hall, Inc., Englewood Cliffs, N.J., 1959.

Jones, E. B., *Instrument Technology*, vol. 1, Butterworth & Co. (Publishers), Ltd., London, 1953.

Kindler and Owens, *Basic Instrumentation Lecture Notes and Study Guide*, Part One, "Measurement Fundamentals," Instrument Society of America, 1960.

——— and ———, *Standards and Practices for Instrumentation*, Instrument Society of America, 1963.

Kirk and Rimboi, *Instrumentation*, American Technical Society, Chicago, 1962.

Leeds and Northrup Co., *pH Meter*.

Linford, A., *Flow Measurement and Meters*, E. & F. N. Spon Ltd., London, 1961.

Ohmart Corporation, *Radiation Techniques for Process Measurements*.

Permutit Co. and Fischer & Porter Co., *Ranarex Instruments for Gas Specific Gravity Measurement*.

Perry, Chilton, and Kirkpatrick (eds.), *Chemical Engineers' Handbook*, 4th ed., McGraw-Hill Book Company, New York, 1963.

Philbrick Researchers, G. A., *Differential Operational Amplifier*.

Philco Technological Center, *Electronic Precision Measurement Techniques and Experiments*, Prentice-Hall, Inc., Englewood Cliffs, N.J., 1964.

Prensky, Sol D., *Electronic Instrumentation*, Prentice-Hall, Inc., Englewood Cliffs, N.J., 1963.

Pressure Gauge Manual, U.S. Gauge, A Division of Ametek, Inc., Sellersville, Pa., 1963.

Rhodes, T. J., *Industrial Instruments for Measurement and Control*, McGraw-Hill Book Company, New York, 1941.

Soisson, Harold E., *Electrical Measuring Instruments*, McGraw-Hill Book Company, New York, 1961.

Spink, L. K., *Principles and Practice of Flowmetering*, The Foxboro Company, 1949.

Stout, Melville B., *Basic Electrical Measurements*, Prentice-Hall, Inc., Englewood Cliffs, N.J., 1960.

Streeter, V. L., *Fluid Mechanics*, 3d ed., McGraw-Hill Book Company, New York, 1962.

Taylor Instrument Co., *Hydrometers*.

Turner, Rufus P., *Basic Electronic Test Instruments*, Holt, Reinhart & Winston, Inc., New York, 1963.

Tyson, C. F., *Industrial Instrumentation*. Prentice-Hall, Inc., Englewood Cliffs, N.J., 1961.

Weber, White, and Manning, *Physics for Science and Engineering*, rev. ed., McGraw-Hill Book Company, New York, 1957.

Appendix A

Useful conversion factors[*]

$\text{Log}_e N = \text{Log}_{10} N \times 2.30258$

Length and Area

1 yard	= 3 feet	= 0.914 meter
1 foot	= 12 inches	= 30.48 centimeters
1 inch	= 25.4 millimeters	
1 meter	= 1.094 yards = 3.281 feet	= 39.37 inches
1 square foot	= 144 square inches	= 0.0929 square meter
1 square inch	= 6.45 square centimeters	
1 square meter	= 10,000 square centimeters	= 10.76 square feet
1 square centimeter	= 100 square millimeters	= 0.155 square inch

Volume

1 cubic yard	= 27 cubic feet	= 0.765 cubic meter
1 cubic foot	= 1,728 cubic inches	= 28.32 liters
		= 28,320 cubic centimeters
1 imperial gallon	= 1.2 U.S. gallons	= 277.4 cubic inches
		= 4.55 liters
1 U.S. gallon	= 0.833 imperial gallons	= 231 cubic inches
		= 3.785 liters
1 liter	= 1000 cubic centimeters	= 0.22 imperial gallon
	= 0.2642 U.S. gallons	= 61.0 cubic inches
		= 0.0353 cubic foot

Weight

1 long ton	= 1.12 short ton	= 2,240 pounds	= 1,016 kilograms
1 short ton	= 0.893 long ton	= 2,000 pounds	= 907 kilograms
1 metric ton	= 0.984 long ton	= 1.102 short ton	= 2,205 pounds
1 pound	= 7,000 grains	= 0.454 kilogram	
1 gram	= 1,000 milligrams	= 0.03527 ounce	= 15.43 grains

[*] See also Table 2-4.

Pressure

1 atmosphere (British) = 14.7 pounds per square inch = 29.92 inch mercury
 = 1.1013×10^6 dynes per square centimeter
 = 760 millimeters of mercury (mm Hg)
 = 1,013 millibars
1 atmosphere (metric) = 1 kilogram per square centimeter
 = 14.22 pounds per square inch
 = 10 meters head of water = 735.5 mm Hg
1 pound per square foot = 0.1924 inch water = 4.88 kilograms per square meter
1 pound per square inch = 2.036 inches mercury = 2.309 feet head of water
 = 0.0703 kilogram per square centimeter
1 inch water gauge = 5.2 pounds per square foot
1 foot head of water = 0.433 pound per square inch
1 inch mercury = 0.491 pound per square inch
 = 13.61 inches water gauge
1 bar = 1,000 millibars = 1.0×10^6 dyne per square centimeter

The above conversions are for inches and feet of water at 62°F (16.7°C), millimeters and meters of water at 39.2°F (4°C), and inches, millimeters, and meters of mercury at 32°F (0°C).

Power and Heat

1 kilowatt (kw) = 738 foot-pounds per second = 1.34 horsepower (British)
 = 1.36 horsepower (metric)

1 horsepower (hp) = 33,000 foot-pounds per minute
 = 0.746 kilowatthours
 = 1.014 metric horsepower
1 kilowatthour (kwhr) = 3.413 British thermal units (Btu) = 860 calories
 = 3.6×10^6 joules
 = 10^7 ergs
1 newton per meter = 1 joule
 = 10^7 dyne-centimeters

Density

1 cubic foot per pound = 0.0624 cubic meter per kilogram
1 pound per cubic foot = 16.02 kilograms per cubic meter
1 grain per cubic foot = 2.288 grains per cubic meter
1 grain per imperial gallon = 14.26 grains per cubic meter
1 cubic meter per kilogram = 16.02 cubic feet per pound
1 gram per cubic meter = 0.437 grain per cubic foot
 = 0.0702 grain per imperial gallon
Water at 62°F and at 4°C (39.2°F) (minimum density)
1 cubic foot = 62.3 (62.4) pounds = 6.23 imperial gallons
 = 7.48 U.S. gallons

Viscosity

1 poise = 100 centipoise

   = 1 gram per centimeter per second in absolute mass units (cgs)

   = 1 dyne second per square centimeter in absolute force units (cgs)

   = 2.088×10^{-3} pounds second per square foot gravitational units (fps)

   = 0.0672 poundal second per square foot absolute force units (fps)

Temperature

degrees Celsius	= $\frac{5}{9}$(degrees Fahrenheit − 32)
degrees Fahrenheit	= $\frac{9}{5}$(degrees Celsius) + 32
degrees Rankine	= degrees Fahrenheit + 459.7
degrees Kelvin	= degrees Celsius + 273.15

Appendix B

Development of Bernoulli's theorem

Derivation of Bernoulli's equation. Study carefully the two diagrams in Fig. B-1. Consider a very small mass of the fluid in motion and call this dM, whose direction of flow is from left to right in some tapered pipe or conduit. The motion is in the same plane as this page. Let the X–X axis be along the direction of motion inclined at an angle θ to the horizontal. The nomenclature is as follows:

dA = minute surface area at the ends of dM upon which the pressure p_a and $p_a + d_p$ act in opposite directions

dl = minute length of dM along the direction of motion

dW = weight of dM = $w\,dl\,dA$, where w is the specific weight of the fluid

dF_s = minute shearing forces (in pound force units) exerted by the surrounding fluid particles on dM

$\dfrac{dV}{dt}$ = acceleration of dM

$\dfrac{dl}{dt}$ = velocity of dM

It should be noted that $p_a > (p_a + d_p)$ because the motion is from left to right, hence the plus sign is in keeping with the fundamental algebraic conventions. Also $p_a + d_p$ is the pressure resistance immediately in front of the particle dM and opposes the motion.

Now consider the forces acting along X–X, the direction of motion. These forces will be due to:

1. The pressure acting on the end area of dM
2. The shearing forces acting downward along the lateral surfaces
3. The component of the weight of dM (acting downward)

From Newton's law of motion the total algebraic sum of forces is

$$\text{Mass} \times \text{acceleration} = dM\,\frac{dv}{dt}$$

Hence,

$$p_a\,dA - (p_a + d_p)\,dA - w\,dA\,dl\,\sin\theta - dF_s = \frac{w}{g}\,dA\,dl\,\frac{dv}{dt}$$

$$= \frac{w}{g}\,dA\,\frac{dl}{dt}\,dv$$

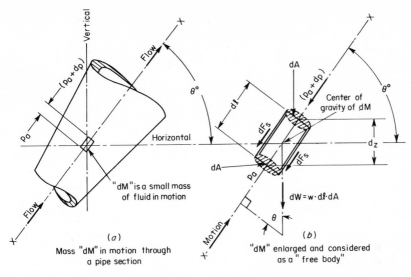

Fig. B-1 *A model of a fluid particle in motion.*

on dividing both sides of the equation by $w\,dA$ and replacing the velocity dl/dt by v, the result becomes

$$-\frac{dP}{w} - dl\sin\theta - \frac{dF_s}{w\,dA} = \frac{v}{g}\,dv$$

Note: $dl\sin\theta = dz$, the difference in elevation of the two ends of dM. Also, the term $dF_s/w\,dA$ represents the resistance to motion along the length dl.

Let τ (tau) be the shear stress:

$$\tau = \frac{dF_s}{\text{lateral area of } dM} = \frac{dF_s}{dl\,dP}$$

where $dl\,dP$ is the lateral area of the element dM, that is, length $\times$ perimeter. The term $dF_s/w\,dA$ now becomes $\tau\,dl\,dP/w\,dA$, and it should be recalled that dA/dP is referred to as the mean hydraulic depth or hydraulic radius (R), which is defined as the cross-sectional area divided by the wetted perimeter. $R = dA/dP$.

The sum of the shearing forces is the result of the energy lost owing to resistance (viscosity). The dimensions and units of $\dfrac{\tau}{w}\dfrac{dl}{R}$ are

$$\frac{[F/L^2]}{[F/L^3]}\frac{[L[}{[L]} = [L]$$

and the units are in feet of head loss. Therefore the head loss

$$dh_l = \frac{\tau}{w}\frac{dl}{R}$$

Reverting to the earlier equation, by rearrangement the fundamental expression is

$$\frac{dp}{w} + \frac{v\,dv}{g} + dz + dh_l = 0$$

Flow of incompressible fluids. As already mentioned, water and liquids, where density variations are insignificant, may be considered as incompressible fluids. The energy equation for incompressible fluid flow becomes, in terms of head of the fluid:

$$\int_{p_a}^{p_b} \frac{dp}{w} + \int_{v_a}^{v_b} \frac{v\,dv}{g} + \int_{z_a}^{z_b} dz + \int_a^b dh = 0$$

By completing the integration and substituting the limits,

$$\frac{p_b - p_a}{w} + \frac{v_b{}^2 - v_a{}^2}{2g} + Z_b - Z_a + h_l = 0$$

Hence, for two sections in the system

$$\frac{p_a}{w} + \frac{v_a{}^2}{2g} + Z_a - h_l = \frac{p_b}{w} + \frac{v_b{}^2}{2g} + Z_b$$

This is practically the same Bernoulli's equation as was deduced when dealing with flow from the orifice of that familiar water tank, except, it will be recalled, that the head loss h_l was ignored.

Flow of compressible fluids in pipes. The relation between pressure and velocity for flow of a compressible fluid through a restriction may be established from the basic law of conservation of energy used in thermodynamics. Assuming that no heat enters or leaves the restriction, no external work is done on or by the fluid. Under such conditions, the process is called adiabatic. Theoretically, the meaning of an adiabatic process is a change of state accomplished without transfer of heat. No heat is gained or lost by the process. The general gas law under adiabatic conditions is

$$pv^k = p_a v_a{}^k = p_b v_b{}^k = \text{constant}$$

where v_a and v_b represent the specific volumes at sections a–a and b–b in Fig. B-2 and where k is the adiabatic exponent and equal to the ratio of the specific heat of the fluid (gas) under constant pressure to that at constant volume

$$k = \frac{C_p}{C_v}$$

If it is assumed, also, that the datum level difference $Z_b - Z_a$ is negligible, the law of conservation of energy in thermodynamics can be written as

$$p_b v_b + \frac{v_b{}^2}{2g} + JE_b = p_a v_a + \frac{v_a{}^2}{2g} + JE_a$$

where J = work equivalent to heat energy
E = internal molecular heat energy
v = specific volume of fluid $1/w$

Applying the definition of enthalpy H as the resultant sum of the internal energy,

$$v_b{}^2 - v_a{}^2 = 2gJ(H_a - H_b)$$

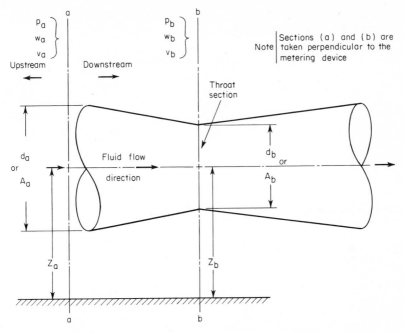

Fig. B-2 Symbols and dimensions of variables for flow measurement of compressible fluids.

For an ideal gas

$$H_a - H_b = \Delta H = \frac{kRT_a}{J(k-1)} \left[1 + \left(\frac{p_b}{p_a} \right)^{(k-1)/k} \right]$$

where R = gas constant for the gas
T = absolute temperature
By substitution in the velocity equation

$$v_b{}^2 - v_a{}^2 = \frac{2gkRT_a}{k-1} \left[1 + \left(\frac{p_b}{p_a} \right)^{(k-1)/k} \right]$$

The equation of continuity for weight flow is

$$W \text{ (lb/sec)} = \frac{A_a v_a}{v_a} = \frac{A_b v_b}{v_b}$$

Alternatively

$$W \text{ (lb/sec)} = A_a v_a w_a = A_b v_b w_b$$

where $v = \dfrac{1}{w}$

Combining the velocity and weight rate of flow equations, the resultant equation for the weight rate of flow for isentropic (a reversible and adiabatic process) flow of ideal gases is

$$W = \frac{\pi}{4} d_a{}^2 \beta^2 C \sqrt{\frac{2gkp_a w_a}{k-1}} \sqrt{\frac{(p_b/p_a)^{2/k} - (p_b/p_a)^{(k+1)/k}}{1 - \beta^4 (p_b/p_a)^{2/k}}}$$

where C is the coefficient of discharge.

A simplification of this equation must be made for flowmetering applications. By using the first two terms of the Binomial expansion series,

$$(1 - x)^n = 1 - nx + \frac{n(n-1)x^2}{1 \times 2} - \cdots$$

and by letting

$$\frac{p_b}{p_a} = 1 - x$$

$$\left(\frac{p_b}{p_a}\right)^{2/k} \cong 1 - \frac{2}{k}\left(1 - \frac{p_b}{p_a}\right) \quad \text{approx}$$

Similarly,

$$\left(\frac{p_b}{p_a}\right)^{(k+1)/k} \cong 1 - \frac{k+1}{k}\left(1 - \frac{p_b}{p_a}\right) \quad \text{approx}$$

Upon substitution of these simplified relations in the weight-flow-rate equation, the expression for compressible-fluid flow becomes

$$W = \frac{\pi}{4} d_a{}^2 \beta^2 C w_a \sqrt{\frac{2g(p_a - p_b)/w_a}{1 - \beta^4 (p_b/p_a)^{2/k}}}$$

For compressible-fluid flow the equation for the weight flow is

$$W = \frac{\pi}{4} d_a{}^2 \beta^2 C w_a \sqrt{\frac{2g(p_a - p_b)}{w_a}}$$

This equation applies only when the change in weight density is small. Using dimensional analysis,

$$\left[\frac{F}{T}\right] = [L^2] \left[\frac{F}{L^3}\right] \left[\frac{(L/T^2)(F/L^2)}{F/L^3}\right]^{1/2} = \left[\frac{F}{L}\right] \left[\frac{L^2}{T^2}\right]^{1/2} = \left[\frac{F}{T}\right]$$

The validity of the weight-flow equation for compressible-fluid flow can be determined by comparison with the incompressible flow rate.

Expansion factor Y

The expansion factor $Y = \dfrac{\text{weight flow rate (compressible flow)}}{\text{weight flow rate (incompressible flow)}}$

Numerically, this factor is given by

$$Y = \sqrt{\frac{(1 - \beta^4)[(p_b/p_a)^{2/k} - (p_b/p_a)^{(k+1)/k}]}{(k - 1/k)(1 - p_b/p_a)[1 - \beta^4(p_b/p_a)^{2/k}]}}$$

The values of the sum of the expansion factor for compressible flow are listed in Table B-1.

In actual flowmetering practice, as recommended in the ASME, ISA, AGA, and similar publications, there is a series of other factors, apart from the expansion factor, that must be considered in order to obtain accurate results. Some of these factors are gas compressibility factor, moisture factor at upstream and downstream conditions, and correction factors for tapping positions and thermal expansion of the metering device, such as the orifice plate.

Table B-1   Some expansion factors for compressible flow

p_b/p_a	K	Ratio of diameters $\beta = \dfrac{d_b}{d_a} = \dfrac{d \text{ (orifice)}}{D \text{ (pipe)}}$			
		0.30	0.40	0.50	0.60
0.95	1.40	0.973	0.972	0.971	0.968
	1.30	0.971	0.970	0.968	0.966
	1.20	0.968	0.967	0.966	0.962
0.90	1.40	0.944	0.943	0.941	0.935
	1.30	0.940	0.939	0.935	0.931
	1.20	0.935	0.933	0.931	0.925
0.85	1.40	0.915	0.914	0.910	0.902
	1.30	0.910	0.907	0.904	0.896
	1.20	0.902	0.900	0.895	0.887
0.80	1.40	0.886	0.884	0.880	0.868
	1.30	0.876	0.873	0.869	0.857
	1.20	0.866	0.864	0.860	0.848

Note: When $p_b/p_a = 1.00$, $Y = 1.00$.

Figure B-3 shows, in graphical form, the expansion ratios plotted against the pressure ratios for $k = 1.4$.

Example. A large closed tank is filled with ammonia under a pressure of 6.3 psig and at 65°F. The ammonia discharges into atmosphere through a small orifice in the side of the tank. If frictional losses are neglected, calculate the velocity of the ammonia leaving the tank assuming (a) Constant density, given that R for the gas = 89.5 ft/°R, and (b) Adiabatic flow conditions and $k = 1.32$.

Solution. (a) Since, from the gas law, $w_a = p_a/RT$

$$w_a = \frac{(6.3 + 14.7)144}{(89.5)(460 + 65)} = 0.064 \text{ lb}_f/\text{ft}^3$$

Apply Bernoulli's equation (flow from the tank to atmosphere)

$$\frac{6.3 \times 144}{w_a} + 0 + 0 = 0 + \frac{V_b^2}{2g} + 0$$

Hence, by substitution for w_a,

$$V_b = \sqrt{\frac{2g \times 6.3 \times 144}{0.064}}$$
$$= 900 \text{ ft/sec} \qquad \text{approx}$$

(b) Absolute pressure heads must be used in calculations where weight density is not constant. Velocity in the tank $(V_a) = 0$; also, $Z_a = Z_b = 0$. For

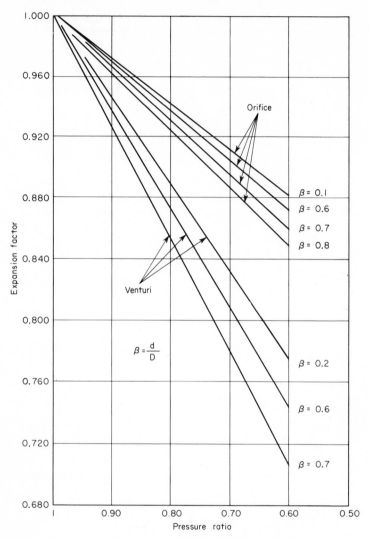

Fig. B-3   Expansion ratios plotted against pressure ratios for k = 1.4.
(Data from *ASME Fluid Meters, Their Theory and Application, 1959*)

adiabatic conditions, Bernoulli's equation is

$$\frac{k}{k-1}\frac{p_a}{w_a}\left[1-\left(\frac{p_b}{p_a}\right)^{(k-1)/k}\right]=\frac{V_b^2}{2g}$$

$$\frac{1.32}{0.32}\frac{21.0}{0.064}\left[1-\left(\frac{14.7}{21.0}\right)^{0.242}\right]=14,000=\frac{V_b^2}{2g}$$

Hence

$$V_b = 950 \text{ ft/sec}$$

Appendix C

Temperature conversion table[*]

Read known temperature in boldface type. Corresponding temperature in degrees Fahrenheit will be found in the column to the left. Corresponding temperature in degrees Celsius (centigrade) will be found in the column to the right.

°F	°C	°F	°C	°F	°C
......	**-350**	-212.22	......	**-260**	-162.22	-274.0	**-170**	-112.22
......	**-348**	-211.11	......	**-258**	-161.11	-270.4	**-168**	-111.11
......	**-346**	-210.00	......	**-256**	-160.00	-266.8	**-166**	-110.00
......	**-344**	-208.89	......	**-254**	-158.89	-263.2	**-164**	-108.89
......	**-342**	-207.78	......	**-252**	-157.78	-259.6	**-162**	-107.78
......	**-340**	-206.67	......	**-250**	-156.67	-256.0	**-160**	-106.67
......	**-338**	-205.56	......	**-248**	-155.56	-252.4	**-158**	-105.56
......	**-336**	-204.44	......	**-246**	-154.44	-248.8	**-156**	-104.44
......	**-334**	-203.33	......	**-244**	-153.33	-245.2	**-154**	-103.33
......	**-332**	-202.22	......	**-242**	-152.22	-241.6	**-152**	-102.22
......	**-330**	-201.11	......	**-240**	-151.11	-238.0	**-150**	-101.11
......	**-328**	-200.00	......	**-238**	-150.00	-234.4	**-148**	-100.00
......	**-326**	-198.89	......	**-236**	-148.89	-230.8	**-146**	-98.89
......	**-324**	-197.78	......	**-234**	-147.78	-227.2	**-144**	-97.78
......	**-322**	-196.67	......	**-232**	-146.67	-223.6	**-142**	-96.67
......	**-320**	-195.56	......	**-230**	-145.56	-220.0	**-140**	-95.56
......	**-318**	-194.44	......	**-228**	-144.44	-216.4	**-138**	-94.44
......	**-316**	-193.33	......	**-226**	-143.33	-212.8	**-136**	-93.33
......	**-314**	-192.22	......	**-224**	-142.22	-209.2	**-134**	-92.22
......	**-312**	-191.11	......	**-222**	-141.11	-205.6	**-132**	-91.11
......	**-310**	-190.00	......	**-220**	-140.00	-202.0	**-130**	-90.00
......	**-308**	-188.89	......	**-218**	-138.89	-198.4	**-128**	-88.89
......	**-306**	-187.78	......	**-216**	-137.78	-194.8	**-126**	-87.78
......	**-304**	-186.67	......	**-214**	-136.67	-191.2	**-124**	-86.67
......	**-302**	-185.56	-349.6	**-212**	-135.56	-187.6	**-122**	-85.56
......	**-300**	-184.44	-346.0	**-210**	-134.44	-184.0	**-120**	-84.44
......	**-298**	-183.33	-342.4	**-208**	-133.33	-180.4	**-118**	-83.33
......	**-296**	-182.22	-338.8	**-206**	-132.22	-176.8	**-116**	-82.22
......	**-294**	-181.11	-335.2	**-204**	-131.11	-173.2	**-114**	-81.11
......	**-292**	-180.00	-331.6	**-202**	-130.00	-169.6	**-112**	-80.00
......	**-290**	-178.89	-328.0	**-200**	-128.89	-166.0	**-110**	-78.89
......	**-288**	-177.78	-324.4	**-198**	-127.78	-162.4	**-108**	-77.78
......	**-286**	-176.67	-320.8	**-196**	-126.67	-158.8	**-106**	-76.67
......	**-284**	-175.56	-317.2	**-194**	-125.56	-155.2	**-104**	-75.56
......	**-282**	-174.44	-313.6	**-192**	-124.44	-151.6	**-102**	-74.44
......	**-280**	-173.33	-310.0	**-190**	-123.33	-148.0	**-100**	-73.33
......	**-278**	-172.22	-306.4	**-188**	-122.22	-144.4	**-98**	-72.22
......	**-276**	-171.11	-302.8	**-186**	-121.11	-140.8	**-96**	-71.11
......	**-274**	-170.00	-299.2	**-184**	-120.00	-137.2	**-94**	-70.00
......	**-272**	-168.89	-295.6	**-182**	-118.89	-133.6	**-92**	-68.89
......	**-270**	-167.78	-292.0	**-180**	-117.78	-130.0	**-90**	-67.76
......	**-268**	-166.67	-288.4	**-178**	-116.67	-126.4	**-88**	-66.67
......	**-266**	-165.56	-284.8	**-176**	-115.56	-122.8	**-86**	-65.56
......	**-264**	-164.44	-281.2	**-174**	-114.44	-119.2	**-84**	-64.44
......	**-262**	-163.33	-277.6	**-172**	-113.33	-115.6	**-82**	-63.33

Conversion Formulas

$$°C = \tfrac{5}{9}(°F - 32) \qquad °F = \tfrac{9}{5}°C + 32$$

Interpolation values for above conversion table

F°	1.8	3.6	5.4	7.2	9.0	10.8	12.6	14.4	16.2	18.0	36.0	54.0	72.0	90.0
Inc.	**1**	**2**	**3**	**4**	**5**	**6**	**7**	**8**	**9**	**10**	**20**	**30**	**40**	**50**
C°	0.56	1.11	1.67	2.22	2.78	3.33	3.89	4.44	5.00	5.56	11.11	16.67	22.22	27.78

[*] Reproduced by permission of Minneapolis-Honeywell Regulator Co.

Temperature conversion table (continued)

°F		°C	°F		°C	°F		°C
−112.0	−80	−62.22	+82.4	+28	−2.22	276.8	136	57.78
−108.4	−78	−61.11	+86.0	+30	−1.11	280.4	138	58.89
−104.8	−76	−60.00	+89.6	+32	+0.00	284.0	140	60.00
−101.2	−74	−58.89	+93.2	+34	+1.11	287.6	142	61.11
−97.6	−72	−57.78	+96.8	+36	+2.22	291.2	144	62.22
−94.0	−70	−56.67	+100.4	+38	+3.33	294.8	146	63.33
−90.4	−68	−55.56	+104.0	+40	+4.44	298.4	148	64.44
−86.8	−66	−54.44	107.6	42	5.56	302.0	150	65.56
−83.2	−64	−53.33	111.2	44	6.67	305.6	152	66.67
−79.6	−62	−52.22	114.8	46	7.78	309.2	154	67.78
−76.0	−60	−51.11	118.4	48	8.89	312.8	156	68.89
−72.4	−58	−50.00	122.0	50	10.00	316.4	158	70.00
−68.8	−56	−48.89	125.6	52	11.11	320.0	160	71.11
−65.2	−54	−47.78	129.2	54	12.22	323.6	162	72.22
−61.6	−52	−46.67	132.8	56	13.33	327.2	164	73.33
−58.0	−50	−45.56	136.4	58	14.44	330.8	166	74.44
−54.4	−48	−44.44	140.0	60	15.56	334.4	168	75.56
−50.8	−46	−43.33	143.6	62	16.67	338.0	170	76.67
−47.2	−44	−42.22	147.2	64	17.78	341.6	172	77.78
−43.6	−42	−41.11	150.8	66	18.89	345.2	174	78.89
−40.0	−40	−40.00	154.4	68	20.00	348.8	176	80.00
−36.4	−38	−38.89	158.0	70	21.11	352.4	178	81.11
−32.8	−36	−37.78	161.6	72	22.22	356.0	180	82.22
−29.2	−34	−36.67	165.2	74	23.33	359.6	182	83.33
−25.6	−32	−35.56	168.8	76	24.44	363.2	184	84.44
−22.0	−30	−34.44	172.4	78	25.56	366.8	186	85.56
−18.4	−28	−33.33	176.0	80	26.67	370.4	188	86.67
−14.8	−26	−32.22	179.6	82	27.78	374.0	190	87.78
−11.2	−24	−31.11	183.2	84	28.89	377.6	192	88.89
−7.6	−22	−30.00	186.8	86	30.00	381.2	194	90.00
−4.0	−20	−28.89	190.4	88	31.11	384.8	196	91.11
−0.4	−18	−27.78	194.0	90	32.22	388.4	198	92.22
+3.2	−16	−26.67	197.6	92	33.33	392.0	200	93.33
+6.8	−14	−25.56	201.2	94	34.44	395.6	202	94.44
+10.4	−12	−24.44	204.8	96	35.56	399.2	204	95.56
+14.0	−10	−23.33	208.4	98	36.67	402.8	206	96.67
+17.6	−8	−22.22	212.0	100	37.78	406.4	208	97.78
+21.2	−6	−21.11	215.6	102	38.89	410.0	210	98.89
+24.8	−4	−20.00	219.2	104	40.00	413.6	212	100.00
+28.4	−2	−18.89	222.8	106	41.11	417.2	214	101.11
+32.0	±0	−17.78	226.4	108	42.22	420.8	216	102.22
+35.6	+2	−16.67	230.0	110	43.33	424.4	218	103.33
+39.2	+4	−15.56	233.6	112	44.44	428.0	220	104.44
+42.8	+6	−14.44	237.2	114	45.56	431.6	222	105.56
+46.4	+8	−13.33	240.8	116	46.67	435.2	224	106.67
+50.0	+10	−12.22	244.4	118	47.78	438.8	226	107.78
+53.6	+12	−11.11	248.0	120	48.89	442.4	228	108.89
+57.2	+14	−10.00	251.6	122	50.00	446.0	230	110.00
+60.8	+16	−8.89	255.2	124	51.11	449.6	232	111.11
+64.4	+18	−7.78	258.8	126	52.22	453.2	234	112.22
+68.0	+20	−6.67	262.4	128	53.33	456.8	236	113.33
+71.6	+22	−5.56	266.0	130	54.44	460.4	238	114.44
+75.2	+24	−4.44	269.6	132	55.56	464.0	240	115.56
+78.8	+26	−3.33	273.2	134	56.67	467.6	242	116.67

Temperature conversion table (continued)

°F		°C	°F		°C	°F		°C
471.2	244	117.78	644.0	340	171.11	816.8	436	224.44
474.8	246	118.89	647.6	342	172.22	820.4	438	225.56
478.4	248	120.00	651.2	344	173.33	824.0	440	226.67
482.0	250	121.11	654.8	346	174.44	827.6	442	227.78
485.6	252	122.22	658.4	348	175.56	831.2	444	228.89
489.2	254	123.33	662.0	350	176.67	834.8	446	230.00
492.8	256	124.44	665.6	352	177.78	838.4	448	231.11
496.4	258	125.56	669.2	354	178.89	842.0	450	232.22
500.0	260	126.67	672.8	356	180.00	845.6	452	233.33
503.6	262	127.78	676.4	358	181.11	849.2	454	234.44
507.2	264	128.89	680.0	360	182.22	852.8	456	235.56
510.8	266	130.00	683.6	362	183.33	856.4	458	236.67
514.4	268	131.11	687.2	364	184.44	860.0	460	237.78
518.0	270	132.22	690.8	366	185.56	863.6	462	238.89
521.6	272	133.33	694.4	368	186.67	867.2	464	240.00
525.2	274	134.44	698.0	370	187.78	870.8	466	241.11
528.8	276	135.56	701.6	372	188.89	874.4	468	242.22
532.4	278	136.67	705.2	374	190.00	878.0	470	243.33
536.0	280	137.78	708.8	376	191.11	881.6	472	244.44
539.6	282	138.89	712.4	378	192.22	885.2	474	245.56
543.2	284	140.00	716.0	380	193.33	888.8	476	246.67
546.8	286	141.11	719.6	382	194.44	892.4	478	247.78
550.4	288	142.22	723.2	384	195.56	896.0	480	248.89
554.0	290	143.33	726.8	386	196.67	899.6	482	250.00
557.6	292	144.44	730.4	388	197.78	903.2	484	251.11
561.2	294	145.56	734.0	390	198.89	906.8	486	252.22
564.8	296	146.67	737.6	392	200.00	910.4	488	253.33
568.4	298	147.78	741.2	394	201.11	914.0	490	254.44
572.0	300	148.89	744.8	396	202.22	917.6	492	255.56
575.6	302	150.00	748.4	398	203.33	921.2	494	256.67
579.2	304	151.11	752.0	400	204.44	924.8	496	257.78
582.8	306	152.22	755.6	402	205.56	928.4	498	258.89
586.4	308	153.33	759.2	404	206.67	932.0	500	260.00
590.0	310	154.44	762.8	406	207.78	935.6	502	261.11
593.6	312	155.56	766.4	408	208.89	939.2	504	262.22
597.2	314	156.67	770.0	410	210.00	942.8	506	263.33
600.8	316	157.78	773.6	412	211.11	946.4	508	264.44
604.4	318	158.89	777.2	414	212.22	950.0	510	265.56
608.0	320	160.00	780.8	416	213.33	953.6	512	266.67
611.6	322	161.11	784.4	418	214.44	957.2	514	267.78
615.2	324	162.22	788.0	420	215.56	960.8	516	268.89
618.8	326	163.33	791.6	422	216.67	964.4	518	270.00
622.4	328	164.44	795.2	424	217.78	968.0	520	271.11
626.0	330	165.56	798.8	426	218.89	971.6	522	272.22
629.6	332	166.67	802.4	428	220.00	975.2	524	273.33
633.2	334	167.78	806.0	430	221.11	978.8	526	274.44
636.8	336	168.89	809.6	432	222.22	982.4	528	275.56
640.4	338	170.00	813.2	434	223.33	986.0	530	276.67

Conversion Formulas

$$°C = \tfrac{5}{9}(°F - 32) \qquad °F = \tfrac{9}{5}°C + 32$$

Interpolation values for above conversion table

F°	1.8	3.6	5.4	7.2	9.0	10.8	12.6	14.4	16.2	18.0	36.0	54.0	72.0	90.0
Inc.	1	2	3	4	5	6	7	8	9	10	20	30	40	50
C°	0.56	1.11	1.67	2.22	2.78	3.33	3.89	4.44	5.00	5.56	11.11	16.67	22.22	27.78

Temperature conversion table (continued)

°F		°C	°F		°C	°F		°C
989.6	532	277.78	1832.0	1000	537.78	2804.0	1540	837.78
993.2	534	278.89	1850.0	1010	543.33	2822.0	1550	843.33
996.8	536	280.00	1868.0	1020	548.89	2840.0	1560	848.89
1000.4	538	281.11	1886.0	1030	554.44	2858.0	1570	854.44
1004.0	540	282.22	1904.0	1040	560.00	2876.0	1580	860.00
1007.6	542	283.33	1922.0	1050	565.56	2894.0	1590	865.56
1011.2	544	284.44	1940.0	1060	571.11	2912.0	1600	871.11
1014.8	546	285.56	1958.0	1070	576.67	2930.0	1610	876.67
1018.4	548	286.67	1976.0	1080	582.22	2948.0	1620	882.22
1022.0	550	287.78	1994.0	1090	587.78	2966.0	1630	887.78
1040.0	560	293.33	2012.0	1100	593.33	2984.0	1640	893.33
1058.0	570	298.89	2030.0	1110	598.89	3002.0	1650	898.89
1076.0	580	304.44	2048.0	1120	604.44	3020.0	1660	904.44
1094.0	590	310.00	2066.0	1130	610.00	3038.0	1670	910.00
1112.0	600	315.56	2084.0	1140	615.56	3056.0	1680	915.56
1130.0	610	321.11	2102:0	1150	621.11	3074.0	1690	921.11
1148.0	620	326.67	2120.0	1160	626.67	3092.0	1700	926.67
1166.0	630	332.22	2138.0	1170	632.22	3110.0	1710	932.22
1184.0	640	337.78	2156.0	1180	637.78	3128.0	1720	937.78
1202.0	650	343.33	2174.0	1190	643.33	3146.0	1730	943.33
1220.0	660	348.89	2192.0	1200	648.89	3164.0	1740	948.89
1238.0	670	354.44	2210.0	1210	654.44	3182.0	1750	954.44
1256.0	680	360.00	2228.0	1220	660.00	3200.0	1760	960.00
1274.0	690	365.56	2246.0	1230	665.56	3218.0	1770	965.56
1292.0	700	371.11	2264.0	1240	671.11	3236.0	1780	971.11
1310.0	710	376.67	2282.0	1250	676.67	3254.0	1790	976.67
1328.0	720	382.22	2300.0	1260	682.22	3272.0	1800	982.22
1346.0	730	387.78	2318.0	1270	687.78	3290.0	1810	987.78
1364.0	740	393.33	2336.0	1280	693.33	3308.0	1820	993.33
1382.0	750	398.89	2354.0	1290	698.89	3326.0	1830	998.89
1400.0	760	404.44	2372.0	1300	704.44	3344.0	1840	1004.4
1418.0	770	410.00	2390.0	1310	710.00	3362.0	1850	1010.0
1436.0	780	415.56	2408.0	1320	715.56	3380.0	1860	1015.6
1454.0	790	421.11	2426.0	1330	721.11	3398.0	1870	1021.1
1472.0	800	426.67	2444.0	1340	726.67	......	1880	1026.7
1490.0	810	432.22	2462.0	1350	732.22	......	1890	1032.2
1508.0	820	437.76	2480.0	1360	737.78	......	1900	1037.8
1526.0	830	443.33	2498.0	1370	743.33	......	1910	1043.3
1544.0	840	448.89	2516.0	1380	748.89	......	1920	1048.9
1562.0	850	454.44	2534.0	1390	754.44	......	1930	1054.4
1580.0	860	460.00	2552.0	1400	760.00	......	1940	1060.0
1598.0	870	465.56	2570.0	1410	765.56	......	1950	1065.6
1616.0	880	471.11	2588.0	1420	771.11	......	1960	1071.1
1634.0	890	476.67	2606.0	1430	776.67	......	1970	1076.7
1652.0	900	482.22	2624.0	1440	782.22	......	1980	1082.2
1670.0	910	487.78	2642.0	1450	787.78	......	1990	1087.8
1688.0	920	493.33	2660.0	1460	793.33	......	2000	1093.3
1706.0	930	498.89	2678.0	1470	798.89	......	2010	1098.9
1724.0	940	504.44	2696.0	1480	804.44	......	2020	1104.4
1742.0	950	510.00	2714.0	1490	810.00	......	2030	1110.0
1760.0	960	515.56	2732.0	1500	815.56	......	2040	1115.6
1778.0	970	521.11	2750.0	1510	821.11	......	2050	1121.1
1796.0	980	526.67	2763.0	1520	826.67	......	2060	1126.7
1814.0	990	532.22	2786.0	1530	832.22	......	2070	1132.2

Temperature conversion table (continued)

°F		°C	°F		°C	°F		°C
......	2080	1137.8	....	2560	1404.4	......	3040	1671.1
......	2090	1143.3	....	2570	1410.0	......	3050	1676.7
......	2100	1148.9	....	2580	1415.6	......	3060	1682.2
......	2110	1154.4	....	2590	1421.1	......	3070	1687.8
......	2120	1160.0	....	2600	1426.7	......	3080	1693.3
......	2130	1165.6	....	2610	1432.2	......	3090	1698.9
......	2140	1171.1	....	2620	1437.8	......	3100	1704.4
......	2150	1176.7	....	2630	1443.3	......	3150	1732.2
......	2160	1182.2	....	2640	1448.9	......	3200	1760.0
......	2170	1187.8	....	2650	1454.4	......	3250	1787.7
......	2180	1193.3	....	2660	1460.0	......	3300	1815.5
......	2190	1198.9	....	2670	1465.6	......	3350	1843.3
......	2200	1204.4	....	2680	1471.1	......	3400	1871.1
......	2210	1210.0	....	2690	1476.7			
......	2220	1215.6	....	2700	1482.2			
......	2230	1221.1	....	2710	1487.8			
......	2240	1226.7	....	2720	1493.3			
......	2250	1232.2	....	2730	1498.9			
......	2260	1237.8	....	2740	1504.4			
......	2270	1243.3	....	2750	1510.0			
......	2280	1248.9	....	2760	1515.6			
......	2290	1254.4	....	2770	1521.1			
......	2300	1260.0	....	2780	1526.7			
......	2310	1265.6	....	2790	1532.2			
......	2320	1271.1	....	2800	1537.8			
......	2330	1276.7	....	2810	1543.3			
......	2340	1282.2	....	2820	1548.9			
......	2350	1287.8	....	2830	1554.4			
......	2360	1293.3	....	2840	1560.0			
......	2370	1298.9	....	2850	1565.6			
......	2380	1304.4	....	2860	1571.1			
......	2390	1310.0	....	2870	1576.7			
......	2400	1315.6	....	2880	1582.2			
......	2410	1321.1	....	2890	1587.8			
......	2420	1326.7	....	2900	1593.3			
......	2430	1332.2	....	2910	1598.9			
......	2440	1337.8	....	2920	1604.4			
......	2450	1343.3	....	2930	1610.0			
......	2460	1348.9	....	2940	1615.6			
......	2470	1354.4	....	2950	1621.1			
......	2480	1360.0	....	2960	1626.7			
......	2490	1365.6	....	2970	1632.2			
......	2500	1371.1	....	2980	1637.8			
......	2510	1376.7	....	2990	1643.3			
......	2520	1382.2	....	3000	1648.9			
......	2530	1387.8	....	3010	1654.4			
......	2540	1393.3	....	3020	1660.0			
......	2550	1398.9	....	3030	1665.6			

Conversion Formulas

$$°C = \tfrac{5}{9}(°F - 32) \qquad °F = \tfrac{9}{5}°C + 32$$

Interpolation values for above conversion table

F°	1.8	3.6	5.4	7.2	9.0	10.8	12.6	14.4	16.2	18.0	36.0	54.0	72.0	90.0
Inc.	**1**	**2**	**3**	**4**	**5**	**6**	**7**	**8**	**9**	**10**	**20**	**30**	**40**	**50**
C°	0.56	1.11	1.67	2.22	2.78	3.33	3.89	4.44	5.00	5.56	11.11	16.67	22.22	27.78

Appendix D

Thermocouple temperature–millivolt equivalents

Iron-Constantan, Type J*

(Degrees Fahrenheit vs. millivolts,† reference junction 32°F)

°F	−300	−200	−100	−0	+0	100
			MILLIVOLTS			
0	−7.52	−5.76	−3.49	−0.89	−0.89	1.94
5	−7.59	−5.86	−3.61	−1.02	−0.75	2.09
10	−7.66	−5.96	−3.73	−1.16	−0.61	2.23
15	−7.73	−6.06	−3.85	−1.29	−0.48	2.38
20	−7.79	−6.16	−3.97	−1.43	−0.34	2.52
25		−6.25	−4.09	−1.56	−0.20	2.67
30		−6.35	−4.21	−1.70	−0.06	2.82
35		−6.44	−4.33	−1.83	+0.08	2.97
40		−6.53	−4.44	−1.96	+0.22	3.11
45		−6.62	−4.56	−2.09	+0.36	3.26
50		−6.71	−4.68	−2.22	0.50	3.41
55		−6.80	−4.79	−2.35	0.65	3.56
60		−6.89	−4.90	−2.48	0.79	3.71
65		−6.97	−5.01	−2.61	0.93	3.86
70		−7.06	−5.12	−2.74	1.07	4.01
75		−7.14	−5.23	−2.86	1.22	4.16
80		−7.22	−5.34	−2.99	1.36	4.31
85		−7.30	−5.44	−3.12	1.51	4.46
90		−7.38	−5.55	−3.24	1.65	4.61
95		−7.45	−5.65	−3.36	1.80	4.76
100		−7.52	−5.76	−3.49	1.94	4.91

* Reproduced by permission of Minneapolis-Honeywell Regulator Co.

† Temperatures are based on the international temperature scale of 1948; emf is expressed in absolute millivolts.

Note: Instruments calibrated to these curves have scales identified accordingly.

Type J (continued)

°F	200	300	400	500	600	700
			MILLIVOLTS			
0	4.91	7.94	11.03	14.12	17.18	20.26
5	5.06	8.10	11.18	14.27	17.34	20.41
10	5.21	8.25	11.34	14.42	17.49	20.56
15	5.36	8.40	11.49	14.58	17.64	20.72
20	5.51	8.56	11.65	14.73	17.80	20.87
25	5.66	8.71	11.80	14.88	17.95	21.02
30	5.81	8.87	11.96	15.04	18.11	21.18
35	5.96	9.02	12.11	15.19	18.26	21.33
40	6.11	9.17	12.26	15.34	18.41	21.48
45	6.27	9.33	12.42	15.50	18.57	21.64
50	6.42	9.48	12.57	15.65	18.72	21.79
55	6.57	9.64	12.73	15.80	18.87	21.94
60	6.72	9.79	12.88	15.96	19.03	22.10
65	6.87	9.95	13.04	16.11	19.18	22.25
70	7.03	10.10	13.19	16.26	19.34	22.40
75	7.18	10.25	13.34	16.42	19.49	22.55
80	7.33	10.41	13.50	16.57	19.64	22.71
85	7.48	10.56	13.65	16.72	19.80	22.86
90	7.64	10.72	13.81	16.88	19.95	23.01
95	7.79	10.87	13.96	17.03	20.10	23.17
100	7.94	11.03	14.12	17.18	20.26	23.32

°F	800	900	1000	1100	1200	1300	1400	1500
				MILLIVOLTS				
0	23.32	26.40	29.52	32.72	36.01	39.43	42.96	46.53
5	23.47	26.55	29.68	32.89	36.18	39.61	43.14	46.71
10	23.63	26.70	29.84	33.05	36.35	39.78	43.32	46.89
15	23.78	26.86	30.00	33.21	36.52	39.96	43.50	47.07
20	23.93	27.02	30.16	33.37	36.69	40.13	43.68	47.24
25	24.09	27.17	30.32	33.54	36.86	40.31	43.85	47.42
30	24.24	27.33	30.48	33.70	37.02	40.48	44.03	47.60
35	24.39	27.48	30.64	33.86	37.20	40.66	44.21	47.78
40	24.55	27.64	30.80	34.03	37.36	40.83	44.39	47.95
45	24.70	27.80	30.96	34.19	37.54	41.01	44.57	48.13
50	24.85	27.95	31.12	34.36	37.71	41.19	44.75	48.31
55	25.01	28.11	31.28	34.52	37.88	41.36	44.93	48.48
60	25.16	28.26	31.44	34.68	38.05	41.54	45.10	48.66
65	25.32	28.42	31.60	34.85	38.22	41.72	45.28	48.83
70	25.47	28.58	31.76	35.01	38.39	41.90	45.46	49.01
75	25.62	28.74	31.92	35.18	38.57	42.07	45.64	49.18
80	25.78	28.89	32.08	35.35	38.74	42.25	45.82	49.36
85	25.93	29.05	32.24	35.51	38.91	42.43	46.00	49.53
90	26.09	29.21	32.40	35.68	39.08	42.61	46.18	49.70
95	26.24	29.37	32.56	35.84	39.26	42.78	46.35	49.88
100	26.40	29.52	32.72	36.01	39.43	42.96	46.53	50.05

Chromel-Alumel, Type K*

(Degrees Fahrenheit vs. millivolts,† reference junction 32°F)

°F	0	100	200	300	400	500	600	700
	MILLIVOLTS							
0	−0.68	1.52	3.82	6.09	8.31	10.57	12.86	15.18
5	−0.58	1.63	3.94	6.20	8.42	10.68	12.97	15.30
10	−0.47	1.74	4.05	6.31	8.54	10.79	13.09	15.41
15	−0.37	1.86	4.17	6.42	8.65	10.91	13.20	15.53
20	−0.26	1.97	4.28	6.53	8.76	11.02	13.32	15.65
25	−0.15	2.09	4.40	6.65	8.87	11.13	13.44	15.76
30	−0.04	2.20	4.51	6.76	8.98	11.25	13.55	15.88
35	+0.07	2.32	4.63	6.87	9.09	11.36	13.67	16.00
40	+0.18	2.43	4.74	6.98	9.21	11.48	13.78	16.12
45	+0.29	2.55	4.86	7.09	9.32	11.59	13.90	16.23
50	0.40	2.66	4.97	7.20	9.43	11.71	14.02	16.35
55	0.51	2.78	5.08	7.31	9.54	11.82	14.13	16.47
60	0.62	2.89	5.20	7.42	9.66	11.94	14.25	16.59
65	0.73	3.01	5.31	7.53	9.77	12.05	14.36	16.70
70	0.84	3.12	5.42	7.64	9.88	12.17	14.48	16.82
75	0.95	3.24	5.53	7.75	10.00	12.28	14.60	16.94
80	1.06	3.36	5.65	7.87	10.11	12.40	14.71	17.06
85	1.18	3.47	5.76	7.98	10.22	12.51	14.83	17.17
90	1.29	3.59	5.87	8.09	10.34	12.63	14.95	17.29
95	1.40	3.70	5.98	8.20	10.45	12.74	15.06	17.41
100	1.52	3.82	6.09	8.31	10.57	12.86	15.18	17.53

°F	800	900	1000	1100	1200	1300	1400	1500
	MILLIVOLTS							
0	17.53	19.89	22.26	24.63	26.98	29.32	31.65	33.93
5	17.64	20.01	22.37	24.74	27.10	29.44	31.76	34.05
10	17.76	20.13	22.49	24.86	27.22	29.56	31.88	34.16
15	17.88	20.24	22.61	24.98	27.34	29.67	31.99	34.28
20	18.00	20.36	22.73	25.10	27.45	29.79	32.11	34.39
25	18.11	20.48	22.85	25.22	27.57	29.91	32.22	34.50
30	18.23	20.60	22.97	25.34	27.69	30.02	32.34	34.62
35	18.35	20.72	23.08	25.46	27.80	30.14	32.45	34.73
40	18.47	20.84	23.20	25.57	27.92	30.25	32.57	34.84
45	18.58	20.95	23.32	25.69	28.04	30.37	32.68	34.96
50	18.70	21.07	23.44	25.81	28.15	30.49	32.80	35.07
55	18.82	21.19	23.56	25.93	28.27	30.60	32.91	35.18
60	18.94	21.31	23.68	26.05	28.39	30.72	33.02	35.29
65	19.06	21.43	23.80	26.16	28.50	30.83	33.14	35.41
70	19.18	21.54	23.91	26.28	28.62	30.95	33.25	35.52
75	19.29	21.66	24.03	26.40	28.74	31.07	33.37	35.63
80	19.41	21.78	24.15	26.52	28.86	31.18	33.48	35.75
85	19.53	21.90	24.27	26.63	28.97	31.30	33.59	35.86
90	19.65	22.02	24.39	26.75	29.09	31.42	33.71	35.97
95	19.77	22.14	24.51	26.87	29.21	31.53	33.82	36.08
100	19.89	22.26	24.63	26.98	29.32	31.65	33.93	36.19

* Reproduced by permission of Minneapolis-Honeywell Regulator Co.
† Temperatures are based on the international temperature scale of 1948; emf is expressed in absolute millivolts.

Type K (continued)

°F	1600	1700	1800	1900	2000	2100	2200	2300	2400
	MILLIVOLTS								
0	36.19	38.43	40.62	42.78	44.91	47.00	49.05	51.05	53.01
5	36.31	38.54	40.73	42.89	45.01	47.10	49.15	51.15	53.10
10	36.42	38.65	40.84	42.99	45.12	47.21	49.25	51.25	53.20
15	36.53	38.76	40.95	43.10	45.22	47.31	49.35	51.35	53.30
20	36.64	38.87	41.05	43.21	45.33	47.41	49.45	51.45	53.39
25	36.76	38.98	41.16	43.31	45.43	47.52	49.55	51.54	53.49
30	36.87	39.09	41.27	43.42	45.54	47.62	49.65	51.64	53.59
35	36.98	39.20	41.38	43.53	45.64	47.72	49.76	51.74	53.68
40	37.09	39.31	41.49	43.63	45.75	47.82	49.86	51.84	53.78
45	37.20	39.42	41.60	43.74	45.85	47.93	49.96	51.94	53.87
50	37.31	39.53	41.70	43.85	45.96	48.03	50.06	52.03	53.97
55	37.43	39.64	41.81	43.95	46.06	48.13	50.16	52.13	54.06
60	37.54	39.75	41.92	44.06	46.17	48.23	50.26	52.23	54.16
65	37.65	39.86	42.03	44.17	46.27	48.34	50.36	52.33	54.25
70	37.76	39.96	42.14	44.27	46.38	48.44	50.46	52.42	54.35
75	37.87	40.07	42.24	44.38	46.48	48.54	50.56	52.52	54.44
80	37.98	40.18	42.35	44.49	46.58	48.64	50.65	52.62	54.54
85	38.09	40.29	42.46	44.59	46.69	48.74	50.75	52.72	54.63
90	38.20	40.40	42.57	44.70	46.79	48.85	50.85	52.81	54.73
95	38.32	40.51	42.67	44.80	46.90	48.95	50.95	52.91	54.82
100	38.43	40.62	42.78	44.91	47.00	49.05	51.05	53.01	54.92

Platinum–Platinum plus 13% Rhodium, Type R*

(Degrees Fahrenheit vs. millivolts,† reference junction 32°F)

°F	0	100	200	300	400	500	600	700
	MILLIVOLTS							
0	−0.089	0.220	0.596	1.030	1.504	2.012	2.547	3.103
5	−0.076	0.237	0.616	1.052	1.529	2.038	2.575	3.132
10	−0.062	0.255	0.637	1.075	1.553	2.065	2.602	3.160
15	−0.049	0.272	0.657	1.098	1.578	2.091	2.630	3.188
20	−0.035	0.291	0.678	1.121	1.603	2.117	2.657	3.217
25	−0.021	0.308	0.700	1.144	1.628	2.144	2.685	3.245
30	−0.006	0.327	0.721	1.167	1.653	2.170	2.712	3.273
35	+0.009	0.345	0.742	1.191	1.678	2.197	2.740	3.302
40	+0.024	0.363	0.763	1.214	1.703	2.223	2.768	3.330
45	+0.039	0.381	0.785	1.238	1.729	2.250	2.796	3.359
50	0.055	0.400	0.807	1.261	1.754	2.277	2.823	3.387
55	0.071	0.419	0.828	1.285	1.779	2.303	2.851	3.416
60	0.086	0.438	0.850	1.309	1.805	2.330	2.879	3.445
65	0.103	0.457	0.872	1.333	1.831	2.357	2.907	3.473
70	0.119	0.476	0.894	1.357	1.856	2.384	2.935	3.502
75	0.135	0.496	0.917	1.381	1.882	2.412	2.963	3.531
80	0.152	0.516	0.939	1.406	1.908	2.438	2.991	3.560
85	0.169	0.536	0.962	1.430	1.934	2.466	3.019	3.589
90	0.186	0.556	0.984	1.455	1.960	2.493	3.047	3.618
95	0.203	0.576	1.007	1.480	1.986	2.520	3.075	3.647
100	0.220	0.596	1.030	1.504	2.012	2.547	3.103	3.677

°F	800	900	1000	1100	1200	1300	1400	1500
	MILLIVOLTS							
0	3.677	4.264	4.868	5.488	6.125	6.773	7.436	8.116
5	3.706	4.294	4.899	5.519	6.156	6.805	7.470	8.150
10	3.735	4.324	4.930	5.551	6.188	6.838	7.503	8.184
15	3.764	4.354	4.960	5.582	6.220	6.871	7.537	8.218
20	3.794	4.384	4.991	5.614	6.252	6.904	7.571	8.253
25	3.823	4.413	5.022	5.645	6.285	6.937	7.605	8.287
30	3.852	4.443	5.053	5.677	6.317	6.970	7.639	8.322
35	3.882	4.473	5.084	5.709	6.349	7.003	7.672	8.356
40	3.911	4.503	5.115	5.741	6.381	7.037	7.706	8.391
45	3.941	4.533	5.145	5.773	6.414	7.069	7.740	8.426
50	3.970	4.563	5.176	5.805	6.446	7.103	7.774	8.460
55	3.999	4.593	5.208	5.837	6.479	7.136	7.808	8.495
60	4.029	4.624	5.238	5.869	6.511	7.169	7.842	8.530
65	4.058	4.654	5.270	5.901	6.544	7.202	7.877	8.565
70	4.087	4.685	5.301	5.933	6.577	7.235	7.911	8.599
75	4.116	4.715	5.332	5.964	6.609	7.269	7.945	8.634
80	4.146	4.746	5.363	5.996	6.642	7.302	7.979	8.669
85	4.175	4.776	5.394	6.028	6.674	7.336	8.013	8.704
90	4.205	4.807	5.426	6.060	6.707	7.369	8.047	8.739
95	4.235	4.837	5.457	6.092	6.740	7.403	8.081	8.774
100	4.264	4.868	5.488	6.125	6.773	7.436	8.116	8.809

* Reproduced by permission of Minneapolis-Honeywell Regulator Co.
† Temperatures are based on the international temperature scale of 1948; emf is expressed in absolute millivolts.

Type R (continued)

°F	1600	1700	1800	1900	2000	2100	2200	2300
				MILLIVOLTS				
0	8.809	9.516	10.237	10.973	11.726	12.488	13.255	14.027
5	8.844	9.552	10.274	11.011	11.765	12.526	13.293	14.065
10	8.879	9.587	10.310	11.048	11.802	12.564	13.332	14.104
15	8.914	9.623	10.347	11.085	11.840	12.602	13.371	14.142
20	8.949	9.659	10.383	11.122	11.878	12.641	13.409	14.181
25	8.984	9.694	10.420	11.160	11.916	12.679	13.448	14.219
30	9.019	9.730	10.456	11.197	11.954	12.718	13.486	14.258
35	9.054	9.766	10.493	11.235	11.992	12.756	13.525	14.296
40	9.090	9.802	10.529	11.273	12.029	12.795	13.564	14.335
45	9.125	9.838	10.566	11.310	12.068	12.833	13.602	14.374
50	9.161	9.874	10.603	11.348	12.105	12.871	13.641	14.412
55	9.196	9.910	10.639	11.385	12.144	12.909	13.679	14.451
60	9.232	9.946	10.676	11.424	12.182	12.948	13.718	14.490
65	9.267	9.982	10.712	11.461	12.220	12.986	13.756	14.528
70	9.303	10.019	10.749	11.499	12.258	13.025	13.795	14.567
75	9.338	10.056	10.786	11.537	12.296	13.063	13.833	14.606
80	9.374	10.092	10.823	11.575	12.335	13.102	13.872	14.644
85	9.409	10.129	10.861	11.613	12.373	13.140	13.911	14.683
90	9.445	10.164	10.898	11.651	12.411	13.178	13.949	14.721
95	9.481	10.201	10.936	11.689	12.450	13.216	13.988	14.760
100	9.516	10.237	10.973	11.726	12.488	13.255	14.027	14.798

°F	2400	2500	2600	2700	2800	2900	3000	
				MILLIVOLTS				
0	14.798	15.568	16.340	17.110	17.875	18.636	19.394	
5	14.837	15.607	16.378	17.148	17.913	18.674	19.432	
10	14.875	15.645	16.417	17.186	17.951	18.712	19.470	
15	14.914	15.684	16.455	17.225	17.989	18.750	19.508	
20	14.952	15.722	16.494	17.263	18.027	18.788	19.545	
25	14.991	15.761	16.532	17.301	18.065	18.826	19.583	
30	15.029	15.800	16.571	17.340	18.103	18.864	19.621	
35	15.068	15.838	16.610	17.378	18.141	18.902	19.659	
40	15.107	15.877	16.648	17.416	18.179	18.940	19.697	
45	15.145	15.915	16.687	17.455	18.218	18.978	19.735	
50	15.184	15.954	16.725	17.493	18.255	19.016	19.773	
55	15.222	15.992	16.764	17.532	18.294	19.054	19.811	
60	15.261	16.031	16.802	17.569	18.332	19.092	19.848	
65	15.299	16.070	16.842	17.608	18.370	19.129	19.886	
70	15.338	16.108	16.880	17.646	18.408	19.168	19.924	
75	15.377	16.147	16.918	17.685	18.446	19.205	19.962	
80	15.415	16.185	16.957	17.723	18.484	19.243	19.999	
85	15.454	16.224	16.995	17.761	18.522	19.281	20.037	
90	15.492	16.263	17.033	17.799	18.560	19.318	20.075	
95	15.531	16.301	17.072	17.837	18.598	19.356	20.112	
100	15.568	16.340	17.110	17.875	18.636	19.394	20.150	

Platinum–Platinum plus 10% Rhodium, Type S*

(Degrees Fahrenheit vs. millivolts,† reference junction 32°F)

°F	0	100	200	300	400	500	600	700
				MILLIVOLTS				
0	−0.092	0.221	0.595	1.017	1.474	1.956	2.458	2.977
5	−0.078	0.238	0.615	1.039	1.498	1.981	2.484	3.003
10	−0.064	0.256	0.635	1.061	1.521	2.005	2.510	3.029
15	−0.050	0.274	0.655	1.083	1.545	2.030	2.535	3.056
20	−0.035	0.291	0.676	1.106	1.569	2.055	2.561	3.082
25	−0.021	0.309	0.696	1.128	1.593	2.080	2.587	3.108
30	−0.006	0.327	0.717	1.151	1.616	2.105	2.613	3.135
35	+0.009	0.346	0.738	1.173	1.640	2.130	2.638	3.161
40	+0.024	0.364	0.758	1.196	1.664	2.155	2.664	3.188
45	+0.040	0.383	0.779	1.219	1.688	2.180	2.690	3.214
50	0.056	0.401	0.800	1.242	1.712	2.205	2.716	3.240
55	0.071	0.420	0.822	1.264	1.736	2.230	2.742	3.267
60	0.087	0.439	0.843	1.287	1.761	2.255	2.768	3.293
65	0.104	0.458	0.864	1.311	1.785	2.281	2.794	3.320
70	0.120	0.477	0.886	1.334	1.809	2.306	2.820	3.347
75	0.136	0.496	0.907	1.357	1.833	2.331	2.846	3.373
80	0.153	0.516	0.929	1.380	1.858	2.357	2.872	3.400
85	0.170	0.535	0.951	1.404	1.882	2.382	2.898	3.426
90	0.187	0.555	0.973	1.427	1.907	2.407	2.924	3.453
95	0.204	0.575	0.994	1.450	1.931	2.433	2.951	3.480
100	0.221	0.595	1.017	1.474	1.956	2.458	2.977	3.506

°F	800	900	1000	1100	1200	1300	1400	1500
				MILLIVOLTS				
0	3.506	4.046	4.596	5.156	5.726	6.307	6.897	7.498
5	3.533	4.073	4.623	5.184	5.755	6.336	6.927	7.529
10	3.560	4.100	4.651	5.212	5.784	6.635	6.957	7.559
15	3.587	4.128	4.679	5.241	5.813	6.394	6.987	7.589
20	3.614	4.155	4.707	5.269	5.842	6.424	7.017	7.620
25	3.640	4.182	4.735	5.298	5.871	6.453	7.046	7.650
30	3.667	4.210	4.763	5.326	5.899	6.483	7.076	7.681
35	3.694	4.237	4.790	5.354	5.928	6.512	7.106	7.711
40	3.721	4.264	4.818	5.383	5.957	6.542	7.136	7.742
45	3.748	4.292	4.846	5.411	5.986	6.571	7.166	7.772
50	3.775	4.319	4.874	5.440	6.015	6.601	7.196	7.803
55	3.802	4.347	4.902	5.469	6.044	6.630	7.226	7.834
60	3.829	4.374	4.930	5.497	6.073	6.660	7.257	7.864
65	3.856	4.402	4.959	5.526	6.102	6.689	7.287	7.895
70	3.883	4.430	4.987	5.555	6.131	6.719	7.317	7.925
75	3.910	4.457	5.015	5.583	6.161	6.749	7.347	7.956
80	3.937	4.485	5.043	5.612	6.190	6.778	7.377	7.987
85	3.964	4.512	5.071	5.640	6.219	6.808	7.407	8.018
90	3.991	4.540	5.099	5.669	6.248	6.838	7.438	8.048
95	4.019	4.568	5.128	5.698	6.277	6.867	7.468	8.079
100	4.046	4.596	5.156	5.726	6.307	6.897	7.498	8.110

* Reproduced by permission of Minneapolis-Honeywell Regulator Co.

Type S (continued)

°F	1600	1700	1800	1900	2000	2100	2200	2300
				MILLIVOLTS				
0	8.110	8.732	9.365	10.009	10.662	11.323	11.989	12.657
5	8.141	8.764	9.397	10.041	10.695	11.356	12.022	12.690
10	8.172	8.795	9.429	10.074	10.728	11.389	12.055	12.724
15	8.203	8.827	9.461	10.106	10.761	11.423	12.089	12.757
20	8.234	8.858	9.493	10.139	10.794	11.456	12.122	12.790
25	8.265	8.890	9.525	10.171	10.827	11.489	12.155	12.824
30	8.296	8.921	9.557	10.204	10.860	11.522	12.189	12.857
35	8.327	8.953	9.589	10.237	10.893	11.556	12.222	12.891
40	8.358	8.984	9.621	10.269	10.926	11.589	12.256	12.924
45	8.389	9.016	9.654	10.302	10.959	11.622	12.289	12.957
50	8.420	9.048	9.686	10.334	10.992	11.655	12.322	12.991
55	8.451	9.079	9.718	10.367	11.025	11.689	12.356	13.024
60	8.482	9.111	9.750	10.400	11.058	11.722	12.389	13.058
65	8.513	9.143	9.782	10.433	11.091	11.755	12.423	13.091
70	8.545	9.174	9.815	10.465	11.124	11.789	12.456	13.124
75	8.576	9.206	9.847	10.498	11.157	11.822	12.490	13.158
80	8.607	9.238	9.879	10.531	11.190	11.855	12.523	13.191
85	8.638	9.270	9.912	10.564	11.224	11.888	12.556	13.224
90	8.670	9.302	9.944	10.597	11.257	11.922	12.590	13.258
95	8.701	9.333	9.976	10.629	11.290	11.955	12.623	13.291
100	8.732	9.365	10.009	10.662	11.323	11.989	12.657	13.325

°F	2400	2500	2600	2700	2800	2900	3000	3100	3200
					MILLIVOLTS				
0	13.325	13.991	14.656	15.319	15.979	16.637	17.292	17.943	18.590
5	13.358	14.024	14.689	15.352	16.012	16.670	17.324	17.975	18.622
10	13.391	14.058	14.722	15.385	16.045	16.702	17.357	18.008	18.655
15	13.425	14.091	14.755	15.418	16.078	16.735	17.389	18.040	18.687
20	13.458	14.124	14.789	15.451	16.111	16.768	17.422	18.073	
25	13.491	14.157	14.822	15.484	16.144	16.801	17.455	18.105	
30	13.525	14.191	14.855	15.517	16.177	16.834	17.487	18.137	
35	13.558	14.224	14.888	15.550	16.210	16.866	17.520	18.170	
40	13.591	14.257	14.921	15.583	16.243	16.899	17.552	18.202	
45	13.625	14.290	14.954	15.616	16.275	16.932	17.585	18.235	
50	13.658	14.324	14.988	15.649	16.308	16.965	17.618	18.267	
55	13.691	14.357	15.021	15.682	16.341	16.997	17.650	18.299	
60	13.725	14.390	15.054	15.715	16.374	17.030	17.683	18.332	
65	13.758	14.423	15.087	15.748	16.407	17.063	17.715	18.364	
70	13.791	14.457	15.120	15.781	16.440	17.095	17.748	18.396	
75	13.825	14.490	15.153	15.814	16.473	17.128	17.780	18.429	
80	13.858	14.523	15.186	15.847	16.506	17.161	17.813	18.461	
85	13.891	14.556	15.219	15.880	16.538	17.194	17.845	18.493	
90	13.924	14.589	15.253	15.913	16.571	17.226	17.878	18.526	
95	13.958	14.623	15.286	15.946	16.604	17.259	17.910	18.558	
100	13.991	14.656	15.319	15.979	16.637	17.292	17.943	18.590	

Copper–Constantan, Type T*

(Degrees Fahrenheit vs. millivolts,† reference junction 32°F)

°F	−300	−200	−100	−0	+0	100
			MILLIVOLTS			
0	−5.284	−4.111	−2.559	−0.670	−0.670	1.517
5	−5.332	−4.179	−2.645	−0.771	−0.567	1.633
10	−5.379	−4.246	−2.730	−0.872	−0.463	1.751
15		−4.312	−2.814	−0.973	−0.359	1.869
20		−4.377	−2.897	−1.072	−0.254	1.987
25		−4.441	−2.980	−1.171	−0.149	2.107
30		−4.504	−3.062	−1.270	−0.042	2.226
35		−4.566	−3.143	−1.367	+0.064	2.346
40		−4.627	−3.223	−1.463	+0.171	2.467
45		−4.688	−3.301	−1.559	+0.280	2.589
50		−4.747	−3.380	−1.654	0.389	2.711
55		−4.805	−3.457	−1.748	0.499	2.835
60		−4.863	−3.533	−1.842	0.609	2.958
65		−4.919	−3.609	−1.934	0.720	3.082
70		−4.974	−3.684	−2.026	0.832	3.207
75		−5.029	−3.757	−2.117	0.944	3.332
80		−5.081	−3.829	−2.207	1.057	3.458
85		−5.134	−3.901	−2.296	1.171	3.584
90		−5.185	−3.972	−2.385	1.286	3.712
95		−5.235	−4.042	−2.472	1.401	3.839
100		−5.284	−4.111	−2.559	1.517	3.967

°F	200	300	400	500	600	700
			MILLIVOLTS			
0	3.967	6.647	9.525	12.575	15.773	19.100
5	4.096	6.786	9.674	12.732	15.937	19.269
10	4.225	6.926	9.823	12.888	16.101	19.439
15	4.355	7.066	9.973	13.046	16.264	19.608
20	4.486	7.208	10.123	13.203	16.429	19.779
25	4.617	7.349	10.273	13.362	16.593	19.949
30	4.749	7.491	10.423	13.520	16.758	20.120
35	4.880	7.633	10.574	13.678	16.924	20.291
40	5.014	7.776	10.726	13.838	17.089	20.463
45	5.147	7.920	10.878	13.997	17.255	20.634
50	5.280	8.064	11.030	14.157	17.421	20.805
55	5.415	8.207	11.183	14.317	17.588	
60	5.550	8.352	11.336	14.477	17.754	
65	5.685	8.497	11.490	14.637	17.921	
70	5.821	8.642	11.643	14.799	18.089	
75	5.957	8.788	11.797	14.961	18.257	
80	6.094	8.935	11.953	15.122	18.425	
85	6.232	9.082	12.108	15.284	18.593	
90	6.370	9.229	12.263	15.447	18.761	
95	6.508	9.376	12.418	15.610	18.930	
100	6.647	9.525	12.575	15.773	19.100	

* Reproduced by permission of Minneapolis-Honeywell Regulator Co.

Nickel Resistance Thermometer Bulb, Type A*

(Degrees Fahrenheit vs. ohms†)

Temp. °F	Resist. Ohms	Temp. °F	Resist. Ohms	Temp. °F	Resist. Ohms	Temp. °F	Resist. Ohms	Temp. °F	Resist. Ohms
		−100	347.9	0	466.4	100	600.2	200	751.9
		− 95	353.5	5	472.7	105	607.3	205	759.9
		− 90	359.1	10	479.0	110	614.5	210	768.0
		− 85	364.8	15	485.4	115	621.7	215	776.2
		− 80	370.5	20	491.8	120	629.0	220	784.4
		− 75	376.3	25	498.4	125	636.3	225	792.7
		− 70	382.0	30	504.9	130	643.7	230	801.0
		− 65	387.8	35	511.5	135	651.2	235	809.4
		− 60	393.7	40	518.1	140	658.7	240	817.9
		− 55	399.5	45	524.8	145	666.2	245	826.4
		− 50	405.4	50	531.5	150	673.8	250	834.9
		− 45	411.4	55	538.3	155	681.4	255	843.6
		− 40	417.3	60	545.0	160	689.0	260	852.2
		− 35	423.3	65	551.8	165	696.7	265	861.0
		− 30	429.4	70	558.6	170	704.5	270	869.8
		− 25	435.5	75	565.4	175	712.3	275	878.6
		− 20	441.6	80	572.3	180	720.1	280	887.5
		− 15	447.7	85	579.2	185	728.0	285	896.5
−110	336.8	− 10	453.9	90	586.2	190	735.9	290	905.5
−105	342.3	− 5	460.1	95	593.2	195	743.9	295	914.6
−100	347.9	− 0	466.4	100	600.2	200	751.9	300	923.8

* Reproduced by permission of Minneapolis-Honeywell Regulator Co.
† Temperatures are based on the international temperature scale of 1948; resistance is expressed in absolute ohms.

Appendix E

Color coding and resistance data for standard thermocouple extension wire[a]

Thermocouple concerned		Extension wire data										
				Conductor material		Color coding			Resistance in ohms per double foot			
I.S.A. Symbol	Calibration	I.S.A. Symbol	Grade	Positive	Negative	Pos.	Neg.	Overall	#14 ga.	#16 ga.	#18 ga.	#20 ga.
J	Iron-constantan	JX	Regular	Iron	Constantan	White	Red	Black[b]	0.090	0.147	...	0.360
J	Iron-constantan	JX	Premium	Iron	Constantan	Gray	Red	Gray	0.090	0.147	...	0.360
K	Chromel-alumel[c]	KX	Regular	Chromel	Alumel	Yellow	Red	Yellow	0.150	0.235	...	0.600
K	Chromel-alumel	WX	Regular	Iron	Cupronel	Green	Red	White[d]	...	0.078		
R and S	Platinum-platinum rhodium	SX	Regular	Copper	Copper-nickel alloy	Black	Red	Green[d]	...	0.008		
T	Copper constantan	TX	Regular	Copper	Constantan	Blue	Red	Blue[e]	...	0.122	0 193	0.300
	Chromel constantan	...	Regular	Chromel	Constantan	Tan	Red	Tan	...	0.278	...	0.700

[a] Reproduced by permission of Minneapolis-Honeywell Regulator, Inc.
[b] Except for lead or armor-covered extension wire.
[c] Trade-mark registered, Hoskins Corp.
[d] Except for lead or rubber-covered extension wire.
[e] Except for rubber-covered extension wire.

Answers to odd-numbered problems

Chapter 1
1-5 $\frac{1}{758}$
1-11(b) 1.0%

Chapter 2
2-3 100 lb$_f$
2-5 3 lb$_f$
2-7 88.3 newtons
2-11 $k\sqrt{\dfrac{g}{L}}$ or $2\pi\sqrt{\dfrac{g}{L}}$

Chapter 3
3-3 0.25 g/cm³
3-5 2.68
3-7 18.8 cm
3-9 0.58

Chapter 4
4-3 20.0 ft of oil
4-5(a) 2.6 psi
   (b) 2.6 psi
4-11 11.5 m
4-13 514 ft³
4-15 73.6 cm
4-21 305 psi
4-23 150 lb$_f$
4-27 4.1 in. Hg
4-29(b) 20.3 psia; 5.6 psig

Chapter 5
5-3 10.2 in. Hg
5-7 2 in.
5-15 4.9×10^5 dynes/cm²
5-17 0.94 lb
5-19 5.6 in.

Chapter 5 (*Continued*)
5-23 10,500 lb$_f$
5-25 1.8 in.
5-27 1.63 in.
5-31(a) 0.042 psi
   (b) 1.16 in. w.g.
5-33(c) 19°
5-37(c) 18 lb$_f$
5-41 5.15 psig
5-43(a) 0.142 psi
   (b) 10 g/cm²
   (c) 7.3×10^3 microns Hg
5-45(c) 3.6×10^{16} (approx)
5-47 2 mm Hg
5-49(b) 0.37 cm Hg
5-53 22 liters

Chapter 6
6-5(b) 4.3 to 21.5 psi; 4.3 psi
6-7 3.79 psi
6-13 Vacuum of 0.74 psi

Chapter 7
7-3(b) 1.58×10^{-4}
   (c) 1.79×10^{-4}
7-7 1.07×10^{-2} poise
7-9 962 psi
7-13 1.2×10^{-3} ft²/sec
7-15 96 poises

Chapter 8
8-1(b) 0.2 ft/sec
8-3(c) Fuel oil, $v_c = 0.20$ ft/sec;
        water, $v_c = 0.05$ ft/sec

Chapter 8 (*Continued*)

8-5(a) Turbulent
  (b) Laminar
8-7 12.6 ft
8-9(b) 12-in. section, $v = 3.75$ ft/sec;
      10-in. section, $v = 5.40$ ft/sec
8-11 $v = 80$ ft/sec
8-15(a) 9.0 ft w.g.
  (b) 3.9 psi
8-19 $C = 2.2$ (approx)
8-23 $C_v = 0.98$
8-25 83 ft³/sec
8-27 1.7 ft³/sec
8-35(c) 26.0 ft/sec
8-37(b) 495,000 ft³/hr
8-41 21,360 gal/hr
8-45(b) 14.14 g
8-53(a) 726,000 (605,000)
  (b) 755,000 (628,000)
8-55(b) 4.83 ft³/sec

Chapter 9

9-1(b) 10.067 in.; 10.11 in.
9-3(b) 0.0000228 per °C
9-7(b) 0.24°C
9-13 168 psig
9-15 33.6 psia = 18.9 psig
9-17 600 ohms
9-23 $a = 2.83$, $b = -8.06$; 14.45
    volts
9-25 3.75, 0.45; 4.19 mv
9-31(a) 14.0858 mv
  (b) 72.7 microvolts
9-33 1386°C

Chapter 11

11-1 2,200 coulombs
11-3 0.99 ohms
11-5(b) 11 ohms
11-7(b) 0.1 mho
  (c) 0.1 mho/mil-ft
11-9 2.73 ohms

Chapter 11 (*Continued*)

11-11(b) 30 ohms
11-13 2.2×10^{-4} amp
11-15 1.4 sec
11-17(a) 1.2 amp/sec
  (b) 1.5 amp
  (c) 1.25 sec
11-25 170 volts
11-27 8.5 amp
11-29(b) 1.3 amp, $-74.2°$
11-31(b) 24 ohms; 19 ohms
11-35(a) 1.9 amp
  (b) 180 watts
11-37(b) 600 volt-amp, 450 watts,
    0.75
11-39 32.4 kc/sec
11-41(a) 5.0 kilohms
  (b) 1.7×10^4 radians/sec
11-43 1.080 ohms, 5.0 henrys

Chapter 12

12-5 108 volts, 17 volts
12-9 0.201 ohms, 4,950 ohms
12-11(b) 0.12
12-13(b) 36 ohms
12-17(a) 550 volts
  (b) 22 volts

Chapter 13

13-5 25

Chapter 15

15-3 1.37×10^{-3} lb/ft³
15-5 55%
15-11(a) 0.15207 psia
  (b) 0.000474 lb_m/ft³
  (c) 0.0065 lb_m steam/lb_m ai
Chapter 16

16-3 11.364
16-7 No
16-9 Helium

Index